# Craft Work

How can human flourishing arise from what the poet Mary Oliver called 'good work/ongoing'? In its attentiveness to the material, form and purpose of distinct, well-made things, craft epitomizes good work. In its disciplined and quiet giving over to the repetitions of tradition, craft is ongoing. Perhaps more than any other practice, craft work reveals the intimacy between a manifest sense of self, making and using things and the imperative of its common expression. In a world where work is broken into shuttered units, each separated from the other for the purpose of measured comparison and control, Robin Holt argues that craft work can produce the unassigned remainder that refuses being broken up: it generates its own sufficiency and joy.

Robin Holt is Professor of Strategy and Aesthetics at the University of Bristol, and Adjunct Professor at the Graduate School of Management, Kyoto University, from where he investigates the nature of organizational form. Having worked in Scandinavia, the UK and Japan, he has studied the emergence of new organizations like entrepreneurial ventures; the shaping of organizations through strategic practice; and in this, his latest work, the intimacy between organizational form, work practice, ethics and aesthetics. He has written and edited ten books, including *The Poverty of Strategy* with Mike Zundel (Cambridge University Press, 2023) and *Strategy without Design* with Robert Chia (Cambridge University Press, 2009) and *Organization as Time* with François-Xavier de Vaujany and Albane Grandazzi (Cambridge University Press, 2023).

# Craft Work
*Making Form in a Broken World*

Robin Holt
*University of Bristol*

Shaftesbury Road, Cambridge CB2 8EA, United Kingdom

One Liberty Plaza, 20th Floor, New York, NY 10006, USA

477 Williamstown Road, Port Melbourne, VIC 3207, Australia

314–321, 3rd Floor, Plot 3, Splendor Forum, Jasola District Centre, New Delhi – 110025, India

103 Penang Road, #05–06/07, Visioncrest Commercial, Singapore 238467

Cambridge University Press is part of Cambridge University Press & Assessment, a department of the University of Cambridge.

We share the University's mission to contribute to society through the pursuit of education, learning and research at the highest international levels of excellence.

www.cambridge.org
Information on this title: www.cambridge.org/9781009165822

DOI: 10.1017/9781009165839

© Robin Holt 2026

This publication is in copyright. Subject to statutory exception and to the provisions of relevant collective licensing agreements, no reproduction of any part may take place without the written permission of Cambridge University Press & Assessment.

When citing this work, please include a reference to the DOI 10.1017/9781009165839

First published 2026

Cover image: Cover photograph: 'Made in Spode' Piper Press © Katya de Grunwald

*A catalogue record for this publication is available from the British Library*

*Library of Congress Cataloging-in-Publication Data*
Names: Holt, Robin, 1966– author
Title: Craft work : making form in a broken world / Robin Holt, University of Bristol.
Description: Cambridge : Cambridge University Press, 2026. | Includes bibliographical references and index.
Identifiers: LCCN 2025036352 (print) | LCCN 2025036353 (ebook) | ISBN 9781009165815 hardback | ISBN 9781009165839 ebook
Subjects: LCSH: Form (Aesthetics) | Ruskin, John, 1819–1900 | Morris, William, 1834–1896
Classification: LCC BH301.F6 H65 2026 (print) | LCC BH301.F6 (ebook)
LC record available at https://lccn.loc.gov/2025036352
LC ebook record available at https://lccn.loc.gov/2025036353

ISBN 978-1-009-16581-5 Hardback
ISBN 978-1-009-16582-2 Paperback

Cambridge University Press & Assessment has no responsibility for the persistence or accuracy of URLs for external or third-party internet websites referred to in this publication and does not guarantee that any content on such websites is, or will remain, accurate or appropriate.

For EU product safety concerns, contact us at Calle de José Abascal, 56, 1°, 28003 Madrid, Spain, or email eugpsr@cambridge.org

For Morven

# Contents

| | | |
|---|---|---|
| *List of Figures* | | *page* ix |
| *Acknowledgements* | | xiv |
| 1 | Gothic | 1 |
| | Plague Clouds | 5 |
| | The Coniston Mechanics Institute | 7 |
| 2 | Rudeness and the Raw | 19 |
| | The Smallness of the Renaissance Mind | 19 |
| | The Being of Things | 23 |
| | Regions | 29 |
| | Experiment | 36 |
| | Reluctance and Functional Excellence | 44 |
| | The Golden Bowl | 45 |
| | Raku Tea Bowls | 47 |
| 3 | Changefulness and Variety | 51 |
| | Material and Limits | 51 |
| | Contingency | 60 |
| | Design | 67 |
| | Visibility and Invisibility | 69 |
| | War | 76 |
| | The Taskscape | 81 |
| | Skill and Expertise | 88 |
| | Rule Following | 91 |
| | Apprenticeship as the Synthesis of Skill, Habit and Tradition | 96 |
| | The Hermeneutics of Writing | 101 |
| | Colour | 109 |
| | Things as Pattern and Fold | 115 |
| 4 | Naturalism | 122 |
| | The Correlations of Natural Things | 122 |
| | Speculative Realism | 131 |
| | *Mingei* | 141 |
| | *Afro-Mingei* | 153 |
| | Form and Natural Form | 159 |
| | Grace and the Body | 163 |
| | Language, the Digital and the Analogue | 169 |

| | | |
|---|---|---|
| 5 | **Disturbed Imagination** | 179 |
| | The Grotesque | 182 |
| | Errant Bodies | 188 |
| | Inverse Hierarchies | 193 |
| | Wild Clay | 196 |
| | The First Studio Pottery | 198 |
| | Interrupting Function | 203 |
| | Outsider and Folk Art | 206 |
| | Metempsychosis and Repetition Revisited | 210 |
| | Urne Burial | 213 |
| | Vegetal Life | 216 |
| 6 | **Obstinacy** | 221 |
| | Functionality | 221 |
| | *Gestalt* | 225 |
| | Authenticity and Being with Things | 231 |
| | Cibachrome | 240 |
| | The 'Me', the 'I' and the Craft Venture | 244 |
| | The Venture and the Community | 250 |
| | The Workshop as a Scene of Progress | 258 |
| | Eutopia | 263 |
| | Mairet and the Biotechnics of Wool | 269 |
| 7 | **Redundancy and Plenitude** | 278 |
| | Mechanization Takes Control | 278 |
| | Patterns of Surplus | 286 |
| | Robbery and Societies | 295 |
| | News from Nowhere | 298 |
| | Some Hints on Pattern Designing | 302 |
| | In between Presence and Absence: The Infrathin | 308 |
| | Profane Objects | 311 |
| 8 | **Making Form in a Broken World** | 317 |
| | *Index* | 340 |

# Figures

1 Joseph Mallord William Turner, *Inverary Pier, Loch Fyne: Morning*, ca. 1845. Oil on canvas. Yale Center for British Art, Paul Mellon Collection, B1977.14.79. — *page* 4
2 John Ruskin and Frederick Crawley, right-hand register of the bas-relief on the north transept door of the Cathedral of Notre-Dame, Rouen, 1854. Daguerreotype. 1996D0084. © The Ruskin, Lancaster University. — 15
3 Charles Herbert Moore, *San Giorgio Maggiore, Venice, from the Lagoon*, 1876. Pencil, watercolour and bodycolour. 1996P037. © The Ruskin, Lancaster University. — 20
4 John Ruskin, *Venice – San Giorgio Maggiore*, 1876. Pencil drawing. 1996P1628. © The Ruskin, Lancaster University. — 21
5 Ursula Munch-Petersen, jug. Stoneware, white glaze. Photography: Author. — 25
6 Bellarmine jug, 1660–1680. Salt-glazed stoneware. The Metropolitan Museum of Art: 10.113 / Gift of M. Harris, 1910. — 34
7 Alison Britton, *Blue Lines*, 2022. © The Artist / Michael Harvey. Courtesy of Oxford Ceramics Gallery. — 37
8 Walter Keeler, thrown, altered, salt-glazed teapot. Courtesy of Walter Keeler/York Museums Trust (CC-BY-SA 3.0). — 38
9 Gillian Lowndes, *Collage with a Cup*, 1986. Stoneware, mixed media. Courtesy of The Sunday Painter. Photography: Ollie Hammick. — 40
10 Gillian Lowndes, *Collage with Tomato Root*, 1990. Stoneware, mixed media. Courtesy of The Anthony Shaw Collection. Photography: Philip Sayer. — 41
11 Robin Dalman, 210 stainless steel (63 hrc) gyuto. Octagonal tapered wa handle in torched ash. Photography: Robin Dalman. — 45
12 Glaze recipe from Michael Cardew's notebooks, Abuja, 1955. From the collections of the Crafts Study Centre, University for the Creative Arts. MAC/2/2. — 63

| | |
|---|---|
| 13 Jaejun Lee, test glazes for celadon, 2022. Photograph taken in Cardiff studio. Photography: Author. | 63 |
| 14 Michael Cardew's technical notes, 1958. From the collections of the Crafts Study Centre, University for the Creative Arts. MAC/1/2. | 64 |
| 15 Suwa Sozan, glaze recipes, 2019. Kyoto. Photography: Yutaka Yamauchi. | 64 |
| 16 Seikado workshop, 2019. Kyoto. Photography: Yutaka Yamauchi. | 66 |
| 17 Josef Hoffmann, *Light*, 1904–1906. Photography: © MAK Museum of Applied Arts, Vienna. | 69 |
| 18 Advert for gridwork flower vase designed by Josef Hoffmann. Photography: © MAK Museum of Applied Arts, Vienna. | 70 |
| 19 Lucie Rie, tea service, ca. 1936. Earthenware, unglazed burnished surface. Photography: Charles Saumarez Smith. © Estate of the Artist. | 71 |
| 20 Interior of Purkersdorf Sanatorium. Photography: © MAK Museum of Applied Arts, Vienna. | 73 |
| 21 Jan Lutma (goldsmith), *Rembrandt van Rijn*, 1656. Etching, engraving and drypoint. Rovinski, 276 (3rd state). 270b Oliver Wendell Holmes Collection. Library of Congress, Prints and Photographs Division. | 87 |
| 22 Märta Måås-Fjetterström AB, *Bruna Heden* (Brown heath), 1931. Rölakan flatweave. Wool. Photography: Anette Nilsson. © martamaasfjetterstrom. | 97 |
| 23 Illustration from Japanese pattern book for kimono designs. Labelled 'Ito nishiki' (yarn brocade). Textile design drawings, Japanese, Colour, 1750–1900. Library of Congress, Prints and Photographs Division [reproduction number LC-DIG-jpd-01056]. | 103 |
| 24 Michael Cardew's kiln book/diary/technical notes (1941–1958). From the collections of the Crafts Study Centre, University for the Creative Arts. MAC/1/2. | 104 |
| 25 Carlo Crivelli, *Madonna and Child*, ca. 1480. Tempera and gold on wood. The Metropolitan Museum of Art: 49.7.5 / The Jules Bache Collection, 1949. | 112 |
| 26 Joos van Cleve, *Virgin and Child*, ca. 1525. Oil on wood. The Metropolitan Museum of Art: 1982.60.47 / The Jack and Belle Linsky Collection, 1982. | 113 |
| 27 Circle of Michel Erhart, *Christ Child with an Apple*, ca. 1470–1480. Willow with original paint and traces of gold. The Metropolitan Museum of Art: 2012.449 / The Cloisters Collection, 2012. | 114 |

List of Figures xi

28 Shinsa Ryūryūkyo (1764–1820), *Temari no aki no tsuki* (Crescent moon in the footfall), 1815–1825. Folded kimono in a box. From series: *Shunkyō osana hakkei: Eight views of New Year's children*. Library of Congress, Prints and Photographs Division [reproduction number: LC-DIG-jpd-02302]. 117
29 Asakura Mitsuko, *Orimagaru*, 2014. Silk and wool, 83 × 127 cm. © The Artist. 119
30 Asakura Mitsuko, *Motion*, 2018. Silk, bamboo, driftwood in the Kurobe River. © The Artist. 119
31 Asakura Mitsuko, *Mandara*, 2020. Silk, 200 × 173 cm. © The Artist. 121
32 Alvar Aalto, *Sketch*, 1936. Paper, crayon, ink. Photography: Alvar Aalto Foundation. 123
33 Alvar Aalto, Paimio Sanatorium Lecture Room. Photography: Gustaf Welin, Alvar Aalto Foundation. 1933. 134
34 Hokkei Totoya (1780–1850), Noh actors as Yamauba (mountain women), 1830–1835. Woodcut. Library of Congress, Prints and Photographs Division [reproduction number: LC-DIG-jpd-0072]. Photograph: www.loc.gov/item/2009615064/. 144
35 Japanese pavilion at the 1873 Vienna Exposition. © Transcendental Graphics / Getty Images. 148
36 David Drake, storage jar, 1858. Alkaline-glazed stoneware. Metropolitan Museum of Art: 2020.7 / Purchase, Ronald S. Kane Bequest, in memory of Berry B. Tracy, 2020. 156
37 Elizabeth Fritsch, *Piano Pot with Counterpoint, Black Diamonds*, 1978. Stoneware with coloured slips. Image courtesy of Adrian Sassoon, London. Photography: Sylvain Deleu. 162
38 Lucie Rie, *Vase*. Porcelain, brown/black glaze over pale body with sgraffito bands. Photograph: Jane Coper. © Estate of Jane Coper / Estate of Lucie Rie. From the collections of the Crafts Study Centre, University for the Creative Arts 2002.26.365.6a. 172
39 David Kindersley, lithograph from Curwen Press, 1971. Lithograph on paper. Printed at Curwen Studio. 174
40 John Ruskin, Plate XIV, *Seven Lamps of Architecture*. In *Complete Works of John Ruskin*. Vol. VIII. Plate XIV. p. 216. © The Ruskin, Lancaster University. 180
41 Zhong Kui (Shoki in Japan) *On a Tiger Assailed by Demon*. Ink on paper. Edo period. Freer Gallery of Art Collection. Smithsonian, Washington. 186

42  Tamsin Van Essen, *Psoriasis*, 2007. Slip cast earthenware, pink glaze. Photography: Tamsin Van Essen. 189

43  Barnaby Ash and Dru Plumb, fractured and mended cauldron vessel in English oak from Kent. Patinated through fire and lime wash, finished with linseed oil and local beeswax. Stitched with waxed linen thread. © Ash & Plumb. 190

44  Rupert Williamson, side table. Osage orange and sycamore wood. The Fitzwilliam Museum, Cambridge. 1990. Photography: Rupert Williamson. 194

45  Maria Bang Espersen, *Home*. Christmas Platters made by Royal Copenhagen and B&G, covered with red clay and fired. 2018 – ongoing project. Glass maker's own. Photography: Maria Bang Espersen. 195

46  Robert Wallace, Underwater grotesque, 1880. Salt-glazed stoneware. Martinware Collection, Ealing Council. © Southall Library, London. Ealing Council. 200

47  R. W. Martin and Brothers, jar in the form of a bird, 1888. Glazed stoneware with wood mount. The Metropolitan Museum of Art: 2013.239.5a,b / Robert A. Ellison Jr Collection, Gift of Robert A. Ellison Jr, 2013. 201

48  Otagi Nenbutsu-ji Temple. Photography: Author. 206

49  Frontispiece to Sir Thomas Browne, *Urne Burial. Religio medici: Urn burial and Christian morals*, 1902, p. 84. Courtesy of Wellcome Collection. 214

50  Fergus Ferguson wearing gansey sweater, Oct 1911. The Wick Society Johnston Collection. www.johnstoncollection.net. 219

51  Martin brothers, failed pot, 1885. Salt-glazed stoneware. © Southall Library, London. Ealing Council. 224

52  The tomb of Gertrude Jekyll by Lutyens with her gardening fork. © Mary Evans Picture Library/The Annabel Watts Collection. 246

53  Patrick Geddes, 'The Notation of Life'. Plate V in A. D. Defries, *The Interpreter Geddes: The Man and his Gospel* (Routledge & Sons, 1927). Courtesy of Archives and Special Collections, University of Strathclyde Library. 267

54  Ethel Mairet, thick, hand-spun, white wool and fine white cotton weft, black and white machine-spun cotton warp, plain weave, spaced reeding, 1930s (T.74.11). From the collections of the Crafts Study Centre, University for the Creative Arts. 276

55  Ethel Mairet, hand-woven wall hanging with stripes in natural linen, clear cellophane and black cotton, plain weave,

| | |
|---|---:|
| warp and weft strips, 1940s (T.74.116). From the collections of the Crafts Study Centre, University for the Creative Arts. | 276 |
| 56 Albrecht Dürer, *Adam and Eve*, 1504. Engraving. The Metropolitan Museum of Art: 19.73.1 / Fletcher Fund, 1919. | 279 |
| 57 Jacob Epstein, *Rock Drill*, 1913–1916. Plaster and rock drill machinery. Destroyed (replica made 1974). © Ben Stansall / Stringer / AFP / Getty Images. | 283 |
| 58 William Morris, *Wandle*. Cotton fabric, block printed. © William Morris Gallery, London Borough of Waltham Forest. | 292 |
| 59 William Morris, Strawberry Thief. Dyed with natural indigo and madder rose. Designed by William Morris. 1883. Block-printed cotton. © William Morris Gallery, London Borough of Waltham Forest. | 293 |
| 60 Edmund Hort New, *The Chintz Printing Rooms, Merton Abbey*, 1898. Pen and ink on paper. D 57. © William Morris Gallery, London Borough of Waltham Forest. | 305 |
| 61 Unknown photographer, *May Morris*, early 1890s. Cyanotype. © National Portrait Gallery, London. | 307 |
| 62 Ludwig Wittgenstein, door handle. Photograph. Doorhandle from Haus Wittgenstein, Vienna. 2024. Photography: Max Ronnersjö. | 337 |

# Acknowledgements

This book has been long in the writing. Many people have been so generous with their advice, and willing to share their experience and to discuss with insight and some candour the nature of craft work, how it might persist and what it reveals about our understanding of goods and the nature of the good. From them all I have learned so much.

Without any sense of priority or hierarchy (hence in lexical order) I would like to thank:

Alvar Aalto Foundation
Clemens Apprich
Asakura Mitsuko
Noro Asano
Manuhuia Barcham
Greta Bertram
Armin Beverungen
Timon Beyes
Dinah Birch
Nils Borch
British Library
Craft Study Centre
Robin Dalman
Catherine Raben Davidsen
Ealing Library
Endo Takahiro
Maria Bang Espersen
Tamsin van Essen
Max Ganzin
Christina Garsten
Rick Gerner
Mike Goldmark
Goldmark Gallery
Märta Måås-Fjetterström AB
Mai Miyake
MAK, Vienna
Makimasa Imai
Masayuki Imai
Anne Fabricius Moeller
Mie Molgaard
Ursula Munch-Petersen
Anette Nilsson
Damian O'Doherty
Ann Charlotte Ohlsson
Anders Petersen
Tani Q
The Ruskin Library,
    Lancaster University.
Innan Sasaki
Nao Sato
Charles Saumarez
    Smith
Michael Schäfer
Maximillian Schellmann
Phil Scranton
Annika Skoglund
Anthony Shaw
Shiro Shimizu

# Acknowledgements

Smithsonian Museum
Katya de Grunwald
Demetris Hadjimichael
Nakatomi Hajimi
Per Hansen
Ryoko Hasegawa
Zoe Hendon
Akiko Hirai
Anne Mette Hjortshøj
Róisín Inglesby
Johanne Jahncke
Rasmus Johnsen
Christina Juhlin
Kou Kado
Kutaniyaki Kanazawa
Keigo Miki
Sandra Kemp
Jesper Kouthoofd
Jochem Kroezen
Jaejun Lee
Ann Linneman
Yuichi Fujita & Atsumi Fujita/
  Sokyo Gallery
Roy Suddaby
Sunday Painter Gallery
Sozan Suwa
Kari Svarre
Takehiro Kato
Toki Hata
Tora Urup
Sheena Vachhani
Max Waterhouse
Lone Weiget
Rene Wiedner
Rupert Williamson
William Morris Gallery
Genbei Yamanaka
Ichizo Yamashita
Yutaka Yamauchi
Mike Zundel

I benefitted greatly from grants given by The Swedish Collegium for Advanced Study in Uppsala and The Carlsberg Foundation, Denmark. Their generosity afforded me time, space and a place to begin shaping a book from an eclectic and randomly acquired collection of notes and images gathered over many years of visiting craft workshops and talking with craft workers. Finally, and as ever, I wish to thank all the editorial team at Cambridge University Press who have stood by and supported the book throughout its serpentine gestation.

# 1 Gothic

At the height of a wet summer in August 1879, the ageing John Ruskin looks out over Coniston Lake from the study window of Brantwood, his Victorian home in the English Lake District. He has been up early, losing himself to the tattered web of febrile thoughts at which he has been poking and pulling with his pen, as though by catching them occasionally in black ink he might find respite from his low mood. A storm has been gathering, the air is 'a loath-some mass of sultry and foul fog, like smoke', rain has been falling in unreliable fits, the clouds lour, unfold and envelop him:

Quarter to eight, morning. – Thunder returned, all the air collapsed into one black fog, the hills invisible, and scarcely visible the opposite shore; heavy rain in short fits, and frequent, though less formidable, flashes, and shorter thunder. While I have written this sentence the cloud has again dissolved itself, like a nasty solution in a bottle, with miraculous and unnatural rapidity, and the hills are in sight again; a double-forked flash … Half-past eight. – Three times light and three times dark since last I wrote, and the darkness seeming each time as it settles more loathsome, at last stopping my reading in mere blindness. One lurid gleam of white cumulus in upper lead-blue sky, seen for half a minute through the sulphurous chimney-pot vomit of blackguardly cloud beneath, where its rags were thinnest.[1]

The observations echo Ruskin's own climate: he has been enduring bouts of despondent hesitancy for months. The campaigning zeal for life in all its untrammelled fecundity that had characterized nearly all his adult life has been deserting him. In bearing witness to the dawn of machine-led industrial capitalism, laissez-faire speculation and godless consumerism, he had spent large parts of his inherited income on experimenting with alternative ways of organizing the consumption and production of material wealth. But of late he has grown frustrated with these experiments. The last of these had begun just over a year ago: the

---

[1] John Ruskin *The Storm Cloud. Lecture 1*. In *Complete Works Vol. XXXIV*. Edited by E. T. Cook and Alexander Wedderburn. London: George Allen. 1908. 37–38.

founding of the Guild of St George, a limited liability association whose primary objective was: 'To determine, and institute in practice, the wholesome laws of laborious (especially agricultural) life and economy, and to instruct first the agricultural, and, as opportunity may serve, other labourers or craftsmen, in such science, art, and literature as are conducive to good husbandry and craftsmanship.'[2]

Ruskin was the 'Master', carrying the duty to encourage and goad others into handing over portions of their wealth to fund the Guild. In turn, the Guild would fund land purchases, build museums, schools and workshops, and give workers, peasants or labourers a 'University education, wide as the fields, true as the laws, and fruitful as the roots of the earth, to all, without distinction, who desire to enjoy the happiness proper to men, and to fulfil the duties assigned to them'.[3] The students of this universal education were to be stewards of their own enjoyment and character as much as the soil, and the Guild was dedicated to the development of both.

The Guild has been Ruskin's most ambitious attempt at instituting what has been a consistent message throughout his life: think hard why you make and use what you do, consider how it gives to life, and if its existence has diminished life in any way, then refuse it. By life he means all life, that of the trees and Lakeland fells as much as human lives, a blending of life forms to which he has been inured from an early age.[4] A good life was a life led as close to nature as was possible, for here, in a state of 'constant watchfulness', was the source of all sustenance and stimulation: curtail nature and you curtail yourself.[5]

It has been a struggle towards closeness and truthfulness, one which he first witnessed in the painter J. M. W. Turner whose unmatched watchfulness had been by Ruskin's analysis the wellspring for a series of canvasses that revealed human nature to itself like no other medium. The greatest of these was *Slavers Throwing Overboard the Dead and Dying – Typhoon Coming on*, an 'accurate' and 'fearless' composition revealing the 'deathfulness' of the ocean alongside the dreadfulness of trade: the slaves 'do not rise everywhere, but three or four together in wild groups, fitfully and furiously, as the under strength of the swell compels or permits them;

---

[2] John Ruskin *The Guild of St George*. In *Complete Works Vol. XXX*. Edited by E. T. Cook and Alexander Wedderburn. London: George Allen. 1907. 12.

[3] John Ruskin *The Guild of St George*. 8, 17.

[4] 'It is the widest, as the clearest experience I have to give you; for the beginning of all my own right artwork in life, (and it may not be unprofitable that I should tell you this,) depended not on my love of art, but of mountains and sea.' John Ruskin *Eagle's Nest*. In *Complete Works Vol. XXII*. Edited by E. T. Cook and Alexander Wedderburn. London: George Allen. 1906. §41. 153.

[5] John Ruskin *Praeterita*. In *Complete Works Vol. XXXV*. Edited by E. T. Cook and Alexander Wedderburn. London: George Allen. 1908. §49. 285.

# 1  Gothic

leaving between them treacherous spaces of level and whirling water', whilst the slaving ship: 'labours amidst the lightening of the sea, its thin masts written upon the sky in lines of blood, girded with condemnation in that fearful hue which signs the sky with horror, and mixes its flaming flood with the sunlight, and, cast far along the desolate heave of the sepulchral waves, incarnadines the multitudinous sea'.[6]

He had owned the painting for decades, and had hung it in his study, until 1872, when he sold it, unable to bear its weight.

Seven years later, as he writes in his diary, accompanied by the storm clouds smudging his window, a weight remains. He half remembers that it had been with Turner he had experienced his last sunset, three years previously. The smoke had been there then too, on the horizon, but it had been incipient, an occluding denouement to the sun's descent which it hid 'through gold and vermillion'. Now the smoke came in brumous stacks that stained everything: 'Blanched Sun, – blighted grass, – blinded man'.[7] The strain is telling. Ruskin no longer knows where to turn; the clouds are everywhere. Not even the prospect of the 'ziggy zaggy' path at the garden entrance to Brantwood – seven twisting switchbacks leading up a plant-strewn embankment, each turn encouraging a gradual loosening from the weight of worldly sin – was offering him release.

It had not always been thus. He recalls how, in *Modern Painters*, his written paean to Turner, he had once been able to write quite differently about clouds:

Often in our English mornings, the rain-clouds in the dawn form soft level fields, which melt imperceptibly into the blue; or when of less extent, gather into apparent bars, crossing the sheets of broader cloud above; and all these bathed throughout in an unspeakable light of pure rose-colour, and purple, and amber, and blue, not shining, but misty-soft, the barred masses, when seen nearer, found to be woven in tresses of cloud, like floss silk, looking as if each knot were a little swathe or sheaf of lighted rain.[8]

This is a typical piece of Ruskinian text: closely observed descriptions alive with their own considered, often exuberant fugue-like progressions. Attend closely, observe and listen, touch and smell, and you

---

[6] John Ruskin *Modern Painters II*. In *Complete Works Vol. III*. Edited by E. T. Cook and Alexander Wedderburn. London: George Allen. 1903. §39. 572. Ruskin owned hundreds of Turners but only ever one oil painting, this one, as though only this one reached a state of truth that warranted fixing in such a present medium.

[7] John Ruskin *The Storm Cloud. Lecture 1*. 40.

[8] John Ruskin *The Storm Cloud. Lecture 2*. In *Complete Works Vol. XXXIV*. Edited by E. T. Cook and Alexander Wedderburn. London: George Allen. 1905. 44. Quoting from John Ruskin *Modern Painters*. In *Complete Works. Vol. VII*. Edited by E. T. Cook and Alexander Wedderburn. London: George Allen. 1904. 179.

Figure 1 Joseph Mallord William Turner, *Inverary Pier, Loch Fyne: Morning*, ca. 1845. Oil on canvas. Yale Center for British Art, Paul Mellon Collection, B1977.14.79.

become aware that all that is beautiful, true and good comes from the earth. The human species would only flourish fully if it realized this intimacy and concourse with the earth and its teaming life: '[N]o air is sweet that is silent; it is only sweet when full of low currents of under sound – triplets of birds, and murmur and chirp of insects, and deep-toned words of men, and wayward trebles of childhood.'[9] No one painted clouds better than Turner because he painted them in concourse with humans; he painted the truthfulness of an experienced event rather than an isolated object. He painted clouds as they were felt (Figure 1).

It is this entwined connexion with natural things that Ruskin fears to be on the wane. Humans, or at least those living in the places to which he has been most attentive – the parts geographically named as: the valley at Chamonui, the Italian cities of Verona and Venice, much of Switzerland, London, Scotland and the English Lakes – are steadily

---

[9] John Ruskin *Unto This Last*. 1862. §82. In *Complete Works Vol. XVII*. Edited by E. T. Cook and Alexander Wedderburn. London: George Allen. 1905. 111.

losing the capacity for encounters with nature. It has left him feeling increasingly isolated. Closely observed, the ragged, loathsome clouds underscore this fear. They are plague clouds.

## Plague Clouds

Five years later, in 1884, Ruskin excavated these parts of his diaries to form the narrative structure of two lectures given in London. The intervening years had provided him with space to reflect and expand upon the incipient feelings of gloom, to the point where, now, he had a full-blown thesis. The plague clouds were manifest, they were empirically present in the vapours, mists, dust and light seeping into the brick of the lecture hall and the bodies of the attendees. If those listening to him talk couldn't sense the plague clouds, then perhaps he could assist by pointing them out. After all, unless one has practised the watchfulness for which Ruskin prided himself, it was notoriously difficult to trace the edges of a cloud and to say with any definiteness that a cloud is there, or not there. Clouds are elusive, and if not seen might still be there, lurking. As well as rocks, buildings, temperaments, ornament, withered leaves and worked landscapes, Ruskin had spent years observing clouds, watching how they formed from the air eddying on the leeward side of cold mountaintops, or how they would emerge along the front between cold and warm air in a slow turmoil of rivalling densities. Now they were gathering and streaking the sky across industrialized nations, and with impunity, blurring and deadening the light. Not just the light by which to see, but the inner light of the soul. As well as in the air, the plague clouds settle upon human souls as these too belonged to biological life and were dependent upon 'a disposition of molecules to swing', an oscillating vitality coursing through all life forms.[10]

In writing *Modern Painters*, he had been able to tap into this swing, to create almost as readily as a cloud is created, to experience the formation of a work authored as much by the surrounding perturbations of air as the internal agitations of thought. Ruskin, in all seriousness, attributed the potency of his greatest work as much to the prevailing weather as he did the genius of those he wrote about, or his own genius; it was all one great atmosphere. Which was why, by 1879, when the climate had changed so irrevocably, so had he, and so had his audience. Whilst hour by hour occasional spots of weather might elicit the odd memory

---

[10] John Ruskin *The Storm Cloud. Lecture 1.* 60.

of a past harmony, the prevailing scene was a doom-riven murk through which any sun could only shine like a crooked, false coin.[11]

Though he felt he was writing alone, others were also associating the industrial acceleration and expanding material wealth of the 1870/80s with moral demise. Mark Twain, for example, had christened it a Gilded Age, a time of rapid machine-led commercial growth in which plenty lived cheek by jowl with extreme deprivation.[12] The earth had become an open, measured space traversed by telegraph wires announcing the arrival of railroads, factories, modern management systems, trading exchanges, entertainment halls, glass arcades and mineral mines, all of which was being put place under the direction of joint-stock holding companies and other such novel, impersonal organizational forms. The gilding was everywhere, a surface sustained by poverty and exploitation. But Ruskin's is a distinct voice. He, and he alone, has been able to set the unfortunate coupling of industrialized prowess and social injustice against a backdrop of creeping, atmospheric despoilation that potentially covered the entire world. Ruskin's plague clouds are not metaphorical: they are ecological phenomena emerging through the cracks of a newly broken world; their poison was real, lasting and global.[13] The clouds built and built, fusing with the sky, leaving nothing untouched by their pall. Where the clouds settled, they left residues marking the soil

---

[11] John Ruskin *The Storm Cloud. Lecture 1.* 40. Ruskin laments to his audience that were they to imagine how the sun might look in the company of the plague clouds they had only 'to throw a bad half-crown into a basin of soap and water'.

[12] Mark Twain and Charles Dudley Warner *The Gilded Age: A Tale of Today.* London: Penguin. 2001.

[13] It was not until 2009, however, with the founding of the Anthropocene Working Group, that science caught up with Ruskin and formally acknowledged the world-changing effects of these clouds. Established by the International Commission on Stratigraphy, the Working Group was commissioned 'to examine the status, hierarchical level and definition of the Anthropocene as a potential new formal division of the Geological Time Scale' (see Anthropocene Working Group of the Subcommission on Quaternary Stratigraphy (International Commission on Stratigraphy) Newsletter 1 December 2009, https://quaternary.stratigraphy.org/). Accepting a 'new formal division' was a deeply ambivalent act, perhaps as conceited as it was self-effacing. Geological time periods are hewn into layers of rock, each following the other in before and after bands of colouration and striation. They mark vast, archaic reaches of time and their names as just as distant: Cambrian, Ordovician, Silurian, Devonian, Carboniferous, Permian, Triassic, Jurassic, Cretaceous, Palaeocene, Eocene, Oligocene, Miocene, Pliocene, Pleistocene, Holocene. Compared to these, the Anthropocene is utterly juvenile, barely 300 years old, still being weaned on the pocketed residues of the Carboniferous, one period looping into and feeding off another. The Working Group suggested the formal division began in spasms of technological speculation that gathered steam and gained momentum, accelerating fast, heedless of anything other than the possibility of a more forceful, controlled industrial capitalism: full steam ahead. The acquisitive urge of humans had been catalysed by ingenuity, clarified by the principles of engineering and organized through relations of acquisition and legal title to a point of total planetary coverage.

and the oceans, and where there remained aloft, they altered the chemical texture of the air. And they were being replenished and expanded by the steam and smoke which stained the earth, tainted the water, and laced the air with particulates that stunted natural growth and restricted breathing. Their expansion was accompanied by an expanded cadre of managers and clerks who oversaw the breaking of labour into increasingly smaller units set within an urban sprawl that knew no restraint. They address one another not just through machinery, but as machines: they push, tap, vibrate, stop, dream, fight and incur loss at the behest of machines. The machinery mediating human life is of a totalizing order: it is the ecological setting by which all relations might take their cue, becoming as homogenized as the soured elements of vapour that permeate their offices, factory floors and streets.[14]

His two lectures on the storm cloud are delivered as a warning to those in the audience who fail to glimpse the enormity of this transformation. Rather than communicate a clear and direct thesis in easily consumed terms, however, Ruskin's instinct is to surround his audience in a flock of confused, discordant phrases which peck at their sensibility as relentlessly as crows might peck at a carcass. Those who attend – the industrialists, merchants, politicians and financiers whose concerted, collective efforts had given birth to this world-breaking technology – are to hear the truth, and the truth is a splintering of the old order. They believe themselves in control, pre-eminent, and they remain quite unaware of the quiet and creeping domination of the cloud-producing machinery they have installed. Far from being a prosthesis designed to augment human powers, Ruskin hints otherwise; his very delivery, the shards of grammar, evoke the deranging effects of this handing over to machine life.

### The Coniston Mechanics Institute

After delivering his warning about the plague clouds, Ruskin returned to Brantwood, and to his study window looking out over Coniston. Guild business still gave him brief spasms of hope, and the pathways in his garden had not failed him completely; their climbing power, though sporadic, was still felt. He (with his retinue of gardeners) had been working on the garden, steadily. It was a place in which he felt able to show his credentials as a thinker and writer who acts and implicates himself in his own edicts. In his 1881 report to the Guild, he had described his own efforts at land improvement in some detail:

---

[14] Tim Ingold *The Perception of the Environment: Essays on Livelihood, Dwelling and Skill.* London: Routledge. 2000: 294.

Leaving the emergent crags, the bosquets of heath, and the knolls of good sheep pasture untouched, as well as the deeper pieces of morass which are the proper receptacles of rainfall and sources of perennial streams, I have attacked only the plots of rank marsh grass which uselessly occupy the pieces of irregular level at the banks of the minor rivulets, and the ledges of rock that have no drainage outlet. The useless marsh grass, and the soil beneath it, I have literally turned upside-down by steady spade labour, stripping the rock surfaces absolutely bare (though under accumulations of soil often five or six feet deep), passing the whole of this loose soil well under the spade, cutting outlets for the standing water beneath, as the completely seen conformation.[15]

Under the gathering clouds, he carried on. He could work in small ways, noticing how natural growth might still bloom amid the broken world to which he was repeatedly calling attention.[16]

As well as working to improve the land, he was also reminded that the investments he had made in revivifying small, local ventures were not always failing, and that his writing had not gone completely unheeded.[17] One such venture lay just across the water from his study: the Coniston Mechanics Institute, for whose survival Ruskin had organized a public subscription in 1876, and to which he had been donating monies and materials to assist in the running of woodwork classes. These were led

---

[15] John Ruskin *The Guild of St George*. 50.
[16] Anna Tsing 'On Nonscalability: The Living World Is Not Amenable to Precision-Nested Scales', *Common Knowledge*. 2012, 18, 3, 505–524.
[17] On his death in 1900, for example, *The Spectator* published an article on Ruskin and Modern Business.

> Seeing that the essence of Mr. Ruskin's gospel, as distinct from its vagaries, was a simple demand for honesty in the first place, and for the relation of economic production to the wider aims of human life, these objections seemed to reflect on British commerce and the business situation, as implying that they could not quite be conformed to honest dealing, or that buying and selling were things by themselves, having no relation to all the other aspects of human life ... Ruskin, with a modesty which he did not always exhibit, derived his ideas on social questions from Carlyle. Now, in economics Carlyle's great remedy for the evils of society was to get the great 'captains of industry' to be really captains, to lead their battalions of workers, to sympathise with them, to care for them, while commanding them in their conflict with the forces of Nature. From that simple germinal idea Ruskin deduced a kind of 'whole duty of man' in regard to economics, and so evolved a new system of industry based not, as is ignorantly supposed, on the abolition of machinery, but on the twofold principle of complete honesty and veracity in production and exchange, and in a due subordination of the production of wealth to the wider aims of man. The question is whether this is feasible?
>
> That question has been answered by the report, balance sheets, and statement of accounts, of the firm of Messrs. William Thomson & Sons Limited, of Huddersfield, which lie before us. This is a woollen firm employing one hundred and fifty persons, and reorganized on what may broadly be called Ruskinian principles. The prime agent in the conversion of the firm, Mr. George Thomson, is both a sincere and intelligent disciple of Ruskin, his moral nature grasping Ruskin's essential ideas, and his business instinct knowing what to reject as impracticable or unimportant.

Reprinted in John Ruskin *The Guild of St George*. 333–334.

by Susanna Beever and W. G. Collingwood, both of whom were evergreen supporters of Ruskin's projects and members of the Guild. One of the ad hoc lecturers at the Institute was Arthur Simpson, trained as an apprentice in wood carving at the nearby furniture makers of Gillows in Lancaster. Simpson was an avid reader of Ruskin, taking to heart the claims that it was through craft or hand work that people might best bring about the good in life, and that everyone, by dint of a universal education, should 'learn to take a straight shaving off a plank, or draw a fine curve without faltering, or lay a brick level in its mortar'.[18] Folk like Simpson were, felt Ruskin, living proof of his assertion of the intimacy between craft work, personal flourishing and civic rectitude. To make and use things well is to live well, not just personally, but as part of a flourishing community to whose health one bound oneself, as a worker bee is bound by both the hive and the flowers.

The proof lay not just in Coniston but further afield, in sixteenth-century Florence for example, a city that thrived, he argued, because

for the provision of things necessary in domestic life, there developed itself, together with the group of inventive artists exercising these nobler functions [sculpture and painting, and histories], a vast body of craftsmen, and, literally, manufacturers, workers by hand, who associated themselves, as chance, tradition, or the accessibility of material directed, in towns which thenceforward occupied a leading position in commerce, as producers of a staple of excellent, or perhaps inimitable, quality; and the linen or cambric of Cambray, the lace of Mechlin, the wool of Worsted, and the steel of Milan, implied the tranquil and hereditary skill of multitudes, living in wealthy industry, and humble honour.[19]

These craft workers occupied what Ruskin likened to a Third Estate, a body of upright citizens committed to public enterprise, to compliment the other two estates of the knights (state) and priests (religion). The city – along with other Italian cities – flourished from the thirteenth century until the Reformation, at which juncture people lost faith in both the ethical and spiritual integrity of their city, a situation made all the worse by the gradual exploitation of craft work by crass mercantilism. Florence became tainted by

the pride of the knights, the avarice of the priests, and the gradual abasement of character in the craftsman, changing him from a citizen able to wield either tools in peace or weapons in war, to a dull tradesman, forced to pay mercenary troops to defend his shop door, are the direct causes of common ruin towards the close of the sixteenth century.[20]

---

[18] John Ruskin *Time and Tide*. In *Complete Works Vol. XVII*. Edited by E. T. Cook and Alexander Wedderburn. London: George Allen. 1905. §133. 426.
[19] John Ruskin *Val D'Arno*. In *Complete Works XXIII*. Edited by E. T. Cook and Alexander Wedderburn. London: George Allen. 1906. §69. 45.
[20] John Ruskin *Val D'Arno*. §73. 46.

Through the vigour and independence of each city reflected a similar state in their craft workers, those who had 'accurate knowledge of their business in all respects; the ease and pleasure of unaffected invention; and the true sense of power to do everything better than it had ever been yet done, coupled with general contentment in life, and in its vigour and skill'.[21] Uphold craft work and one upholds the social, cultural and political relations that give to life, but uphold the interests of money and one elevates the idle, aggressive and elitist instincts of those who assume privilege a natural right.

The craft workers teaching and learning at the Coniston Mechanics Institute understood this too. But in contrast with Florence, they were working under the pall of industrialism, making the job both more urgent and far harder. The Institute drew people in from all walks of life. Simpson was very explicit in this attempt to entice even the most reluctant and unskilled into craft work. He developed self-assembly kits for basic pieces like trays, whilst encouraging the more gifted to learn carving and embossing (in leather, pewter and copper). His maxim of instruction was to encourage a form of learning in which error had a pre-eminent place, for to err is to take imperfection into one's nature, and to find there a spur to learning. Simpson's pedagogy was infused with Ruskin's advice: the teacher's role was to begin with whatever rough and ready capacity the student possessed, and 'to look for the thoughtful part of them, and get that out of them, whatever we lose for it, whatever faults and errors we are obliged to take with it. For the best that is in them cannot manifest itself, but in company with much error.'[22]

The intent was to lead them to a place where, rather than being satisfied with neat, narrow accomplishment, they felt skilled and confident enough to take things on for themselves, to expand upon their growing capacity rather than settle back into the complacency of easy success.

Simpson applied the same principles to himself. By 1885 he had set up a handicrafts workshop in the nearby town of Kendal, employing apprentices and making furniture on commission. From the start he committed, where possible, to using quarter sawn oak. The tree is cut in such a way that the growth rings run through the thickness of the board, setting them perpendicular to the cut, rather than the much flatter angles found in plain sawn oak. Quarter sawing makes the wood more moisture resistant and less prone to twisting and cupping. It also reveals medullary rays that flare and leap across the surface in unruly

---

[21] John Ruskin *Val D'Arno*. §78. 48.
[22] John Ruskin *The Stones of Venice, Vol. II*. In *Complete Works Vol. X*. Edited by E. T. Cook and Alexander Wedderburn. London: George Allen. 1904. §11. 191.

and arresting patterns. It is more laborious and hence expensive to cut oak this way, and the resulting planks are restricted in width to a quarter of the tree's girth, but the resulting furniture lasts for as long as users wish to care for and use it. The pieces emerging from the workshop followed basic principles which Simpson had distilled from Ruskin's advice; above all, a commitment to an honest complicity with made things. The joints were exposed rather than hidden, unashamedly revealing the process of making, whilst also using the maximum possible depth of the timbers, making for stronger joins. The contrasting grain patterns also drew the eye and hand, they wanted to be seen and touched, as ornament, but ornament that belonged to the wood itself. It was not added, and unlike some forms of ornamentation using painting and gilding it was created by revealing and not concealing the raw material. Further ornament emerged from an attentiveness to function. Bookcases, for example, were made on a cascading principle, so smaller shelves at the top, widening as they descended, with the largest at the bottom, stood on feet that widened further still, providing both a waterfall effect and stout foundations when the shelves were loaded. Each shelf was bracketed to prevent bowing and hinged with a small vertical flap along the top that could be raised to accommodate the books, then lowered, preventing dust from gathering.

The quiet zeal shown by Simpson and his ilk was, for Ruskin, an adequate response to the broken world. The craft worker belonged to traditions that lay askance from a mechanized present intent upon breaking the human experience of the world into isolated compartments that could be managed predictably, irrespective of time and place. Craft workers were untimely because they resolved to remain placed. What gave them resolve, in Ruskin's eyes, was their disciplined capacity to use rather than conquer space and time. They were patient, they struggled to think and to see as clearly as they might how things could connect, they worked patiently and curiously, they refused to be caught up in the speed of capital transformation, they understood the value of lingering with things and appreciated their provocation.

A fool always wants to shorten space and time: a wise man wants to lengthen both. A fool wants to kill space and kill time: a wise man, first to gain them, then to animate them. Your railroad, when you come to understand it, is only a device for making the world smaller: and as for being able to talk from place to place, that is, indeed, well and convenient; but suppose you have, originally, nothing to say.[23]

---

[23] John Ruskin *Modern Painters III*. In *Complete Works Vol. V*. Edited by E. T. Cook and Alexander Wedderburn. London: George Allen. 1903. §35. 382.

The problem with industrial capitalism and its technologies was the furious, fast-paced urge to spread its reach, to corral as much space as possible, in as little time as possible, and to do so through processes of standardization whose uniformity was disguised by the superficial circulations of fashion.[24] More distressing still was the relentless 'using up' of workers entailed by this speed and spread. The plague clouds emerge from the machinery of divided workers, their whole being has been segmented to a point where they are not even capable of making a chair or table, but only a leg, and then only at the behest of a mean pattern from which deviation is an unimaginable liberty. Workers are no longer workers, but belong to the machine, they are a new form of life, they have 'sunk into an unrecognized abyss, to be counted off into a heap of mechanism numbered with its wheels, and weighed with its hammer strokes'.[25] Even where work is more complex, such as glass making, where the emphasis is on a cleanliness of line and tight, smooth edges, the worker becomes a prisoner of arithmetic.

Ruskin's Lake District had been no stranger to industrial capitalism, or what decades earlier William Wordsworth, in his poem *The Excursion*, called 'the local summons to unceasing toil', a bell which called

> Men, Maidens, Youths
> Mother and little Children, Boys and Girls
> Enter, and each the wonted task resumes
> Within this temple – where is offered up
> To Gain – the Master Idol of the Realm
> Perpetual sacrifice.[26]

Those working there were not incorporated into nature, but the factory. The children were working the bobbin mills, slate mines, gunpowder factories. Wordsworth observes closely the scouring effects of machines and work patterns dedicated to the production of a form of wealth built on sacrificed health and diminishing prospects. There was no diffusion of wealth and any chance for betterment remained with the better classes. Wordsworth felt keenly how industrial capitalism cast a pall of powerlessness over workers, conditioning them to a deadening similarity in outlook.

---

[24] Even where things are handmade, fashion corrupts. If, Ruskin asks, those with wealth enough to have gold or silver plate, insist on having it melted down and re-fashioned in the latest style, then what is the effect on the goldsmith? They will not invest themselves 'but a little quick handicraft – a clever twist of a handle here, and a foot there, a convolvulus from the newest school of design'. And to melt down the work of goldsmiths where they have invested themselves is to eradicate an intellectual achievement, it is to deny them their skill. John Ruskin *Joy Forever*. In *Complete Works Vol. XVI*. Edited by E. T. Cook and Alexander Wedderburn. London: George Allen. 1905. §45. 45.
[25] John Ruskin *The Stones of Venice, Vol. II*. §15. 195.
[26] William Wordsworth *The Excursion Book 8*. In *Collected Poems*. London: MacMillan. 1896. 180–185.

Ruskin took up the refrain, and in craft work found a riposte. Craft work had the poise to play with the surplus that lay within all human bodies. The surplus associated not just with labour power, but the experience of hitherto untapped potential and enthusiasm, the feeling of excess that resides in us, would we learn to tend it through the acquisition of skill. What is being made in craft work are human beings as much as useful objects, and in both cases these made things refuse to be reduced to the co-efficient of utility; they are as pointless as they are purposeful, as endless as they are finite.

In preparing his lectures on the plague clouds Ruskin had spent hours walking around central London observing for just how long the sun shone. Less than an hour each day. Like Turner, Ruskin had always been interested in reading the sky: it was mercurial, vast, inscrutable, and its provocation was immense and enduring. Would we only attend to it now and then, the sky:

is fitted in all its functions for the perpetual comfort and exalting of the heart, for soothing it and purifying it from its dross and dust. Sometimes gentle, sometimes capricious, sometimes awful, never the same for two moments together; almost human in its passions, almost spiritual in its tenderness, almost divine in its infinity, its appeal to what is immortal in us is as distinct, as its ministry of chastisement or of blessing to what is mortal is essential. And yet we never attend to it, we never make it a subject of thought[27]

The sky, what John Constable called 'the chief organ of sentiment',[28] shows the way in the interplay of light and dark, emptiness and volume, cold and warmth, beginnings and endings, still and frenzied. The sky was the undefined yet very present thing that drew us in and on, whose undiminished potency allowed us to live alongside the rough errors of noble failure that would inevitably accompany ambition. It was the unreachable mark by which human beings might call upon themselves to become more than they are. There was a religiosity to Ruskin's sense of the sky, a sense that it was here, if anywhere, that humans might teach themselves of their own capacities, might, like the poet George Herbert looking out from a church porch, apprehend the intimacy between nature and belief:

> Sink not in spirit; who aimeth at the sky
> Shoots higher much than he that means a tree?
> A grain of glorie mixt with humblenesse
> Cures both a fever and lethargicknesse.[29]

[27] John Ruskin *Modern Painters II*. In *Complete Works Vol. IV*. Edited by E. T. Cook and Alexander Wedderburn. London: George Allen. 1903. §3. 344.
[28] John Constable *Letter to Revd John Fisher, 23 October 1821*. In *Life and Letters of John Constable*. Edited by C. R. Leslie. London: Chapman and Hall. 1896.
[29] George Herbert *The Temple: The Church Porch*. LVI *The English Poems of George Herbert*. Boston: Houghton Mifflin. 1916. 29.

With industrial capitalism, the likelihood of the sky remaining such a stirring provocation was diminishing day by day. The urge to discover and refine the material uses of all things meant humans were no longer looking at the clouds; worse still, they had 'got the clouds packed into iron cylinders' so they might power belts and cranks and pistons in a ceaseless motion that in turn stained the air with poisonous soot.[30]

Just as the sun broke the London cloud, briefly, for an hour or so each day, so craft work breaks through the surface of an industrial landscape like a flower through the surface of a tarred road. Ruskin may have lamented how meagre was the interlude but, equally, been transfixed by the contrasts that it could set in play. Craft workers no longer run an entire city, but craft work might still create small, beguiling worlds of unabashed surfaces, hidden niches, occasional bright flashes and resilient persistence made possible by the 'taking of the one nature into another', a hypostatic union whose animating power Ruskin distilled into the concept of Gothic (Figure 2). Though derived largely from his obsessive attention to the stonework of Medieval cathedrals and Venetian Palazzos, Ruskin's views on Gothic extend in broader application to the forms of craft work that held economic uniformity in abeyance. As objects, Gothic buildings revealed themselves in a gathering of distinct qualities for which Ruskin used the following categories: savageness; changefulness; naturalism; grotesqueness; rigidity; and redundance. In isolation, none were sufficient. It was only in concert they amounted to something distinct, and the builders, in turn, bore Gothic sensibility when they held within them an embodied assembly of related human characteristics: rudeness, love of change; love of nature; disturbed imagination; obstinacy; and generosity.

To be rude was to entertain what was wild and remote with as much care as the familiar and habituated. To love change was to find in the order of tradition the rudiments of disorder, and to expose oneself to the free orders of variation. To love nature was to refuse the humanist conceit that civilization progressed only as far as it walled itself off from the accident and blind force of an indifferent, cold and mute world. To disturb the imagination was to be enticed by the irregular and broken and to embrace the deficient, for it was from fragments rather than 'wholes' that one might learn anew. To be obstinate was to commit to the grounding values of consistency and integrity. And to be generous was to create things that continued to give with repeated and renewed use; nothing is exhausted or discarded and what is made contributes to, rather than depletes, the available stocks of wealth.

---

[30] John Ruskin *Modern Painters III*. §37. 383.

# The Coniston Mechanics Institute

Figure 2 John Ruskin and Frederick Crawley, right-hand register of the bas-relief on the north transept door of the Cathedral of Notre-Dame, Rouen, 1854. Daguerreotype. 1996D0084. © The Ruskin, Lancaster University.

16   1   Gothic

Reading craft work through these qualities is itself, much like the making of craft objects, a risky undertaking. Ruskin's reading of Gothic was highly idiosyncratic. Through patient and attentive observation heightened by his skills in drawing, Ruskin came to develop his own systems of classification that were just as likely to take lines of flight from the orthodox divisions of style and technique as they were to admit them. His analysis and reasoning were often eclectic and advanced in leaps and lurches rather than the gradual, systemic and transparent movements that characterized typical scholarly efforts to ensure the variability and reliability of knowledge claims. He barely stopped to consider alternate arguments to his own.

The accepted understanding of the Gothic was an architectural style of the Middle Ages, sitting between the Romanesque and the Renaissance. As Christianity spread throughout Europe and became the hearth around which all spiritual, cultural and social life gathered, larger cathedrals were being built. The use of pointed arches aligned in arcades, flying buttresses, spires and rib vaulting allowed the buildings to encompass large congregations and to reach upwards towards God. The point – and it was a style that excelled in the use of points – was to prove the presence of God on earth by providing believers with weighty, vertical evidence of the hierarchical chain of being, with God at the top, then the angels, the saints, the rulers, the priests and so on down to the smallest of sentient life.[31]

---

[31] See for example Erwin Panofsky's seminal text *Gothic Architecture*. Pierre Bourdieu prefers Panofsky's version to Ruskin's because, whilst it too originates in immediate impressions – a carving is arresting or rude, a chapel window uplifting – these feelings are subjected to second-order analysis, whereas Ruskin stayed with the feeling. To remain with first-order 'demonstrative concepts' signifying emotional responses such as delight and fear, describing felt sensations such as the coldness of the surface or the enveloping play of light is to eschew the demands of analysis. Good analysis requires such feelings and meanings are settled into wider awareness of cultural, social and economic structures. Ruskin's generalities distil or crystalize the first-order experiences, rather than generalize from them, whereas Panofsky begins with a phenomenal order out of which, through methodological analysis, structures (institutional fields) emerge. These fields structure thought and action, they permit, 'the sense of the sense'; they create fact. Yet unlike other structural studies content to discover homologies through the location of connexions between first- and second-order concepts, Panofsky's *Gothic* goes further still, able to argue for a deep affinity between Thomist Scholasticism and Gothic architecture, a common temperament that befalls all, wittingly or otherwise, across diverse practices. He accounts for the logic and existence of homologies across multiple experiential spaces, practices, symbols. The binding affinities of work, activity and thought are woven by scholastic institutions whose function is to transmit a collective heritage, consciously and subconsciously, to individuals and collectivities expressed through their culture and even more engrained, their habitus. In this way, arguments for god (sole authority), ways of arguing (reasoned disputation to clarify and reconcile contraries), the spaces for disputation (universities organized through secular and religious

Yet it is precisely because of his refusal to fall in with this standard reading of Gothic that he gained a passionate readership. Ruskin's popularity lay with those willing to question a class system of styles and tastes whose only virtue was an upright rigidity. His readers were tempted to become edge dwellers, and they found in Ruskin someone who authorized this precarious position by dint of his own example. Here was someone unafraid of pursuing the unanswerable questions of meaning with infectious gusto, someone who seemed willing to challenge establishment belief, to recognize how religion might be little more than what the poet Philip Larkin was later to describe as that 'vast moth-eaten musical brocade/Created to pretend we never die'.[32] Ruskin did not hide away amongst the pews of the establishment (though at times his own Christianity drifted into an occluding orthodoxy) and nor did he pursue their plaudits, preferring instead to pursue things with which he might link and love. He wrote and spoke as he felt fit, and he did so tirelessly and to as many of his readers and listeners as he might. There is an ego at play here of course, a desire to be heard and be at the centre of conversations, yet the self-love is more in the way of what Rousseau called *amour de soi*, a natural, robust concern with what allowed human beings to flourish. Ruskin used hard-phrased maxims whose weighty, stentorian tone was sifted with, and lightened by, looping, ornate prose that allowed what might otherwise be ponderous in meaning to float and settle with an unplanned abandon. The effect was more akin to the spread of dandelion seeds than the planting of sturdy trees, an effect which exemplified his version of Gothic, a version that was committed to a broad, enveloping thesis: the happiness and integrity of all organization rests in the free interplay of disciplined imagination and manual expression of individuals bound to one another in common, playful industriousness.

It is towards this realization that any concern with craft work and its organization must turn. Ruskin's work on Gothic was isolated by William Morris as 'one of the few necessary and inevitable utterances of the century' for it outlined 'a new road upon which the world should travel', a road that might only be taken would we first realize:

timetables, disciplinary distinctions and hierarchical titles/offices) combine as an entire structuring worldview, covering theologians, builders and believers alike, though they be worlds apart at the phenomenal level. See Pierre Bourdieu's postface to his French translation of Erwin Panofsky, *Gothic Architecture and Scholasticism*. In Bruce Holsinger *The Premodern Condition: Medievalism and the Making of Theory*. Chicago. 2005. 221–243. 233.

[32] Philip Larkin Aubade. In *Collected Poems*. London: Faber and Faber. 1988.

that art is the expression of man's [sic] pleasure in labour; that it is possible for man to rejoice in his work, for, strange as it may seem to us to-day, there have been times when he did rejoice in it; and lastly, that unless man's work once again becomes a pleasure to him, the token of which change will be that beauty is once again a natural and necessary accompaniment of productive labour, all but the worthless must toil in pain, and therefore live in pain. So that the result of the thousands of years of man's effort on the earth must be general unhappiness and universal degradation – unhappiness and degradation, the conscious burden of which will grow in proportion to the growth of man's intelligence, knowledge, and power over material nature.[33]

It is, Morris continues, curious to think how unhappiness grows in strict sympathy with the progress of science and industry, and it is, he continues, an absurdity to embrace a laissez-faire system of material wealth production in which assets and rents are procured on the prospect of others' immiseration, a sadness which is kept at bay by the persistent and proliferating divisions that break the world up into assets.

Nothing much has changed. We continue to take satisfaction in a broken world, not just of things being broken to make way for newer things, but of broken relations, a world diminished in the spirit of which Gothic speaks. Ruskin's advocacy of Gothic is a diagnosis of this anomaly: in dividing thought from activity, imagination from logic, spirit from materiality, the body from thoughtfulness, and management from labour, we have, following Morris' prediction, continued to work and consume with little heed for the sustained pleasure to be had in making (and using) things well, in giving them good form.

The advocacy of craft work in this book is an attempt to use Ruskin's Gothic to conceptualize the nature of such pleasure in such a way that it might make sense to reconnect with Morris' warning, and to think anew what it means to make and use things well, to work well, and why.

---

[33] William Morris *Preface to Nature of Gothic*. Reprinted in John Ruskin *The Stones of Venice, Vol. II.* Appendix 14. 460.

# 2  Rudeness and the Raw

### The Smallness of the Renaissance Mind

Rudeness permits the wild and un-managed to roam the surfaces of civility, and for rough work to persist alongside the smooth as undeniably rough work. Its ranging, sidestepping strides seem to mock those who aspire to produce something organized into a state of tidy completeness. To open up for perfection is to shut down on the imagination. Take the seventeenth century Renaissance architects working in Venice as an example, the ones whose work, for many, represented the acme of civilized expression, but in which Ruskin saw only lifeless symmetry. These architects were, he argued, imprisoned in their own intellectual devices and mental blueprints: 'Imperatively requiring dexterity of touch, they gradually forgot to look for tenderness of feeling; imperatively requiring accuracy of knowledge, they gradually forgot to ask for originality of thought. The thought and feeling they despised departed from them, and they were left to felicitate themselves on their small science and their neat fingering.'[1]

They associated perfection with an ordered and neat organization of substances, voids and planes that had been combined in the service of an idea which belonged to them, and them alone. Their buildings were to imitate their designs, and their designs were derived from the first principles of their profession – architecture – of which they were the foremost exponents and custodians. Empirical questions of the different ways their buildings might be used were utterly secondary: the intentional ideas in the design were primary. On first viewing, the resulting buildings might offer immediate gratification, but in this they succeed only in hollowing out the elevation of their own status. Having been diagrammatically laid out, the perfect realization of their design requires all things – materials, builders, users – to fall into their assigned places; yet, as the focal details

---

[1] John Ruskin *The Stones of Venice, Vol. III*. In *Complete Works Vol. XI*. Edited by E. T. Cook and Alexander Wedderburn. London: George Allen. 1904. 15.

20    2 Rudeness and the Raw

Figure 3 Charles Herbert Moore, *San Giorgio Maggiore, Venice, from the Lagoon*, 1876. Pencil, watercolour and bodycolour. 1996P037. © The Ruskin, Lancaster University.

of a perfectly functioning building become ever sharper in their script, its character becomes ever more boring and anodyne. It is not that Ruskin abhors order, but that he witnesses its excesses. Too much emphasis on lawful discipline brings about a lifeless conclusion.

Ruskin reserved his fiercest hostility for the often-admired church of St Giorgio Maggiore. It owed its significance, argued Ruskin, to the isolated position it held at the head of Venice's Grand Canal, and how the lagoon took up its reflection (Figure 3). The building itself was nothing more than an ego trip of its architect, Palladio, whose classical design, inspired by ancient Greek temples, went completely untroubled by the locale of its setting and the variety of its purpose. 'The traveller' suggested Ruskin:

> should especially notice in its façade the manner in which the central Renaissance architects (of whose style this church is a renowned example) endeavoured to fit the laws they had established to the requirements of their age. ... It is impossible to conceive a design more gross, more barbarous, more childish in conception, more servile in plagiarism, more insipid in result, more contemptible under every point of rational regard.[2]

---

[2] John Ruskin *The Stones of Venice, Vol. III.* 381.

The Smallness of the Renaissance Mind                                    21

Figure 4 John Ruskin, *Venice – San Giorgio Maggiore*, 1876. Pencil drawing. 1996P1628. © The Ruskin, Lancaster University.

And here is Ruskin's sketch (Figure 4); he can hardly bring himself to depict it, reducing it to scribbled lines.

The smallness of Palladio's science and the neatness of his fingering created a design for which he assumed responsibility and might take the credit. The church, by implication, belonged to him because without him it would have had no life. Though Palladio died in 1580, and the church was not completed until 1610, it remained his church based on his models. Ever since Vitruvius had lain down the orders in *De Architectura*, the architect was to be regarded as a first mover, a creator, a fabricator of mental images that infuse mute matter with life. Good building work became the realization of an idea that had been thought through according to timeless initiating principles whose ratios should remain explicit in the completed work. The more perfect the reasoning and its ordered fabrication, the more civilized the life on offer. Palladio, who took this to his cold heart, had become carried away with his own civilizing force and the cultural symbols it was able to produce. The pinnacles of San Giorgio Maggiore were testimony to such lofty self-aggrandizement. One only had to look, and to see. Ruskin had looked and urges us to do so, and to look behind our initial enthusiasm with the church's comforting proportions which are, he suggests, a substitute for real life. Instead of something that belongs to the earth and the things of the earth, Palladio had imposed a self-sufficient object which could have been placed anywhere and which assumed the materials used in its construction wanted nothing more from their existence than to conform to his ideas.[3] Palladio's work is set in a very restricted and exploitative relation to all things, especially to the masons, carpenters, surveyors and sculptors working on its construction. These workers suffered under the repetitious yoke of back-and-forth movements which invited nothing in the way of personal or collective consideration. The plan gave them no room to own the design, to take it on. The greatest ill that can befall a worker is to be forced, with their head downwards, to operate without a sense of involvement:

> It is not that men [sic] are ill fed, but that they have no pleasure in the work by which they make their bread, and therefore look to wealth as the only means of pleasure. It is not that men are pained by the scorn of the upper classes, but they cannot endure their own; for they feel that the kind of labour to which they are condemned is verily a degrading one.[4]

Despite its superficial beauty, the materials and workers who built St Giorgio Maggiore were degraded. Their bodies were being 'racked into the exactness of a line'[5] defined by the designs of an elite class dedicated to the furtherance of a mental idea that sets itself against the world as though it were 'out there', passively awaiting the ministrations of an architect's forming intelligence. It has set itself against the earth, and its beguiling neatness makes it dangerous: with every plaudit the freedom of things on earth withers.

Imagine, asks Ruskin, two stonemasons working on the capitals of columns. One is working on a concave surface and having to be careful not to damage the work as he goes along, which will necessarily protrude and be vulnerable to knocks. He plans ahead, setting down a design that can be followed and replicated with skilful exactness. The other, working on a convex surface, is freer to experiment as they go along. Her work is not so exposed, and she can sketch, amend and experiment. When compared,

> we shall assuredly find the two families of capitals distinguished, the one by its symmetrical, thoroughly organised, and exquisitely executed ornament, the other by its rambling, confused, and rudely chiselled ornament: But, on the other hand, while we shall often have to admire the disciplined precision of the one, and as often to regret the irregular rudeness of the other, we shall not fail to find

---

[3] Yuk Hui *On the Existence of Digital Objects*. Minneapolis: University of Minnesota Press. 2016. 60–61, expands upon this aspiration in discussing hylomorphism – the propensity of matter to take on form in order to actualize itself – whereas it is equally likely, and perhaps more compelling, to think of craft work, or good craft work, as when form arises out of an attentiveness to matter. To have form dominate matter is to pursue an idealization that culminates, in the machine age, with an ascendency of the perpetual struggle to correct irregularity and uncertainty through a reaching after ever more refined form.
[4] John Ruskin *The Stones of Venice, Vol. II.* §15. 194.
[5] John Ruskin *The Stones of Venice, Vol. II.* §14. 193.

balancing qualities in both. The severity of the disciplinarian capital represses the power of the imagination; it gradually degenerates into Formalism; and the indolence which cannot escape from its stern demand of accurate workmanship, seeks refuge in copyism of established forms, and loses itself at last in lifeless mechanism. The licence of the other, though often abused, permits full exercise to the imagination: the mind of the sculptor, unshackled by the niceties of chiselling, wanders over its orbed field in endless fantasy; and, when generous as well as powerful, repays the liberty which has been granted to it with interest, by developing through the utmost wildness and fulness of its thoughts, an order as much more noble than the mechanical symmetry of the opponent school, as the domain which it regulates is vaster.[6]

The craft work of the second mason does much to disturb the ease and familiarity with which the human being presumes to use the skilled acquisition of repeated patterns to set itself against the things of the world. Even the work of the first mason, being craft work, remains honest enough, insofar as it is a practical response to the shape of the stone. The corruption sets in, as Ruskin would have it, when the balance of discipline and liberty is lost, and work takes up residence in the comfortable 'refuge of copyism' whose motions quickly degenerate into those of a 'lifeless mechanism'. In its suspicion, though not hostility, of the mechanical craft work permits the intrusion of rudeness (and accepts the riskiness of doing so) and so counteracts the slinky, confident spread of the complete and perfect idea that demands it be copied out into life. Hesitation and chance event are given voice and the unfinished or untouched becomes a scene of delight and provocation. Moreover, if there are mistakes, so be it, they are a sign of effort, of having tried, of throwing oneself into the difficulties of working things out. The small eruptions on a glaze, the subtleties of colour in woven willow, the exposed, weathering surfaces of brick or stone, the undulating surfaces of glass blown using wooden moulds, these are examples of rudeness that enhance our relations to things because they are signs of a freer, more open sense of how things can be, and remain, beyond the law. Craft work admits to being puzzled by the question of how things come into being because, but also outside of human order and design, how is it they just are, or come to have form, as if from nowhere, like a wind filling the sails, without heed of a destination?

### The Being of Things

It is a question to which the philosopher Martin Heidegger dedicated his *Being and Time*, a large, single-authored book made up of two divisions

---

[6] John Ruskin *The Stones of Venice I*. In *Complete Works Vol. IX*. Edited by E. T. Cook and Alexander Wedderburn. London: George Allen. 1903. §39. 382.

with numbered sections and numbered lines. Yet whilst it might appear as a written equivalent to Palladio's church, the typographical neatness is open or exposed in its intent. Its precision is dedicated to an understanding of how things can be understood outside of the precise definitions by which they were typically confined. It is a book whose central concern is with how meaning emerges from the 'being there' of specific things, with how something comes from nothing and with how Being itself – life – comes into being through the being of that thing which uses, or 'has' language: the human being, or *Dasein*. In these concerns, it is a book that enquires into similar puzzles motivating craft work: how can things be left to be themselves whilst still being made and found to be made well?

For a craft worker, like the potter Ursula Munch-Petersen, the puzzle of the everyday 'being there' of things like clay, glaze, fire, voids, handles and liquids forms an everyday prompt that guides her work. She talks of asking herself continually, and even suspiciously, what it is that makes, say, a cup a cup, or a jug a jug. How can a jug stand (not sit, curiously) over there, on the wooden surface of a table, and emit its jug-ness (Figure 5)? Or how can two jugs standing side by side on a tabletop remain distinct things but also be sufficiently similar and sympathetic to belong together as objects of the same kind? In what ways can a pair of jugs be said to be properly standing on the wooden surface, and not loosely, or wrongly? The struggle in craft work is to respond to such questions, and the response comes in the form of the next jug she makes: 'Is this how they are then?' 'Perhaps.' Then try again. Can a jug have a lid, for example, is that too far? Maybe not if it is used, like Simpson's hinged strips of wood, to stop dust landing on the contents, rather than to hide the void, but then maybe hiding the void is also a possibility?

Rather than discount questions and responses like Petersen's as too empirical and practical to equate to an inquiry into truth and the nature of 'being', Heidegger would take them as serious attempts to discover how it is that in 'being there', things appear and acquire meaning. The questions and responses have philosophical heft because they disturb what, for centuries, had been the standard way of considering how it was that things came to be.

Prior to *Being and Time*, the existence of things like jugs on a table (or anything material placed 'on' another material thing) had been considered, thanks to the seminal, if somewhat anxiety-laden work of Rene Descartes, an objective condition of what was called 'extension'. In a Cartesian world system, argues Heidegger, the 'being' indicated by two jugs would be 'a definite objective presence of two objectively present *res extensa* [material, extended body] next to each other. The relation of

Figure 5 Ursula Munch-Petersen, jug. Stoneware, white glaze. Photography: Author.

their movements is itself a mode of extension that primarily characterizes the objective presence of the corporeal thing.'[7] The reality of the jugs is grounded in their substance, and the nature of substance is grounded in the attribute of its extension in space (length, breadth, depth): being is *res extensa*. Extension is the *a priori* of thingly being. Without extension, all the other qualities of 'being' (hardness, weight, colour, motion, decay, form or *Gestalt*) cannot appear. These qualities (in which further

---

[7] Martin Heidegger *Being and Time*. Translated by Joan Stamburgh. New York: State University of New York., 2010. I, III, 97.

qualities such as being useful, approachable, obstinate, graceful or flexible gain their footing) are, in essence, quantified modifications of this primal mode: no 'thing' 'is' and no 'thing' can 'be there', without *extension*. The talk of function and appeal that peppers the assessment of crafted things like jugs can only make sense once their extensive structure, and the grounding qualities resulting from that extension, have been substantiated.[8]

Those who enquire into this condition of extension become authorities on being and begin to authorize its proper conditions. Hence it is the presumed primacy of extension that gives figures like Palladio their authority. As an architect, an exponent of the first (*arche*) mode of knowledge, he could think upon and express perfect forms of extension, forms which were, though themselves without substance, given they were the product of the mind (*res cogitans*), a template to which those things with extension should conform. For Heidegger, it is this presence of a 'should' that hints at a profound problem with Descartes' views: they expose us to two worlds. The seat of human consciousness and intelligence, the mind, had no extension, but could represent and imagine things with extension (Palladio's blueprints), and through reasoning and designing, it thought of things that were more efficient and beautiful than those currently existing. Lacking the essence of extension, human intelligence could roam freely, securing itself in spaces of representation (symbols) and classification, which gave rise to meaning. The more constant and acceptable the representations, the more authoritative the structures of meaning into which the mute, material things 'out there' were placed. The meaning of things was given to them by human design, so any enquiry into the meaning of things became an enquiry into the structures of cognition (*res cogitans*) by which meaning was structured. Descartes had instituted two worlds, the mute world of *res extensa* and the active, thoughtful world of *res cogitans*. It was the job of *res cogitans* to ascertain and school others in those qualities of the world that were most persistent and certain, the primary of these being the certain sense of one's own inner being, one's own mind. In casting the mind at the centre of being, Descartes had placed the ontic (a stated idea of a thing, such as Palladio's design for St Giorgio Maggiore, or Descartes maxim 'I doubt, therefore I am') as prior to the ontological (the actual, manifest thing), resulting in a moratorium on enquiry into the meaning of Being itself. Being, the quality of existence of earthly things, had been sterilized of meaning, it had been reduced to the constant objective idea of quantity. Meaning

---

[8] Martin Heidegger *Being and Time*. I, III, 99.

came from elsewhere, from the mental world of the meaning-giving subject (the thinking architect, the thinking – doubting – philosopher). This was only as it should be (at least for Descartes, who seemed to have had a torrid time trusting his own experiences, let alone others') because if it was to material things that we looked for meaning, then all we could experience was uncertainty. The everyday world of material experience is little more than a circulation of indifferent, chance and accidental events and to rely upon any constancies it displays is to invite betrayal. Truth cannot emerge from such things as jugs on tables. It can only come from ourselves, through the disciplined use of categories and concepts that represent *res extensa* in the form of designs and ideas, such as Palladio's designs, which proposed that buildings be made according to the strict, apparently timeless, smooth principles discovered by the architectural genius Vitruvius.

The idiocy of, and damage done by, this breaking up of the world is well attested by Ruskin. His critique of Renaissance architecture is overly polemical because he wishes to make us realize that, if it is a calculating, designing mind that is elevated to a primary and exclusive role in the realization of meaning, then it is as a pall bearer who bears truth towards its grave with a sturdy, idiotic dignity. In their love of laws, maxims, plans and ratios, Renaissance architects suffered from an illusion of purity, and in consequence the society for which they designed also suffered. To break this illusion required rudeness. The rude has a way of upsetting the confidence of *res cogitans* by revealing the particularity of the being of things, and how it is in the rough passage of their 'use' that they lived and acquired meaning. Heidegger too warns us against setting ourselves at a measured distance from material things, as though it was only by removing ourselves from their immediate company that we could get a proper perspective upon them. Far better to get close, and to consider how it is things are when we are alongside them, like neighbours. What is it, after all, that motivates us towards a condition of meaning if not becoming more aware of what surrounds us, what penetrates us, what mediates us, whether dark clouds or sunlight? *Being and Time* was an attempt to restore meaning to Being itself, to give things a place by setting the ontic and ontological in equivalence. If Descartes' sense of the two jugs is a diagrammatic representation of their position and dimensions made by a separate mind, Heidegger inspires a qualitatively different understanding of the scene, one which proposes different kinds of questions. How are the jugs appearing in nearness to me, emerging from the hidden reveals, how are they standing there as well as in here, pulling me into them? In response, Heidegger considers how it is that things appear *as such*, and conjectures on the basic structure of these appearances. The basic structure was linguistic, language was the all-encompassing atmosphere into which all inquiry was pitched and through which all things were disclosed.[9] It was Heidegger's project to put language back into the world, rather than regard it as a means of separating *res extensa* and *res cogitans*. He wished to acknowledge the rudimentary, linguistic work inherent in any appearance appearing as some*thing*: language situated us amongst things by bringing being into something that presents itself as a presence.[10]

Here, *res extensa* gives way to the existential, an awareness that a grounding aspect of being in general (or Being) is the horizon of its possible intelligibility as it is experienced through the repeated (and so, historical) appearance as a 'this' or a 'that'. Measured distance was just one of many ways in which a thing appears, and not at all the dominant one. To understand things like ceramic jugs standing on a wooden tabletop became an experience of attentive apprehension rather than a calculated demonstration. A jug comes to us whole, and by 'us' Heidegger meant each individual as a 'there being' (*Dasein*), a relational condition that he was to elaborate on as 'being' that was configured as a relational organism consisting of 'thing-tool-work'.[11] Though we only see the jugs from one perspective or other, we sense a whole scene, along with the background against which the jugs stand in relief, or into which they bleed, depending on how light refracts on both the glazed

---

[9] For an illuminating foray into the intimacy between Heidegger's sense of language and craft work, see Lesley Chamberlain 'Heidegger: An Aristotle of the Village?', *The Journal of Modern Craft*. 2019, 12, 3–12.

[10] Heidegger's reading of Descartes remains contentious not simply intellectually, but because of the tone. Sidonie Kellerer writes a revealing piece comparing a re-written essay (*The Age of the World Picture*, published 1950) which was originally a 1938 lecture Heidegger gave when Rector of Frieberg University having been appointed by the Nazi party. She reveals Heidegger's complicity in National Socialist ideology which had been partly redacted or mollified. Where the 1950 essay has Descartes as an intellectual precursor for what became the eventual handing over of science to industrial technology, the earlier lecture rails against the Frenchman Descartes for displaying a 'degenerative' superficiality of thought compared with the (German) power of 'Leibnitz, Kant, Fichte, Hegel and Schelling'. See Sidonie Kellerer 'Rewording the Past: The Postwar Publication of a 1938 Lecture by Martin Heidegger', *Modern Intellectual History*. 2014, 11, 3, 575–602. See also Robin Holt and Mike Zundel *The Poverty of Strategy*. Cambridge: Cambridge University Press. 112–117; 158–173.

[11] The full quote is: 'The clearing must ground itself in its open realm and has need of what maintains it in openness, and that is in each case and in different ways a being (thing-tool-work).' To have a sense of being alive as a self, as an organism, was to experience being as a space, or clearing, for the emergence of presence itself, which could not, however, be separate from making things present as something. Martin Heidegger *Contributions to Philosophy (Of the Event)*. Translated by Richard Rojcewicz and Daniela Vallega-Neu. Bloomington: Indiana University Press. 1989. §243. 307.)

surface and wooden grain. We sense the way the clay walls gather in vertical poise because of the flattish, horizontal plane of a table from whose subdued background they gain their distinction. We sense the way the handles await hands and bear the memory of having been handled in their patina. Depending on our upbringing, we sense the many ways jugs have been used and the things they may have contained. As indications of being, these are all as legitimate as the measured extent of the tabletop surface or the uprightness of the clay body. More broadly still, any apprehension of the jugs will also immerse itself in the assembly of things and forces into which the jugs have been gathered in scenes of mutual affect.[12] The nearness, say, of a window that overlooks a garden from which flowers have been freshly cut and which might soon be placed into one of the jugs along with some water; the window being oriented towards the east, giving morning light into the room, a colder warmth, which belongs to this part of the house; and this awareness of an east-facing room is set within the broader assembly of associations with other houses and buildings, with the generational passage of people using jugs in traditional ways, with the reliability of weather patterns. We cannot rid ourselves of this broad and broadening experience of the jugs, it comes to us unbidden: in its intimacy, our perception is passive, and massive. The advocates of *res extensa* for whom manifest extension is the primary condition of being for mute things may well try and dismiss this looser, felt and unedged awareness of being as a crude, unreasoned experience, and instead force themselves into a technical language that isolates the really 'real' aspects of the scene: the measured ones that can be calculated and shared. But far from getting to the really 'real', all their effort amounts to is a diminishment of experience grounded in deception. We cannot divorce from circumstance; and language, far from removing us from the world, is the embodied means by which we acknowledge our complicity and dependency with it: it is, suggests Heidegger, 'the house of Being'.

## Regions

'Strictly speaking', says Heidegger 'there "is" no such thing as a useful thing ... A useful thing is essentially "something in order to".'[13] There are different ways in which jugs might be used in order to do something. They

---

[12] This immanence of effect to cause is toyed with by Gilles Deleuze in *The Logic of Sense* (New York: Columbia University Press. 1990. 69–72), one being co-extensive with the other, and neither having a boundary to one another.
[13] Martin Heidegger *Being and Time*. I, III, 69.

can, for instance, be comforting, provocative, helpful, handy or practical, but always in and amid a regional array of other things, traditions and events from which they are continually taking their cue. 'On the basis of this' argues Heidegger 'an "organization" shows itself, and in this organization any "individual" useful thing shows itself. A totality of useful things is always already discovered before the individual useful thing.'[14] As when say, a jug is made a certain size, like Kaj Frank's cream jugs made by Arabia of Finland, which were made to sit neatly between the double glazing in the kitchen window, keeping the contents cool. The dimensions were critical, but these did not give meaning to the jug. Meaning came through a circulation of cream, jug, glaze, foot, window, glass, gap, weather, clay, kiln etc., each of which emerges only in regional relations with the other, an ongoing organization that becomes apparent when, through the concern and solicitude of their consideration, the craft worker or user becomes attuned to how things like jugs are accommodating other things, orchestrating a scene of mutual action – or work – within which the individual things, if they too are working, disappear from conscious attention. Even when they are noticed, they are not noticed in isolation, but in terms of the roles they are playing in the practices by which the human is finding itself placed in the world, again and again.[15] Placing the flowers in one of the jugs on the table in the room filled by light from the east-facing window, for example, brings a distinction to the objects, yet only in the regional settings by which objects like flowers are arranged. The jug is made to carry liquid and can, on occasion, also be used to sustain displays of cut flowers and foliage. The flowers connect the user and maker of the jug to a larger world of which they are a part, though here, in the room, somewhat apart, they also hint at a lingering and enjoyable hedonism to which we, in our encounter with the jugs, will be, more or less, attuned, depending on the mood we bring with us from earlier scenes in the day. What flowers mean, what types, in which bunches, and where and when they are placed, constitutes a grammar of ornament whose subtleties we can become, more or less, aware of depending on our regional experience.

Humans have always related to things from within these relations of use. Placing flowers in a jug is but one of many acts of overturning the earth and directing it towards our own human interests. The budding and flaring open of the petals alludes to a natural world of fecundity, growth, colour and scent that gives a sense of peace, or exuberance, and if bought from a florist the flowers have been grown for these effects, and

---

[14] Martin Heidegger *Being and Time*. I, III, 69.
[15] Martin Heidegger *Introduction to Metaphysics*. Translated by Gregory Fried and Richard Polt, 2nd edn. New Haven: Yale. 2014. 174.

in being arranged in jugs on a table these effects of the outdoors have been within the setting of a private home. Those cutting and making the arrangement, and those who, in noticing the arrangement as they pass by the table, or even lingering momentarily to take it in become aware of its balance, its tension, its sense, only because they belong to the circling rhythms of use encircling all things.

Heidegger called these assemblies of use 'regions', as if to maintain their fixity whilst only loosely defining the edges: (…/jug/table/flowers/room/window/house/town/community/…). Those who can hazard at what comes after the last slash or before the first slash of this listed representation of a regional assembly, those who can make a good guess at what might plausibly be entailed by the conjunction of these things, can only do so because they share the same regions as the jug and they too have placed jugs on tables in specific rooms for well-known, practical reasons such as displaying flowers, reasons that have stayed firm. These assemblies will always exhaust language, though it is in language that the referential connexions between an 'in order to' (cutting the flowers to fit in the jug, placing water in the jug to keep the flowers temporarily 'alive') and a 'what for' (calm, distraction, delight) is agreed upon and sustained within the totality of useful things.[16] The shape of a jug has changed little over the millennia of use, it has found its shapes, its *Gestalt*, and has kept within these regions. Petersen, for example, experiments by using declivities rather than handles on the smaller jugs, but their shape retains the impress of the human grasp. Most of the things with which craft work concerns itself are of a similarly stubborn form: there are cups amongst the grave goods found in excavations of the ancient Greek city of Etruria which are the spitting image of a teacup. There has been a modicum of slow evolution in the type of clay used and techniques of firing, but the shape has been fixed for millennia. The same with knives, glasses, the coat, the shoe, the pen, the curtain, the bed, the lamp. They are things whose functional range and expressive form have been settled upon and become settled into the geological layers of human practice. Yet in each encounter the jug appears, or 'dawns' to use a phrase of the philosopher Ludwig Wittgenstein, for the first time. It is not simply there but emerges and in use is 'taken on' from within a regional situation, and each time uniquely.

Within regions, things often cohere quite naturally, and language (that is, the ordinary language of conversation) acknowledges our faith in the ongoing stability of this coherence in its grammar, allowing words to slip between referents with the ease of a slow-gliding stream. Jugs have a body, lip, foot, they can hold themselves upright, and typically

---

[16] Martin Heidegger *Being and Time*. I, III, 77.

without ostentation, they have a darker inner life and an outside more easily read, notably when turned to the light. The surface can appear flat but on closer looking can be pock-marked and ridged, undulating in minute valleys, wrinkling and spreading, and the patina can vary with age, whilst still holding that which it was made to hold. All of this can also be said for the lipped and footed humans that 'use' them. The pot redounds with human qualities, as evoked beautifully in George Eliot's novel *Silas Marner*:

> It was one of his daily tasks to fetch his water from a well a couple of fields off, and for this purpose, ever since he came to Raveloe, he had had a brown earthenware pot, which he held as his most precious utensil among the very few conveniences he had granted himself. It had been his companion for twelve years, always standing on the same spot, always lending its handle to him in the early morning, so that its form had an expression for him of willing helpfulness, and the impress of its handle on his palm gave a satisfaction mingled with that of having the fresh clear water. One day as he was returning from the well, he stumbled against the step of the stile, and his brown pot, falling with force against the stones that overarched the ditch below him, was broken in three pieces. Silas picked up the pieces and carried them home with grief in his heart. The brown pot could never be of use to him anymore, but he stuck the bits together and propped the ruin in its old place for a memorial.[17]

Helpful, reliable, but needing the concern and solicitude that Silas, eventually, momentarily, failed to give. The pot breaks down and is let go, unable to contain itself, or anything else. The memorial is a reminder of the honesty, dependability, resilience (despite its fragility) of things that never attempt to hide themselves or be something they are not. It indicates a further region still, that of life and death, from which jugs and earthenware pots acquire both their solidity and fragility, and from which what they hold also takes their cue, as objects being brought from the outside to bring life into an interior, whether as an essential for life, like

---

[17] George Eliot *Silas Marner*. Edited by David Carroll. Harmonsworth: Penguin, 2003. 13. Sara Ahmed (*What's the Use? On the Uses of Use*. Durham: Duke University Press. 2019. 6–10) finds this episode equally provocative, notably as an indication of how, in being used, an object impresses itself upon the character of those using it, a distributed influencing that weaves instrumentality and affection, and which is patterned in all manner of often-complicated and political relations associated with willingness, helpfulness, belonging and sympathy. The brown pot reappears at the end of the novel. Silas, having found a small child, Eppie, on his hearth and raised her as his own:

> Silas sat down now and watched Eppie with a satisfied gaze as she spread the clean cloth, and set on it the potato-pie, warmed up slowly in a safe Sunday fashion, by being put into a dry pot over a slowly-dying fire, as the best substitute for an oven. For Silas would not consent to have a grate and oven added to his conveniences: he loved the old brick hearth as he had loved his brown pot – and was it not there when he had found Eppie? The gods of the hearth exist for us still; and let all new faith be tolerant of that fetishism, lest it bruise its own roots.

water, or as a contemplative aside, like flowers.[18] It was only as the pot breaks that these feelings start to emerge. In picking up the three pieces, Silas was not giving the scene meaning, he was searching for a foothold within it, trying to excavate sense by adjusting to a situation that has to be accepted, but which nevertheless extends his relation to the pot, for what emerges is its potential as a ruin, its role as a strange shibboleth.

It is within these regional settings (and many more might be attributed to the 'being' of the things called jugs, depending on where and when they are placed, and how they have been made and used) that the form, the materials, the purposes and the traditions of making coincide as a 'jug'. Neither the jug nor its maker can sever completely from the combined historical influence of these gatherings of form, material, purpose and tradition. For example, all jugs should really be glazed on the insides so they might hold water, milk, cider or oil, and, on occasion, flowers. To hold is often also to pour. Much like the body of a fish is shaped by the water in which it swims, the shape taken by pouring liquid defines the shape of the lip, typically made by a suggestive and simple, upward pinch in the clay by strongly palmed fingers. The body is often made straight, typically with a stabilizing outward flare to the base, slightly restrained as though attentive to the potential presence of other tableware with which it might join company, but always with distinction. The outer glazes and slips can be freer than the interior ones, even absent, thought typically they too are made to take the knocks of use, such as the salt-glazed Bellarmine jugs (Figure 6) made throughout Rhineland Europe until the nineteenth century, but centred in Frechen, Germany, a concentration of activity where the potters learned to make standardized, differently scaled stoneware forms embellished by adding a caricatured face of a bearded man to the necks.[19]

Uses change. The potter Phil Rogers, for example, was always quick to accept that hardly any of his customers really needed to buy a big Bellarmine-style jug these days. People no longer used them for oil, water, ale or cider. So why buy them? Because many of the regional settings remain in place. The user wants to feel a connection to the maker, and because they are witnessing a line, a shape, an orchestration, a historical connexion to past use, even though they will never pour from these larger jugs, they might still belong to the tradition of doing so. So, a large jug by Rogers retains its proper qualities. It should not be heavy, even if it is

---

[18] Martin Heidegger *Being and Time*. I, III, 103. Also see Christian De Cock, and Damian O'Doherty, Ruin and Organization Studies. *Organization Studies*, 2016, *38*, 1, 129–150.

[19] These *Bartmannkrüge* contrast with the tall and narrow Baluster jugs used to hold beer without it going flat and to be tucked into the limited floor space of cellars. Others, like the big-bellied German Bellarmine or *Bartmann* jugs (*Bartmänner*, bearded man, whose features were often sprigged or impressed onto the necks) popular until eighteenth century were used to hold a huge variety of liquids, including mercury and witches' potions.

Figure 6 Bellarmine jug, 1660–1680. Salt-glazed stoneware. The Metropolitan Museum of Art: 10.113 / Gift of M. Harris, 1910.

not to be used, it could be, and the resulting thin wall then makes it very hard to get the shape right, which takes a lot of working up and down to get the sides firm, and a specific stiffness to the clay. The jug is, indeed, glazed inside so it can hold liquids without seepage and be more easily washed, and the handle is strong enough to bear lifting. Had a handle not been attached, and the jug remained a vase, Rogers may have been able to charge more for it, but he is making jugs because jugs need to be made still. There is something intimate about a jug, especially the larger ones, that arcs back to a time when questions of storage were ones of survival.

The jug, like many crafted things, fosters relations with distant peoples, it once afforded folk the ability to move whilst taking their preserved food and drink along with them, or to preserve it for leaner seasons, to share a meal, or to trade. The jug connects, largely because, in itself, it is not all that notable; it contains. Unlike weaponry like arrows or spears, it does not isolate a target and give birth to a narrative of killing, surviving and overcoming, though the sides of some Grecian urns depict such. Typically, there is nothing glamorous or memorable about the use of a container.

These differences between things-in-use can be quietly significant. Accepting the basic thesis that we relate to things largely as being there for us, as things to be put to use, and that these uses frame a long-standing sense of our own sense of being, the novelist Ursula Le Guin pondered on what it might be like were the origin myths of the human species grounded in the use of things that were not so aggressive or assertive, in containers rather than weapons: 'a leaf a gourd a shell a net a bag a sling a sack a bottle a box a container. A recipient. The first cultural device was probably a recipient.'[20] How might the things of the world have appeared to us in our histories if a gourd, woven bag or earthenware pot were the object from which relations were mediated? The spear is, Le Guin admits, a more compelling option. The hunter, male, alone, a heroic figure trading in lives, returns with a kill and a tale, and the tale authorizes his distinction, it elevates and sediments the elevation.

It is hard to tell a really gripping tale of how I wrested a wild-oat seed from its husk, and then another, and then another, and then another, and then another, and then I scratched my gnat bites, and Ool said something funny, and we went to the creek and got a drink and watched newts for a while, and then I found another patch of oats ... No, it does not compare, it cannot compete with how I thrust my spear deep into the titanic hairy flank white Oob, impaled on one huge sweeping tusk, writhed screaming, and blood spouted everywhere in crimson torrents, and Boob was crushed to jelly when the mammoth fell on him as I shot my unerring arrow straight through eye to brain.

That story not only has Action, it has a Hero. Heroes are powerful. Before you know it, the men and women in the wild-oat patch and their kids and the skills of the makers and the thoughts of the thoughtful and the songs of the singers are all part of it, have all been pressed into service in the tale of the Hero. But it isn't their story. It's his.[21]

To restore the vessel, the recipient, the object into which gathered things are put as the 'first cultural device', to examine two jugs side by side on a table and to think of their form belonging to the opening of human civilization, is to re-calibrate the regional history to which jugs, and craft work, belong. It is no longer a grammar of victors and vanquished, of a subject who in lunging, thrusting, retreating, capitulating, overcoming, staking and claiming overcomes nature. It is a story of orienting and observing, collecting, of storing and waiting, of finding useful, edible and arresting things that can be brought into company with other things, and into a family space, a home, a community, and

---

[20] Ursula Le Guin *A Carrier Bag Theory of Fiction*. In *Dancing at the Edge of the World*. New York: Grove Atlantic Press. 1989.
[21] Ursula Le Guin *A Carrier Bag Theory of Fiction*. 149–150.

shared and used and replaced. History becomes a story of gathering, not killing, of keeping things in a rude or raw state because not all the things in this growing company are apparently useful, but there they are anyhow, having been gathered and stored in vessels and now lying in wait, with their potential concealed on the underside, awaiting the accident of revelation from a clumsy movement or an uncommon angle of the light.

As a vessel, the jug authorizes an alternate form of cultural common sense in which the meanings immanent to use are ones of containment rather than domination, and makers and users can intrude into these regions of the commonplace with the kind of questions Ursula Munch Petersen, and all other craft workers ask. These questions animate the regional gathering of things with small pauses of gathered consideration, pauses which serve to heighten the scene of use, to bring it, as a scene, nearer, much like small bronze speckles of manganese might direct attention to the smooth off-white glaze of a jug into which they are set: the hero has no place in such stories.

## Experiment

The questioning over use can go on and on, and sometimes become quite extreme, to a point where it begins to press hard upon the regional arrangements that shape our relations to things. For example, when a potter like Alison Britton starts building a jug-like vessel from slabs of hand-pressed clay rather than on the wheel, and she deliberately enlarges or restricts the standard proportions, or when she decorates the jug to force the conjunction of colour and plane to the fore, and repress the void, the habituated integration of thing, tool, and work begins to stutter. The form emerges from an effortful and active process of thought and experiment rather than from the more purposeful, functional tradition of making jugs for use. Extension is revisited, but as an inherent rather than measured quality, symmetry is twisted, and balance something that warrants suspicion. In a 1990 catalogue for an exhibition of Alison Britton's pots, Tanya Harrod recalls being struck by their mobility and openness, by how they resisted the role of being used easily, but nevertheless grew out of a deep familiarity with these uses; unable to shed the ontology of being containers, they were nevertheless not contained, nor were they containing. Their rudeness or rawness arises from them being both objects that are active and objects that are contemplative, and refusing to settle into either register: look at them and they entice you into use, and take them up and they elicit the gaze.[22] They teeter, and would tease the Cartesians: extensa

---

[22] Tanya Harrod *Alison Britton: Ceramics in Studio*. London: Bellew. 1990. 32.

Figure 7  Alison Britton, *Blue Lines*, 2022. © The Artist / Michael Harvey. Courtesy of Oxford Ceramics Gallery.

fuses with cogitans, function with idea, without hierarchy. Their lips roam and their edges pitch and spilt, sometimes their sides are stretching out to a point where they might even give way to gravity and topple, and some

38   2   Rudeness and the Raw

Figure 8 Walter Keeler, thrown, altered, salt-glazed teapot. Courtesy of Walter Keeler/York Museums Trust (CC-BY-SA 3.0).

have insides that tend towards becoming outsides. In reaching towards the outer reaches of function, a rawness emerges from a process of closely wrought, thoughtful making where each piece, being on the edge of the region, stands somewhat alone (Figure 7).[23]

A further variation on deviance or waywardness comes in the work of Walter Keeler whose jugs and teapots nevertheless retain a strict geometry, whilst bearing strong echoes of other forms. A ceramic teapot can

---

[23] Theodor Adorno argued that what separated Beethoven and Mozart was the relationship between the form their music took in relation to tradition. Mozart, heir to the old traditions, was so confident in his having absorbed the proper limits to a symphony, or mass, that he allowed the centrifugal forces of sound free reign, sure that the organized integrity would hold fast: unity came from the inheritance and replication of form. For Beethoven form, and the unity it brings, was not an inheritance one absorbed, but an executed idea, that had to be asserted though the making of each piece. See, Theodor Adorno *Aesthetic Theory*. Edited by Gretel Adorno and Rolf Tiedemann. Translated by Robert Hullot-Kentor. New York: Continuum. 1970/2002. 141. For Alison Britton the jug gains more of the qualities Adorno associates with Beethoven than in the hands, say, of a ceramicist like Kylliki Salmenhaara working for Arabia, Finland. For Britton jugs do not carry or indicate something in addition to their own distinction, whereas for those working at Arabia the carrying function was brought to the fore. Salmenhaara's tableware jugs were made in relatively large numbers within a factory setting, yet they occupy the proper limits ascribed to tableware objects with an incomparable force. The unifying force of tradition was absorbed into each jug with such sensitivity and strength that time and time again the simple became arresting.

be more like an oilcan made from bent sheets of galvanized tin, and the spout made to resemble a gun barrel (Figure 8). A jug can be like a section of pipe, pinched along one rim and bent in the middle, a cup a hollowed-out coil, its handle an errant offshoot, barely touching the side.

With Britton and Keeler, and many others, the inquiry raised by the question of being begins to exclude or re-negotiate the wider regional forces of functional need, logics of economy and traditional appearance. The thing itself is made more immediate, it becomes an overtly aesthetic experience; what is present is being made present through an intellectual and sensory engagement with material things and the possibilities they yield by interrogating their limits and their resemblances. Tradition remains very present in the acquisition of training and the very firm sense of working in response to the work of others, but the acquired learning is considered less as a yardstick than a propulsive force, and the future is being anticipated in an as yet unrealized array of new forms. Britton and Keeler excel in an aesthetic capacity to explore, enact and extend the complexity and minuteness of the differentiations in the relations between things, and between humans and things, not to discover and enforce 'better' or more productive relations, but to foster and enjoin themselves to new relations. It is in this way, suggests the American pragmatist philosopher John Dewey, that each new piece of work attempting to realize new form becomes an inauguration of life itself, with the creation of difficult, unusual, rude form: '[T]he designs of living are widened and enriched. Fulfilment is more massive and subtly shaded'.[24]

Another potter, Gillian Lowndes was tireless in her enquiry into the multiplicities of form that things might become, not just one thing, but multiple things, often found things that were fused, broken, joined, twisted without regard for classificatory distinctions or methodological standards (Figure 9). The forms might be awkward, and were certainly raw, yet because they retained, in part, a semblance of what they once were they carried the 'user' along with them. She had been inspired to use found things in her pottery having encountered the Yoruba tradition in Nigeria, in which artistic media could be anything: discarded shopping bags, the husks from cracked nuts, rusting munitions, wire, plastic toys or clay. Clay was the mainstay, the original material, that from which life came and to which it returned, but it was never privileged, neither in Yoruba work, nor hers, and was often mauled and splintered so that it barely held itself together. The resulting pieces become

---

[24] John Dewey *Art as Experience*. New York: Minton Balch & Co. 1934. 11–17, 23. Dewey is speaking of artists, yet in his pragmatic way, he rarely differentiates between artist and artisan.

Figure 9 Gillian Lowndes, *Collage with a Cup*, 1986. Stoneware, mixed media. Courtesy of The Sunday Painter. Photography: Ollie Hammick.

a deliberate and delicate paean to the unclassified and voiceless forms that life takes when it is barely begun or barely remains.

Here work is cosmic, in that its concern is with the start and end of life. It is at these extremities that things are at their most enigmatic and fragile, or their most dishevelled and experienced. Shorn of proper purpose, they barely fit in anymore. Yet for Lowndes it is in this state of near abandonment that they can reveal themselves, albeit not in their original capacity as useful things, but as found things from whose unlikely persistence new openings are possible.[25] The things have passed through or as yet not reached the useful stage: they have broken down and lost their place in everyday practices, or failed to find grip there. The cup has stopped holding liquid, the fork has stopped spearing food, the cloth has never wrapped anything, the nail never joined anything. Yet in this loss and severance they have gained an independence that attracts a ceramicist who experiments with how new forms can emerge by placing such things in motley company. Fuse the shards of a cup with found wire

---

[25] Anthony Shaw and David Whiting *Seeing with Another Eye*. Stuttgart: Arnoldsche. 2024. 140.

Experiment 41

and harshly fired cement and a queer assembly of differences emerges. Before they were fused, the raw materials had little in common, and as much as they can complement one another, they also antagonize, yet the final piece nevertheless coheres as 'bone-china', a spinal column that gathers its own life to itself. Lowndes remarks how she had little idea beforehand of what might emerge; there is no blueprint, no *res cogitans*. She works through the raw materials rather than imposes ideas upon them. The meaning of the piece emerges from this collaboration of craft worker, form and raw materials mediated through collective memories of different forms of use. The broken and re-fused cup reveals an intimacy between different surfaces whose conjunction evoke a once-upright human body that has been felled. Showing backbone is no longer showing backbone.

In *Collage with Tomato Root* Lowndes reveals very directly how a craft worker becomes alive to how humans are continually attempting to use things to expand their sensory potential and the criteria of meaning (Figure 10). Where for many a used plant, once dead, becomes waste to be cast aside, for Lowndes it becomes a reminder of how forms integrate with and rely upon one another. The *Collage with Tomato Root* reveals the form a root system was afforded by its surrounds, before it was pulled from the

Figure 10 Gillian Lowndes, *Collage with Tomato Root*, 1990. Stoneware, mixed media. Courtesy of The Anthony Shaw Collection. Photography: Philip Sayer.

earth, vitrified in dry air and fused with wire-bound clays that take the form of an open hulled pod being hauled onto land; a vessel that can only hold things because it is being held and supported. One form organizes the other, transferring life back and forth and in witnessing this the viewer is provoked into thinking through the prevalence of such interdependencies of form and how they too are being held onto by ostensibly dead forms: their entombed ancestors, their photographed memories of youth.

As a piece of work, Lowndes' collage is stripped back to raw elemental things that reveal the incipient beginnings of culture. The aesthetic response of a plant to its environment spliced to that of an artist in which sensuous form begins to firm up, but without reaching anything complete or even recognizable. Its hybridity is touching, fragile and will face the resistance of derision or indifference when presented as a finished piece. It lacks solidity, representational familiarity, definite order, it is as much movement as it is still, and whilst it is organized and ordered in time and space it hesitates, wondering if there is space and patience enough for it to eke out its spare connexions. As well as tomato plant, broken ceramic, metal wire and mesh, it is a collage of sensuous feelings, perceptions and emotional intensities, an ensemble that has undergone alteration in human hands and continues to do so under the gaze of viewers. Like any useful thing, it too is a form undergoing the struggle between itself and its environment, one initiated and tended by a craft worker for whom the appreciative effort of learning and training, of sourcing, combining and disassembling things, of breaking things up and starting again, of joining, working against accident and of finishing and presenting, has itself to be appreciated by others. The collage is consummated in execution and then once again in reception and in being received the viewer must somehow work against the urge to judge it according to the comforting criteria of recognition and use-value, whilst all the while having the solidity of these criteria re-enforced by the sheer effort of working against them.

Lowndes' extremities are a reminder that to recognize something as an object is an act of perception that has been formed. Lowndes goads our perception into perceiving itself as that which is already, naturally turning toward pre-given categories. We sense ourselves perceiving her made things as an expression of technical skill, or a representation of other things, or an object that has been authored by a signature and that can be sold on that basis alone, or a now defunct functional device, and as many other things. She reveals how, because of this immediate, instinctual categorization, the work becomes lost to itself because nothing is at stake any longer, the thing has been classified, objectified. The perception has been immediately canalized by categories, and so the possibilities for exploring the richness and nuance of its form get lost.

Whilst it is not possible to rid oneself of the language by which the thing makes itself apparent as an object, its named appearance need not be of a clear and definitive form. As Ruskin notes 'It does not much matter what things are in themselves, but only what they are to us; and that the only real truth of them is their appearance to, or effect upon us'.[26] The world we perceive exists as a form of grip on appearance, and objects still rely on appearance: they are not 'out there'. The grip is not an all-embracing one: objects (and events for that matter) will always appear differently, depending upon the mix of regional settings that structure the experience. Hence appearing need not always be, or only be, an act of settled recognition, there is room for the kind of disruptive experiment made by Lowndes. Her work is a conscious assembly of objects that resists proper objectification, and which appears in ways that upset the habituated inclination to equate recognition with naming. The collage of things provides a space for both the craft worker and viewer to explore the limits of what has hitherto been agreed upon as an acceptable expression of harmonious form. It is the consciousness (in maker and user) by which this shuttling between what is being created and how it is being perceived that distinguishes Lowndes' collage from the found objects of which it consists, and it is the deliberation with which she (and her viewer) refuses to allow the piece to settle into an easily read, settled perception, and the making of perception itself something perceived, that distinguishes its aesthetic charge (it looks to expand and enrich the struggle for such settlements of recognition).[27]

The value of these liminal experiences in making form is how they gather the association of meaning and use into a kind of joust animated by a slightly macabre humour. Typically, the union of meaning and use goes hidden. The jug pours or helps the flowers gather in a bunch, all is as it should be. But when a jug is made to topple under the slightest touch or intrudes upon the scene by disturbing proportional norms (of the kind deliberately investigated by Alison Britton and Walter Keeler), the naturalness of the union falls into question: its naturalness becomes almost a petulance. In a more drastic way still, when a form is broken and reassembled 'wrongly', and when apparent contraries are merged into a weird hybrid form, and yet something still appears, it becomes apparent not as a thing-in-use, but divested of use, and so as something whose reluctance to con-form reminds us of the hold that regional settlements have on our perception.

[26] John Ruskin *Modern Painters III*. In *Complete Works Vol. V*. Edited by E. T. Cook and Alexander Wedderburn. London: George Allen. 1903. 162
[27] John Dewey *Art as Experience*. 48. Dewey continues: the aesthetic is always moving towards completeness without ever reaching the complete state, in its moment of perfection it runs asymptotic to any endpoint.

## Reluctance and Functional Excellence

Reminders can also appear when things are so well made that, in use, the thing stands out because of its excellence. Rather than pushing uses to the edges of what is normal, the thing becomes apparent by encouraging an intensification of its normal use. The yaw between made things that make themselves present as something of which the user must take note, and those that fit so readily into use they go unnoticed, is far from smooth, and the regional setting in which presence and absence vie with one another is more agonal than it is consensual. A well-wrought kitchen knife, for example, one that chops and slices with minimal, graceful effort, is a thing that encourages the user to concentrate on the job of dicing vegetables or slicing flesh. There are specialist knives for cleaving a carcass or for splitting large tubers, for filleting fish, de-boning meat or slicing tomatoes, and if they are well-made, they require skilled use, but even a general-purpose knife can elicit the consideration of its user, indeed require it. The knife does not disappear into a habituated arc of blade, hand, body movement; it becomes very obviously present. The blades of these knives are often made from high carbon steel (the more carbon, the harder the steel, with high being between 0.75 and 1.5 per cent), and some have a mix of different steels, with the cutting edge made from steel soft enough to be sharpened to a keen edge, from the tip to the heel of the blade, whereas harder steels are used to form a resilient backbone along the blade's spine. Forging like this takes time as the different steels are twisted, heated and beaten repeatedly before being shaped, ground and polished. The Swedish knife maker Robin Dalman uses a distal tapering of the spine (the blade thins as it moves from the heel to the tip) and then grinds gentle concave hollows along both sides of the primary bevel and both sides of the blade bevel (Figure 11). The result is an undulating 's' profile which allows thinly sliced food to fall away rather than stick to the blade surface, and being thinner the blade encounters less resistance, allowing the edge to cut rather than relying on the thickening of the bevel to wedge or cleave the food apart.

How to care for such a knife must be learned. The knife becomes a thing of which the user becomes conscious. It requires attention, and with attention it retains its prominence, even beauty, but only if it is looked after. If not, it will quickly go wild, it will cease to perform properly, it will not make itself available for use.[28] Carbon steels are prone to rust and so the knife must be cleaned immediately after use, and then stored dry or with a light coat of mineral oil. Responding to this obstinacy, a bladesmith can use stainless steel instead (the steel has 11–13 per cent chromium added)

---

[28] Martin Heidegger *Being and Time*. I, III, 88.

Figure 11 Robin Dalman, 210 stainless steel (63 hrc) gyuto. Octagonal tapered wa handle in torched ash. Photography: Robin Dalman.

which will not rust, and the modern versions like AEBL or Magnacut hold an edge just as well as carbon steel, if not better, though they take longer to work. Either way, the knives still need regular sharpening, and often, which means the use of a sharpening stone, the use of which, like the knife, takes time. Stones too have different grades and qualities. Different types of grinding can add further subtleties to the blade. Using such tools in the home is perhaps excessive. They are not cheap, and even hard to find, but they will last a lifetime if properly looked after. Cheaper knives are more convenient, but something is perhaps lost in this convenience as the knife begins to disappear; rather than impress itself upon the user, it integrates itself into use seamlessly and obediently, and is no longer present in the activity of chopping as a provocation or obstacle. It becomes just a knife, and chopping is just chopping.

**The Golden Bowl**

A further way that craft work can reveal and work productively with the rudeness and rawness of things is through the presence of flaws. Flaws have great potency, a force that is played upon with some effect in Henry James' short novel *The Golden Bowl*. The bowl first appears in the collection of an antiques shop in Bloomsbury, London. It is being sold at what appears to two of the main characters – Charlotte and the Prince, who have been out strolling and happened upon the shop – to be a very reasonable price. That is until the shopkeeper admits, eventually, there is a hairline crack, unseen, but revealed when the bowl was 'rung': on striking its sides with a fingernail, the note was hollow, ending abruptly. Those few 'susceptible to registration' might spot the flaw, but for the majority the bowl remains as it is first introduced by the shopkeeper: an object whose mystery is capped by a gilded, crystalline allure. Glass and metal had been fused through a 'lost art' that swithered between the transparent lucidity of crystal and opaque lucence of gold. Cleverly, the shopkeeper hints that, as he procured it for less than its real value, he might also let it go for less. After all, the flaw prevents him from charging more, and surely these customers – to whom he has revealed the flaw, because they, being persons of intelligence, could absorb the understanding that flaws accompany all things as inevitably as do their shadows – were from that special class of person who could live with the bowl properly, alive to its merits as a cracked thing-in-itself. They were the kind of customer who could sense how, once unwrapped from its box and placed upon a satin mat, like a small sun, its monetary value became incidental, and its real value shone through; the flaw provokes attention and so enhances rather than detracts from its presence.

Momentarily, Charlotte considers the shopkeeper's offer, then demurs. Its attraction is not strong enough to commit to its purchase as a wedding gift for the Prince and his fiancé Maggie Verver. The bowl is re-boxed and tucked away. Yet its effect lingers, seeding the germ of a further flaw: illicit love. Charlotte's protracted and irresolute refusal had communicated the possibility of an affair between her and the Prince in a way words never could, and once opened up by their having stood in such close proximity looking upon the flickering glow of the bowl's surface, the affair beckoned, and they had little control over the matter, for their agency was no longer, and had never been, at the centre of things, because nothing is ever central, nothing holds firm, not their morals, not their probity and not their self-assured command of character. The bowl, alluring yet flawed was resisted; the affair, alluring and flawed, was not.

The bowl reappears later in the novel, now purchased by Maggie, who wanted a gift for her father, Adam Verver, who is marrying Charlotte. It is displayed on a mantelpiece, only to be smashed in a facile gesture of support for Maggie on her discovery of the affair between her husband, the Prince, and her friend and now stepmother, Charlotte. Within the gravitational pull of this occasional circulation of a flawed thing, the protagonists continue to negotiate the regional settings of their precarious positions. The intricate regional mesh of relations (friends, betrothed, blood ties), social mores and morals, commerce, class, abstracted, unspoken duties, desire, are held within the void of a bowl. The bowl cannot be fixed, the crack is minute but fatal, and so it can do nothing but bear its flaw with a profound patience, becoming in the meantime the only source of constancy as in the story it intrudes into the novel's small intricacies, both as an indication of broken and breakable truths, and as a means for disturbing and breaking these truths further by pushing what is already broken to its limits, as it too is pushed from above the fireplace. The bowl becomes rude, unruly: precisely because of its flaw it has a potency lacking in a perfect (and so reliable) version. It evokes the lustre of desired but shameful possibilities that will stain and crack the very fidelity of the relations to which it is being offered up as a token, a symbol, an assurance. The bowl draws the gaze of the Prince and Charlotte and they cannot now withdraw it, but they must withdraw, forcing them to the edges of their disciplined habit, then nudging them over, from which open, disorienting space their only recourse is to latch onto empty formality and the confinements of secrecy, much as they would cling to stray lifebuoys in a restless, featureless sea. Whereas Silas can lament the breaking of the water pot and the loss of its close and useful company, Maggie's relation to the bowl is more abstract and symbolic, its meaning is not so easily read from its use. It begins as a gift intended to express the love she has for her father and for a friend, and somehow to fuse these different forms of love. Once installed on the mantelpiece, however, it glides into something more equivocal, a scene of uncertainty, and then of crystal-clear betrayal. She senses the loss of her own self-assured sense of being in the middle of her experience, of being in control of what happened to her. Events have occurred over which she had no knowledge or control, and she is dashed to pieces. The fragments of Silas' bowl instil a sense of loss, whereas those of the Golden Bowl are created from loss, and they retain a compelling hold, charging Maggie with the gilded, variable and wavering duty to keep quiet, preserve decorum, hold herself aloof from those she once held dear, in order that the flaw cleaving her family is concealed: the bowl shows her a way through, back to the manners and mores of her station, but now emptied of their everyday fluidity and heft. The regional habits verge on meaninglessness, but they are all that are left to her, those and love itself, rather than love directed towards a specific person.

**Raku Tea Bowls**

As well as revealing itself in obstinacy, and in keeping what is broken in play, crafted things can also remain present in a raw or rude form when being used in formal rituals during which they take to the stage, such as the tea bowl in the Japanese tea ceremony. The ceremony requires of the participants an attentive patience and abeyance to ritualistic procedures whose purpose remains unspecified but whose structure remains as clear as when they were first mooted by the Tang dynasty Chinese poet Lu Yu (733–804 CE) in his treatise on tea drinking. Many forms of drinking tea exhibit a ritualistic side and can be etched with a habituated discipline acquired from earlier generations as uncritically and thoughtlessly as one inherits eye or hair colour. In the UK the tea 'ceremony' might extend to warming the pot, putting the milk into the cup first (or after, or no milk), letting the leaves steep (or mash), and, if a certain type of guest is expected, using the best china cups, which normally sit quietly on a cupboard shelf. In Japan the rituals are more intricate and orchestrated, more consciously and collectively abstracted. The ceremony sits outside of the everyday, it is indifferent to the bustle, the things become conspicuous. It is an indifference that indicates self-sufficiency, a severing from normal busyness, one whose rigours elide from the interference of specific interests and so remain what they are: a bone-hard calibration of a cultural event.

Movements are scripted, objects are placed and then used in a strict order: the steam from the hot water held in the small tea pot is given vent for a requisite number of seconds, the different teas are legion, requiring a variety of tools for mixing, spooning and stirring the leaves or powder. At the centre of the performance is the tea bowl, or *chawan*, which awaits both the tea and the lips with an inscrutable calm whose very stillness makes it the most present of present things in the ceremony. All the senses are employed: the hands feeling the undulations of its sides, the shifting subtleties of taste, the aroma suffusing the head as it leans to drink, the sound of tools being laid to rest, the colour of the tea reflecting the glazes.

Raku versions of the tea bowl are especially present.[29] The original raku bowls emerged in the late sixteenth century. A tile maker, Chojiro, was commissioned by a tea master, Sen no Rikyū, in the sixteenth century to make a tea bowl. Chojiro then took the name Raku (meaning enjoyment), and laid down the patterns of making each bowl, to be followed by his descendants, each succession repeating the shapes, exploring small differences, from a small workshop in Kyoto, now over fifteen generations old. The bowls are moulded by the hands rather than turned. The outward, centrifugal force of a wheel is replaced by the centripetal force of the hands pushing inwards, a smooth disc of clay shaped by the curl

---

[29] There are two types of tea ceremony: *cha-no-yu* that serves matcha (powdered green tea); and *sen-cha* servicing regular tea with tea leaves. Raku bowls are used with the former.

of fingers, the slap of the palm, the warmth of the blood, the form revealing itself as the potter goes along. Sometimes the near-finished bowl is stood on a small wooden platform that can be turned, but it is more often the hand itself that continues to hold the bowl and to twist this way then that, as the other hand works away at the clay, playing with the inevitable irregularities that ensue as the hand cups and presses the clay, pinching and pressing the surfaces with subtle declivities, the sides slope slightly rather than deferring to a vertical upright, a small world is being made. The bowl is then shaved with self-made scrapers and in places it begins to lose its smoothness, it becomes angular, though only ever minimally. The shaving creates sharper edges, notably along the lip. To the eye they are subtle, to the lips they are definite. Subtle horizontal facets or bands can appear in the bowl's wall, both inner and outer. The base is an especial site of interest: how does it stand? Finally, the very top of the lip is smoothed with a stick and the pot brushed. To cope with the thermal shock of rapid heating and cooling, the body clay is often mixed with heavier clay or grog. Once dried, a glaze – made from ground, dark purple-black pebbles gathered from the Kamo (duck) River – is painted on in gestural movements, up to ten times, drying between each layer. Some clay is left bare, especially round the base. The bowl is fired in a single setting, and each one separately, in a covered chamber only big enough to house a single bowl, surrounded by a heap of oak charcoal. Once lit, traditionally the fire was tended by a team of specialist 'firers', all of whom had, like the potter, inherited the job from their forbears. One worked the bellows, others dragged the charcoal over the chamber, all of them assessed the colouration in the burning wood, the silvery sound of heat taking hold of dry matter. Nowadays the potter does much of this work alone, or with a far smaller team. Once the colour, sound and heat have reached a particular intensity and pitch, the chamber is uncovered and the bowl removed using long tongs and then placed on a board and left to cool in the open air. The next bowl is placed into the chamber. As they cool, the bowls darken, the glaze deepening to dark reds and blacks.

Its form is a standard form, a bowl, for drinking from, but also for holding, for feeling, for pondering. It is not just that it holds hot liquid, but how it holds it. Its role in the tea ceremony is to demand and instil an attentiveness to the reflections and reverberations of colour, aroma and light, the way it gives to and yet refuses the hand and lips, the patience with which it sits on its foot, waiting, but not at all a supplicant. It cannot be too weighty, too present, as though dominating the scene; it must bear itself lightly. As must the maker, whose restraint refuses to force the clay. The maker is present, barely, adhering to the time-worn patterns with curious deference. The clay too has been allowed to speak.

As has the fire in the kiln, recalled in the steam from the tea. The bowl conforms to standards of what it is to be a bowl. It can be picked up comfortably, it holds liquid, it sustains itself in re-use. Yet it disturbs this handiness. The colouration is of no obvious palette, the decoration follows no deliberate design, the clay conforms but then resists the standard shape, the absence of explicit design is palpable yet it is clearly set in a lineage that stretches back to Tang dynasty (618–907 CE) China.[30] The closer one attends to its presence the more it withdraws into its own rude state and brings the user along with it, out of themselves. The prepositional grammar circuiting the bowl ('it', 'this', 'the', 'a') starts to shimmer and then crack, like the charcoal, and behind the language the tea drinker witnesses a thing in the raw. A thing that has its own life and that holds other lives and that cannot be understood with the usual standards of beauty or use. The raku bowl contains tea, but also the conventions of prevailing regions; they become apparent precisely at the point where they begin to loosen and stutter, unable to properly fix the bowl as being this or that. Conventionally, we go about life without questioning whether a bowl is a bowl. Periodically though, we might encounter a bowl as something more than an object that fits into a practice in an appointed way. The bowl ceases to be present in habit and becomes present in both body and thought. It is a presence that confounds our habits. This loosening, however, cannot be witnessed outside of practice, but through its intensification, and so is immanent to the regional setting rather than separate from it. The limits of these regions are revealed by intensifying them in formal rituals rather than opposing them. The formal emptiness yields an opening, a clearing, where things become just things, beyond our language and yet still somehow present.

---

[30] Tang dynasty earthenware lead-glazed ceramics are often decorated with painted rivulets of leaf green and subdued ochre, leaving patches of pale cream to slip underneath (known as three colours, or *sancai*). All manner of elaborate shapes and sculptures were made, often for grave goods, as well as lidded boxes and ornate bowls, possibly for tableware, though the lead glaze was poisonous, and the earthenware often broke. A more minimal, austere and contemplative stoneware gained ascendency in the mid eighth century, along with the tea ceremony itself recounted by Lu Yu's *Chajing*. The green hue of the Yue ware was said to enhance the lucent colour of green tea. Siliceous stoneware was higher fired, could take under and over glazes and slips as it was better able to cope with thermal shock, and survived the knocks of use. Judging from the shipwrecked finds from the Changsha kilns, there is a strong affinity between the green and brown colouration and the gestural natural decorative forms of foliage, animals and fish, and the Twentieth Century Studio Pottery movement initiated by Yanagi, Hamada and Leach. See Liu Yang *Tang Dynasty Changsha Ceramics*. https://asia-archive.si.edu/wp-content/uploads/2017/10/10Liu.pdf.

# 3 Changefulness and Variety

### Material and Limits

Speaking on the role of science in craft at a conference at Dartington Hall, Devon in 1952, the potter Michael Cardew began by bemoaning the tendency amongst many craft workers – as amongst many humans – to look for easy ways through. Was it, he wondered, acceptable for potters to buy their clay and glazes ready-made and to use electric or gas kilns with refined temperature knobs so that they might then leave their creative personality free to pursue the 'higher things'. This parsing of creativity from material preparation and getting dirty was anathema for Cardew. Human nature, he argued, didn't work in compartments. Moreover:

> A personality that dodges difficulties isn't going to be a particularly edifying personality even if it does flow freely into the chosen medium. The expression is not going to be awfully interesting. And there's an even more difficult point to make, which I always find difficult to express, that the expression you make with the materials is inseparable from the materials, in some very indescribable way. That there isn't one thing – the expressing artist and another – the expressed material. The material really takes charge, I think. And you've got to study the nature of the material as profoundly as you're capable of and with all your five wits not necessarily only with your analytical or your mathematical faculties – but all your five wits. In other words, scientific knowledge about your technical materials isn't really different in kind from your artistic knowledge.[1]

In both science and art, there are those who avoid contact with raw materials and those who relish it, those who yearn for the experience of thoughtfully apprehending the creation of form as it is occurring in all its phases, and those who hanker for the clean lines of convergence and necessity that overlay and shroud the made things. In short, there are those who experiment in an artisanal way, and those who have a firm

---

[1] Michael Cardew *The Craftsman's Use of Scientific Development*. In *Proceedings of The International Conference of Craftsmen in Textiles and Pottery*. Dartington Hall. 1952.

sense of the necessary laws to which things ought to cohere, whether these laws are those of aesthetics and beauty, or of physics and force. What puzzles and irritates Cardew is not that there are these distinct tendencies, but that there is an implied hierarchy between them, and that craft work was in danger not only of absorbing it uncritically, but of accepting its place in the lower categorical region of imperfection. If only craft practice could be more like art, more elevated, less in thrall to the edges of functionality, it would then become more meaningful. Or if only craft could be more like science and be more exact in the direct production of stable objects that are less wasteful.[2] No. Craft should resist such hierarchies, and delight in this resistance.

The problem lay with an uncritical acceptance of the categorization of work distinguishing the location of 'hand' (body, *res extensa*) on one side and 'head' (mind, *res cognitans*) on the other. Cardew recognized that in its pursuit of what were assumed to be 'higher things', craft work would only ever be a subaltern to art and science, either a loyal appendage to the body of fine art that occupied the apex of the western cultural cannon, or an anachronistic form of technical production. Art both conferred and challenged standards of beauty and industrialized science did the same for truth, both striving for the essential, whereas the best craft work might aspire to was as an art of the workshop or the home, that was processed through smaller galleries and shops and destined for the table, window, floor or sideboard. Compounding this secondary status was a further institutional trajectory of having outsourced the 'thinking' aspects of practical making to the professions associated with engineering and academic training, leaving craft workers formally bereft of a body of knowledge through which they might claim recognition and status.[3] If it accepted its distinction from art on one side and science on the other, craft work would be left raising objects upon a fault line between functionality and decoration. Far better, suggests Cardew, to ignore the distinction, and enlist art and science into thinking through materials in ways that, to recall Ruskin, enhance life.

---

[2] The philosopher of technology Gilbert Simondon talks of industrialization as progression toward the determinate, technical object. Artisanal work shows a weak correlation between science and technology, its functional awareness is often lax and willing to indulge multiple interpretations, whereas industry progresses through the production of concrete objects that narrow the interval between science and technology (Gilbert Simondon *On the Mode of Existence of Technical Objects* Translated by Cécile Malaspina and John Rogove. Minneapolis: Univocal Publishing. 2017. 40).

[3] See Glenn Adamson on the emergence of the practice 'craft work' in *The Invention of Craft*. London: Bloomsbury. 2013. On the association of a body of knowledge, status, institutions and the professions, see Andrew Abbott 'Linked Ecologies: States and Universities as Environments for Professions', *Sociological Theory*. 2005, 23, 3, 245–274.

And Lowndes is a peerless example. Whilst her pieces are stilled by thought and the need for thought, they remain in respectful abeyance to materials, rather than to ideas or symbols: she thinks though discarded and recovered materials of the everyday, and through techniques, and not words. They are empirical inquiries, like science, or at least like the scientific practice advocated by Johann Wolfgang von Goethe, which was nothing if it did not take seriously the job of making imaginative connexions: 'either one brings together and connects, in the gloom of fantasy and with the cunning of mysticism, things that are worlds apart, or one isolates what belongs together by a disintegrating, in reality unintelligent, analytical procedure.'[4] The job of science, then, was to ascertain connexions: how, for example, when observing nature through what Goethe called 'active empiricism' (blending sight with imagination) the scientist witnesses how parts are continually giving forth to other parts, and by following these trajectories one discloses the inherent structures by which nature is developing. Even improbable connexions can be made, given there is no 'thing-in-itself': all things exist by virtue of relations. In this the scientist is like the artist: both have an intuitive feel for the transitions between things, and how these movements are far from logical and sequential, but overlap and inhere within one another, as an immanent totality, revealing nature to a unity forever generating new forms.[5] For Cardew this is also the job of craft work: to reveal the potential in nature through active empiricism.

In his book *Art as Experience* John Dewey had also puzzled over why fine art had sought to sever itself from the normal processes of living. It was, he supposed, a natural progression from the assumption that 'design, plan order, pattern, purpose, emerged in distinction from and relation to the materials employed in their realization', and that the idealization inherent to fine art immunizes it from the partial, temporary and uncertain activities associated with leading a useful life.[6] Attempts to enforce the separation are 'a pathetic, even a tragic, commentary on life as it is ordinarily lived. Only because that life is usually so stunted,

---

[4] Johann Wolfgang von Goethe quoted in R. Stephenson 'Binary Synthesis: Goethe's Aesthetic Intuition in Literature and Science', *Science in Context*. 2005, 18, 4, 553–558.

[5] In examining every appearance of nature, but especially in examining an important and striking one, we should not remain in one spot, we should not confine ourselves to the insulated fact, nor dwell on it exclusively, but look round through all nature to see where something similar, something that has affinity to it, appears: for it is only by combining analogies that we gradually arrive at a whole which speaks for itself, and requires no further explanation.

Goethe *Theory of Colours*. Translated by Charles Eastlake. London: John Murray. 1840. §228.

[6] John Dewey *Art as Experience*. New York: Minton Balch & Co. 1934. 26.

aborted, slack, or heavy laden, is the idea entertained that there is some inherent antagonism between the process of normal living and the creation and enjoyment of aesthetic art.'[7] Stunted because it fails to appreciate, or even apprehend, that culture, far from being the product of a mind, is the culmination of a prolonged and intense interaction between humans and their environment: art is continuous with the natural processes of living, or it is nothing. Dewey is insistent that without access to, and thinking through, sensuous, emotional and instinctual feeling, art voids itself of experience, and becomes little more than a circulation of dead formulae.

And if, as in the previous chapter, the supposed distinction between the higher realm of ideas and lower realm of experience is pursued uncritically, the pursuit quickly slips into grammatical quicksand. A distinction works by establishing what the anthropologist Gregory Bateson calls a relation of effective difference: 'differences in texture are *different* (a) from differences in colour. Now note that differences in size are *different* (b) from differences in shape.'[8] The difference being established is relational. It is only in comparison that a difference comes into being, and the comparison is made as part of our natural history, as part of the way in which we have historically isolated certain occurrences as notable ones

> I suggest to you, now, that the word 'idea,' in its most elementary sense, is synonymous with 'difference.' Kant, in the *Critique* of *Judgment* – *if* I understand him correctly – asserts that the most elementary aesthetic act is the selection of a fact. He argues that in a piece of chalk there are an infinite number of potential facts. The *Ding an sich*, the piece of chalk, can never enter into communication or mental process because of this infinitude. The sensory receptors cannot accept it; they filter it out. What they do is to select certain *facts* out of the piece of chalk, which then become, in modern terminology, information.
>
> I suggest that Kant's statement can be modified to say that there is an infinite number of *differences* around and within the piece of chalk. There are differences between the chalk and the rest of the universe, between the chalk and the sun or the moon. And within the piece of chalk, there is for every molecule an infinite number of differences between its location and the locations in which it *might* have been. Of this infinitude, we select a very limited number, which become information. In fact, what we mean by information – the elementary unit of information – is *a difference which makes a difference.*[9]

Bateson is modifying the reasoning of Immanuel Kant by considering idea as something that is felt; difference is a question of experience, of resonance, and those potters, or other craft workers, who excel are those

---

[7] John Dewey *Art as Experience*. 27.
[8] Gregory Bateson *Steps to an Ecology of Mind*. Northvale, NJ: Jason Aronson. 1987. 324.
[9] Gregory Bateson *Steps to an Ecology of Mind*. 321.

who are able to allow difference 'in' by attending to material with their 'five wits', by understanding that what is already known is so only by virtue of its having closed itself off to differences that, were they given a voice, would surely disturb the known facts to a point where they were no longer so well known, and experiment would once more take precedence. By remaining with the inchoate half-truths and dimly lit, yet sometimes explosive feelings, craft work is able to fold experience upon itself with attentive and disciplined concern to the point where an experience is created. From amid the haphazard and ad hoc flow of impressions comes a gathering of material things, emotional connexions and purposive order whose self-sufficiency is experienced as a consummation and maturing of movement, a 'rounding out' in which closeness and distance, the massive and meagre, the inner and outer, the fore and aft, the recalled and the dreamt, the intense and dispersed are expressed in spatial and temporal experience.[10]

The art of the writer W. G. Sebald was peerless in this capacity to 'round out' experience. His media – words and images – lay strewn on the page in unlikely yet carefully settled drifts, or took themselves off in serpentine twists, having been teased and encouraged by his cultivated attentiveness to place, people and event. His stories follow patterns that appear like scents, sometimes barely there but for the care of the author, sniffing out their conjunctions and concentrations, throwing us the reader into a maze of felt, emergent connexions whose movements cohere long enough to reveal how our life too is full of such overlapping interludes and small, out of the way associations that we so often fail to acknowledge and pursue.

I gazed farther and farther out to sea, to where the darkness was thickest and where there extended a cloudbank of most curious shape, which I could barely make out any longer, the rearward view, I presume of a storm that had broken over Southwold in the late afternoon. For a while the topmost summit regions of this massif, dark as ink, glistened like the icefields of the Caucasus, and as I watched the glare fade, I remembered that years before, in a dream, I had once walked the entire length of a mountain range just as remote and just as unfamiliar ... It was a scene that felt familiar in an inexplicable way and for weeks it was on my mind until at length I realized that, down to the last detail, it matched the Vallüla massif, which I had seen from the bus through eyes drooping with tiredness, a day or so before I started school, as we returned home from an outing to the Montafon. I suppose it is submerged memories that give to dreams their curious air of hyper-reality. But there is something else as well, something nebulous, gauze-like, through which everything one sees in a dream seems, paradoxically, much clearer. A pond becomes a lake, a breeze becomes a storm,

---

[10] John Dewey *Art as Experience*. 35–38; 208–209.

a handful of dust is a desert, a grain of sulphur is a volcanic inferno. What manner of theatre is it, in which we are at once playwright, actor, stage manager, scene painter and audience?[11]

In such 'rounding out' Sebald could almost be channelling Ruskin here. It is this experience of 'rounding out' that Cardew feels is lost in craft work when the potter shies away from the difficulties of preparing their own materials or avoids the risk of failures in form and firing by controlling the process as tightly as possible. Potters talk of the subtle differences between throwing and casting; the slight imbalance in the former reveal the process of making: the pulling and settling, whilst the exactitude of the latter is mute. The more the craft work concerns itself with the predictable realization of exact shapes, the more it removes from itself. Cardew was directing his ire towards those interested in using standardized units, slips and moulds. At some point the potter stops being a potter and becomes an amalgam of designer and manufacturer for whom the proper ordering of relations between humans and their materials is judged by the costs of application and the attainment of results set against a pre-given goal. The making is judged from these abstracted points of view, and not from the process itself.

When did craft work slide into manufacture, or, perhaps, when did craft work begin to emerge as a category of work in response to the growing dominance of manufacturing? Maybe with the arrival in England of Dutch silversmiths, the Elers brothers, around 1680. They made metal teapots. Ornate, arresting, but thermally inefficient when compared to the Chinese redware teapots from Yixing being imported irregularly (and so expensively) by the Dutch East India Company. How, then, to replicate more functional Chinese teapots using cheaper local materials and existing skill sets? They experimented with red clay found in Bradwell, Staffordshire, producing imitations of the Yixing teapots more cheaply. The new teapots were unglazed redware, decorated in sprigged relief, and made not on the wheel or from coil but by casting in moulds and then turning them on the lathe when they were 'leather hard'. The techniques were common to pewter making, but revolutionary in ceramics, originating what became, during the eighteenth century, a vastly scaled manufacturing of ceramics. Alive to the risk of what became known as industrial espionage, the brothers tried to guard the secrets of manufacture by employing, in their words, only the stupidest of workers, but agents of their rivals gained employment by pretending to be idiots, and the process was made public. The clay was

---

[11] W. G. Sebald *Rings of Saturn*. Translated by Michael Hulse. London: Verso. 2002. 79–80.

poured, not felt by hand, and the forms were units, not unique, especially when refinements in mould making technique made lathe turning and hand sprigging obsolete. The work could be scaled using division of labour and machine-based tasks: organizationally, the use of moulds was mould breaking.[12] The moulds, whilst they emerged from a profound level of skill and productive nous, created lines of production destined to be followed again and again, without variation.

The making to which Cardew is drawn, in contrast, nurtures an intense will to be amid things, moments and places, and to charge this experience with what Dewey calls 'accumulations of long-gathered energy', making the felt presence of materials the subject of unique, ongoing experimental drama to which they, as workers, belong bodily as well as thoughtfully. In craft work this belonging is at its most intense when working with materials. In art, the isolation of a pristine idea or a specific form can become more prominent than the experience of material immersion, but nevertheless, as the artist Tacita Dean attests, 'any artist who works in paint or chalk or film or whatever knows that sometimes the medium itself will give you something entirely unexpected, and something far better than what you intended … And at that point you follow the medium.'[13] Hence her own stubborn commitment to materials: to the petroleum blues and flickering glitches of 16mm film, to the fragility of time-sensitive chalk, to the bleeding effects of ink on thickly woven paper depicting hazy golden reflections in the windows of a now-vanished building. A deliberate loosening of artistic control pervades everything, the medium resists and pushes back. '[D]igital media', she continues 'do not have that resistance and I think that is a big problem … nothing can really happen in digital that is not intended.' What marks digital media is a tendency towards pervasive invisibility, to a point where they become indistinct from processes of organization. Dean is alive to what the media theorist John Durham Peters notices is the prime medium of digital media, organization: 'digital media traffic less in content, programs, and opinions than in organization, power, and calculation. Digital media serve more as logistical devices of tracking and orientation than in providing unifying stories to the society at large. Digital media revive ancient

---

[12] Gordon Elliott *John and David Elers and their Contemporaries*. London: Jonathan Horne. 1998.

[13] Tacita Dean. Interviewed by Tim Adams in *The Observer*, 11 March 2018. Dean works extensively on small editions made in collaboration with craft workers, notably the printer Niels Borch Jensen, based in Copenhagen, who is adept at working within and across multiple mediums and techniques. The direct physicality and unguarded subtleties of the made things belie the idea of these editions being just repetitious multiples. Each repetition bears the marks of its having resisted, of being its own thing. (Interview between author and Niels Borch Jensen, 9 October 2019).

58     3  Changefulness and Variety

navigational functions: they point us in time and space, index our data, and keep us on the grid.'[14]

Physical media are visible, they come alongside, they cajole and disappear awhile, re-appearing unexpectedly, pulling one into reverie and possibility. It was in struggling with 16mm celluloid film that Dean was provoked into playing about with it, scratching onto the surface as though it were an etching plate, using adapted apertures on cameras, and to recording onto only one half of the stock, then reloading to shoot on the other half of each frame elsewhere, in one case moving film physically between Cornwall and Wyoming, exposing both her and the film to the kinds of unassigned occurrence that Sebald's all-consuming theatre was so adept at revealing.[15]

Often unruly, materials make it possible for a craft worker to follow forces into these digressive associations. Marbled with practical know-how and what Richard Sennet calls the 'rhythms of routine', the repetitions of working movements are, nevertheless, freed from being exact copies because each movement is materially unique. Repetitions are etched into the filmmaker's body. Again and again, frame after frame, spooling the empirical sensations onto a reel of experience which grows thicker over time, each frame an episode of small distinction in a unifying event. The physicality of film tape and its use force the routine to take on shapes that differ; though sometimes only ever so slightly.

The composer and musician Eliane Radigue makes similar observations about working with magnetic tape, remembering her work as an assistant to the composer and musician Pierre Henry in the early 1960s. She was presented with a pile of recorded tape and asked to make a montage using only the attacks of the sounds [i.e. the sharp beginning of certain sounds, the equivalent of an opening consonant in speech]:

> So you had a 'ta-ta-ta-ta' sound. Believe me, making three minutes of that, I know what it is to cut! But I preferred what was left after the attack – if you cut the sound of a bell just after the attack, you have this beautiful gain of the harmonic, and the ear is not 'attacked' by it.
>
> ... I realized that the last piece I did [2010] with electronics, using a sound programme – like Digidesign – I had the feeling that they were not as sensitive

---

[14] John Durham Peters *The Marvelous Clouds: Toward a Philosophy of Elemental Media*. Chicago: University of Chicago Press. 2015. 7.

[15] Dean has made work about Sebald, including the quoted material from *Rings of Saturn* in a catalogue published in 2003 in which she documents her inquiry into her ancestors' involvement in the execution of the Irish nationalist Roger Casement by the British, an event that also drew Sebald's attention. She also made a documentary about Sebald's close friend and translator Michael Hamburger teasing out a narrative from serpentine movements through his home (using shots of the house that also crop up in Rings of Saturn), natural places and historical recollection.

as when I was doing it by hand, because with these programmes you see and you draw the line and that's it. But when I was doing that with a potentiometer I could pause, slow or accelerate the fades.[16]

Like Dean, Radigue has used chalks, inks, tapes, splicers, glues, potentiometer, fader dials, to acquire a toothy, empirical know-how of magnetic tape and how its oily, fragile surface, its curling, linear shapes, its willingness to be spliced and reluctance to be pulled straight, and its capacity to hold onto and replay sound once a source sound has dissipated enforce a state of uncertainty within the recording studio. In intimate company with her ARP 2500 synthesizer, she can alter, quicken stretch, slow and linger awhile (an instruction to musicians playing one of Radigue's pieces is as follows: 'listen to a note until you no longer wish to change the note, then change the note'), hazarding where the sound may go, as it emerges from the air. The emphasis is always on the process, layering, the adjacencies and diversions and splits. Slowness is immanent to the work: she weaves intricate patterns that echo the disciplined attentiveness that guides their creation.

With both Radigue and Dean, what is made by the 'rhythms of routine' are loops and sequences of images and sound in which the abrupt and perceptible gives way to barely discernible differences in patterns that are discovered as the making goes along. Sennett isolates two aspects to rhythm: beat and tempo, both being musical, the stress on a beat structures the form to which then tempo anticipates a shift, taking the structure out of itself.[17] Dean's and Radigue's work expands upon this anticipatory quality of rhythm, finding confidence to work with the insubstantial, meandering elements of material as much as the substantial, the click of the tape as it passes through the reels and over the feed sprockets before hitting the tape head or gate, the flicker of a frame.

The sculptor Barbara Hepworth was equally alive to how rhythm excavated what was most fleeting about a material and gave it a grave and arresting presence. When her friend Priaulx Rainier composed *Rhythms of the Stones* inspired by the sounds of tools at work on the figures for *Contrapuntal Forms* (1950–1951), Hepworth suggested that the composer's notation of the chisels, hammers and mallets working the Irish blue limestone was no less materially present than the finished sculpture.[18] With pieces like *Contrapuntal Forms* Hepworth

---

[16] Elian Radigue. Interviewed by Paul Schütze in *Frieze* 142, 1 October 2011. See also Julian Cowley, 'Radigue: Analogue Elegist', *The Wire*, 180. February 1999 and Louise Gray 'The Sound before Sound', *Gagosian Quarterly*, Summer 2024.

[17] Richard Sennett *The Craftsman*. London: Allen Lane. 2008. 177–178.

[18] See Eleanor Clayton *Barbara Hepworth: Art and Life*. London: Thames and Hudson. 2021. 172. *Contrapuntal Forms* was made for the Festival of Britain (her assistants were

had pioneered the technique of direct carving (rather than the more exact pointing method, which uses a plaster cast template as a guide). She had brought an immediacy to the form whose completeness was decided upon by sound; she could hear when the shape was emerging in the 'right' way. Letter carvers also talk of the rhythmic quality of their work, how when it is going well there is a specific percussive alertness to the strikes, and how they're to listen for a certain ring when the stone is about to give way.[19] The following year Hepworth began combining this direct technique with the use of repeated forms, allowing her to experiment with space and its dynamic arrangements as similar shapes were placed in different choreographed conjunctions, as when humans are engaged in intricate work tasks or in dance. Concentrating on the rhythm allowed her to reveal: 'the unconscious grouping of people when they are working together, producing a spatial movement which approximates to the structure of spirals in shells or rhythms in crystal structures; the meaning of the spaces between forms, or the shape of the displacement of forms in space, which in themselves have a most precise significance'.[20] Groupings that allowed her to play with the limits of the block itself, that allowed her, as she put it, to 'extend the forms beyond the capacity of stone and wood', to play with how to 'swing upwards and outwards when feeling cannot be contained by the block'.[21] Her struggle to convey and then transgress the limits of the material then took her away from using a block. She turned to sheet metals: 'I bent and twisted the sheets under tension until I found out the nature of its construction and forced it to express what I wanted by its nature, not against its nature.'[22]

### Contingency

By escaping from the block into new materials, Hepworth's craft work, as with Dean's, Radigue's and Cardew's, was transgressing its own expertise, learning anew, not from scratch, but pushing itself into

---

the St Ives artists Dennis Mitchell, John Wells and Terry Frost) and then gifted by the UK Arts Council to Harlow New Town in 1953. It still stands outside a block of unassuming flats in Glebelands, Harlow.

[19] David Kindersley *Mr Eric Gill* [italics as this is the title of the book]. Cambridge: Cardozo Kindersley Editions. 1990. 11.

[20] Quoted at Kettle's Yard www.kettlesyard.cam.ac.uk/objects/three-personages/. See also Barbara Hepworth *Writings and Conversations*. Edited by Sophie Bowness. London: Tate. 2015.

[21] Quoted in Eleanor Clayton *Barbara Hepworth: Art and Life*. 195.

[22] Barbara Hepworth *The Sculptor Speaks*. In *Writings and Conversations*. Edited by Sophie Bowness. London: Tate. 2015. 158. Also in Eleanor Clayton *Barbara Hepworth: Art and Life*. 197.

encounters with the unfamiliar whilst being able to count on a growing assuredness of experience and skill. The unfamiliar can also be cultivated by sharing techniques across different crafts. Some plates made by potter Akiko Hirai, for example, make use of a carving technique called *Kohiki* derived from Kamakura-bori, an old folkcraft of wood carving based in Kamakura in Japan: petals floating on a pond. Though the pieces are high fired stoneware, they retain a slightly porous state, meaning they change colour over time, taking on a darker, mottled hue. The water darkens, the flower fades. This is one of myriad examples of cross-fertilization: lacquerware (urushi) makers and glass-blowers, carpenters and blacksmiths, lace makers and cobblers, weavers and computer coders.

Breaking free from the standard materials or techniques allows the craft worker to experience what for Ruskin, was the

> second most essential element of the Gothic spirit, that it broke through that law wherever it found it in existence; it not only dared, but delighted in, the infringement of every servile principle; and invented a series of forms of which the merit was, not merely that they were new, but that they were capable of perpetual novelty.[23]

Ruskin lauded Gothic because of its almost wanton embrace of change:

> Undefined in its slope of roof, height of shaft, breadth of arch, or disposition of ground plan, it can shrink into a turret, expand into a hall, coil into a staircase, or spring into a spire, with undegraded grace and unexhausted energy; and whenever it finds occasion for change in its form or purpose, it submits to it without the slightest sense of loss either to its unity or majesty.[24]

Gothic culminated in a 'great system of perpetual change which ran through every member of Gothic design, and rendered it as endless a field for the beholder's inquiry as for the builder's imagination.'[25] It was not random, it was a 'system' of change that relied upon the rhythmic repetitions by which the builders could embody the laws they might then freely, and delightedly, contest. The repetition was characterized by an urge towards changefulness, a restlessness that works towards one 'rounding out' after another, so they come with the irregular pattern of sea waves, one after another emerging from the horizon, an undulating company of diverse lines rising to eclipse one another in recursive loops, sometimes affable, sometimes reluctant, sometimes with angry gusto.

---

[23] John Ruskin *The Stones of Venice, Vol. II.* §31. 208.
[24] John Ruskin *The Stones of Venice, Vol. II.* §38. 212.
[25] John Ruskin *The Stones of Venice, Vol. II.* §38. 212–213.

What animates and gives life to these recursive loops is contingency: the falling short or going awry which overspills attempts at prediction, but which, however, still might be imagined. The contingent exhausts probabilistic measurement and it cannot be confined by naming it a 'possibility', if by the 'possible' is meant the occurrence of an event that can be imputed from past circumstances. The possible can be predicted, whereas contingent patterns have an anticipatory pattern that is more phenomenal than measurable. Contingency appears almost out of nowhere, but its texture is more organized than chance because rather, being happenstance, it is catered for by the 'rhythms of routine' searching for footholds.

Craft work is a process of settling into and making peace with contingency. When one of his pots emerged from the kiln, Cardew talked of a solidified merger of glaze and body brought about through a combination of concomitant effects that applied uniquely to each firing, but which emerged from a gathering of independent factors that, were one able to isolate them in a laboratory setting, would have a deterministic quality. That quality is not lawlike but is experienced in repeating patterns that a potter learns as they go. They learn how it is that materials interact, their likely effects, for example as when body and glaze clays are mixed with manganese to strengthen the resulting pot, but also speckle the surface, making it appear like an eggshell, or a pebble, that is if the pot ought to appear 'like' something else. Some potters will experiment with the possibility of the spots flaring, congregating in constellations, or isolating, but it is as much to the alchemy of the fire, clay, glaze, kiln, or temperament of the maker, as it is design. Other metals have different effects, and as they too are experimented with the manganese can behave differently, and rather than strengthen the pot it can then crack, or the glaze go muddy rather than mottle. These 'failures' are acceptable signs of having worked towards the limits of the current understanding of the material – recalling Goethe's 'active empiricism' – where other limits are then encountered, as they are with 'successes' too, and either way further experiment ensures through further routines that channel the materials as a musical core channels voices, carrying forth in a company of overlapping, polyphonic sound.

The results of each firing, each experiment, are often recorded in recipe books and these are cross referenced with pieces from test firings in which different quantities of material fired at different temperatures, with different rates of cooling and heating have been logged, assessed and stored in tables, text, sketches, lists and test pieces (Figures 12–15). The books and tests convey the experience of the material qualities that will only ever be imperfectly given to the senses as the work proceeds. As records they follow Goethe's desire for a conventional language, by

31/8/64. New (Aug '64) Zircon Glaze Correction. (2 parts 1964 Zr, 1 part 1963 Zr) mixed with equal ...
Recipe to Formula.

| Material | Percent | Formula wt. | | KNaO | CaO | $Al_2O_3$ | $SiO_2$ | $ZrO_2$ |
|---|---|---|---|---|---|---|---|---|
| K felspar | 45.000 ÷ | 609 = | 0.07389 | 0.07389 | – | 0.07389 | 0.51176 | – |
| Saleh Gida clay | 7.917 ÷ | 475.5 = | 0.01665 | 0.00200 | 0.00233 | 0.01665 | 0.08025 | – |
| Kaolin | 4.583 ÷ | 258 = | 0.01776 | – | – | 0.01776 | 0.03553 | – |
| Limestone | 15.000 ÷ | 100 = | 0.15 | – | 0.15 | – | – | – |
| Quartz | 15.833 ÷ | 60 = | 0.26388 | – | – | – | 0.26388 | – |
| Zircon | 11.667 ÷ | 183 = | ~~0.63754~~ 0.06375 | – | – | – | ~~0.63754~~ 0.06375 | ~~0.63754~~ 0.06375 |
| Totals. | 100.000. | | | 0.07589 | 0.15233 | 0.10830 | 0.95517 | 0.06375 ~~0.63754~~ |
| RO = 0.22822 | | | | 0.33 KNaO. | 0.67 CaO. | 0.475 $Al_2O_3$. | 4.185 $SiO_2$ | 0.28 $ZrO_2$. |

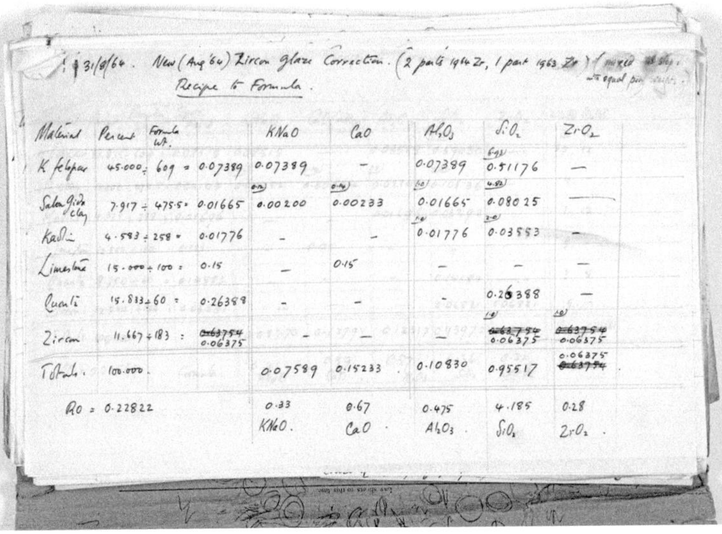

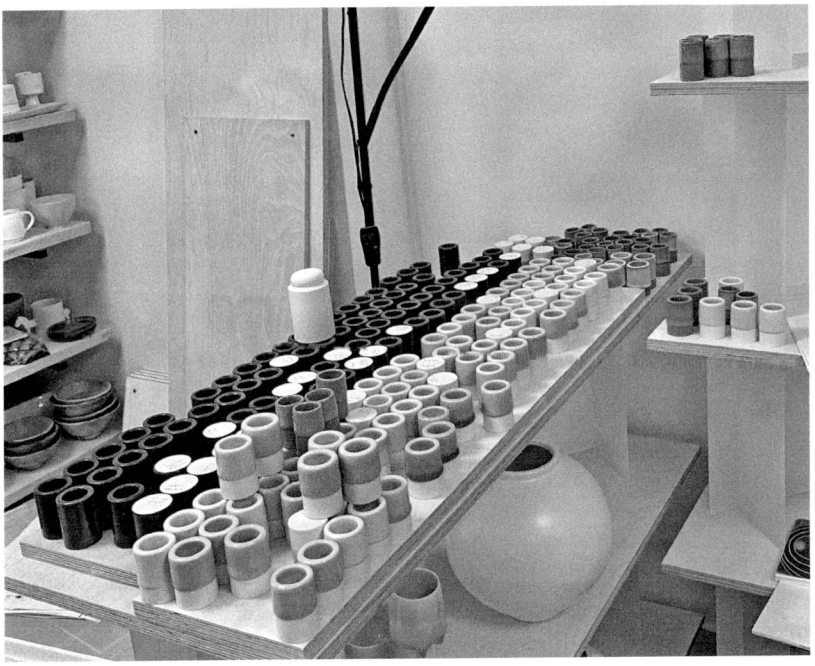

Figure 12 Glaze recipe from Michael Cardew's notebooks, Abuja, 1955. From the collections of the Crafts Study Centre, University for the Creative Arts. MAC/2/2.

Figure 13 Jaejun Lee, test glazes for celadon, 2022. Photograph taken in Cardiff studio. Photography: Author.

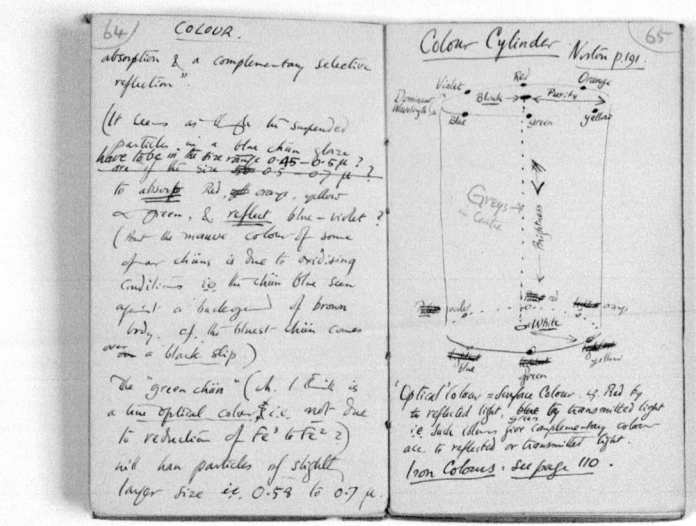

Figure 14 Michael Cardew's technical notes, 1958. From the collections of the Crafts Study Centre, University for the Creative Arts. MAC/1/2.

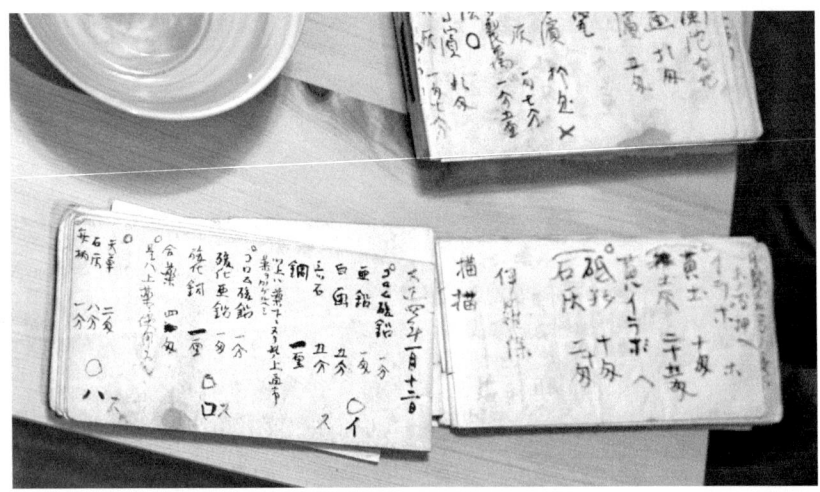

Figure 15 Suwa Sozan, glaze recipes, 2019. Kyoto. Photography: Yutaka Yamauchi.

which he meant one grounded in elementary formulae and symbols that remained as close to the province of work itself.[26]

The information being noted down and consulted does not refer to a settled state of affairs so much as initiates the process of giving form, a process that, in turn, far from being read as a linear representation of cause-and-effect relations, remains immanent to moments of making. The information (what Bateson called the differences that make a difference coursing through the coordinated cycles of hand-eye-tool-material-workshop interactions) is not of the same quality as formal, numerical data; it is meaning in continual formation. It informs and becomes a record of the rhythm of the workshop or studio where work is marked by bouts of thoughtful activity stratified by irregular pauses that stiches the material, milieu and organism (a maker) together as a recurring scene of evaluation, accident, absorption and control.[27] The looping flows of information embodied in the recursive interaction are the basic means by which any organism becomes different to its current state: it grows, develops, learns, dies back, splits, re-groups. Contingencies arise from within these recursive patterns, appearing as further difference-making differences, which in turn belong to future repetitions. This intimacy between recursion and contingency reveals what the philosopher Yuk Hui calls the ontogenetic nature of organization. In other words, far from canalizing or ordering life, organization of the kind embodied by the 'rhythms of routine' becomes the condition of its emergence, its in-forming: it is only through organization that difference emerges.[28]

Difference erupts in all craft work, even where material tolerances are so strict there is no discernible distinction between the making of one piece and another, as with the as with the pewter cylinders of the Kyoto-based tea caddy maker Seikado. The smoothly milled, inner smoothly milled, inner sides of the lid rest so neatly onto the body that it descends gently to a close under its own weight. Too proximate and smooth and the sides will bond molecularly, like Jo blocks, and so stick, but too distant and the lid loses its touch and wobbles when

---

[26] In writing, the artist and scientist needs be careful of the word when describing the powers that are ever in movement in nature: Yet, how difficult it is to avoid substituting the sign for the thing; how difficult to keep the essential quality still living before us, and not to kill it with the word. With all this, we are exposed in modern times to a still greater danger by adopting expressions and terminologies from all branches of knowledge and science to embody our views of simple nature.' Goethe *Theory of Colours*. §754.

[27] Yuk Hui *Receptivity and Contingency*. London: Rowman and Littlefield. 2019. §4.

[28] Yuk Hui *Receptivity and Contingency*. §1.

66   3 Changefulness and Variety

Figure 16 Seikado workshop, 2019. Kyoto. Photography: Yutaka Yamauchi.

in place. To keep the tea in good condition the fit needs to be just so, a union that occurs through minute adjustments made by the hand using bench tools, the eye and a mix of electric and window light (Figure 16). Fatigue, changes of weather and season, differences in materials all still play out in the making of these carefully measured things. The milling machines react to different room temperatures, the movements are held within tolerances set by limiting rods which judder, the cutting edges heat up as they are being used and their sharpness dulls, and they can pull and jar if they meet irregularities in the metal's grain. It is an assembly of movements and forces interacting through feedback loops to reach a state of homeostatic balance which is temporary, even precarious. Within this recursive looping the craft worker – the sentient organism – adds the further complication of double looping. They react by learning, and so are able to reflect upon as well as experience contingency, adjusting continually to the presence of things including themselves, reciprocally acknowledging and modifying a convergence of sensory feeling, emotion, thought and activity that allows for the emergence of further differences that feed further looping. Where the machinery is set to work towards balance within tolerances, the presence of a craft worker creates the possibility of individuation. The work is animated by a struggle to finish something, to complete a work rather than simply go on and on, a process which Hui describes as actualizing the potentials and virtuals of energy and matter that ground experiences of unsettlement (the variety induced by contingency) heralded in the arrival of information. The push, then pull of the plane, the slight applications of pressure applied to the lathe or sanding belts, the angling of the chisels that shave off strands of the soft metal as delicate as hair, are all punctuated with skilled hesitation and thoughtfulness that gathers in the memory of a working body that refuses to be pulled into the past without first having made something complete that can be thrown into the world freed from the repetitions of work from which it was made, and free from the stipulations of use to which well-designed, manufactured objects are consigned.

## Design

Contingency cannot be pre-figured, it cannot be planned for or designed into the process of making or using. It lies outside of design, and it is now design, rather than craft work, that determines how most objects are to be made and should be used. Rather than tease out contingencies, design looks to close them down. By combining an archival knowledge of things and materials with a curiosity for how it is that humans might be persuaded, goaded or nudged by the array of things that are already moving them to move differently, designers look to improve everyday life. There is an intelligence in designed things, they anticipate the range of possible uses to which they might be put, and they can make allowances for ill use. Married to this precautionary principle is a proactive quality of making room for the possible as well as the planned.[29] In both registers, the precautionary and proactive, designers use objects to solve problems by bringing things and users into more intimate, harmonious, intuitive, engaged and so effortless relations.[30] They create the futures into which we will step, they are little gods growing apples upon which we are being encouraged to bite, falling into newly contrived, human-made arrangements. The designed thing begins to work at the point it begins to insinuate itself into a lived life not randomly, or suggestively, but with the authorization that it contributes to an articulated purpose to which

---

[29] See Cameron Tonkinwise 'Design Studies – What Is It Good For?' *Design and Culture*. 2014. 6, 5–43 and Cameron Tonkinwise 'Failing to Sense the Future: From Design to the Proactionary Test Drive', *Social Research*. 83, 597–624.

[30] Beatriz Colomina and David Wigley *Are We Human? Notes on an Archaeology of Design*. Zürich: Lars Müller. 2016. 163.

the designer and user have become committed: the regional gathering of things is being set upon by objectives, and things become objects, contingency is snuffed out in use, a death by iteration that is only hastened by co-creation. Over time, the continuing use of these objects transforms an individuated life into an aggregated lifestyle, one that dampens the very forms of singularity to which good design vows its allegiance.

Like craft work, design accepts that in any attempt to ask itself the question 'What am I?' the human has always involved things, or objects. Where design differs, however, is in reading this question as a problem that needs solving. 'What am I?' becomes a question of engineering, whereas in craft work it remains somewhat existential. Rather than keep the human dependency upon things under questionability, design not only assumes it, but tends to use this as a justification for realising a more correct, more compelling, more reliable and progressive relationship between humans and objects.[31]

The almost compulsive urge to ease the burden of living through an active design of 'the totality of useful things' makes for a more accomplished, because efficient and effective, life, yet it also encourages a state of human desire in which it is objects, and the possession of these objects, that fill out and fulfil an idea of the self, which is itself an object of design. Under the impress of design, life begins to pass through objects, through prostheses, and a noetic individuality emerges, an individual conceived in nous, in problem-solving intelligence fed by a desire for as seamless and as untroubled a union of user and used thing as is possible, a union authorized by the designer (rather than by anything necessary to the object itself). The ideal design is invisibly stitched into the material of human practice, either passing unnoticed in inconspicuous, immersive use, or vaunted as an idealized thing. In its dedication to problem solving, design concerns itself with task alignment: the *res cogitans* (the idealized form imagined by the designer) is coupled to *res extensia* (the organization of human practice) with the 'aim to manage, govern, control, and orient … the behaviors, gestures, and thoughts of human beings'.[32] The goal is an all-embracing positivity of communication, awareness and production in which the great enemy is negativity, absence, disorder. The vectors by which this goal is pursued are of two types: one towards visibility, the other towards invisibility.

---

[31] Beatriz Colomina and Mark Wigley *Are We Human?* 164.
[32] Giorgio Agamben *What Is an Apparatus? And Other Essays*. Translated by David Kishik and Stefan Pedatella. Stanford: Stanford University Press. 2009. 12.

## Visibility and Invisibility

Visibility comes from a concerted effort to strip back the superfluous, deviant and excessive elements in any design. By concentrating on fewer, more perfectible elements, the designer might at least approximate an alignment between an ideally conceived thing and its empirical realization. The work of the Wiener Werkstätte, founded by Friz Waerndorfer, Koloman Moser and Josef Hoffmann in 1903, was an early adopter of this decluttering spirit. Hoffmann's metalwork vases and lights for example, are studies in harmony between use and form manifest in gridded restraint (Figures 17 and 18).

They evoke and then distil a style that is smooth, inducing calm, surety, efficiency, sanitation. the removal of variable and intense

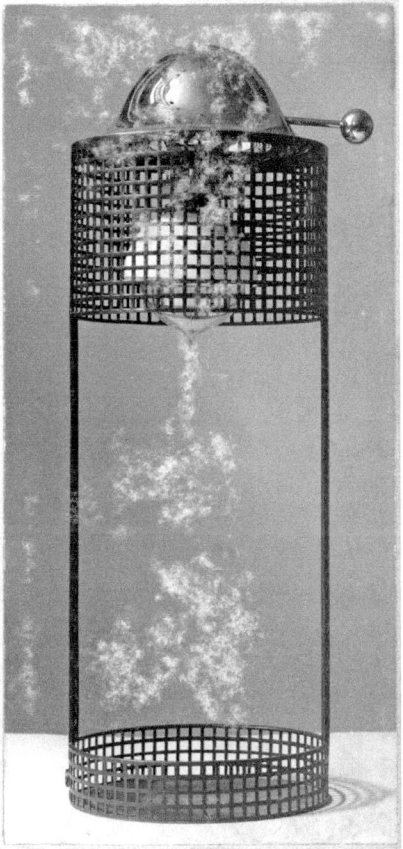

Figure 17 Josef Hoffmann, *Light*, 1904–1906. Photography: © MAK Museum of Applied Arts, Vienna.

Figure 18 Advert for gridwork flower vase designed by Josef Hoffmann. Photography: © MAK Museum of Applied Arts, Vienna.

Visibility and Invisibility 71

Figure 19 Lucie Rie, tea service, ca. 1936. Earthenware, unglazed burnished surface. Photography: Charles Saumarez Smith. © Estate of the Artist.

feeling. Hoffman's objects are assured and without need for the arresting noise of clashing colours and forms and sounds found on many of the Fin de Siècle objects with which his designs were competing. They have been stripped back from superfluity, from bourgeois displays of virtuous taste. Modern humans have a different nervous structure, a different sensibility, they are no longer able to cope with excess, in the presence of ornament they feel nausea and nervousness. They need smooth, uncluttered, forms that speak of cleanliness, a stripping away of superfluousness.

This tea set from the mid 1930s was made by Lucie Rie, heavily influenced by Hoffmann (Figure 19). The teapot has a geometric, simple shape, with a short spout. The piece is pure restraint, a formal flat glaze on the insides and a burnished red clay outer (*terra sigillata*).[33] Its function is to do more than hold and pour hot liquid, which it does not do well. The tea would spill easily and lose all its heat in the cup, the meagre spout of the pot would drip, the milk bowl would barely take the strain of a spoon or pouring. Their value is as much in the values they exude as their utility. Their form induces an urban calm and surety, efficiency, sanitation, it removes disturbance, the shapes repeat with comforting rhythm, the rounded handles echo the rounded lid and edges. It exudes what Beatriz Colomina and Mark Wigley call anaesthesia: the removal of excessive feeling, a suspension of the nerves and anxieties besting industrialized life, a protective gauze, insulating the nerves from shock, from the arresting noise of clashing colours and forms and sounds.[34]

---

[33] Similar to the Elers' redware, see p. 56–57.
[34] Beatriz Colomina and Mark Wigley *Are We Human?* 89–126.

Hoffmann was designing in Vienna at the same time as Sigmund Freud was working through the rudiments of psychoanalysis, a science of the soul which would, if properly organized, reveal the inner workings of the self to the self. The desires of the id, the reprimands of the super ego and the reconciliations offered by the ego formed a potentially self-sustaining trinity of forces by which the thing called a human being was able to adequately respond to the question 'What am I?' Through the talking cure, psychoanalysis could reveal the inner nature of the desires and urges that had, hitherto, been repressed by a bourgeois obsession for decorum and decoration. Psychoanalytic techniques would then clarify and manage this inner state, correcting the mental disturbances that beset so many, restoring human things to a more determinate, settled state. Design would perform a similar role for the interior and exterior environments occupied by humans: it would create objects that would induce the transparency, flexibility and cleanliness necessary for good living. Calm, well cut, uncluttered dress and industrially produced objects for both domestic, public and commercial uses whose clear and consistent lines evoked a robust reliability and efficiency. Through the *Wiener Werkstätte* Hoffman even took it upon himself to design an entire regional setting (architecture, interiors, finishes, décor, furniture) for the Purkersdorf Sanatorium, a private clinic treating nervous disorders (Figure 20). White, clean, untroubled ambience, plenty of glass, transparent settings behind which nothing can be hidden. The atmosphere was one of settled, rational and cleansing exactness: modern design managing modern disorders, as Leslie Topp puts it.[35] The vulnerable body and vulnerable mind need to be calmed, embalmed with linear vectors, smooth surfaces, incubated interiors.

This 'less is more' logic has taken a hold of design practice: the intent is to clear away the superfluous and redundant aspects of objects, leaving only what works to meet the needs of users. Ornament and appearance remain part of those needs, but guardedly so, and not so as to crowd out and detract from the visible, productive alignment between functional objects and functioning human beings. The alternate vector runs the other way.

---

[35] In the 2009 exhibition at the Welcome Institute in London, *Madness and Modernity* the curators (one of which was Topp) placed the objects associated with mental health disorders and care alongside design objects from the *Wiener Werkstätte*. Hoffmann's designs were accompanied by more archaic objects taken from Freud's study, the contents of which had found their way to London after the Nazis had been welcomed into Austria in 1938, forcing a Jewish exodus, many to London, including to Lucie Rie. See Leslie Topp *The Mad Objects of Fin-de-Siècle Vienna*. In *Journeys into Madness: Mapping Mental Illness in the Austro-Hungarian Empire*. Edited by Gemma Blackshaw and Sabine Wieber. New York: Berghahn Books. 2012. 10–26.

# Visibility and Invisibility

Figure 20 Interior of Purkersdorf Sanatorium. Photography: © MAK Museum of Applied Arts, Vienna.

If the trend towards visibility concerned itself with the health-giving effects of transparency, and with the glassy ambition of realising a predictable, well managed, constructive life, there has also been a trend towards invisibility. Ostensively this is a counter move, yet one that further enforces the main objective of design: to move towards more determinate, settled relations to objects so that one might improve the experience of living. Invisibility has become necessary. As objects have become more complex and technology has expanded in its reach and insinuating detail, as diseases have morphed and their spread accelerated, and as the global environment starts to buckle under the burden of over-use and toxicity, so the general human capacity to understand how objects work, or even to recognize objects, diminishes. To confront this growing ignorance, design starts to create black boxes. Peer into a laptop, or under the bonnet of a car, then withdraw: the warranty is invalidated as soon as the parts are touched by an 'unqualified' hand, the components are no longer visible even, sensors blink like small life forms allied to unknown forces. The design does not encourage curiosity. Instead, stay with the surfaces. The user of a car can engage with the air conditioning, ergonomic seats and prompts from the infotainment system. After all, why wrestle with the loose wires of detail? Let others deal with the technicalities of locomotion; the role of the user is to be moved, perhaps whilst doing other things, preferably browsing and consuming, making the car more like a large smartphone into which one can be placed. Rather than use design to baffle the destabilizing conditions besetting the species – burnout, depression, precarity, attention deficit disorder, dislocation, exile, allergies, self-delusion – maybe it is better to use it as a distraction. Rather than transparency, the power of design comes from compensating users for their ignorance by persuading them that this weakness is, in fact, a strength. Friedrich Nietzsche argued similarly: the power of Christianity lay in its ability to persuade believers that ignorance, sinfulness and weakness were a source of great power. Designers, like priests, encourage users to follow the rituals of using objects, without asking how or why these rituals might work. The wider the uptake of these objects, the more integrated the lives of users into what Giorgio Agamben calls 'apparatuses'. These are: 'literally anything that has in some way the capacity to capture, orient, determine, intercept, model, control, or secure the gestures, behaviours, opinions or discourses of living beings', and Agamben casts a deliberately wide net: kitchen appliances, cars, exercise devices, timepieces, heating systems, street lighting, neighbourhood watch organizations, transport and navigation systems, voting booths, school attendance records, dating apps and the pen, computer, paper, words and grammar that he was using to write his polemical essay on the apparatus. Though mass uptake an apparatus invisibly clarifies experience into sequences of predictable behaviour for which there is no foundation, no reason, other than its income-generating repetition.[36] To the extent the use becomes so invisible that it is as thoughtless as breathing, the apparatuses can be said to produce the user, and it is the user, and not the used object, who becomes the object of use value, because it is through the scroll, the tap, the glance, the push – in these micro-moments of ascent – that the paymasters of design generate immense profits.[37]

Between them, these two vectors of visibility and invisibility channel how design defines the relationship between humans and objects. Design works by creating a world of objects that use precise tolerances and defined purpose to cushion users from shock, and it is into this world that users are being encouraged, with their hopes and their happiness.[38]

---

[36] Giorgio Agamben *What Is an Apparatus? And Other Essays*. 11, 14.
[37] Alexander Galloway 'The Cybernetic Hypothesis', *Differences*. 2014, 25, 1, 107–131. 126.
[38] Beatriz Colomina and Mark Wigley point out (*Are We Human?* 90) that Charles and Ray Eames defined design as a shock absorber, a definition that is grounded in their own original designs for plywood leg splints to aid soldiers injured during

Objects are either clear and immediate, or they disappear into apparatuses, and as they trend towards these extremes – they are 'all show', or they are seamless – the horizons of experience that have been drawn out by the passageways of common sense and local accumulations of tradition dissolve. Instead of local experience, users occupy the regions of design, the design that strips things of their idiosyncrasy and distinction, and which attends exclusively to what is explicit enough to be organized, and what is universal enough to be placed anywhere.

Those refusing or suspicious or unable to properly access these proper regions of design – the hackers, bricoleurs, up-cyclers and vagrants, those for whom making, escaping and surviving run cheek by jowl – must make do from within, whilst not belonging to such a well-designed world.[39] They are too unruly, smelly, patchy and frayed to be acceptable users, and succeed by unpredictable expressions of situational intelligence; they are tacticians, those who feed off and disturb the provisions of design, but without ever threatening its strategic dominance. The tactician is weak, they can only ever appropriate what already exists, but it is precisely this ability for re-appropriating the proper use of an object that enables the tactician to survive without having to bear the weight of possession. Their inventiveness can never lead to a new proper space, but then why is this needed if one can work inventively with the scraps? Tacticians look for *la perruque*, the phrase used to describe how workers can disguise their activity sufficiently well to divert employers' resources towards their personal ends, and which Michel de Certeau uses more broadly to describe how tacticians can graft themselves onto the circulation of cultural objects and the proper spaces imposed by dominant forms of design, and exploit what they find there, albeit momentarily.[40] They reassemble code so it attacks itself, they overload complaint systems, they traverse

---

World War II. The Eames, endlessly modern, untroubled, smiling, removed from sadness, an anaesthetic, a removal from sensation, which is ironic given aesthetics concerns sensation. The design aesthetic became, with figures like the Eames, a deliberate attempt to actively manage human emotion and sensation so that it remains within a tight band of contentment that is bridged by the outline of a fixed smile.

[39] Using bespoke pentalobe screws which require specialist screwdrivers, gluing components so they shatter if separated, copyrighting repair manuals, using encryption to prevent copying or altering of operating code etc. See *The Guardian*, 8 May 2019.

[40] Michel de Certeau *The Practice of Everyday Life*. London: University of California Press. 1998. 36–37. Michel Anteby defines la peruque thus:

> A 'homer' [«perruque» in french] is an artifact that a worker produces using company tools and materials outside normal production plans but at the workplace and during workhours. Despite legal, artistic and ethnographic evidence of their existence, silence surrounds [perruques] … this silence is not linked just to the marginal and illegal quality of these artifacts. [Perruques] shed light on a high degree of 'complicity' between employees regardless of their position in the hierarchy.

the formalities of practice with an ironic touch, they experiment with leftovers, they pass things under the counter, they duck, weave and skew, all of which acts as an irritant to design, yes also a provocation, affording those designing proper space the opportunity to go again along the vectors of invisibility and invisibility.[41]

**War**

Given its intent to clarify, simplify and expand the certainties and comforts of human life, design rarely meets much hostility. There is bad design, but design per se is not bad. Design suits the kind of human beings many of us have become; namely, beings whose lives are lived in the wake of World War I. Though largely a European and North American war, it extended into the colonies, and more significantly, it was a war dominated by the relentlessness of machinery. Though they stilled lived, Walter Benjamin said of those returning from World War I they had been denuded of experience, and could no longer experience, because the barbarism they had experienced was not just bloody and deathly, but ministered by machinery that was utterly indifferent to place and history. Even during his lifetime technology had, observed Walter Benjamin, trained the human sensorium into a jostling acceptance of rapid-fire bodily and cognitive stimulus on the one side, and managerial and bureaucratic abstraction on the other. The soldiers in battle, like the clerks in offices and workers in factories, had come to accept and endure the mechanical rhythms of production and destruction. These rhythms, he observed, were both linear and automatic: a trigger is pulled and bullets fire indiscriminately, a conveyor belt is switched on and objects appear and disappear from the workers' fixed workplace, a ledger is opened and signs are entered and erased within cell-like, representational divisions. Benjamin continues by quoting Karl Marx,

It is a common characteristic of all capitalist production …,' wrote Marx, 'that the worker does not make use of the working conditions. The working conditions make use of the worker; but it takes machinery to give this reversal a technically concrete form.' In working with machines, workers learn to co-ordinate 'their own movements with the uniformly constant movements of an automaton.'

> in *Sociologie du travail*, 2003, 45, 453. Quote taken from *La Peruque* website, a type magazine made from the unused strips from the sheets used for offset printing in print shops. Each edition is a strip of 1 by 90 cm long, along which different designers show their experiments with typeface, it is a magazine made from the margins, and placed in the margins. http://la-perruque.org/about.html.
> [41] Michel de Certeau, *The Practice of Everyday Life*. 25.

The worker works without allure, and with futility; their hand gestures nothing more than unskilled, trigger-quick repetition quickly absorbed into relentless drill of the second hand. There is no difference in this repetition, the movement does not accumulate and then riff off the past, tick, tick, tick, an endless succession of new moments to which consciousness has been sublimated and the worker is left in thrall to a strict mimesis of action that gathers nothing in its onwards movement, held fast under the aegis of a 'liquidated memory'. The soldier and officer worker too, so that not only manufacturing, but the values, purposes and identities cementing the societies fed by capitalist industrialism and to whose preservation martial investment was dedicated, had been denuded of their progressive force. 'Never' Benjamin continued:

has experience been contradicted more thoroughly: strategic experience has been contravened by positional warfare; economic experience, by the inflation; physical experience, by hunger; moral experiences, by the ruling powers. A generation that had gone to school in horse-drawn streetcars now stood in the open air, amid a landscape in which nothing was the same except the clouds and, at its center, in a force field of destructive torrents and explosions, the tiny, fragile human body.[42]

As if in response to Benjamin, in his *Helden* paintings the artist Georg Baselitz figuratively imagines what these returnees from World War I might look like. Their tiny, alone-ness is magnified onto huge canvases. They are splintered, maimed, their muddied clothes tattered, their heads, devoid of thoughts, stand shrunken, whilst feet and hands, their means of basic bodily function, have become enlarged, as if it has been by trudging and scraping alone they have managed to escape the scene of war, only to spill into something equally callous, though not at all as apparent. They have been wandering, but are now at rest, impaled upon bare branches, utterly lost. Some squat near the earth, unsure of their place, where others stand standing upright on crude, knurled prostheses not at all like the smooth, curvaceous plywood marvels invented by Charles and Ray Eames. Even in pairs these 'new types' are alone. They, like Baselitz, have emerged from a destroyed people, a sundered culture, and rather than rebuild their old order they must start again, from the ruins of a stunted forest floor draped in a carpet of reddened soil and blasted stumps.

This tiny fragile body writ large is the 'new type', the new human being from which we begin again, the source of the new age, the age of design

---

[42] Walter Benjamin *Experience and Poverty*. In *Selected Writings. Vol. II. Part 2*. Edited by Michael Jennings, Howard Eiland, Gary Smith. Cambridge, MA: Belknap Press. 2005. 731–736. 732.

to which the founders of the German Bauhaus School dedicated themselves, the school through which a newly minted human could be fashioned, one that no longer had to endure the pain and maiming of war, no longer had to endure time even. The Bauhaus became dedicated to forms of rational thinking that would place the power of machinery and its capitalist, industrial organization at the behest of designers for whom the human and its activity was, like Palladio's churches and Hoffmann's lamps, an object of proper ordering.[43] From the ruins of war-torn bodies, humans could be re-imagined and be properly managed with their bodies restored to proper proportions. Oscar Schlemmer, professor of drawing, had been one such new type, a damaged figure having served as a soldier on the Western front, and now with the opportunity to redeem experience by turning away from the vicissitudes of war and towards a well-planned and proportioned body and mind. In 1928 he established the interdisciplinary course Der Mensch, the human being, where students would study what it was to be human, a formal body moving rhythmically within, along and across curved and flat spaces, a biological body busy with metabolic need, a philosophical body ordered by reason. He drew humans as diagrammatic repetitions of movement, almost indistinguishable from one another, but unlike Baselitz's figures whose homogeneity in appearance was secured by their having equally blank gazes and featureless expanses of loosened, wasted clothing, with Schlemmer's the repetition is quick, efficient, purposeful.

The language of design is one of formal proportions and attributed functions packaged into housing solutions, calibrated utensils, glass – 'the enemy of secrets' – and steel products, and clean white ceramics which shed any traces of their use with a frigid calm. The post-war human begins again without reference to regional history or sense of place, without a knapsack of home provisions. There is now neither inclination nor capacity to invoke and use fables. These have given way to representations that make things both visible (the clear edges and relations by which things are placed into alignments whose order is tethered by clearly stated aims) and invisible (the superlatives describing the effects that await the user should they submit to preformed, easy patterns of use). No longer tethered by aphoristic reminders whose gentle irony was aimed at those who forget their natural-born limits, the modern, well-designed human works to annul experience,

---

[43] Beatriz Colomina and Mark Wigley *Are We Human?* 155–157. Colomina and Wigley detail how from Schlemmer onwards designers became increasingly interested in providing essentialist answers to the question of 'what makes us human?' Essentially the human is a scene of organic proportions that edge toward perfection and from which all other objects might take their cue.

seeking acclamation for recognising the shortest route to efficiency. At the behest of design, the user abandons experience gladly, for it is shattered anyhow, and concentrates instead on speed: 'engraving, lacquer work or paintings in which a series of thin, transparent layers are placed one on top of the others – all these products of sustained, sacrificing effort are vanishing, and the time is past in which time did not matter. The modern person only works at what can be abbreviated.'[44]

Benjamin is not wholly set against this transformation. The shards were a wasteland from which new things might grow. Artistic creations were attracting mass audiences; in the cinema and magazines the 'aura' was sidelined, making way for collective bodily experiences that shiver and pulsate with pleasures and diversions as intense as the divine movements of the Quakers and Shakers. The new media – film stock, photographic reproductions – foreclose on the possibility of having an origin and an original, but what they lack in authenticity they gain in communicability, and reach. Their job is no longer to reveal the essence of a thing, but to document experience. A painted portrait bears the mimetic weight of having a human subject of which it is an intimate representation. The expression of loss in the eyes, say, if caught by the genius of the artist, gives it immense emotional power; it speaks of a substantial and placed life that will forever be receding, but which remains forever there. Early photographs imitated painting, as though they too were trying to catch what was unique about a subject. Yet the photography that Benjamin admired, that of Eugène Atget and others, the photography suitable for the new post-war types emptied of bourgeois pretensions, revealed another trajectory, no longer mimetic, but documentary, no longer an object requiring intense, private contemplation, but a piece of public evidence, reality unmasked. By concentrating on what was small, overlooked and bypassed Atget removed the aura from objects.

> Atget almost always passed by the 'great sights and so-called landmarks.' What he did not pass by was a long row of boot lasts; or the Paris courtyards, where from night to morning the handcarts stand in serried ranks; or the tables after people have finished eating and left, the dishes not yet cleared away – as they exist by the hundreds of thousands at the same hour;[45]

In these leftover scenes, the misty distance of aura dissolved away: rituals give way to details. The stains on the buildings remain just that,

---

[44] Paul Valery quoted in Walter Benjamin *The Storyteller*. In *Illuminations*. Edited by Hannah Arendt. Translated by Harry Zohn. New York: Schoken Books. 1961. 92–93.

[45] Walter Benjamin Little History of Photography. In *Selected Writings. Vol. II. Part 2*. Edited by Michael Jennings, Howard Eiland, Gary Smith. Cambridge, MA: Belknap Press. 2005. 507–530. 519.

the squares are vacated from history, left vacant. What appears has no urge to be remembered. The commandeering appeal to belong to posterity is stripped away, leaving objects documented with a clean eye in the here and now. The pall left by posterity's strange twisting of time and space lifts, the distance that habitually insinuates itself between the viewer and the viewed is shut down, the photograph is a testament to the direct observation of a democracy of things and it is in making this sameness apparent and uncluttered by equivocation that Atget's craft excels. To be alike, to belong, to have access, to settle in the here and now as a universal condition. The object is released from the weight of its having an origin, or of being related to an original, and so it circulates freely and without diminishment, immediately available, no longer woven into rituals.

Benjamin's enthusiasm, however, was short lived, as consumerism took hold. Mass entertainment collapses into what Theodore Adorno called communications: an excess of unrestrained production whose legitimacy was secured in the atmospheric pressure generated by repeated performative expression.[46] With the onset of abundant consumerism, the things we own have no real edges, they are always being replaced and updated, liquid then liquidated. Their rightful place is a modulated temporariness, they feel transient in our home, as does our home itself, and those with whom we share it. Yet without possessions we collapse into a state of profound dependency, a prospect that spurs and so authorizes the system of property relations by which the relations between production and consumption are animated and accelerated.[47] It was a system of relations normalized by the measured and goal-oriented repetitions of modern design. The emphasis on images and symbols rather than material things, and on aspirations and not practical intelligence, took industrial capitalism out of the factory and into the bright, open spaces of the consumer society: the arcing, mirrored plenum of a

---

[46] Benjamin was not averse to owning things, indeed he would obsess over certain rare editions of books and was an avid collector of children's toys. The collector can remove things from the circulation of exchange, can discipline desire into curiosity, can become a steward for the fate of things. As a practice collecting is characterized by dialectics that 'combine with loyalty to an object, to individual items, to things sheltered in his care, a stubborn subversive protest against the typical, the classifiable'. Walter Benjamin quoted in Hannah Arendt *Walter Benjamin 1892–1940*. Translated by Harry Zohn. New Yorker. 1968. Reprinted in *Men in Dark Times*. New York: Harcourt Brace. 1968. 153–206. 199. Arendt goes on to remark, laconically: 'That a certain destructive force was active even in this passion for the past, so characteristic of heirs and latecomers, Benjamin did not discover until much later, when he had already lost his faith in tradition and in the indestructibility of the world.' (Arendt *Walter Benjamin 1892–1940*. 194).

[47] Theodor Adorno *Minima Moralia: Reflections from a Damaged Life*. Translated by E. Jephcott. London: Verso. 1951/2005. §39.

mall, the house as a machine for living, the car interior as both enclave and prospect. Nothing went untouched; even personal spaces became scenes of intervention.

## The Taskscape

Like tacticians, craft work sits askance from these vectors of visibility and invisibility, but unlike tacticians, it does so by using its own resources, for which it looks back and enlists the past, in the institutional form of tradition. In the Diapsalmata at the opening of *Either/Or*, the philosopher Søren Kierkegaard also looks back, to what he calls the time of folk literature and the traditional fable, whose tracing of human desire was untouched by contemporary ideas of betterment grounded in fashionable relations of envious comparison. He urged readers to recall how:

> [T]he tremendous poetic power of folk literature finds expression in, among other ways, its having the strength to desire. Compared to it, the desire of our own time is both sinful and boring because what it covets is the neighbour's. That other desire knows very well that the neighbour no more than itself has what it seeks. And when its desire is sinful it is on such a titanic scale as to make man tremble. It won't let its price be beaten down by the cold probabilities of a sober reason.[48]

The desire of our own time, like Kierkegaard's, is organized in relations of comparison between things that have identifiable causes and effects, and that are dated and dateable. Design encourages these comparative relations. It gives things a story, authors them, fills them with desired qualities, before suggesting further things that are slightly better. Out with the old, in with the new, trade up, improve. Working as an advisor to a London auction house, the writer Bruce Chatwin observed how 'All civilisations are by their very nature "thing-oriented" and the main problem of their stability has been to devise new equations between the urge to amass things and the urge to be rid of them.'[49] Fashion is the organization of one such equation, augmented by attributions of style, status and taste. Fashion accentuates and then obliterates the distinct qualities of a thing; it declares the thing 'in' or 'out'. The idiosyncratic manner in which some bowls can sit upon a flat surface, the flicker of candlelight in the surface of a glass, the curved resilience of a wooden board, the shape of a coat that has begun to echo the body of its user, none of these values have value when compared to the comparative

---

[48] Søren Kierkegaard *Either/Or: A Fragment of Life*. Translated by Alastair Hannay. London: Penguin. 1843/1992. 45.
[49] Bruce Chatwin *Anatomy of Restlessness: Uncollected Writings*. London: Picador. 1997. 171.

value of a things being 'in' or 'out' of fashion. In design, any inner 'thing power' or presence is concealed as the modern user – impressed upon by envy of the neighbour – looks beyond each thing for comparisons with yet other things, things which others might also covet, and it is these things that come to make up the desirable, secure, predictable, easy-to-use modern home whose occupants catch the eye of one another now and then, each glance alive with envy.

The 'other' desire to which Kierkegaard alludes – the archaic desire – acknowledges the thing itself, and is compelled by it, rather than by the repetitions of desire circulating as fashion and the fashionable. But the thing itself is elusive. Benjamin also had a reverence for the folk tale, the evening fables that hold a community fast of an evening, the homilies and nursery rhymes which gather and condense practical wisdom, the ironies of doggerel verse that refuse excellence the ease of certitude, the well-timed, rhythmic proverb that transforms a situation by taking possessing of and distilling experience into bright kernels that gather the patina of use, enriching the communal soil of tradition.[50] These experiential aspects of culture have been hard won. They are the residue from having struggled towards sense, they are frayed and stained cultural things taken up by those for whom making sense of experience has been a scene of 'haphazard groping, of putting out and withdrawing feelers in formless surroundings, of bedazzlement, of sorties into the illimitable'.[51]

Folk literature, as Kierkegaard and Benjamin express it, is of the body, place and its material nature, and its fantastical, even strange nature, belongs to the world, but where precisely? Its origins are misty, and its settings are elusive. It speaks of desires that are powerful, equivocal and personal but which refuse to declare themselves in comparative terms, and who speaks? The characters are both ordinary and magical, human and non-human, ancient and naive, and the tales are without authors, they are collectively owned and taken on, warped and accentuated and half forgotten. They are mongrel tales and as tough and malleable as mongrels. There are common themes: an uprooting (being tossed up to the moon seventeen times, ascending the bean stalk, climbing a rope of hair) which is also a deviance, and even a violence. There is often an extravagance of materiality – golden straw, glass slippers, rich foods, warm porridge, overgrowing

---

[50] Walter Benjamin *On Proverbs*. In *Selected Writings. Vol. II. Part 2*. Edited by Michael Jennings, Howard Eiland, Gary Smith. Cambridge, MA: Belknap Press. 2005. 582.

[51] Paul Valery *The Crisis of the Mind*. In *The Collected Works of Paul Valery Volume 10*. Translated by Denise Folliot and Jackson Mathews. New York: Pantheon Books. 1962. 14. 'in the beginning was the fable', 43.

gardens – in which to take pleasure and from which to recoil. There is a shaking of the order of things, a breach into unknown, alien and occult territories often made possible by the presence of a threshold thing (an egg, a nut, a lamp, a seed, an apple) that serves as a portal but also, in its ordinariness, to remind the protagonists of the naturalness of this estranging experience. After the protagonist has been seduced into experiencing the 'other' place, there is no going back to the innocence of the earlier time: their experience has bolted into the shadows to hide, but also to find a fantastical understanding which hardens and sharpens into practical wisdom. Rather than a recovery, their return is a mature restoration, a sense of having lived and of the traditions they once took for granted having had to bend and twist to accommodate new understandings. But there is no destruction or complete transformation. This is how experience grows, by the fits and starts of errant desire that animate, disturb and settle back into tradition, a process amazingly and disturbingly accentuated and distilled in Angela Carter's *The Bloody Chamber* in which she takes episodic elements from folk tales as spurs for new stories, new patterns feeding off the latent content of old tales. Jaques Derrida had a similar relationship to the classics or the cannon. Like folk tales, it was a body of writing whose status was a function of is resilience and robustness in the face of continually vivid, errant and even mischievous use.

The traditions invoked by craft work can follow such similar patterns. The forms of well-made things – bottles, rugs and stools – are like folk takes, often authorless, replete with ordinary qualities, and potentially slightly strange and surprising. The repetitions in form are not linear or predictable in nature; the sense of acknowledging and building on what has gone before is not progressive, neither in style nor technique. Rather, each succession builds from within the attainments of earlier generations, and truth is passed between them, from one to the next, as much by events of individual effort as by the rules being sanctioned by protecting institutional structures like guides and guilds.[52] Recalling Hui's distinction between the repetitions in a system

---

[52] The debate on guilds and innovation in craft work is contested. Hannah Arendt comments on the equivocal relation guilds have to improvements, how, whilst they allowed craft work the method of trial and error to improve their methods they 'stressed the continuity rather than the progress of craftsmanship [sic]'. See Hannah Arendt *The Life of the Mind*. Edited by Mary McCarthy. Indiana: Harcourt. 1978. 318. Other theorists counter that guild structures promote efficient use of resources because they fostered co-ordinated action amongst disparate agents, giving both skills and commercial and political influence to otherwise powerless workers. Sheilagh Ogilvie comes out on Arendt's side, though with more spleen, arguing that whatever efficiencies guilds were

of interacting machinery and the contingencies of a system into which a craft worker is placed, the rules of craft work, as of art work more generally, do not prescribe their own extension and execution. The rules are inherently under-determining, and it is the necessity of this openness that brings the individual worker to the fore in artistic practice. It is why, suggested Kant, art is so often associated with individual artists:

> the concept of fine art does not permit a judgment about the beauty of its product to be derived from any rule whatsoever that has a concept as its determining basis, i.e., the judgment must not be based on a concept of the way in which the product is possible. Hence fine art cannot itself devise the rule by which it is to bring about its product. Since, however, a product can never be called art unless it is preceded by a rule, it must be nature in the subject (and through the attunement of his powers) that gives the rule to art; in other words, fine art is possible only as the product of genius.[53]

But where Kant attributed the artistic impetus and impulse to what lay within an individual artist touched by ineffable and inimitable insight (often described as the gift of the muse) the rules by which craft work progress require no such genius, indeed they demand its suppression. As a craft worker, said Annie Albers, as a weaver 'I believe that it is right to lose yourself in your work, to lose your self-awareness and thereby the self-insistence that we know so well in the subjectiveness of the much discussed, and/or verbalized, art scene.'[54] There is an aversion to individuals standing out as inspired carriers of truth, as though touched by a divine tongue and caused to speak thereof. Kant argued that artistic power was conferred by nature directly. After all, if it was not, if instead it emerged from the effortful repetition of acceptable patterns of work

---

able to extract to raise economic rents for craft workers, it was always a small elite of craft workers that benefitted, and they in turn did much to keep their elite clients in place; they enforced rather than challenged hierarchies and social divisions. In her 2006 Tawney Lecture she reminds her audience that, 'Empirical micro-studies of guilds' actual activities – as opposed to the rhetorical advocacy of their benefits in literature and legislation – show how they underpaid employees, overcharged customers, stifled competition, excluded women and Jews, and blocked innovation.' And even where they were able to foster the development of technical knowledge, it was typically at the expense of extracting monopoly rents for members, enforcing high barriers to entry, insisting that craft workers form clusters in tight geographic areas, forcing journey workers to travel long distances and stipulating which apprenticeships transmitted which techniques. Sheilagh Ogilvie '"Whatever Is, Is Right"? Economic Institutions in Preindustrial Europe'. Tawney Lecture 2006. Cesifo working paper no. 2066. 13, 18–19.

[53] Immanuel Kant *Critique of Judgment*. Translated by Werner Pluhar. Indianapolis: Hackett. 1987. §46. #308.
[54] Annie Albers Talk to the Colloquium of Associated Artists of Pittsburg, February 12 1964, www.albersfoundation.org/alberses/teaching/anni-albers/craftsmanship.

and the following of authoritative design, then it ceased to be art, for then it was the rule and not the artist that made the work. Art could not proceed by imitation alone, and whilst the products of individual genius provide others coming after them with a form and impetus they might imitate, the artist cannot be imitated; they are, by definition, a unique force.

Craft work, being close to what Kant called the mechanical arts, is more sanguine about the gifts of imitation and how these might be seeded with originality. The tradition within which it works is far from a formal, scholarly catalogue of categories and concepts, and more akin to that what Hubert Dreyfus calls the acquisition of skill. The acquisition of skill in craft work requires a steady immersion in the activities and norms of a practice characterized by shared understandings that have a deep-set intensity but no distinguishable edges. Dreyfus argues that to be skilled a worker acquires a shared and unspoken awareness of 'what it is to be a person, an object, an institution', and the ground of this acquisition is unspoken, it is acquired without an explicit conferring of status which only happens in retrospect, once it is already agreed that the craft worker has attained a requisite level of skill. Level, though, is a misleading metaphor, because it is nothing like a plumbline or yardstick. The understanding lies beyond language: experts 'dwell in the equipment, practices and concerns' often without 'noticing them or trying to spell them out'; as such, any attempted explication of expertise 'can never be complete because we dwell in it ... it is so pervasive as to be both nearest to us and farthest away.'[55]

Yet craft work is experienced as more than bouts of immersed flow elicited through a reasoned, situational responsiveness, and Dreyfus' sense of skill struggles to absorb the punctuations and bumps to which many exponents of craft work attest as they go about their tasks scattered in what Tim Ingold calls a 'taskscape'. The allusion to landscape is deliberate. Within a taskscape there is concern for the explicit arrangements of materials, actions, memories and symbols through which those undertaking the tasks can read the regional contexts into which they have been thrown. These regions are rough, uneven, they undulate, and whilst much of what becomes the task involves following the existing flows of energy that follow the lie of the land, as might a river both create and follow a valley, this 'going along' or 'wayfaring' is far from unconscious. It may aver from the 'sober' dictates of design,

---

[55] Hubert Dreyfus *Being-in-the-World: A Commentary on Heidegger's Being and Time*. Cambridge, MA: MIT Press. 1999. 22, 22, 90.

but it is not thereby its embodied contrary.[56] For a start, the tradition by which craft work finds its footing acts as a warrant, it authorizes the work by virtue of previous expressions of work: 'insofar as the past has been transmitted as tradition', argues Hannah Arendt, 'it possesses authority; insofar as authority presents itself historically, it becomes tradition.'[57] It is in tradition that authoring and authority collude with a knowing familiarity that is spoken of and agreed upon and in these agreements the tasks become legitimate. As a craft worker repeats tasks they silently invoke, and are exposed to, a common sense and to a commonplace into which they have settled and have found there a security that comes from being in possession of rounded skills that they have mastered and embodied.[58]

It is this sense of settlement that pervades Rembrandt's etching of Johannes Lutma (1584–1669) (Figure 21). Working from Amsterdam and a friend of Rembrandt, Lutma was a silversmith and goldsmith renowned for a technical facility that blended classical order with an indigenous ornamentalism (*kwabstijl*) into pieces with an expressive restraint. He is surrounded by his tools: a hammer, a beaker full of punches, a *kwabstijl* chased dish or drinking bowl and a candlestick. In Dutch, *Kwab* evokes undulating folds of skin, curling mists, a twinning of what is inside and outside such that neither settles into a dominant presence, a stretching and deforming of outline, and it was with risk-taking goldsmiths like Lutma that the style gained distinctiveness. The restless outlines of their ornamentation refused to indicate their referent with any loyalty: it might be a mouth agape or a gaping cavern, a bushel of straw or plait of hair: the lustre and play of light along the curvaceous surface took precedence.[59] Though Rembrandt was also immersed in *kwabstijl* often including the pieces in his own paintings, in his etching of Lutma the outlines are stable, even the glass flask in the recess of the windowsill is marked with clearly etched lines, and his drinking bowl is pushed by the hatching into half-shadow. His cap slouches with a nonchalant poise atop a half-closed gaze is allowed to drift in the middle distance, he sits as though suffused by what Ruskin

---

[56] See Tim Ingold 'Work, Time, and Industry', *Time and Society*. 1995, 4, 5, 5–28.
[57] Hannah Arendt *Walter Benjamin*. In *Men in Dark Times*. New York: Harcourt Brace. 1968. 193–195.
[58] Jochem Kroezen, Davide Ravasi, Innan Sasaki, Monika Żebrowska and Roy Suddaby 'Configurations of Craft: Alternative Models for Organizing Work', *Academy of Management Annals*. 2021, 15, 2, 502–536.
[59] Allison Stielau *Fit Vessel: Kwab at the Rijksmuseum*. Review of exhibition 'Kwab: Dutch Design in the Age of Rembrandt'. *West 86th*. 2019, 26, 1, 110–132. See also Peter Thornton *Form and Decoration. Innovation in the Decorative Arts 1470–1870*. London. 1998. 96.

Figure 21 Jan Lutma (goldsmith), *Rembrandt van Rijn*, 1656. Etching, engraving and drypoint. Rovinski, 276 (3rd state). 270b Oliver Wendell Holmes Collection. Library of Congress, Prints and Photographs Division.

called 'the spirit of touch', holding loosely, but closely, onto one of the many pieces he has wrought over the years; he is an embodiment of the successful habitation of a tradition.[60]

[60] John Ruskin *The Stones of Venice*, Vol. II. §21. 200.

### Skill and Expertise

The habituated fitting in within a landscape of tradition brings forth the vexed question of creativity and originality in craft. Dreyfus' characterization of expertise as an immersive fit with the demands and possibilities inherent in a practice begs the question of how that practice disturbs and transforms itself? For Richard Sennett it is a question of critique. An expert subjects their own and others' skill to critical reflection, improvisation and experiment: in the taskscape of craft work, absorbed coping is animated by serious thought. As much as it requires and encourages a state of immersed situationally attuned action, it also curries an almost wilful recalcitrance.[61]

It is a form of recalcitrance that Sennett describes, by way of offering some daylight between design and craft, as the transition from problem solving to problem creating.[62] To be sure, Sennett defines craft skill practically: to become an expert requires the repetitions in practice that emerge from sustained, embodied movements. His examples of craft work drift across a range of activities: playing the cello, dancing, software programming or baking. Whilst the concept of craft might often be hefted to the hand working of specific materials like clay or wood, it is Sennett's conviction that it applies to many different work practices. What distinguishes the movements of craft work are a closeness to, and disciplined awareness of, the material medium: stone, coding language, soundwaves, coupled to an intimacy with tools, so they augment the body. As they absorb the rules of technique and acquire an understanding of the consistencies and quirks of different raw materials, form begins to emerge naturally from the craft worker's practice. Not easily necessarily, but as it should be. The material and tools merge with a tutored awareness of patterns, shapes and use-value to constrain but not determine the form: already made things, the work process, the maker, the materials, the workshop, the standards, the small, personal and communal histories, all cohere in dynamic feedback loops or what the philosopher Maurice Merleau-Ponty called 'intentional arcs'. The immersive discipline of rhythmic repetition (e.g. the up-and-down and side-to-side motion of a weaver's arms in echo to the shuttling of the loom and the weft and warp of the cloth is less iterative (repetitious) than what Tim Ingold calls itinerative (a journey, a discovery)).[63] As the experience of

---

[61] Richard Sennett *The Craftsman*. 279–289; Harry Collins 'Studies of Expertise and Experience', *Topoi*. 2018, 37, 67–77.
[62] Richard Sennett *The Craftsman*. 282–285.
[63] Tim Ingold *Being Alive: Essays on Movement, Knowledge and Description*. London: Routledge. 2011. 239.

making matures in taking these journeys, so does the ability to calibrate and corroborate the appropriate response (from a rich and varied repertoire of available responses) as situations unfold, allowing the craft worker to realize states of 'maximal grip' (recalling the earlier discussion of finding footholds). Their intentional force does not arise from any separate 'thinking subject' (there is no controlling *res cogitans*) but through a succession of meaningful attempts to arrive at states of skilled coping with the small problems of making.

Yet expertise requires more than this: skill is enhanced the more the craft worker questions, dwells upon and ranges over their experiences of coping.[64] Barbara Montero, for example, argues that expert dancers, no matter how immersed in the flow of their movement, nevertheless pepper the performance with interruptions in which questions are being posed, not answered.[65] The vitality of skill requires the agitations of thought. Without them being in place, the novel or untimely act is only ever an immature lurch from one impulse to another. It is a style of thought that acknowledges and questions the dependency on maximal grip. Intentional arcs might feel like endings, yet in delineating themselves they also mark out, albeit in the negative, those unavailable activities that have been overlooked, avoided or cast into history as anachronisms. The expertise can be revisited, re-aligned, deliberately marginalized even, and any sense of accomplishment is embraced then made the subject of concern, prompting a learning after other materials or techniques for realizing effects, which are marginally, or massively, different. How, to recur to the weaver, do similar patterns appear in differing colour combinations, differing weights of thread, differing yarns and upon different machines? The flow is being broken into eddies, a reconsidering takes place, a thoughtful pause fosters breaks in the rhythm where the craft worker thinks themself into the task and broader 'taskscape'.[66] From

---

[64] Maurice Merleau Ponty *Phenomenology and Perception*. Translated by Colin Smith. London: Routledge. 2005. In accepting the presence of the 'question', Ponty is alive to the potency of disturbance, noticing how 'Sometimes a new cluster of meanings is formed; our former movements are integrated into a fresh motor entity, the first visual data into a fresh sensory entity, our natural powers suddenly come together in a richer meaning, which hitherto has been merely foreshadowed in our perceptual or practical field, and which has made itself felt in our experience by no more than a certain lack, and which by its coming suddenly reshuffles the elements of our equilibrium and fulfils our blind expectation.' 177.

[65] Barbaro Montero 'Practice Makes Perfect: The Effect of Dance Training on the Aesthetic Judge', *Phenomenology and the Cognitive Sciences*. 2002, 1, 413–425.

[66] This understanding of how craft workers become experts upends somewhat the seminal work of Hubert Dreyfus. With Dreyfus, becoming skilled is a process of trained submission: first, being taught formal rules detailing what to do and why; second, gradually submitting one's body to required movements, to the point they become instinctual,

these small thoughtful perturbations in approach, more disturbing ones can also be pursued, as when the weaver Sheila Hicks asks: what if yarns are made from featherweight acrylics, and what if the loom becomes a makeshift, temporary construction made from found materials, what is it to concentrate on and emphasize the space between the threads, giving absence priority over presence, and what is it to think of threads as an alphabet in three dimensions and textiles as texts?[67]

The nature of these thoughtful intercessions, is not a distancing from the experience of making, but an intensification of awareness within it. The pauses induce an imaginative response to the intentional arcs without the intercession of overt designs or interests. The expert has got to the point in their learning where the skilled movements and procedures that have etched themselves into their body, where the prevailing attitudes that they assume as naturally as they breathe, and where the affective loyalties that colour and tone their affections, have themselves become the overt subject matter of an imaginative, conscious way of working. The glassmaker and writer Erin O'Connor documents how skill is acquired through this reciprocal working through of practice and imagination. The state of immersed flow is not a singular experience. First comes a reciprocity between body and tools, second comes a growing material sensitivity, then third comes an imaginative an active, willed attention.[68] Citing Gaston Bachelard, she suggests that once a glass-blower experiences all three, they are in a place of direct communication with: 'images of matter, direct images of matter. Vision names them, but the hand knows them. A dynamic joy touches them, kneads them, makes them lighter. One dreams these images of matter substantially, intimately, rejecting forms – perishable forms – and vain images, and the becoming of surfaces. They have weight, they are a heart.'[69]

---

no longer mediated by conscious decision; and third, the body, mind and tradition are enjoined, each expressing the other. Though the practice can be difficult and technical, Dreyfus' expert experiences increasing surety in an accomplished *automaticity*, allowing them to instinctually follow the affordances of a situation. See Hubert Dreyfus 'Refocusing the Question: Can There Be Skilful Coping without Propositional Representations or Brain Representations?' *Phenomenology and the Cognitive Sciences*. 2012, 11, 59–68.

[67] See Jennifer Higgie 'Fibre Is My Alphabet: Interview with Sheila Hicks', *Frieze*. 169. 20 February 2015.

[68] Erin O'Connor *The Centripetal Force of Expression: Drawing Embodied Histories into Glassblowing*. In *Ethnographies of Artistic Work*. Edited by Howard S. Becker and Marie Buscatto *Qualitative Sociological Review*, III, 3, 113–134.

[69] Gaston Bachelard *The Poetics of Reverie: Childhood, Language and the Cosmos*. New York: Orion Press. 1969. 11. See also Erin O'Connor *Embodied Knowledge in Glassblowing: Meaning and the Struggle towards Proficiency*. In *Embodying Sociology: Retrospect, Progress and Prospects. The Sociological Review Monograph*. Edited by Chris Shilling. London: Wiley. 2007. 126–141.

The images are not designs imposed upon the glass, they are not even thought about during the making of the glass. Rather, the expert glass-blower, having become sensitive to the limits of possibilities of the material, is thinking of how glass moves and shapes under the different heats that can be induced by a furnace and the cooling jacks, how bowls emerge from alterations in heat on the blown surface. O'Connor rather beautifully, because carefully, attends to the difference as one of thinking through the material rather than of the material. Expertise in craft work stems from a gradual awareness that the material, form and tools have means of thought already contained within them. Expertise is more than the deployment of refined motor skills in the exacting fulfilment of the norms and operations of an established practice. It extends to a disciplined knowledge of the quality and range of the behaviour of form and material, coupled to an exacting and conscious consideration of the feelings of attraction and repulsion elicited by this behaviour.

**Rule Following**

The interventions of Sennett and O'Connor offer themselves as a pause for thought. If the acquisition of expertise in craft work is marked by states of immersed flow, it is enhanced and developed when the experience of making is pockmarked with moments of thoughtful distancing. But what is the nature of this distancing? It might be called a distancing from within (O'Connor uses Heidegger's term 'de-distancing'), an internal severance echoed in Peter Sloterdijk's comment that real expertise has the virtuosity of being 'able to learn what can be learned until it takes the risk and plunges into achievements that cannot be learned'.[70] The plunge inwards, a deepening of involvement that cannot be fully contained by concepts such as 'flow' or thoughtless 'ease', and which requires, in addition, a willed aspect to what the ancient Greeks called *technē*: working techniques and skill. Alva Noë talks of it as a continual adjustment in the skills, attitudes and affections grounding perception as craft workers (or any practitioner) struggle to get things to come into view. In craft this coming into view is also a coming into being; there is an achieving of, and an evaluation of, the object in the moment of its unfolding into life. On this the cusp of their appearance, these made things are mediated by the bodily skill of craft workers, by the values and routines toning the tradition of making, and by

---

[70] Peter Sloterdijk *The Aesthetic Imperative*. Translated by Karen Margolis. London: Polity Press. 2017. 255.

the instinctual feelings of attraction and repulsion that pull and push at a craft worker's loyalties and concerns. Being 'on the cusp', the things need not be associated with firm and fixing concepts, and often the craft worker finds themselves in an aesthetic predicament where perception needs adjusting: things are perceived anew, the concealed is revealed, the nonsensical becomes sensible.[71] These adjustments are typically iterative and native to the entanglements of the taskscape: the breakdown of habit is part of habit, the traditions revivify themselves.

Such thoughts on skill and expertise dissolve the more typical distinction between mind (brainwork) and body (handwork) to which analysis of craft expertise has long been prone (sometimes with the addition of a middle classification of 'knowing', which covers the commitments of the heart). It is a distinction that reaches at least as far back as Aristotle, but in its modern, commonsensical guise is attributed to Gilbert Ryle's separation of 'knowing that' (e.g. knowing the names of stitches, cuts and types of cloth that might combine well to make different uniforms in a tailoring apprenticeship) from 'knowing how' (e.g. the way cloth falls over a body, or how a suit embodies a specific character).[72] The former is largely propositional, explicit and definitional whilst the latter is practical, tacit and engaged. It is a distinction to which Dreyfus' understanding of expertise implicitly subscribes, though it reverses the presumed hierarchy, by arguing for the priority (and implied superiority) of the embodied knowing how, the form of knowledge at which craft work is presumed to excel.

But once thought through the examples offered by Sennett and O'Connor's interventions, Ryle's distinction dissolves. To know that a business suit can convey a certain 'character', for example, is a loose form of propositional knowledge that invokes an awareness of how the suit is made, which in turn requires a familiarity with making and the value associated with one way of making above another, which then implies an affinity between the making of a suit and making of a character, both of which can be done well or ill. 'Knowing how' and 'knowing that' are knotted in bundles of thoughtful association wrought through the aesthetic effort to perceive and perceive again. Even when the making stops – for example, when a tailor no longer has the manual dexterity to stitch – their know-how stays with them, they can still tell at a

---

[71] Alva Noë *The Entanglement: How Art and Philosophy Make Us What We Are* (2nd ed.). Princeton, NJ: Princeton University Press. 2023. 95–99. 106.
[72] Gilbert Ryle 'Knowing How and Knowing That: The Presidential Address', *Proceedings of the Aristotelean Society*. 1945, 46, 1, 1–16.

glance how a suit fits and they might still teach others of this aesthetic struggle for fit, indeed become adept at such.[73]

Originality only makes sense from within the practice from which it is attempting to cleave itself in distinction: any distancing only occurs because of a profound connexion, the recoil is born from an intense yearning to belong. The re-organization of material and form is startling less in its novelty than in its having distilled meaning to a point of irrefutable objectivity that shines clearly, like crystal. Aesthetic moves that attempt to move the other way and distance themselves from the practice and stand on their own legs will wither because they lack a sustaining atmosphere, they have little against which they might seek to pit themselves, there is no air. The poet T. S. Eliot, for example, thought: 'the poem which is absolutely original is absolutely bad; it is, in the bad sense, "subjective", with no relation to the world to which it appeals'.[74] For Eliot the most compelling poets were necessarily those who were most stylistically alive to the possibilities lying *within* traditions, to the means of thought lying deep within the already existing form and material. Shakespeare's sonnets are written in clear, ordinary language but in such a way that readers bethink to themselves 'Of course it could not have been otherwise'. Here, the aesthetic work of perception, imagination and thoughtfulness is not directed towards breaking a tradition so much as the struggle of working through its potential and showing others the naturalness of such progression, by deliberately pausing to think through the enlarged possibilities contained within a short word or basic shape. Suddenly what was marginal can become central, what was alien can become kin, or what was lost be found.

Continuing this line of reasoning, Eliot then argued that at its most successful, aesthetic work extricates itself from the thrown condition by which it was first prompted and authorized. The real genius is to extricate oneself from genius, to become timeless, freeing the skill, attitude and feeling from the taint of a regional place and time. The only tradition to which they were to belong was the cannon of poetry itself, and not at all the culturally mongrel and historically inter-penetrating sense of tradition typically experienced within most practice traditions. Nor was the canon that favoured by Derrida, the literary equivalent of a brilliant open-source code made available through close attention for all manner of interpretation. Eliot's poetic tradition was altogether

---

[73] D. G. Brown *Knowing How and Knowing That, What*. In *Ryle*. Edited by O. P. Wood and G. Pitcher. London: Macmillan. 1971. 13–48.

[74] T. S. Eliot *Introduction to Ezra Pound*. In *Selected Poems*. Edited by T. S. Eliot. London: Faber & Faber. 1934. x

less kaleidoscopic, and whilst it was to be written by those who had felt strong emotion and who had formed a strong personality, it consisted of neither emotion nor personality, for these were the products of experience and inheritance, and poetry was the product of labour.[75]

The thoughtful *techne* to which Sennett and O'Connor appeal, however, proffers no such severance from experience and inheritance. Indeed, what would it even be to repress the everyday? Even if Eliot's poet could shed their quotidian ties, they would still be speaking and writing and require an audience, and to the extent they understood Eliot's claim, they would be moved by an emotional force of recognition whose acknowledgement, as an event in time and space, would taint and twist its universality. The thoughtful pause within the processes of craft work is less a repression of the everyday entanglements that sustain these processes than a willed struggle to push oneself into the interstices of the taskscape again and again, and to retrace the techniques, espouse the attitudes and feel the yearning and recoil anew. The expertise is being settled within the taskscape through a multiplicity of traditions that provide the cultural, commercial and social agreements by which any craft worker can make sense of themselves and others in the pursuit of well-made things. Within these traditions, craft workers acknowledge how they relate not only in terms of sharing interests, skills, values and affections, but in sharing the public and institutional conditions by which these perceptual experiences and interests gain support and sustenance. Tradition is a phenomenon of context and criteria, not specific projects and content: it remains 'indifferent to the achievement of any substantive purpose'.[76] Rather than conceiving or enforcing a proper 'object' of choice, its concern is with the ongoing organization of relationships necessary to the satisfaction of any purpose or to the acknowledgment and acceptability of perception. It is the medium of understanding by which they appreciate their entanglement and disclose this reciprocally to other craft workers and users.

Ludwig Wittgenstein used 'language game' to conceptualize this entanglement. To become aware of and appreciate the nature and potential of being entangled is to learn the 'rules' of the game. Craft work is inundated with rules, the most apparent and simple being those of decoration, such as following a motif, learning to detail a Greek key

---

[75] T. S. Eliot *Tradition and the Individual Talent*. In *Selected Essays 1917–1932*. New York: Harcourt Brace. 1932. 3–11. The poet's job is not to express their own emotion but to transform the emotions they find in experience (the raw material) into new, hitherto unexperienced emotions, and for this it is a matter of indifference: it is emotion, transformed, through discipline, rather than 'emotion recollected in tranquility'.10.

[76] Michael Oakeshott *On Human Conduct*. Oxford: Clarendon Press. 1975. 65.

border; for example, one right-angled abutment of strait lines nestling under another, the two then repeated, again and again. The rule is followed, yet through perceptual gestures in which the repetition of the earlier coupling introduces another instance, a gap, what the philosopher Gilles Deleuze calls an interruption that tremors, and which only resolves itself within the overall effect of the pattern, and only then as an absence alluding to something else, something as yet virtual. The 'cause' of this dynamic pause, the gesture, remains unresolved, and it must remain so, for only then can a work be said to be fulfilled, or achieved.[77] The causal power reverberating along the motif is not the equivalent of a logical sequence of the mathematical order '+2', but a translation of signs from one instance to the next and as the sign crosses the interlude there is a brief sense of precarity, the 'productive disparity' of a crossing being made. To learn such a simple decorative sequence is to acquire a sense of established patterns of movement and consideration through a disciplined and intimate co-habitation of routine.[78] Learning dawns from within these acts of repetition. Wittgenstein suggests the comprehension of a rule is akin to setting oneself along a vector: 'Ah, now I can go on'. This 'going on', whilst it is a rhythm of addition, is of a completely different order to abstracted instructions such as '+2'. These instructions are closed systems: they contain all possible instances of their own extension. The assigned value and the rules for assigning the value are synonymous: there is no room for contextual interpretation without a collapse of sense, there is no vector. In contrast, the rules followed in marking out a Greek key motif are being mediated and taken in and absorbed by a body that is gradually and patiently acquiring sensory awareness of how the weight, stiffness, colour, smell and size of threads and tools can gather within a repeating shape. As the apprentice follows the pattern, they bring their own movement into line with the rhythmic weight and lift of the repetitions they are following. 'We learn nothing' suggests Deleuze 'from those who say "Do as I do". Our only teachers are those who say "do with me" and are able to emit signs to be developed in heterogeneity rather than propose gestures for us to reproduce',[79] signs that are bound through effect, one feeling body to another, self-organizing in an unscored concert to which thought is brought by way of an attendance.

---

[77] Gilles Deleuze *Repetition and Difference*. Translated by Paul Patton. London: Continuum Books. 2001. 21.
[78] Alva Noë *The Entanglement*.
[79] See Emma Bell and Sheena Vachhani 'Relational Encounters and Vital Materiality in the Practice of Craft Work', *Organization Studies*. 2020, 41, 5, 681–701.

## Apprenticeship as the Synthesis of Skill, Habit and Tradition

'Do with me' was very much the mantra at the workshops of the weaver Märta Määs-Fjetterström in Båstad, Sweden. After a few years of spinning, the 'yarn girls' were allowed to spend time with a weaver through whose looms the work, drawings or cartoons took life. Different yarns had different textures, robustness and colours: the weft was typically wool, the warp being wool or linen, which can be twisted.[80] The motifs defer to the side-side and up-down orthogonal constraints of working along loom lines, shuttling back and forth, along and back again (Figure 22). The variation on a Greek key emerges, along with other linear, stepped shapes revealing a rhythm whose regularity and order provides a secure space for small differences to come through under the attention of a close eye and touch: its marking out oscillates between engagement and interruption. The Greek key becomes something lifelike, a border around a heathland, the outline of a fern leaf ready to spring forth and to seed new life, it becomes a crude thing: 'crude thinking, this is the thinking of the great' said Bertolt Brecht in his *Threepenny Novel*.[81] It is blunt not because it is shabby but intimate with the process of its execution, it emerges in action and its subtleties and suggestiveness are those immanent to lived movements and not to the refinements of concepts and categories: the crudeness is a roughness and the roughness emerges from the undulations of immersive flow, hesitation, correction and lines of flight.

Thinking through Wittgenstein's comments on rule following, learning in apprenticeships is an experience of absorbing signs into the 'rough ground' of perceptual experience and taking them onwards, which is why it cannot be reduced to the repetition of abstracted movement, one key stroked after another. There is in apprenticeship, as much as in expertise, an ineffable, pre-representational experience of familiarity with tradition and habit, a gathering of signs, that cannot itself be the subject of signs. The rule following occurs against this background, as the apprentice leans in, touches and inserts difference, which is why 'there is something amorous – but also something fatal – about all education'.[82] The rule becomes theirs, the motif of the Greek key becomes theirs, and the others' uses die away, new intensities intrude into the outward abstract surface of the keyed lines whose ordered cadence conceals a distinct,

---

[80] Ingrid Bergman *Märta Määs-Fjetterström En mästare och nyskapare inom textilkonsten*. Högbo: Nordiska Museum. 1990.
[81] Bertolt Brecht, *Threepenny Novel*, Translated by Desmind I. Vesey. Harmondsworth: Penguin Books. 1961. 158.
[82] Gilles Deleuze *Repetition and Difference*. 24.

# Apprenticeship as Synthesis

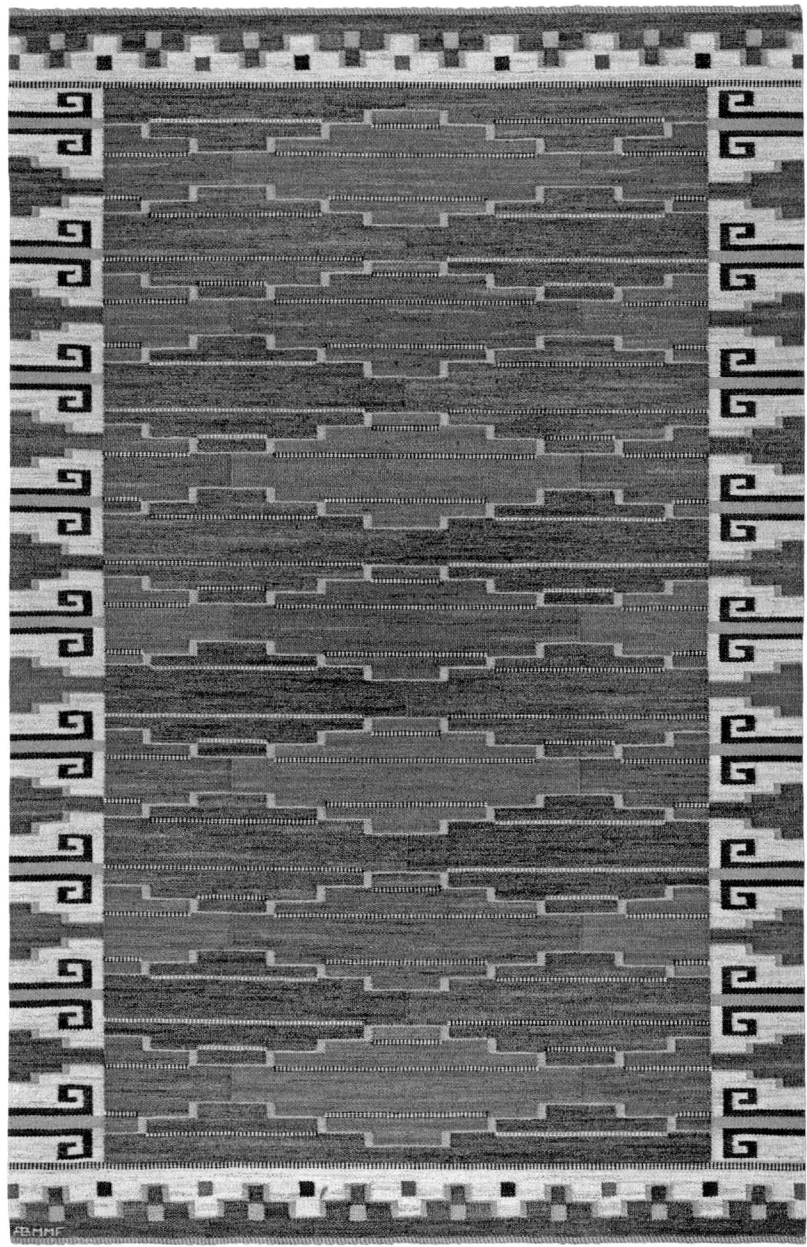

Figure 22 Märta Måås-Fjetterström AB, *Bruna Heden* (Brown heath), 1931. Rölakan flatweave. Wool. Photography: Anette Nilsson. © martamaasfjetterstrom.

dynamic rhythm of a woven repetition that has been received as a vector and that is now being passed onwards under cover of an outward pattern: beneath the rules lies singularities that 'weave their repetitions in the depths of the earth and of the earth where laws do not yet exist'.[83]

The threads on the loom are not only held in organized relations, but suffused with a purposive glow; there may not be an exact end fixed in place, but there remains a profound and consistently felt sense of direction sufficient to enlist the parts into an awareness of a whole towards which they lean, as might the sole of a boot lean into the soil, its tread both an indication of direction and an imprint or memory of passage. Again and again a movement can leave its trace, until a groove is found, a path of desire, of wanting to have gone this way then back along the loom, repeatedly, so that imperceptibly, though very definitively through each repetition, an incision is being made into pattern that is both an ongoing act of marking, a claim to passage, which terminates in the thresholds of commencement and of ending. Yet the repetition and its capture is nothing without its being each time a unique, contingent act in the present, so that the woven pathway of the thread appears in a looping process of self-determining expression: it is made, and in being made overlays and defers to what was once made without losing its immediate distinction as always being under way in repeated movements. In maintaining its distinctiveness, the mark making commits to the end form without being subsumed by it. It is not first a fragment and then a whole, but both/and, which is perhaps what Kant meant by the purposiveness that characterizes all artwork: an atmosphere of expressive direction and motivation that cannot be pinned down by a list of explicit purposes, but which nevertheless enlists the service of each fragmentary act in the service of the whole.

In gathering themselves in the company of signs through acts of repetition, an apprentice is generating a dynamic space in which they immediately and bodily dramatize the instruction and ideas inherent in tradition. In the presence of this repetition the apprentice begins to experience what Deleuze calls 'passive synthesis'. There is no memory here, no active thought, just the operations of imagination through which the present comes to contain the past and future in the form of a contraction or distillation of occurrence; a move from particular to general and back again that remains immanent to the present through the imaginative work of expectation. Noë uses the word 'style' to describe this expressive way of being in which the re-enactment and representation of routines gathers around and within a body that begins to absorb the

---

[83] Gilles Deleuze *Repetition and Difference*. 21.

succession of repetitious events.[84] Each turning move becomes a return, such as one angled line being placed adjacent to another, again and again, or small pieces of bronze and copper being bedded into the rim of a leather hard clay bowl to create red dots which bleed through the glaze during firing,[85] or when a typographer receives the typical instructions 'Demy 8vo, set 101 11/12, 24 em measure, 36 lines to page, r.heads 10/110 italic u/lc. House style' and can picture the printed page immediately, even hankering after something a little less formulaic: Bodoni perhaps, or Caslon, or to discuss ornaments on a title page?[86] Style blends routine with feeling, nestling itself between the subjective and objective, feeling its way into singular instantiations of conformity that ground the body and its sense of self. The self appears wherever there is a system capable of drawing a difference from within a repetition, the self being in its origin a modification, a drawn distinction, whose existence continues only by virtue of further modification; that is, a further act of contemplation by which what it contracts in the extraction of difference is that to which it has a right, a need, a claim, which is carried first by passion and which ends with fatigue. The effect is a drawn-out self, larval, an extension of life in which passive syntheses are accompanied by active ones. Whilst habit affords the texture for life, what allows habit to take hold within 'a life' are intelligence and memory: that which allow the present to pass and so give existence a sense of life, of being alive. This former (re-membered) present is represented in the present, alongside a currently existing present which is also represented, giving rise to an active synthesis that has a double aspect: the reproduction of the former present and reflection upon the present present.[87]

A potter, like Florian Gadsby for example, aware that certain metals create red effects in glazes, slips and bodies when fired, records experiments with how to mix and place them, which temperatures to fire them, which glazes to accompany them, which forms to house them, which alignments to pattern them, and then, in addition, thinks through how the recording of these experiments might also be recollected as prompts for future recall (databases of films, images, written texts). Here action – the activity by which habit is embodied and embedded – is accompanied by contemplation (there is no hierarchy, the body is not primary, it just 'is') and the self, as a self, is contemplation (it does not

---

[84] Alva Noë *The Entanglement*. 150–155.
[85] See Florian Gadsby *Spontaneity or Intention*. www.youtube.com/watch?v=C-dI__shMg8. See also his *By My Hands: A Potter's Apprenticeship*. London: Penguin. 2023.
[86] Michael Clapham 'Typographer and Comp', *Matrix* 18. 1998. 2. Clapham was writing about the craft of comp work at Cambridge University Press in the 1930s.
[87] Gilles Deleuze *Repetition and Difference*. 81.

contemplate itself, there is nothing to contemplate, it *is* the process of contemplation) and only in contemplation does the potter learn as it is in contemplation that difference is extracted from repetition.[88]

All organisms rely on contracts with the earth, water and air held within cycles of repetition and held up to contemplation (the generalities, claims, satisfactions, imagination by which the right and capacity to contract with the broader environment are affirmed). In the repetitions of craft work, the imaginative mind-body has the role of extracting difference from repetition; first it allows for length in repetition, for the qualitative move from an instant of repetition unfolding itself to the actively imagined and remembered repetition of passive synthesis, and second it allows for depth by passing between different experiences of passive synthesis and actively thinking about this passage. There is a range or scope of contemplation whereby the contractions dawn and then dwindle at differing rates, depending on the organism and when it tires and no longer contemplates what it contracts. In states of contemplative wakefulness, the craft worker experiences a sense of lack accompanied by a question, a conception of a negative through which the problem field arises (Sennett's posing of questions) of how and why to realize a piece of work. The passive syntheses, the stylistic repetitions, become agitated by active syntheses of memory and contemplation, which together bed into rich regions of meanings.

Any craft workshop is organically composed of these syntheses, myriad contractions by which life becomes more than occurrence. Craft work feeds from the conserving impress of repetition and the contextual stability this brings: indeed, context (from Latin *con-* together with *texte* – weaving) is a craft-based concept. The contextualization that happens in the workshop is a deliberately and carefully orchestrated scene of repetitious movement tethered by regional awareness. As the experience of Måås-Fjetterström's apprentices became infused with a sense of folklore, the emergence of skilled dexterity in working a loom, with an appreciation of different yarns, with long work hours on low pay, with work deadlines and so on, the structures as well as the content of their understanding was changing. Their bodies changed, their expectations, their sense of community and self, all of which would colour their feeling for fact and skew how the facts appeared and re-appeared in the repetitions of their work. Far from being a series of 'instants', one occurrence after another, the present is expanded through a heighted awareness of what is being handed over from the past and what is being owed to the future.

---

[88] Gilles Deleuze *Repetition and Difference*. 73.

As much as it is grounded by an archival respect for the past, the regional context to which her weavers belonged was also charged and loosened by the future, which intruded into the making through an authorizing force of expectation that the work would be in some way expressive of, rather than an imitation of, a standard design. The dye in the yarn would carry unique tones, the weight of the weave would alter with changes in technique and atmosphere, the sheep from whose backs the wool was shared would be from a different farm, all of them small differences being compressed into repetitious movement. The repetition etched into the body of the weaver was felt as a need: in need repetition finds expression as an expectation, and in expectation the context of passive syntheses is twisted and shaped by what John Dewey calls the emergent ends in view, which dawn and recede as the activity unfolds. The ends in view remain immanent to the task at hand: they feed it as readily as the thread is fed into the loom and emerge from it as tentatively as the changefulness and variety of the pattern. The pattern fixes these expressions of time and preserves their originality. An accomplished weave feels like one of Kierkegaard's old folk tunes: it might have always existed, and might always exist, and it appears and circulates outside of the linear chains of progress and indifferent to the withering ascriptions of taste, motioning to whomever is in view as surely and as freely as when it was first made.

## The Hermeneutics of Writing

Måås-Fjetterström was inspired by the flowers, ponds, forests and heavily tilled soils of southern Sweden, all of which could be distilled into lines, colours, planes and directions that were sketched onto squared paper and held as a library of cartoons from which rugs and tapestries emerged, again and again. The paper is riddled with pin marks where successive weavers have matched paper against yarn. Måås-Fjetterström's immediate, spontaneous imagination that had encountered natural signs (the recognition of a bird call, the upright scent of a flower) had been caught into a living archive that allowed her and her apprentices access to the past again and again, as did the folklore of Sweden to which so much weaving in the past had deferred and from which her own workshop could never sever entirely. The folklore and archive of drawings formed a set of artificial signs emerging from the past that had been mediated by memory, representation and intelligence and which made the workshop a scene of active synthesis where the accrued instinct for making yielded to a process of learning.[89]

---

[89] Gilles Deleuze *Repetition and Difference*. 78.

All instantiations of craft work are recorded in some way. The tacit made explicit, whether as paper patterns and recipes or in the more considered and abstracted form of written manuals. In being considered in writing, the orthopraxis of having repetitively acquired an expertise through bodily practice receives both a textual distillation and hermeneutic analysis. The texts provide a space in which knowledge of the woven 'what' and 'how' can be preserved, qualified, sometimes critically, by considerations of 'why'. Manuals were some of the first books printed in Europe. Moving type and advances in paper making and distribution – the early seeds of industrialization – meant books becoming affordable for those in want of earthly as much as spiritual council and who felt their practical knowledge might be animated by more principled advice.[90] Pre-eminent amongst these writers of manuals on craft work – or more accurately just work, and engineering work – was Albrecht Dürer who wrote on architecture and fortifications, and specifically on geometry and proportion for stonemasons and goldsmiths, as well as for artists, printers and engravers, expounding on measurement techniques, methods of representation or sources of raw material distilled from his own reading and practical experience. Two centuries later these manuals mixing formal knowledge, myth, local custom and bodily technique culminate in Denis Diderot and Jean d'Alembert's immense project *Encyclopédie, ou dictionnaire raisonné des sciences, des arts et des métiers*, an exhaustive survey of European practical arts published between 1751 and 1772. Though craft workers are often reticent when it comes to using the word and thinking through written analysis, there are very few who do not keep notes, and fewer still who have not referred to the writings of their peers and forebears where these do exist.

Beyond manuals and pattern books come more sustained and reflective written, spoken and visual commentaries upon the nature of craft: a body of interpretations set alongside the work by way of thoughtful interpretations (Figures 23 and 24). In his *Conflict of Interpretations*, the philosopher Paul Ricoeur discussed how, by listening to their own commentaries upon on activity or a text, the writer or speaker deepens and enriches their understanding of what is being said, done and thought, fostering what he called a hermeneutics of attentiveness. Hermeneutics – meaning a process of interpretation, from the Greek messenger god

---

[90] Pamela Smith *From Lived Experience to the Written Word*. Chicago: University of Chicago Press. 2022. See also Pamela Smith 'Why Write a Book? From Lived Experience to the Written Word in Early Modern Europe'. *Bulletin of the German Historical Institute*. 2010, 47, 25–50.

# The Hermeneutics of Writing 103

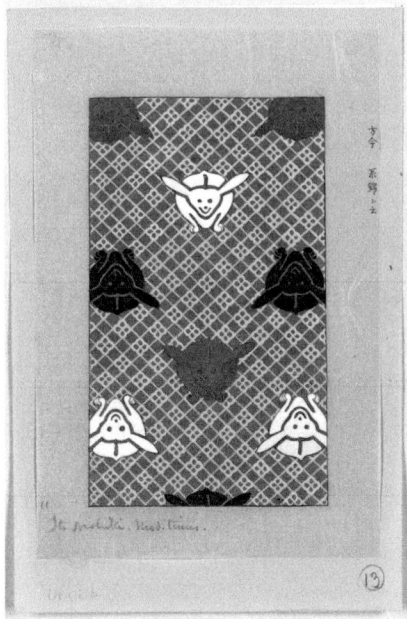

Figure 23 Illustration from Japanese pattern book for kimono designs. Labelled 'Ito nishiki' (yarn brocade). Textile design drawings, Japanese, Colour, 1750–1900. Library of Congress, Prints and Photographs Division [reproduction number LC-DIG-jpd-01056].

Hermes – was grounded in the scholarly explication and interpretation of religious texts, but in Ricoeur's hands it was being expanded to inquiries into the pre-enacted structures by which humans agree upon meanings. Ricoeur was especially concerned with how we became aware of knowing faculties and how these were formed and re-formed within different regional settings. Acknowledging that knowledge, no matter how objective, only emerges because of a prior, pre-epistemological inclination of the human being to relate to the world as a scene of questionability; Ricoeur's hermeneutics of attentiveness equates to an epistemological method for making this basic inclination explicit. It is only because the world arises as a question (the human is a creature for whom occurrence is an incomplete and insufficient experience, it must also be studied and explained, added to, altered) that we come to know things, as opposed to just being aware of them. To understand one must first feel the wobble from finding oneself thrown into a scene of sense. The wobble is given voice in text, imagery or talk, which then serve as evidence that can be further interrogated by those who compile them, setting in train

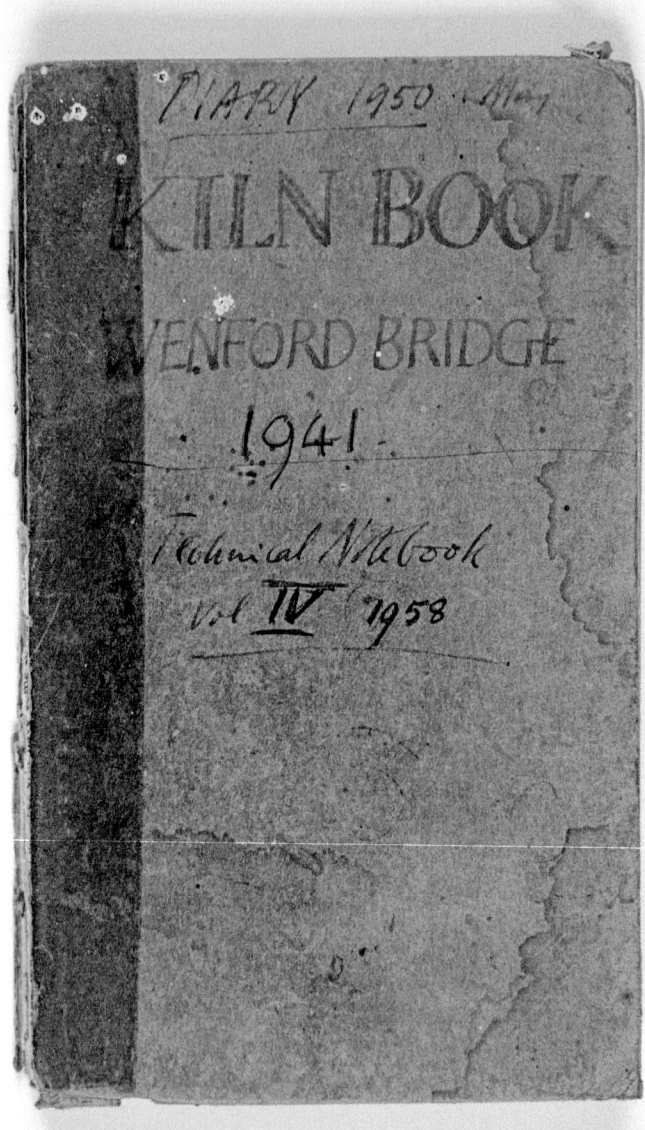

Figure 24 Michael Cardew's kiln book/diary/technical notes (1941–1958). From the collections of the Crafts Study Centre, University for the Creative Arts. MAC/1/2.

a continual circling of questioning through which knowledge becomes both subjective and objective, fluid and fixed, restricting and liberating.

Craft workers writing about craft work has the feel of this hermeneutic circling. They might inquire into their own experience of making, interpreting it anew, making strangers of themselves by questioning these arcs of experience, reaching for what Ricoeur called a 'second naïveté'.[91] If a first naivety described the organized conditions of credulity to which human understanding was prone without sustained and disciplined reflection (and upon which many workshops relied when instructing those setting out to learn on the job), then 'second naïveté' described an approach to work – an epistemological method – in which reflexivity and self-reflexivity were sustained as one worked: they sought to see from different perspectives, to reverse these, and want to do so.[92]

In this vein, one treatise that stands out is David Pye's *The Nature and Art of Workmanship*. It is a hermeneutic inquiry into the nature of skill that interrogates handwork as a series of operations bound by constraints. Pye, woodworker as well as astute and pithy writer, had been prompted into writing by what feels like frustration with those who were uncritically eulogising craft skills. Good work, he insists, emerges by combining a quick, assured, deft use of tools, an intuitive sense of what a material might offer, an idea of how a piece should turn out, and a reticence to pursue an idea to the end. The last of these, the reticence, was critical to developing skill. Reticence allowed room for the worker to intervene and negotiate the constraints in the operations of making: in Pye's case, for the grain in the wood, say, to now and then gain in small ascendency when determining the course of a bowl's declivities with an adze. The repeated strikes on the wood become self-jigging over time, but the early cuts, and perhaps deliberate pauses during later phases, can alter the nature of what is made; that is, if the idea of what the thing will become is not too fixed.[93] The less invasive the jig – a jig guides the tool or shape (like a mould) independently of the worker's skill – the more room for a worker's dexterity, and the more bespoke the made object.[94] The jigged form obviates skill: the outcome is

---

[91] For an insightful foray into how this manifests itself in the creation and management of ventures such as craft business, see Ghislain Deslandes *Posctcritical Management Studies: Philosophical Interpretations*. London: Springer. 2023.

[92] Paul Ricoeur *The Conflict of Interpretations: Essays*. Edited by Don Ihde. Evanston: Northwestern University Press. 1974.

[93] David Pye *The Nature and Art of Workmanship*. Cambridge: Cambridge University Press. 1968.

[94] In woodwork a simple jig would be the plane; in effect a chisel held in a flat jig so it smoothes the surface more reliably than a chisel can by eye, and does so uniformly across different pieces of wood, so each might be paired with the other predictably,

determined, whereas in hand working the constraints are variable, and the skill emerges in-decisions or intuitions of where and how to move. The more skilful, the better the worker is able to control and discipline these movements. Pye breaks them into five types: processing (understanding and manipulating materials); wasting (cutting away, milling, plaining); constructing (jointing, bonding, weaving); forming (forging, folding, pressing); and casting (moulding, setting). Skill emerges from learning, blending and directing these movements in ways that allow for controlled risks: the outcome cannot be predicted, only supposed.[95]

The riskiness could be regulated, depending on the tools and techniques being employed, and work that carried more certainty (the use of machine-cut, routed joints rather than hand cut, for example) still required skill to execute it properly, in accordance with an idea of how the piece should look and work: there is, argues Pye, nothing inherently superior in free over regulated aspects of work. The OP1 synthesizer made by the Swedish company Teenage Engineering provides an interesting example of what Pye might mean by incorporating risk. The OP1 is a digital electronic tool for sampling and sequencing sound, one made through a sustained connexion to the musical artists who use (and stress) the instrument, and who come to care for it. The user (though more commonly referred to as an operator) weaves threads of sound into one another, using splices, overlays, patches, twists, mirroring and a bewildering array of slightly deviant techniques offered by the programmers, but not obviously apparent; they are discovered, or more accurately bumped into. The OP1 looks more like a toy; it is available, it is not obviously a keyboard or synthesizer, it does not fit into the expected forms of 'older gear'. The familiarity with the tool must be earned, it is a carefully made tool for the user's imagination, asking them: 'If you do not have control, then what happens?' Once the tool is learned, surprising and sophisticated assemblies of sound become possible, which provoke and entertain the brain and body. There is one beautiful addition, or refusal, there is no rewind or undo button on the OP1. Make what turns out to be a wrong move, and like an errant blot of ink on fine calligraphy, the work must be made again. With this one feature, not at all an oversight, the engineers (craft workers) recognise and counteract the tendency in work practice towards safety, conformity and certainty.

eliminating the need for 'offering up' of one piece of wood to another. Combined with mechanical saws and similar timber, the worker can make square, flat and straight pieces of wood that become standardized, and useable in different pieces, further removing the need for skill. See David Pye *The Nature & Aesthetics of Design*. London: Herbert Press. 1978. 45–47.

[95] David Pye *The Nature & Aesthetics of Design*. 45–50.

The riskiness could be regulated, depending on the tools and techniques being employed, and work that carried more certainty (the use of machine-cut, routed joints rather than hand cut, for example) still required skill to execute it properly, in accordance with an idea of how the piece should look and work: there is, argues Pye, nothing inherently superior in free over regulated aspects of work. The problem is not regulation or the constraints of limited features, but when these become hegemonic, resulting in a dreary and degrading work environment devoid of textures, nuances and surprise.[96]

This would also be a scene of risk, but one removed from the uncertain eruptions of material or form during production, to the non-creative, non-productive risks associated with a bored and listless workforce, a risk more typical to manufacturer than workshops, and a risk to which manufacturers can add further risks associated with distribution (breakages, say, or customs duties) or with selling (finding a market). In the closed, determining systems of production favoured by manufacturing, these broader risks of economy become more apparent. After all, says Pye 'the primary concern of all manufacturers is not with making things but with getting rid of them afterwards';[97] the 'know how' of the manufacturer tends towards those associated with branding or distributing rather than the actual making, which are given over to machines. In making wooden bowls, for example, their 'know how' would concentrate on which wood resists knocks and blemishes in handling, which woods are hardest on the expensive machine tools, which shapes have market appeal and where, whether customers wish for low cost or durability, which suppliers have greatest political clout in any given market, and these considerations rarely align, indeed they often conflict, making the 'know how' a situational experience of compromise and contestation.

Hermeneutically speaking, Pye's emphasis on technical skill and a pragmatic 'knowing how' is itself a risky move, one that Glenn Adamson neatly questions even on its own terms: if skill equates to an acquired discipline in controlling work processes, then why bother with its acquisition? To become skilled, as Dreyfus was at pains to point out, is to invest oneself, and sense of self, into a process and experience of learning which is at some juncture one of quiet revelation: one becomes an adept in a practice, and in doing so one absorbs the wider cultural and social norms that sustain the distinctiveness and authority of that practice. Skill is imbricated with symbolic meanings that extend well beyond those attending the deft

---

[96] Conversation between author and Jesper Kouthoofd, CEO and Head of Design, Teenage Engineering. 18 March 2021.
[97] David Pye *The Nature & Aesthetics of Design*. 56.

control of machinery and material intelligence, or the practical know-how to negotiate the multiple demands of economy, very real though these are. It emerges when the craft worker attends to the fuller gamut of these regional forces; when, for example, they become aware whether and which skills are valued in wider social settings. Whilst technical in content, social and cultural in form insofar as the purpose of creating the room for risk can be one of status-seeking excellence as much as it is creating an affordable object with functional value and fine appearance.[98]

This extension and expansion of what skill works inwardly too. So not only is expertise an awareness of the regional settings by which techniques are being agreed upon as valuable, it is also, deeper, personally speaking, than the physical experience of making things. Ruskin hinted at this in his definition of skill:

the united force of experience, intellect, and passion, in their operation on manual labour: and under the term 'passion' to include the entire range and agency of the moral feelings; from the simple patience and gentleness of mind which will give continuity and fineness to the touch, or enable one person to work without fatigue, and with good effect, twice as long as another, up to the qualities of character which render science possible – (the retardation of science by envy is one of the most tremendous losses in the economy of the present century) – and to the incommunicable emotion and imagination which are the first and mightiest sources of all value in art.[99]

Skill, as Ruskin envisages it, excites the craft worker's emotional and imaginative capacities, which are direct and elusive experiences that prompt the craft worker into relating to work as thoughtfully and as completely as is possible. Passion touches on the mysterious side, which comes into view when the practical experience and intelligence become unhinged slightly, loosening the effable and affable, making room for the presence of a worker who cares whether they too belong to what is being made.

The poet Seamus Heaney elaborates on this distinction by separating craft and technique. Craft he reserves for a process of technical competence, the acquisition of a voice capable of athletic display, which was, Heaney continues, not to be confused with the finding of a voice. To find a voice requires technique, which

involves not only a poet's way with words, his management of metre, rhythm and verbal texture; it involves also a definition of his stance toward life, a definition of his own reality. It involves the discovery of ways to go out of his normal cognitive bounds and raid the inarticulate: a dynamic alertness that mediates

---

[98] Glenn Adamson *Thinking through Craft*. London: Bloomsbury. 2018.
[99] John Ruskin *Unto This Last*. 1862. §47ftn. In *Complete Works Vol. XVII*. Edited by E. T. Cook and Alexander Wedderburn. London: George Allen. 1905. 67.

between the origins of feeling in memory and experience and the formal ploys that express these in a work of art.[100]

In technique, Heaney is reaching toward a threshold where skill is accompanied by an examined sense of personal complicity in which the experience of making a thing becomes its own object of attention, resulting in the imprint of oneself into that self-awareness through an explicit, disciplined struggle to bring about something complete. With poetic aplomb, Heaney likens it to a watermarking of the 'patterns of perception, voice and thought into the touch and texture of your lines': through the watermark of technique, technical experience is given over to the jurisdiction of form.

## Colour

This reaching for thresholds of understanding within the taskscape can be traced in the search for that most elusive of all aspects of craft work: colour. In Måås-Fjetterström's *Bruna Heden* it is the red in the yarn, not brown, that evokes the Swedish soil, and its extraction. Red oxide, a by-product of the copper ore mining to which Swedish industry around the region of Falun has dedicated itself for centuries, abounds. The country is covered in this red, literally, given it is the base ingredient of the Falu red paint with which nearly all farmsteads have been painted. As with the colours in Måås-Fjetterström's weaving, the hue of the paint is restless: in different lights it can move from a vibrant, sunset dark orange to a dim maroon. It is good at absorbing the sun and the damp without dimming, holding fast by changing as its surroundings change. Made from wheat and rye flour, linseed oil and iron oxides, Falu red not only evokes tradition, it is tradition, and historically the cooking of Falu Röd paint was a staple activity for many Swedes. The colour announces an intimacy between a people and a landscape. But it also speaks of fashion and even envy, for it was a colour that emulated the grander, more substantial brick houses built elsewhere in the more 'advanced' regions of Europe. To paint in red became a status symbol, one backed by a royal imprimatur when in the sixteenth century King Johan III encouraged and even insisted on its use as an expression of the power and reach of the House of Wasa.

The red in the weave redounds with different resonances, as do all colours. There is nothing fixed about colour. Even a red colour swatch which carries a label 'R' belongs to a grammar of use which tolerates equivocation. To point to a red square and say 'This is red' is a culturally

---

[100] Seamus Heaney *Feeling into Words*. In *Finders Keepers: Selected Prose 1971–2001*. London: Faber. 19.

specific activity with which language users become familiar before the statement and illustration make any sense. They have to be aware, for example, that words can refer to objects, that swatches are a specific form of object which carries a representation within itself, that representations can be labelled or carry legends, and that to ostensively define objects with a finger is to isolate an object from a wider background so that the interlocutor concentrates on it, though the finger can also point out a general scene, such as a red sunset. To carry meaning, the red square belongs to one of Wittgenstein's language games, which in the case of the statement and swatch might be the practice of teaching in an apprenticeship, involving teachers, pupils, pedagogic norms, material objects, traditions and so on. In the language game of teaching, 'Red' is being used as a proposition, a description, in which a specific square is being described: the name is a preparation for the description, and the description is a move in the game, a 'showing' rather than a 'telling', and it is in the showing that red gathers meaning; it is a relational achievement in which red as a colour, 'R' as a label, a square swatch set against other coloured squares are associated in a performative display to which others – apprentices – are being encouraged to ascent, or even to dispute: 'Look, here, this is red'. If the apprentices agree the red square continues in its role as a means of representation rather than a thing that is itself represented in conversation about whether other representations might work better, a dyed piece of thread or yarn for example, or a piece of red leather. Stating that the square shows red says nothing about red as such. Rather it is an indication that 'Red' has meaning as a grammatical move, it has nothing to do with the colour in its own right and everything to do with the relational performance in the language game.[101]

Changefulness is built into the meaning, and it is this mercurial mobility that attracts the craft worker who, through apprenticeships (whether formal or informal) that extend well beyond instruction in swatches, becomes attentive to the ways in which colour meanings have been hived within a grammar of use acquired across generations. Some uses remain concealed in obscurity, and others hidden in the plain sites of unquestioned familiarity, and none can be distilled to a core or base state. As Timon Beyes has argued, perhaps, alongside its role as a commodity, a means of manipulating mood, as a mode of standardization, it is the unmanageable elusiveness of colour that constitutes its power to take those who use it towards the very edges of understanding. It attracts in an immediate and visceral way that can be explained, but never fully,

---

[101] Ludwig Wittgenstein *Philosophical Investigations*. Oxford: Blackwell. 1953. §48–51. 23e–25e.

or even properly, and hardly consistently.[102] There is no essence to red, only associations, such as sin. Red was the colour of the apple that Eve had taken from the Garden of Eden. The attraction had been too great, the colour too alluring. The fall beckoned, and was visited upon the human species which was, from then on, cast into a state of dislocation and lack which hangs over us, like the apples in Crivelli's painting, symbols of sin, vying with the redeeming force of a cucumber (Figure 25).

Yet during the Middle Ages the sinful connotations of red were reassessed, indeed transformed, as the role of the apple in Christian myth became more complicated. Rather than being taken by Eve in a burst of unauthorized self-assertion, the red apple indicated something being given back, as when Mary, a second Eve, hands over the symbol of the Fall to a sleeping Christ child in Joos Van Cleeve's painting (Figure 26).

Red becomes a redeeming colour, a symbol of forgiveness as Christ accepts the task of absorbing human sin, taking on the weight as lightly and naturally as might a child hold an apple to its cheek.

This carving from willow wood is of a type used to decorate altars throughout medieval Europe (Figure 27). Those made in Ulm, Germany, in the workshops of Michel Erhart were regarded as the finest. Erhart's workshop was famed for producing figures with a startling, uncanny realism, notably their blushed skin, which under the candlelight of a church interior effulged with calm, inner faith. Erhart's workers were known for their skill in polychromy: the surface colourations that lent the pieces an overall harmony. As a symbol of forgiveness, the form of the red apple is echoed in the round belly, and the palette of its ruddy skin is repeated in the cheeks of the god-child bearing the sins of the world, red aside red, a saviour holding the world, an embodiment of belief and its boons.

The paintings and statues were also channelling the association of red and opulence, entitlement, loftiness. It had been and remained the hardest colour to manage. The mordants used to fix the colour were outcompeted by nature, red being the colour at the most unstable end of the visible light spectrum, the colour most susceptible to fading. Red glass was especially difficult to make, and in medieval stained glass it was often painted onto clear glass rather than being inherent in the material. Recipes had been circulating for centuries, but few could arrive at anything stable. No sooner was it made (usually with a copper oxide) than it started to diminish, losing its struggle with the sunlight. This fickleness made it desirable, especially amongst the European nobles wanting to display their wealth by investing in the production of

---

[102] Timon Beyes *Organizing Color: Toward a Chromatics of the Social.* Stanford: Stanford University Press. 2024. 210–211.

112    3   Changefulness and Variety

Figure 25 Carlo Crivelli, *Madonna and Child*, ca. 1480. Tempera and gold on wood. The Metropolitan Museum of Art: 49.7.5 / The Jules Bache Collection, 1949.

Colour 113

Figure 26  Joos van Cleve, *Virgin and Child*, ca. 1525. Oil on wood. The Metropolitan Museum of Art: 1982.60.47 / The Jack and Belle Linsky Collection, 1982.

red things. Foremost amongst these was Frederick William I, Elector of Brandenburg (1620–1688), who had become so obsessed with red that he had cutting-edge laboratories built in seclusion on Peacock Island

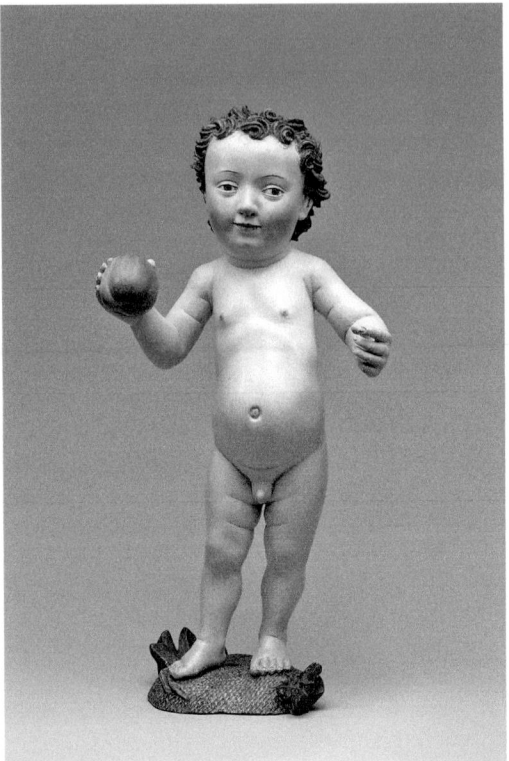

Figure 27 Circle of Michel Erhart, *Christ Child with an Apple*, ca. 1470–1480. Willow with original paint and traces of gold. The Metropolitan Museum of Art: 2012.449 / The Cloisters Collection, 2012.

in the River Havel near Potsdam and installed the German glassmaker and alchemist Johannes Kunckel (1630–1703) with one objective: make red glass.[103] Kunckel had been raised a glassmaker by his father, he knew the processes intimately, and through years of experiment with manganese, copper and hydrochloric acid, had hit upon a technique

---

[103] Not long after, and not far to the south, near Dresden, the Elector of Saxony Augustus (1670–1733) was fueling his *Porzellankrankheit* by 'installing' Frederik Böttger in the fairy tale absurdities of Albrechtsburg Castle in Meissen. It was a thing amongst male aristocrats with an obsession for things to collect the makers as well as the made. See Edmund De Waal *The White Road*. London: Chatto and Windus. 2015; J. Gleeson *The Arcanum*. London: Bantam Books. 1988; Robin Holt, *Luxury and the Entrepreneur: A Story of Meissen Porcelain, Harlequins, and Creative Destruction*. In *The Oxford Handbook of Luxury Business*. Edited by Pierre-Yves Donzé, Véronique Pouillard and Joanne Roberts. Oxford: Oxford University Press. 2020.

using 'purple of Cassius' (tin chloride and gold shavings) with silica, lime and sodium to make what became known as ruby glass.[104] Gold is expensive. There is an alternative using selenium, but this wasn't discovered until 1817 by Jöns Berzelius who had been making sulphuric acid in Stockholm and thought to test the red dusty residue being left in the large vats. Kunckel had to make do with gold, and red glass remained the preserve of the few aristocrats and churchmen who could afford it. With ruby glass came the prestige of controlling an object that others coveted. With the death of William I, Kunkel lost an obsessive patron, and Frederich III, the new elector, refused to extend him the same license to experiment and roam, even demanding monies given by William be repaid. After a fire at his works, Kunckel took up the offer from Charles XI, the King of Sweden, to run the Board on Mines and receive the title Baron Kunckel von Löwenstern. He died in Stockholm in 1703, but not before he oversaw the expansion of the mining for copper ore around Falun, releasing vast quantities of iron oxide onto the market, permitting Sweden to paint itself again and again in its muted, matte red.

The changefulness of colour ranges restlessly over the taskscape: it shapes how craft workers and users sense and organize and it offers itself up for, without ever capitulating to, detailed understanding.[105] Its apprehension is as much a gestural and textural sensitivity to situational tone as it is a sequencing of distinct hues, saturation, brightness, so any knowledge is fleeting, often falling into ruins from which new understanding re-emerges, like a small, buried creature, shaking off the dust as it blinks in the light.

### Things as Pattern and Fold

The insistence of changefulness and variety in Gothic is not a lessening or loosening of order, but its containment in pattern. Gregory Bateson argued patterns were the proper carriers of order because, unlike abstract signs and concepts, they belonged to life rather than being a commentary upon it. Patterns were a source of

---

[104] Leslie B. Hunt. 'The True Story of Purple of Cassius', *Gold Bulletin*. 1976, 9, 134–139. Kunckel describes the recipe thus: 'I take two parts of good aqua fortis and one part of spirits of salt, or failing this some strong salt water. When these are mixed throw in from time to time a little of the purest tin so that it does not heat up but dissolves slowly ... With this solution the gold can be precipitated in such a beautiful colour that it cannot be more beautiful, and thereby can crystal glass be given the finest ruby colour if the gold has previously been dissolved in three parts of aqua regia and one part of spirits of salt.' Quoted in Leslie B. Hunt, 'The True Story of Purple of Cassius', 138.
[105] Timon Beyes *Organizing Color*. 215.

stability from which human practice could learn, beginning with those we encounter in nature, to which, Bateson suggests, there are different orders. First order patterns are the similarities we encounter in what is closest to us, our bodies. One eye, for example, is like the other, or fingers are configured in the same arrangement as toes, or legs and move similarly when walking. Second order connexions are made between bodies across related species or events, as when zebras and donkeys are in proximity, or waves and ripples. Completing the trinity come third-order patterns in which the two groups and their similarities are themselves then compared: can we, for example, associate what brings zebras and donkeys together with what brings waves and ripples together? The stripes on the flank of a zebra are like the disturbance on the surface of water, though one is concealing movement and the other betraying it. The noise of a herd of herbivores pulling at the grass is like the wash of waves as they pull back against small stones on the shore. For Bateson all patterns are stories of association, some more compelling than others, some more bewitching, some so ephemeral they don't last much longer than the time it takes to tell them. Those that last form the background conditions of meaning against which all efforts at distinction – like our own sense of self – must take their cue. We humans are nothing more than distinctions set against these storied patterns: sinful beings awaiting the wrath of god, or his forgiveness; featherless bipeds cued to obsess over prosthetic enhancements; bundles of atoms, or unbundling bundles of affection. Yet these backgrounds are also circulating, albeit barely perceptibly and the slowness becomes mistaken for fixity and with this misguided presumption of meanings being fixed comes a preponderance of linear stories; the direct plot lines etched out in means-end connexions and statements of teleological destiny. In linear stories the end emerges fully clothed from out of the given means and the effect is always indebted to the cause, so that we may conclude the stripes on the zebra's flank evolve in the way they do, whether through natural selection or a more active awareness, to help them disrupt the eyesight of predators and evade capture. The stripes are useful, they have a defined role, they are a dazzle pattern. That is that, end of story, which is to be repeated as fact, hiding its storied origins behind the scales of verification and replication.

Bateson's insistence that order and form are stories that circulate, and that facts are nothing more than a stalling or quieting (not a quitting) of these circulations, recalls Dewey's reminder that all unities are aesthetically governed, and that craft work also issues such a reminder. The made thing continues as something distinctive and definite only as it circulates, drawing in the immediate past and future as measures by

Things as Pattern and Fold 117

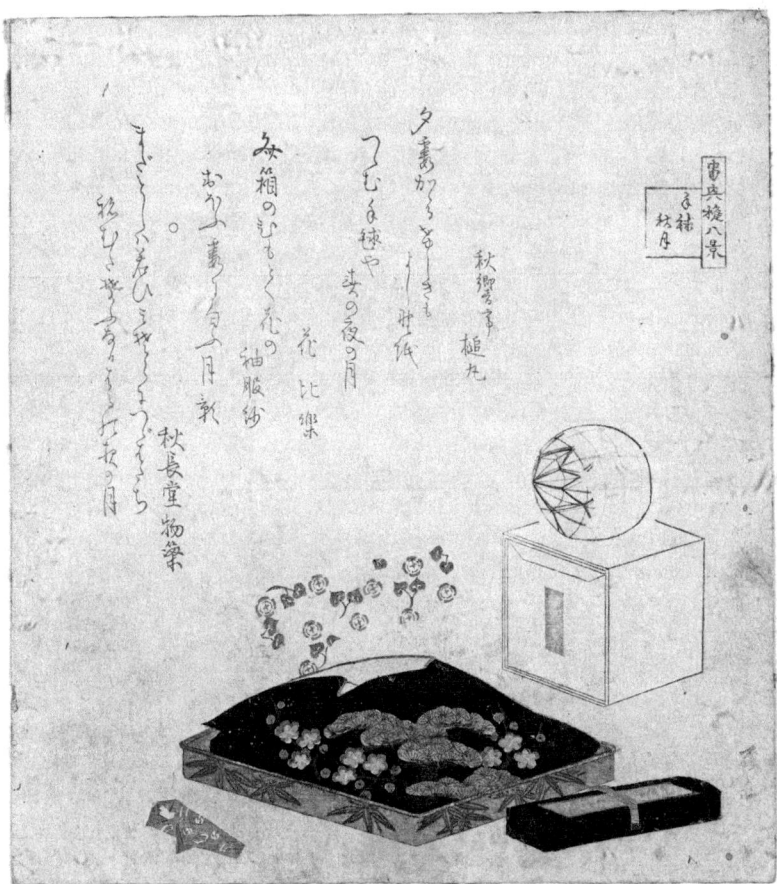

Figure 28 Shinsa Ryūryūkyo (1764–1820), *Temari no aki no tsuki* (Crescent moon in the footfall), 1815–1825. Folded kimono in a box. From series: *Shunkyō osana hakkei: Eight views of New Year's children*. Library of Congress, Prints and Photographs Division [reproduction number: LC-DIG-jpd-02302].

which its presence can be assured, drawing in and giving out to its surroundings as it seeks grip.

Each stage of the making of an obi strip for a kimono, for example, is dependent on the previous one along, each stage acknowledging the work and worth of the other stages in a collective sense of awareness and dependency (Figure 28). Whilst it might appear as a series of linear events, it is really a story of flows and folds rather than stages, and one set to a cultural and social history of use. The process is called *ori*, using threads

118  3  Changefulness and Variety

to create dimensional form in the textile, the *senshoku*, which translates roughly as dying/weaving, which are the two poles of the textile culture, one flowing and folding into the other. Having begun her working career making obi strips, the weaver Asakura Mitsuko has continually explored the circulation of threads, colours and light in her textiles and how the fold enhances these patterns, whilst also making them provisional, how it disguises and then reveals hints of what might lie beneath. Typically, she says, there is no prepared design, the form emerges as she goes along, working on the threads, sensing how they slide into and alongside one another, how the colours take to one another, how they blend. In Japan, she suggests, the fold has a special place: the way clothes sit on the body, or are stored, stems from how kimonos were worn often in layers, the outer more sombre and hiding perhaps more flamboyant inner layers folded away, and how the kimono was carefully fitted and packed away in kimono paper, or the way bought things and gifts are wrapped and un-wrapped in passages of giving and receiving. *Ori* means weaving, but also means folding, and to fold can be to reveal what is otherwise hidden, to bring the edges right to the centre, or to hide what might otherwise show itself, but never completely, hence the pattern is both confirmed and interrupted.[106] A basic weave is a folding through warp and weft at right angles, and these angles can be made acute through further folding, so the rear of the thread and textile become the front, and then back again, each time the surprise of the underbelly assumes as full a role as the front. The bend and the fold are archaic movements, both natural, yet also highly artificial, a binary perfectly embodied by the zigzag pattern, taken from the paper streamers used in Shinto rituals, the *gohei* and *nusa* (Figures 29 and 30).[107]

The rhythm is compelling, a laying down of form, a regularity which from a distance resembles a landscape image taken by a high-altitude aeronautical reconnaissance plane, as Richard Buckminster Fuller when he was teaching architecture at Black Mountain College and came across the weaving of his

---

[106] Following an imperial edict restricting the displays of luxurious cloth to those with aristocratic lineage, the newly wealthy merchant classes in eighteenth-century Japan rebelled by adopting heavily folded, meek, dark outerwear (*uwagi*) which hid extravagant underrobes (*shitagi*) dyed in expensive colours such as beni red, derived from the fermented petals of the benibana flower, which, worn close to the skin, radiated a contained, life-affirming energy. (See Delphine Hirasuna *Hinagata*. Pentagram Papers 31; see also Akira Yamazaki (Japanese, b. 1891), *Book (Japan)*. Paper, thread, silk. Gift of Elizabeth Gordon, 24 February 1964. Cooper Hewitt Museum, New York. Object No. 18451391).

[107] Asakura Mitsuko *Orimaguru*. Kyoto: Seigensha. 2021. 70. 78. Also in an interview with the author, November 2020: 'If you look at what's going on, the weft yarn intersects with the warp yarn at a right angle, which is what weaving is all about, but if it's not at a right angle, but at an acute angle, it shows that the warp and the weft yarn try to intersect at a right angle, and the fabric itself bends.'

Figure 29 Asakura Mitsuko, *Orimagaru*, 2014. Silk and wool, 83 × 127 cm. © The Artist.

Figure 30 Asakura Mitsuko, *Motion*, 2018. Silk, bamboo, driftwood in the Kurobe River. © The Artist.

colleague Annie Albers.[108] Yet looking more closely, the nuances of colour intercede. Whilst from afar colour (*iro*) appears to be flat and a block, from close-up the block recedes and new patterns emerge, a multiplicity, including shadows caused by threads placed alongside one another at differing heights. Mitsuko dyes the threads herself, using the soft water from a well running under her house set between Kyoto Imperial Park (京都御苑, Kyōto Gyoen) and the Kamo River. The well water in Kyoto is very soft, which allows threads to take dye well. To get the bottom colours it is better to use pulling dying (*hikizome*) rather than immersion dying (*tsukezome*) where the colours can be more delicate. She does not confine herself to just natural dyes, and in Kyoto especially there is a tradition of using synthetic dyes to push the possibilities of colour and to innovate with different threads (including mixing them with bamboo and driftwoods) and with how threads 'take' colour and combine (*ori iro*). Natural dyes are analogue, impure and give off an innate variety, whereas synthetic dyes render colour in more abstract, deliberate, uniform way, and they resist decay in the sun, which is important for architectural commissions, for example, where the piece is often in bright settings. The combination of natural and synthetic dyes, and different yarns, create the second-order patterns of different bodies, giving a flexibility to the textile and its use, and allow the form and dimensionality of fabric, its volume and weight and tightness, to reveal itself.

The repetition of motifs within the piece create further second-order connexions; often with Mitsuko it is the circle (*maru*) associated with the shape of the sun, bringer of life, which is then confined to the orthogonal threading of the weave, which in turn is broken from time to time to leave just the vertical warp, so that the sun begins to dip across a horizon, caught in its own reflection (Figure 31).[109] The visibility of the warp is a reminder of first-order connexions to the patterns by which any textile belongs, the similarities in gridded structure, materials and techniques, the squaring off of edges, the manner of hanging and lying flat, all of which are available as limits to be transgressed now and then. Third-order connexions abound in small stories of congregation and the moments of eclipse that come within any gathering, or the mutual transience of light and thread in a dance of appearance and disappearance.

---

[108] Annie Albers *On Designing*. New Haven: The Pellango Press. 1959. The full quote on the blurb reads 'From aeronautical altitudes, the criss-cross grids of Earth's cities seem to be two-dimensional planar arrangements, as do woven fabric surfaces, seen from a distance. Seen from inside the city streets or within the loom, both cities and fabrics disclose multi-dimensional structuring of great complexity. Anni Albers, more than any other weaver, has succeeded in exciting mass realization of the complex structuring of fabrics. She has brought the artist's intuitive sculpturing faculties and the age-long weaver's arts into historically successful marriage.'

[109] Asakura Mitsuko *Orimaguru*. Kyoto: Seigensha. 2021.

Figure 31 Asakura Mitsuko, *Mandara*, 2020. Silk, 200 × 173 cm. © The Artist.

*Oritatamu* reveals bodies whose order, residing in pattern, have, as their core, an irresolution of purpose. They are there, but not determinedly so, and as they are stilled they are also on the move, working within and across different forms of pattern, suggesting, would we listen by looking at them, that perhaps this is how, now and then, we too might act, outside of known or instructed ends, and making our habits yaw and lurch.

# 4  Naturalism

### The Correlations of Natural Things

In 1936 Alvar Aalto entered a competition to design a new glass vase for Iittala, the Finnish interior ware manufacturer, to be made for the World's Fair in Paris the following year. Going by the title of the submitted sketch (*Eskimåkvinnans skinnbyxa*) he based the proposed form on the hem outline of the Sami women's long flowing leather dress or apron. The vases edges imitated the flowing, natural movement of an indigenous, well-crafted object that was then appropriated and refashioned for fashionable interiors. It now goes by the more approachable 'Savoy' vase, named after a restaurant in Helsinki for which Alvar and Aino Aalto designed the interiors in 1937. Its flowing lines were made using an open mould of loose wooden sticks whose gaps allow the glass to fall through a little before hardening, making each one, at least those that are handblown, unique. The deeper ones are used for flowers, primarily tulips, which bunch contentedly into the curves; the shallow ones for small plants or perhaps paperclips.

Aalto drew by eye, the sketched outlines are gestural, and there are no neat, final versions: in its attentiveness to curvaceous flow and the play of light it is like a stripped back, Scandinavian version of the seventeenth century Dutch *kwabstijl* (Figure 32). The suggestion of outline is carried along by a felt sympathy in patterns that might arise between apparently different things: clothing and vases, they both hold things, display them, shape them, they can both fold and curve, neither relies on definite, accurately measured outline. The human and nature are one and the same, and functionally share the same need to bend to coherence, but without submission:

Nature, biology, is formally rich and luxuriant. It can with the same structure, the same intermeshing, and the same principles in its cells' inner structure, achieve a billion combinations, each of which represents a high level of form. Man's life belongs to the same family. The things surrounding him are hardly fetishes and allegories with mystical eternal value. They are rather cells and tissues, living

The Correlations of Natural Things 123

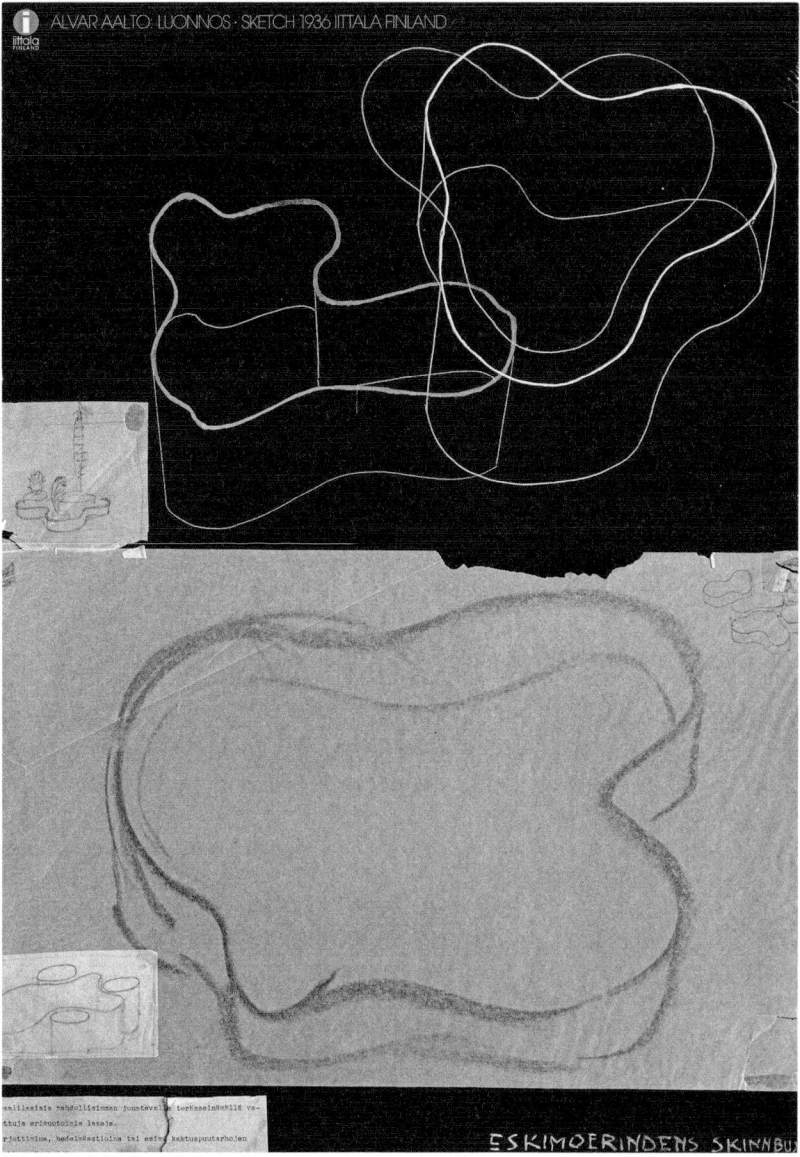

Figure 32  Alvar Aalto, *Sketch*, 1936. Paper, crayon, ink. Photography: Alvar Aalto Foundation.

beings also, building elements of which human life is put together. They cannot be treated differently from biology's other elements or otherwise they run the risk of not fitting into the system; they become inhumane.[1]

Human reason extended into nature, and following nature, meant loosening the strictures of calculation with which the Western sensibility had been blinkered, something that could only come about by engaging our whole body with those of nature in aesthetic empathy. It was a sensibility shared by Ruskin, who when he drew allowed the body and the eye to work free-form:

> All the professors of perspective in Europe could not, by perspective, draw the line of curve of a sea-beach; nay, could not outline one pool of the quiet water left among the sand. The eye and hand can do it, nothing else. All the rules of aerial perspective that ever were written, will not tell me how sharply the pines on the hilltop are drawn at this moment on the sky. I shall know if I see them, and love them; not till then.[2]

The love of linear perspective that had been encouraged in Renaissance painting and architecture had turned our gaze away from the laws of natural vision, which is a scene of curves and appearances, and puts in its place a planar, pictorial language of rational signs from which to construct a perfect image or building. The height, breadth and depth of a form or scene were gathered under a single, systematic, planar space governed by the vanishing point. The entire scene coheres: depths are graded consistently; planes are arranged in orderly hierarchies, objects are placed in the space to fix the proportional harmony, the emphasis is on means and method and upon space as a measured, contained object that exists prior to objects and that expects to be filled by those objects.[3] Gothic had no sense of space as a distinct thing, a container, or of objects as obedient, stable things awaiting proper placement. In Gothic things belong to a flowing, light-sensitive world of movement, they belong with

---

[1] Alvar Aalto *Rationalism in Man*. In *Sketches*. Edited by Göran Schildt. Translated by Stuart Wrede. Massachusetts: MIT Press. 1978. 61.

[2] John Ruskin *The Stones of Venice, Vol. III*. In *Complete Works Vol. XI*. Edited by E. T. Cook and Alexander Wedderburn. 1904. §18. 57. This has echoes of Lao Tsu [Lazoi]: 'Similarly, the Laozi later says, "great fullness is seemingly empty," but "its use is never exhausted," and "great straightness is seemingly crooked."' (Francois Jullien *The Great Image Has No Form, On the Nonobject through Painting*. Translated by Jane Marie Todd. Chicago: University of Chicago Press. 2009. 69, who adds 'just look at the horizon the ocean traces far off in the distance').

[3] Erwin Panofsky *Perspective as Symbolic Form*. Translated by Christopher Wood. New York: Urzone. 1991. 38–40; 48–49; 66. The Renaissance mode of representing space distorts the depths, heights and breadths in equal proportions, and so allows the size of objects to appear as they are in relation to other objects and the position of the viewer. There is no instability, no emphasis, no skewing, no overlooking, in short there is no life.

nature and Gothic masons wished only to express this state of belonging, without concern for the exactness. In Gothic stonework, suggested Ruskin: '[T]here is sensation in every inch of it, and an accommodation to every architectural necessity, with a determined variation in arrangement, which is exactly like the related proportions and provisions in the structure of organic form.'[4]

The sensation is of moving things and of the varying spaces left between them, it is a space of mobilities where things can become unreliable, as in the story re-told in Tanya Harrod's catalogue essay on the potter Alison Britton, about the psychoanalyst Marion Milner who, in her autobiographical *On Not Being Able to Paint*, recalls how, on waking up and still half asleep, she had glanced over at two jugs standing next to one another on a nearby table, their outlines in a mutual echo. 'Without any mental struggle' she continues 'I saw the edges in relation to one another and how gaily they seemed almost to ripple now that they were free from this grimly practical business of enclosing an object and keeping it in its place.' The jugs' edges broke free from being limits of the form because of the repeating patterns by which they had been held in place, and would continue to be so, once sleepiness gave way to thirst and the jug returned to its grim business of holding water. Gothic columns can be equally 'free' flowing, before resolving into the practicalities of creating a plenum.

Ruskin's call for naturalness in the production of things was an attempt to re-institute a sense of ecological connexion, one that he felt had been obliterated by the Renaissance obsession with Man, alone, running a ruler over the world.[5] The novelty and power of the Renaissance perspective lay with its being able to establish consistent distances and sizes across multiple scenes. It was a generalising viewpoint in which objects and relations obtained a proportionally correct place. Yet the rules of proportion were so systematic and all-encompassing as to annihilate any sense of natural occurrence on its own terms. The subjective succumbed to objectification, and with it the presence of all objects became dependent upon a human spatial practice dedicated to calculation and control.[6] The loss is profound,

---

[4] John Ruskin *Seven Lamps of Architecture*. In *Complete Works Vol. VIII*. Edited by E. T. Cook and Alexander Wedderburn. London: George Allen. 1903. Chapter 5, §13. 203.

[5] Under Renaissance proportions life withers whereas Gothic stonework relishes life: the detailing of trees growing and curling around pillars, then become themselves pillars: 'then the branches shot out, and became loaded with leaves; autumn came, the leaves were shed, and the eye was directed to the extremities of the delicate branches;– the Renaissance frosts came, and all perished.' In John Ruskin *The Stones of Venice, Vol. I*. §31. 278.

[6] Erwin Panofsky, *Perspective as Symbolic Form*. 67.

as the persistent and stable (and so artificial, as immutability and stability are against life) gained precedence, and we lost our connexion to the effulgent giving forth of nature: 'there is not a cluster of weeds growing in any cranny of ruin which has not a beauty in all respects nearly equal, and, in some, immeasurably superior, to that of the most elaborate sculpture of its stones.'[7]

To become aware of natural things is to be alive to their being distant to us, as being somehow over there and coming forth on their own productive terms without need of management. The ancient Greeks called it *physis*, the unexplained eruptions and perturbations of life and presence. It is a power that might be apprehended in a glance, but its presence is enigmatic. We are provoked, always provoked, by nature, by the raw light of a grey winter, by the soft bend of neck, by a flash of colour along a riverbank, by the breeze that arrives unbidden on a calm day. *Physis* can inspire yet mock us, and remind us to put working concerns in perspective: 'And why take ye thought for raiment? Consider the lilies of the field, how they grow; they toil not, neither do they spin'.[8] The apparent smallness of a lily, or a bird song, is not of the same order as a measured, made human smallness, and its presence can envelop the most monumental human work: out of nowhere, listening to Ludwig van Beethoven's fifth symphony, Percy Shelly detected what he thought to be the call of a bunting, a bird of a few ounces at the centre of so much cosmic gravity.

Where the Renaissance closed itself off to such *physis*, Gothic exposes itself, fostering a sense of nature to which the human is enjoined, but over which it is not wholly in control. Whilst *physis* remains elusive, it can be apprehended through *technē*, which we might think of as a human equivalent. The Gothic stonemasons were attuned to the intricate feedback systems by which the bones and muscles of the human body, its nervous system, memory, community relations, a tradition of skills, a surrounding and searched-for array of possible things for use and history of uses, can all cohere as they negotiated the environment in which they lived and worked.[9] They embodied a situated *technē* that threw any simple or definite distinction between humanity, animality and nature into serious question.[10] There is wariness in Ruskin's voice though, a sense of precarity that

---

[7] John Ruskin *Seven Lamps of Architecture*. Chapter 2, §19. 81–82.
[8] Matthew 6: 28–33. King James Bible.
[9] Katherine Withy *Heidegger on Being Uncanny*. Cambridge, MA: Harvard University Press. 2015. 123.
[10] Bernard Stiegler *Technics and Time 1. The Fault of Epimethius*. Translated by Richard Beardswoth and George Collins. Stanford: Stanford University Press. 1998. 148; 151.

arose from his having witnessed how such *technē*, such technique, could quickly morph into control of, and violence against, nature.

For Heidegger this progression or descent into control was lamentable but unavoidable. From the very beginning a sharp sense of technological anticipation has been resident in human gesture: in rasping a flint on the angle to generate a sharp, cutting edge, early humans at one stroke created something exterior to them, the prosthetically extended hand which opened up the inherited history of tool-making, as it also opened up an interior: the tool maker constituted in and through this act.[11] The gesture is at once an anticipation and a remembering; the anticipation of a design and purpose that are both inherited but also developed and transformed in the act of making and fabricating.[12] It is not the mark-making itself that constitutes *technē* but its being carried into language, where it is stored, and re-used. Acts gain a certain endurance as operations when they come to stand out, become defined, named and made into rules to be applied in other instances. By becoming part of language, the acts gain distinction from the world from which they emerged, they stand against it in a 'relative and unitary constancy';[13] enduring as tradition. In *technē*, language reveals itself to be the medium by which the human distinguishes itself from nature: it houses humans by equipping them with the means to draw distinctions and attribute intelligibility to actions, events, patterns, sensations and things. 'It is', suggests Heidegger, 'in the word, in language, that things first come to be and are'.[14] What is decisive about *technē* is therefore not its capacity for making and manipulating, but its capacity for revealing, for bringing forth, for unconcealing, and then challenging the world out there – nature – to correlate with the written plans of the central subject which, so obsessed with the (technological) health of its own bios, forgets its regional reliance upon other life forms.[15]

With the onset of industrialization, and especially its capitalist version, this unconcealing language of *technē* has been let loose to create its own world, losing contact with natural things along the way. The meanings bestowed in language have come to suffice because it is in grammar, and not nature, that truth can be locked down and repeated without fear of

---

[11] Bernard Stiegler *Technics and Time 1*. 151. Beatriz Colomina and Mark Wigley *Are We Human?* 66–68.
[12] Bernard Stiegler *Technics and Time 1*. 154.
[13] William McNeill *The Time of Life: Heidegger and Ethos*. New York: State University of New York. 2006. 45.
[14] Martin Heidegger, *Introduction to Metaphysics*. 15/11.
[15] Martin Heidegger *The Question Concerning Technology*. In *Basic Writings*. Edited by D. F. Krell. London: Routledge. 1978. 319.

getting loose. This is not a fault of grammar per se, but of grammar that has committed itself to an idea of truth as a correlation between the word, a mental representation, and reality 'out there' that has been pictured as a coherent mass of calculable force that can be managed in the pursuit of specific human interests made explicit in the form of aims, targets and goals.

To make itself distinct from the *technē* that has morphed into an industrialized massification of logistics and manufacture, craft work must hold onto the possibility of glancing *physis*, as it works and improvises its own and owned *technē* must keep touch with the naturalness of things. Merleau-Ponty offers a succinct expression of experiencing *physis* through *technē*:

> Inside and outside are inseparable. The world is wholly inside and I am wholly outside myself. When I perceive this table, the perception of the top must not overlook that of the legs, otherwise the object would be thrown out of joint. When I hear a melody, each of its moments must be related to its successor, otherwise there would be no melody. Yet the table is there with its external parts, and succession is of the essence of melody. The act which draws together at the same time takes away and holds at a distance, so that I touch myself only by escaping from myself.[16]

The sense of reciprocal identification made possible by this weaving of insides and outsides keeps the subject in touch with things. The craft worker is willing to make do with the crooked timber of their everyday self which invites the attention of other things. Even when they have become experts their knowledge of raw materials, techniques and of long-standing patterns and designs is never definitive, and to know of these materials, methods and forbears is also to be searching for their transgression. And whilst the craft worker is very much an efficacious force – they make decisions and choices and are forever looking for ways to encounter things in all their variety – they consciously de-centre themselves from the scene of making and in this way they are better placed to apprehend what it is things do as they decay, expand, wither, dissolve, explode, all the while accepting that there are things whose productive being in the world – *physis* – lies outside of human 'sayings and doings'. It is accepted and even enjoyed that the 'thereness' of a thing can exceed any attempt to describe it (otherwise it can be reduced to pure function, or pure idea), and the making of the thing cannot be reduced to the method (otherwise it is imitation and manufacture). In the techne of craft work there is an acceptance that things naturally have their own life, that in being made to appear they also disappear.

Most craft workers are intimately aware that a thing cannot be confined or explained by its components nor by its wider setting, neither its

---

[16] Maurice Merleau-Ponty *Phenomenology of Perception*. Translated by Colin Smith. London: Routledge. 2005. 474.

elements nor its relations can exhaust it. They, more than most, remain alive to an almost otherworldly fission of the kind Paul Klee felt when staring into the void of a ceramic pot:

> The interior is infinite, all the way to the mystery of the inmost, the charged point, a kind of sum total of the infinite (the causal). Comparison from nature: the seed. The exterior is finite, i.e. it is the end of the dynamic forces, the limit of their effects, dictated by the causal. One may call it the virtual. The objective. One could also say the erotic-logical eros-logos.[17]

This reversal in which the inner, contained space becomes infinite, and the outer, extending space the measured and restricted space of edges, is how a craft worker refuses the comforts of correlation whilst still committing to the value to be had from experiencing things. No matter how it is approached in use or in theory, no matter how tightly as distinct objects bound by relations in habit or how detailed the analysis, Klee's pot with its void is always escaping, withdrawing to contain itself. It can be an uncanny experience, one of being alongside things that are just beyond the reach of one's skills and even, at times, comprehension. Things can become inscrutable, and the imagination can do nothing other than be open to remaining alongside them, even if it becomes troubling as the things morph into thresholds to which the craft worker can be both sensitive and wary, like the poet Auxilio in Roberto Bolaño's novel *Amulet*, who we find pausing in front of a vase, hesitating:

> when I was a few feet from the vase, I stopped again and said to myself: If it isn't Hell in there, it's nightmares, and all that is lost. All that causes pain and is better forgotten. Then I thought: Does Pedrito Garfias know what's hidden in this vase? Do poets have any idea what lurks in the bottomless maws of their vases?[18]

Yet alongside experiences of the uncanny and hesitation can come those of delighted sympathy, periods where things seem just to cohere with sentient abundance, as though the breath of life coursed through all things. In *A Christmas Carol*, Charles Dickens' descriptions of the groceries being offered on market stalls spill over themselves with abundance.

> There were pears and apples, clustered high in blooming pyramids; there were bunches of grapes, made, in the shopkeepers' benevolence to dangle from conspicuous hooks, that people's mouths might water gratis as they passed; there were piles of filberts, mossy and brown, recalling, in their fragrance, ancient walks

---

[17] Paul Klee *The Notebooks Volume Two*. Edited by Jürg Spiller. Translated by Heinz Norden. London: Lund Humphries. 1973. 149.

[18] Roberto Bolaño *Amulet*. Translated by Chris Andrews. New York: New Directions. 2009. 9.

among the woods, and pleasant shufflings ankle deep through withered leaves; there were Norfolk Biffins, squab and swarthy, setting of the yellow of the oranges and lemons, and, in the great compactness of their juicy persons, urgently entreating and beseeching to be carried home in paper bags and eaten after dinner.[19]

The market is in colourful and generous spate; the produce is complicit in the seasonal goodwill that falls on all life as evenly and indiscriminately as snow. For a while at least, what is joyous with the world eclipses what is drab; it is a seasonal atmosphere of unreasoned and unabated generosity. Humans were not alone, and for a while desire grew untrimmed by the shears of economic reality.

This sensitivity towards the abundance of life, and an intense interest in life, is what drew Deleuze to call on Dickens as a writer of life itself, a writer for whom life – the glowing, struggling, striving force of life, the 'life' to which Ruskin said all work should give itself completely - became a subject in its own right. Life lives, it has its own inscrutable presence, through which humans or Norfolk Biffins can all, equally, be moved. Scrooge, infamous for locking himself into the grimy realities of possession, is confronted with this worldly principle of life's movement by the Ghost of Marley, his erstwhile business partner:

Scrooge fell upon his knees, and clasped his hands before his face.
 'Mercy!' he said. 'Dreadful apparition, why do you trouble me?'
 'Man of the worldly mind!' replied the Ghost, 'do you believe in me or not?'
 'I do,' said Scrooge. 'I must. But why do spirits walk the earth, and why do they come to me?'
 'It is required of every man,' the Ghost returned, 'that the spirit within him should walk abroad among his fellow-men, and travel far and wide; and if that spirit goes not forth in life, it is condemned to do so after death. It is doomed to wander through the world – oh, woe is me! – and witness what it cannot share, but might have shared on earth, and turned to happiness!'[20]

Marley had not walked amongst things enough, he had not moved with the movements of life, and so did what he could, by haunting those that still might.

Naturalism appears through combinations of the uncanny and delight, it agitates and spurs the process of making, whilst allowing things to pull back into a self-contained, natural state, and so maintain a distance from the scaffolding of knowledge through which those who know – the expert, the genius – might otherwise look to elevate themselves above and beyond the world. It also appears when it mocks us, turning away, refusing to give as it once had, unreliable and unwilling,

---

[19] Charles Dickens *A Christmas Carol*. London: Chapman and Hall. 1897. 53.
[20] Charles Dickens *A Christmas Carol*. 24.

and the subject withers away, or departs in questions, as in Patrick Kavanagh's opening of his poem 'The Great Hunger':

> Clay is the word and clay is the flesh
> Where the potato-gatherers like mechanised scarecrows move
> Along the side-fall of the hill – Maguire and his men.
> If we watch them an hour is there anything we can prove
> Of life as it is broken-backed over the Book
> Of Death? Here crows gabble over worms and frogs
> And the gulls like old newspapers are blown clear of the hedges, luckily.
> Is there some light of imagination in these wet clods?
> Or why do we stand here shivering?[21]

## Speculative Realism

'If', the games designer Ian Bogost suggests 'we take seriously the idea that all objects recede interminably into themselves, then human perception becomes just one among many ways that objects might relate. To put things at the center of a new metaphysics also requires us to admit that they do not exist just for us.'[22] All things, not just humans, are *Dasein*. Bogost is one of the more considered exponents of a philosophical thesis labelled 'speculative realism'. Its various exponents argue that hitherto those interested in the grounding reality of things have failed to apprehend how, in the very act of inquiry, they are failing to understand this reality. The root of this failure goes back to Descartes, and Kant, who between them, in their different ways, cemented the idea that the ground and centre of all knowledge and understanding was the correlation between thinking and being enacted by human subjects. The world is nothing outside of the ways in which it correlates with human perception and practice.

This tendency towards the errors of correlation had already been noted by Ruskin, notably in art; he called it 'the pathetic fallacy'. Artists were prone to sheathing experience with metaphors that more closely reflected their own sensibility and context than the nature of the things and events they encountered. As an instance of committing the pathetic fallacy he takes lines from a poem by Oliver Wendell Holmes:

> For instance—
> 'The spendthrift crocus, bursting through the mould
> Naked and shivering, with his cup of gold.'

---

[21] Patrick Kavanagh 'The Great Hunger'. In *Collected Poems*. London: MacGibbon and Kee. 1964. 34.
[22] Ian Bogost *Alien Phenomenology, or What It's Like to Be a Thing (Posthumanities)*. Minneapolis: University of Minnesota Press. 2012. 36.

> This is very beautiful, and yet very untrue. The crocus is not a
> spendthrift, but a hardy plant; its yellow is not gold, but saffron.
> How is it that we enjoy so much the having it put into our heads that
> it is anything else than a plain crocus?[23]

It is because we feel strongly, or identify with the strong feelings of the poet, who, being weak, cannot control the wild, untruthful associations thrown up by his imagination as he forces the small flower into service as a portal for his emotional surges. It is also because of an institutional tendency towards conformity. To the extent Holmes calls on his expertise and the authority of his tradition to warrant the pursuit of specific associations, he frames the appearance of things like a crocus as objects which fit existing knowledge structures associated with technique (rhyme and metre), tools (moulds, cups), standards (spendthrift, gold) and principles (a moral to the narrative); the 'regional' grammar by which the crocus appears always comes first, and it comforts both the poet and reader for this to be so.

Were we to think harder, however, we would be suspicious of our enjoyment and reserve our approbation for those poets who can marry strong feelings with truthful insight. Poets like Dante, suggests Ruskin, who have the genius to concentrate on the fact of their own emotional experience, and upon the fact of a flower's existence, make associations in a measured, discerning and thereby insightful way, as when he describes spirits falling away from the banks of the Acheron 'as dead leaves flutter from a bough'. There is a directness and economy in describing the scattering of these enfeebled souls; and as leaf and soul are joined to intensify the understanding of the scene, neither confuses the other, they remain distinct things.[24] It is Dante who renders a fuller and richer understanding of nature by virtue of a disciplined capacity to stand back from his own emotion, and from things 'out there' and yet maintain both under intense, poetic scrutiny. He takes his own emotional state away from the centre stage, placing it alongside other events and feelings, and attending to all equally, and as far as is possible, on their own terms, rather than steeping them in the immediacy of strongly felt passion.

Speculative realism redounds with appeals for the forms of insight that Ruskin attributes to Dante. Though language cannot be shed, we can go farther than we do to apprehend things outside of human framing, especially the thoughtless, surface framing of strong emotion or prejudice? The restrained, careful impassive use of language grounded in close

---

[23] John Ruskin *Modern Painters IV*. In *Complete Works Vol. V*. Edited by E. T. Cook and Alexander Wedderburn. London: George Allen. 1904, §4. 204.

[24] John Ruskin *Modern Painters IV*. In *Complete Works Vol. V*. §5. 205.

empirical attention gives greater voice to things, it acknowledges their own being, outside of their being hitched to chains of human reasoning. It is an ontological expansion of being that allows things and events to come forth as much on their own terms as on those of the human subject.

It is an expansion that, practically speaking, craft work might be well suited to undertake. More than many other human practices, craft workers encounter the paradox which motivates speculative realism: despite intense interest in the nature of things, they can never apprehend their reality.[25] Yet in craft work, as with Dante, no matter how alive to the raw state of materials and to natural expressions of *physis*, the 'being' of the made thing is still only understood in relation to the maker's or poet's perception. The subject remains in play as an efficient cause, without whom there is neither insight nor its wider, regional resonance. Craft work would not have it any other way. Though alive to the pathetic fallacy, the *technē* of craft work remains firmly in the business of making things so they appear in ways that are sympathetic to broader regional situations.

Indeed, for those alive to the techne of craft work like Aalto this sympathy between a thing and its setting *was* naturalism. He wouldn't just design and have made a table, light fitting or vase, but things-in-relation. Working on the Tuberculosis Sanitorium at Paimo in 1929, for example, Aalto set out to build 'a cathedral to health and an instrument for healing'. Working with the natural air, light and wooded seclusion to create an ordered and calm space for long term, bed-bound patients. Outside air enters the patient's rooms diagonally, gathering radiant heat as it passes between vented pairs of double-glazed windowpanes. The patients' walkways look over the tree canopy, chairs and loungers lined along a pale coloured wall. The chairs had to be light so weakened patients might be able to move them relatively noiselessly and staff could relocate them across different floors and in different rooms. They also needed to be easily cleaned to keep them hygienic, to have no hard

---

[25] The speculative is needed to distinguish them from realist scientists who, when they examine occurrence, tend to fall right away into undermining (to reduce them to constituents or components or elements) or overmining (to expand them into law like patterns, or to combine elements and systems). The same goes for realist philosophers who can appear equally unwilling to cede to objects. They rather look to explain objects via their compositional parts, reducing them downward to real levels (Deleuze's plane of immanence for example, or Democritus' atoms) or upwards (Latour, objects are networked relations, or Foucault, subjects belong to discursive structures of knowledge, etc.). In contrast to these realists, the speculative realists, suggests Graham Harman, urge us to think of objects having their own existence, over and above their being composed of parts and separated from the relations by which they gain a relative sense of distinction. Their unity extends beyond their parts (whether these are primary, i.e. inherent) or secondary (perceived), and they can withdraw from relational settings and remain objects; ontologically, an object is separated from its qualities.

134    4  Naturalism

Figure 33  Alvar Aalto, Paimio Sanatorium Lecture Room. Photography: Gustaf Welin, Alvar Aalto Foundation. 1933.

edges, to be cost effective to fit within the limited budget, and comfortable. Aalto had experimented with the local woodyard, first using a blend of bent steel and wood before hitting on the springy qualities of laminated sheets of local birch that could be scrolled and cantilevered into shape without needing steam, and which would compress gently under the weight of a seated patient, allowing them to lean back gently, expanding their lungs, without pulling heat from their body (Figure 33).

A piece of furniture that forms part of a person's daily habitat should not cause excessive glare from light reflection: ditto it should not be disadvantageous in terms of sound, sound absorption, etc. A piece that comes into the most intimate contact with man, as a chair does, shouldn't be constructed of materials that are excessively good conductors of heat.[26]

The made things are in continual touch with nature, and they glance towards *physis*, if only ever occasionally, and with small accents, a form of living coheres with a form of making and the made form, none of which

[26] Alvar Aalto *Rationalism in Man*. In *Sketches*. Edited by Göran Schildt. Translated by Stuart Wrede. Massachusetts: MIT Press. 1978. 48.

dominates, each of which opens up onto the other, and because of the other, making for a complex and dynamic array of insides and outsides.[27] There was no such naturalism in Hoffmann's Purkersdorf.

Aalto, like Ruskin, still adhered to the phenomenological assumption that what appears does so in relation to the affections, desires, interests and histories with which our lives our irrevocably stained. To get at the truth of nature was to get at a truth that correlated with the life of the human species as it was represented in grammar, a truth that mattered for its flourishing. The naturalness of the trees and light, of the birch wood and its qualities, was sensual; they existed as correlates to acts of consciousness and feeling, as well as to common agreements upon which the legitimacy and authority of the grammatical criteria for naming objects like 'trees' and 'light' are sustained.

Yet what, asks the speculative realist, of those aspects of the tree that do not appear, that are beyond the perception of the designer, carpenter and user, even those who, in the manner of Dante, are disciplined enough to contain and interrogate their own feelings? For speculative realists the tree is more than its sensual appearance, and its relationship to the designer, carpenter and user is different from theirs to it. For the tree, language is not the house of its being, rather it is the 'great outdoors', which is a vast place untouched by human perception. Each object, human and tree is translating the other object in its own terms, endlessly and openly. Humans happen to experience consciousness and thoughtfulness in such processes of translation, but this is nothing more than one amongst many forms of apprehension, there is nothing special about it: human–nature relations are on the same ontological plane as thing–thing relations, and thought is just one form of access, along with sound, song, pressure and heat sensitivity, and myriad other sensory apprehensions of sentient and non-sentient life.

The virtue of this knowledge claim made by speculative realists comes in the form of a reminder: no matter how exhaustive the analysis and understanding of an object, something of the object itself remains free. Human analysis goes one of two ways, and neither way, despite their ambition, apprehends the object fully. First, analysis can break the object into its constituent parts, which in turn consist of yet smaller parts, until at some juncture it arrives at the base condition, what Plato in *Theatetus* called 'simples', the essential things that cannot be reduced any further. Graham Harman, another speculative realist, calls this process

---

[27] For an extended discussion of the resonance between Aalto and Heidegger see Jeff Malpas Heidegger, *Aalto and the Limits of Design*. In *Suchen, Entwerfen, Stiften*. Edited by David Espinet and Toni Hildebrandt. Leiden: Brill | Fink. 2014. 191–214.

'undermining' the object.[28] Second, going the opposite way, analysis proceeds by inserting the object into wider environments and understanding it as a vehicle for larger phenomena like laws, discourses or institutional forces (overmining the object). Often, analysis does both, as, perhaps, when Aalto understands the bentwood chair as a gathering of components, tools and physical forces (freshly cut birch, glues, steam) and as a component within wider systems (within an array of hospital furniture, discourses of health and sanitation, laws associated with cantilevered forces, wooded nature as a retreat). What, asks Harman, of the object itself: 'An object is anything that cannot be entirely reduced either to the components of which it is made or to the effects that it has on other things', and whilst he accepts there are different realities for objects, 'for it is false that dragons have autonomous reality in the same manner as a telephone pole. My point is not that all objects are equally real, but that they are equally objects.'[29] They are equals because they have their own reality: light, tree, chair and Aalto. To Aalto the chair appears as what Harman calls a 'sensual object', which is a perspective one object has of another object, a human of a chair, and the translation from the former to the latter is then extended to other humans: the woodworkers, patients, clinicians and cleaners, all of whom agree, broadly, on the grammar associated with 'chair'. The lightness of the chair, for example, cannot be argued with, nor that it is made from lamina of birch wood, yet these apparently real qualities are anthropological in nature, they have a cultural ground, they emerge from a correlation between thought and being.[30] They do not belong to the object (whose 'real' qualities withdraw from the regions of use) but to the grammar of analysis and use, and to the expertise being acquired in the historically grounded development of practices of inquiry.[31] But why separate the real and the sensual when they belong to the same sea, and why insist that one can only access the real by supressing the sensual and the being of the subject?

Admittedly, it is salutary to argue humans might do better for themselves by accepting their own epistemic limits rather than struggling to place their interests centre stage. Craft workers often confront such

---

[28] In *Philosophical Investigations* (Oxford: Blackwell, 1953, §46, §59) Ludwig Wittgenstein also questions this urge to find the base constituents of which things are composed, the grounding elements that can only be named and not explained. But craft things are not composites in this way, the assembly of their parts does not become them. The presence of a made thing is a unity, not a composition.

[29] Graham Harman *The Quadruple Object*. New York: Zero Books. 2011. 69.

[30] In Ludwig Wittgenstein *Zettel*. Oxford: Basil Blackwell. 1967.

[31] Graham Harman *Object-Oriented Ontology: A New Theory of Everything*. London: Penguin. 2017. 186.

salutary limits, but this as often serves to enhance rather than diminish their expertise. The potter Rupert Spira puts it like this. There are, he suggests, at least three aspects to all pots: its substance (the presence that is its own, its 'alien' material, its ownmost presence, which cannot be reduced to its component parts nor expanded into its functional or symbolic roles) and the consciousness (the potter attentive to the contextualized communication by which material appears as form) and the relation between both the potter and the cultural and social habit (their willingness to accept and yet question habituated symbolism). The relationship between habit, the potter and the enigma of the material is what she, as a potter, is pursuing in her learning, her development. Whilst experience differs uniquely, the fact of its being conscious is a constant, yet this consciousness is not interior to the mind but extends through habit into the contexts of the studio or workshop, and of tradition, and through to material in the form of plastic knowledge. On both counts it is, like Dante's, a situational awareness that thinks and acts across contexts; to reach outwards into what is other than them, into nature. It is then, and only then, that the potter can create 'forms whose inspiration, knowingly or unknowingly, comes direct from consciousness – that is from love, beauty, intelligence – and these objects have a particular capacity to reveal the space of consciousness out of which they arise and into which they vanish. Their purpose is to reveal their source.'[32] The source being not only the consciousness of the potter and their tradition, but also nature, in itself.

To insist one go further than this, further than Dante or Spira's potter, and to insist that the ontological reality of objects is utterly separate to that of humans and their grammatical structures, seems to be slightly absurd: it is to philosophize amid the void. It also feels like avoidance of the basic fact that just as our awareness of objects is always tainted by grammar, so are the ontological claims made by philosophers. The speculative realists make a forceful point when they remind us that philosophers have been too hasty and too assured in converting the impressionistic appearances of sensual and emotional experience into strictly proportioned perception and factual representations; philosophy has traded truthfulness for the presumption of human control. Yet this does not obviate the very real organizational need for involvement. Culturally speaking, if humans are being encouraged to denigrate sensory relations to being just one of many ways objects connect, doesn't this then reduce the aesthetic work of myriad human civilizations to being the equivalent

---

[32] Rupert Spira in conversation with Daphne Astor in Rupert Spira *Bowl*. Norwich: Sainsbury Centre for Visual Arts. 2004. 42.

of the shell made by an oyster, or the murmuration of starlings? In what way does the assertion that object–object relations are the equivalent of subject–object relations foreclose on the admission that the latter offers rich and potentially transformative qualities that the former lacks?

There is a rich strand of phenomenological thinking, such as Merleau-Ponty's, which admonishes the rather frigid effects of seeking strict correlations between empirical occurrence and theoretical explanation, but which nevertheless remains committed to understanding appearances through the framing of sensible objects. This thinking accepts language can never properly contain and convey the perceptual field and accepts further that the perceptual field is never the whole field, but without converting these limits into limitations. There is no privileging of subject–object relations in these studies, nor is there in craft work. It is more a realization that when things emerge from the repetitious processes of making, the subject – the craft worker – reaches what the critical theorist Theodore Adorno called 'coherence, however self-antagonistic and refracted, through which each and every successful work separates itself from the merely existing.'[33] Reaching such a threshold of occurrence does not upgrade the subject relative to other objects, rather it is an attempt to understand and represent it as the subject experiences the dips, elation, schisms, mistakes, boredom, weaknesses, discipline, progressions and intercessions of a working life. Speculative realism seems to be a downgrading of these subject experiences, shaming them almost; that is, if they really do insist that a human being is the ontological equivalent to a lemon or dust mote.

Craft workers, like many other human beings, are acutely and consistently aware that their knowledge of things occupies nothing more than small patches or hesitant arcs of sensory translation between thought, the world and language. They correlate and apprehend the limits of correlation, and do so practically, as they make. They acknowledge the difficulty of accessing the object. Indeed, this is their job, this is what excites and frustrates and moves them on. As when Watt, in Samuel Beckett's eponymous novel, encounters a pot:

Looking at a pot, for example, or thinking of a pot, at one of Mr Knott's pots, of one of Mr Knott's pots, it was in vain that Watt said, Pot, pot. Well, perhaps not quite in vain, but very nearly. For it was not a pot, the more he looked, the more he reflected, the more he felt sure of that, that it was not a pot at all. It resembled

---

[33] Theodor Adorno *Aesthetic Theory*. Edited by Gretel Adorno and Rolf Tiedemann. Translated by Robert Hullot-Kentor. New York: Continuum. 2002. 141. As to craft being a synonym with art, and whether craft work is capable, like art work, of potentially 'severing' from everyday commerce, Adorno is typically skeptical.

a pot, it was almost a pot, but it was not a pot of which one could say, Pot, pot, and be comforted. It was in vain that it answered, with unexceptionable adequacy, all the purposes, and performed all the offices, of a pot, it was not a pot. And it was just this hairbreadth departure from the nature of a true pot that so excruciated Watt. For if the approximation had been less close, then Watt would have been less anguished.[34]

The dance between the approximation and the thing is what gives life to the made thing, and it is always an approximation. But why go further and assert that this difficulty then traduces the reality of the object, what extra work is the stipulation that real things are foreclosed doing? Craft work is inclined to sense the life in things, to confront what appears, and not to confuse this appearance with complete understanding. In the rooting around for raw materials, or in making tools from discarded objects, they partake in a region of appearances that is far from being secure, properly organized and beautified. And in concentrating upon and listening to what occurs in the raw, they place themselves in the drama of natural forms without much in the way of epistemological scaffolding. Yet, as Aalto so amply embodies, they do not judge this to be an impoverished or restricted experience, quite the opposite. They relish it because it puts them in touch with the nature of things, but without drifting into correlationist tendencies. The craft worker speculates by committing to making things rather than quiescently standing back so as to reveal them in writing.

Speculative realism is insistent that the sensory involvement of humans like craft workers is both limited and unseemly because it habitually expects things to appear, and to be approachable. Limited because human thought and consciousness is itself limited (it is just one of many ways in which objects relate) and unseemly because the relish and quizzical delight often felt by the likes of craft workers is an unwarranted and unwanted distraction if one wishes to apprehend the really real situation, which is only available, it seems, to philosophy, and to philosophers of a certain speculating bent. In downgrading the human senses, speculative realism elevates itself as a substitute, as it, not craft work (nor phenomenology, nor physics) can ascertain the real nature of objects. As to how, however, remains vague. Harman suggests the use of poetic, metaphorical glances, but this amounts to little more than a hesitant coupling of linguistic dependency (of the kind that elsewhere he criticizes) with quietism (given its a flat ontology of endlessly and openly relating objects, one has to be careful not to elevate one object above another,

---

[34] Samuel Beckett *Watt*. New York: Grove Press. 81.

or to privilege subjects).³⁵ Other proposed access points to what is, by dint of its own reality, inaccessible, prove equally circular. To propose objects have their own nature only insofar as this nature can never be apprehended ends up getting caught in the very same linguistic thicket it sets out to untangle. Speculative realism criticizes the correlationists who use a set of super concepts to represent a natural order in which claims, referents, truths and experiences cohere as an organized whole. Objects are not part of such a whole, they have their own reality. But to maintain such a natural distinction means trying to represent its essence, and to forget Wittgenstein's advice: 'if the words "language", "experience", "world" have any use value, it must be as humble a one as that of the words "table", "vase", "cloth".'³⁶

By examining things carefully in his search for a vivid concordance (correlation) of mind, body, material, activity and form, Aalto (and those with whom he worked) enjoined himself to the new through an exposure to nature and so was able to consider, again and again, why it was that the world might need yet one more thing. The naturalism that Aalto exhibits (along with many other craft workers) uses a humble, stripped-back language that is hesitant to explain itself, and that is more content to keep quiet. It is a language that is all too alive to the deadening effect of generalising explanations. In language, suggests Kierkegaard there is a risk that:

[T]he sensual is reduced to mere instrument and thus rescinded. If when a man spoke one heard the movements of his tongue, etc., he would speak badly; if when he heard, he heard the air vibrations instead of the words, he would hear badly; if when reading a book one constantly saw the individual letters, one would read badly. Language becomes the perfect medium just at the moment when everything sensual is negated in it.³⁷

---

[35] See Stephen Mulhall 'How Complex Is a Lemon?' *London Review of Books*. 2018, 40, 18. Alexander Galloway wonders whether the democracy of things insisted on by speculative realism is little more than an extension of modern capitalism, which also shares an utter indifference to the different qualities of their sentience or sanctity. For the market, all objects (dreams, coal, parcels of air, stars, freeports) are ontologically equal as (potential) goods. The dogmatic commitment to an equality between all things serves to reduce all things to a point where they are forced to make themselves available to inhuman forces, whether those of real objects or those of the market. Though apparently a human construction, technological mediation has removed the market from human commerce, it is run by machine-governed protocols, its reality is one of object–object, not subject-object, it too is part of the 'great outdoors', beyond language, given it 'consists of the extraction of value based on encoding and processing of mathematical information'. Alexander Galloway 'The Poverty of Philosophy: Realism and Post-Fordism', *Critical Inquiry*. 2013, 39, 2, 347–366. 358.

[36] Ludwig Wittgenstein *Philosophical Investigations*. §41.

[37] Søren Kierkegaard *Either/Or: A Fragment of Life*. Translated by Alastair Hannay. London: Penguin. 1992. 78.

To keep the sensual in play means remaining suspicious of language, and to accept that rather than declaiming or stating, it is better to gesture towards judgments that work thoughtfully into the in-between space. It is form of thoughtful making that acknowledges that in ascribing value to things we also rob things of their own value; we come to know things as objects for our (subjective) estimation; thinking throws us into 'the open region that lights the between within which a relation of subject to object can be.'[38]

## Mingei

If naturalism is less about escaping language altogether than it is about abutting the limits of language in the 'open region', then another way of letting nature 'in', in addition to Aalto's expressive, experimental mode, is to consider how things can find themselves set within the grammar and form of life of an altogether different regional setting. Wrapped in black material, in a black box, hidden away in the Daitokuji Temple, Kyoto is a simple rice bowl from Korea. Its milky glaze is rough, hazed, cracked and pockmarked. Its roughly shaped foot is unglazed. The sides are gently undulating, having born the finger marks of its anonymous maker. For the writer Muneyoshi Yanagi it is a bowl that embodies the form of rustic beauty to which Japan and Japanese sensibility turn most intensely and naturally; indeed, so bewitching is its form, those who touch it are said to be overcome with tremors. In this recovery of a concealed thing the ideal bowl ceases to be the perfect, highly decorated objects emerging from China. From the late sixteenth century, the Ido ware of Korea is preferred by the warring Samurai then assuming control over large swathes of what was to become Japan. The ornate gave way to the beguiling but muted nuances of the ordinary and so began the story of *Mingei* that found its most eloquent apogee in Yanagi's *The Beauty of Everyday Things* published in 1933.[39] The *Mingei* (民藝) movement emerged during the mid 1920s and 1930s, *Min* (民) meaning people or folk and *Mingei* meaning peoples' work ('folk art'), distinguishing it from both high art and manufacturer.[40] The book slowly advances a long list of criteria that Yanagi believed encompassed those things classified as *Mingei*. Their materials and methods were to reflect the regional locale in which they were made, and to show signs of having been made by hand,

---

[38] Martin Heidegger *Letter on Humanism*. In *Basic Writings*. Edited by David Farrell Krell. New York: Harper Row. 1978. 213–265. 229.
[39] Muneyoshi Yanagi *The Beauty of Everyday Things*. London: Penguin. 1933.
[40] T. Matsui *Muneyoshi Yanagi and Mingei in the Present* (柳宗悦と民藝の現在). Yoshikawa Kobunkan. 2005.

and yet it was better that these signs were barely perceptible. There should be few indications of an individual maker. The made things were the products of a collective, community body that gathered its motivation and warrant from nature itself. Like Kierkegaard's and Benjamin's folk tales, it was the traditions in making that afforded the potters the desire and freedom to roam without the impediment of authorship, they become lost in the oral and felt voice of the wider folk that had been locked into the rhythms of work. *Mingei* things were inexpensive, simple, readily available, and part of ordinary homes: they possessed a beauty that could not be disassociated from the patina of use and the years of use to come but could be disassociated from any single maker.[41] Yanagi took his cue from earlier traditions in the East, ones Japan might emulate and accentuate. The iron dark body hidden beneath a milky white slip in a Korean punch'ong bowl or the pale celadon of a Sung dynasty Chinese brush washer carried no trace of an individual mark; in their singular striving to make something as well as it can be made the maker became a medium for object, not vice versa.

The idea of *Mingei* as the expressive outcome of a cyclical, unindividuated organic whole is itself grounded in the native blend of Shinto and Zen Buddhism which have nature as their cathedral and its spirits as gods. In his Nobel acceptance speech *Japan, the Beautiful and Myself* the writer Yasunari Kawabata expounds on this intimacy between nature and the natural dispositions of many Japanese, a relationship he suggests is given profound poise in Eihei Dōgan Kigen's (1200–1253) poem:

> In the spring, cherry blossoms, in the summer the cuckoo.
> In autumn the full moon, in winter the snow, clear, cold.[42]

The seasonal cycles given form by natural things whose presence is transient. The blossom comes apart, though the colour of spring remains fast in the memory, the call of the bird leaves no trace, though its mark is indelible, the moon lights the way into the night, the snow conceals the world with a cold innocence. There is a simplicity and persistence in this natural occurrence, and it arises into language through the disciplined concentration of a poet whose words have been a lifetime in the fashioning, a voice whose edges are lapped by silence, a life in its final throws which, finally, has found itself freed.

Despite the emphasis on letting go of control, on de-centring the human, and on realising the mystery inherent in things, there is a profound

---

[41] Idekawa Naoki *Mingei-Riron no Houkai to Yoshiki no Tanjyo*. Tokyo: Shinchosha. 1998.
[42] Yasunari Kawabata 'Japan, the Beautiful and Myself', *Nobelprize.org*. Nobel Media AB 2014. Web. 27 Apr 2018. www.nobelprize.org/nobel_prizes/literature/laureates/1968/kawabata-lecture.html.

distinction between this naturalism and that of the speculative realists because in Japan the subject and its acquired wisdom remain the grounding concerns. It is a naturalism through which humans learn how consciousness, reflection and imaginative reason agitate the body in the way that water is rippled by a breeze or brought into a maelstrom by hard winds. The human quivers with nature but is not an ontological equivalent. In an arresting flipping and twisting of the speculative realist worldview, the Japanese philosopher Nishida argued that it is the human alone who makes things as things: 'In biological life, things that have been made are not free from the body; in other words, they are not free from the subject ... In historical life, on the contrary, things that have been made (*tsukurareta mono*) are independent from those who make them (*tsukuru mono*).'[43] The things of biological life are not really things at all given they only exist in unmediated processes of natural occurrence that cannot be sensibly parcelled into components.[44] The things of historical life are human made: the homestead and not the beaver's dam, the jack hammer and not the rook's stone, this is where things as things are born because it is here and only here that a negation occurs, a poise and pause that intensifies experience into a singular thing or event, like the masks in Japanese Noh theatre. Carved from a single block of wood, they intercede as stilled moments of concentration (*Komi*) through which a distant folk tale is brought into immediate presence across a bridge of sound. Then the mask moves, tilting, almost imperceptibly, searching for mood. Short sounds suggest surprise, and long sounds yearning or sorrow. The drummers intercede, their clacks and breaks reveal time passing, without control, showing human impotency and transience, they shape the void and leave it there, lingering, stilling the pale face and blackened teeth of the mask, the shadows more substantial that skin and bone. The story is repeated, but the performance is unique, a single event made as a unique thing that cannot be reproduced or imitated. There is attention to one performance, just one performance, the repetition is utterly novel (Figure 34).

In schooling attentiveness away from the confines of habit, the subject can experience nature anew, unmediated by thought, and with the body gaining an ascendency, a pre-conceptual, pre-cognitive state of awareness dawns through the body where the subject and object became

---

[43] Quoted in Sugimoto Kōichi *Tanabe Hajime's Logic of Species and the Philosophy of Nishida Kitarō*. In *Japanese and Continental Philosophy: Conversations with the Kyoto School*. Edited by Bret W. Davis, Brian Schroeder and Jason M. Wirth. Bloomington and Indianapolis: Indiana University Press. 2011. 52–70. 63 (NKZ 8: 501–502).

[44] Robert Chia. *Nishida Kitarō (1870–1945)*. In *The Oxford Handbook of Process Philosophy and Organization Studies*. Edited by Jenny Helin, Daniel Hjorth, Tor Hernes and Robin Holt. Oxford: Oxford University Press. 2014. 287–302.

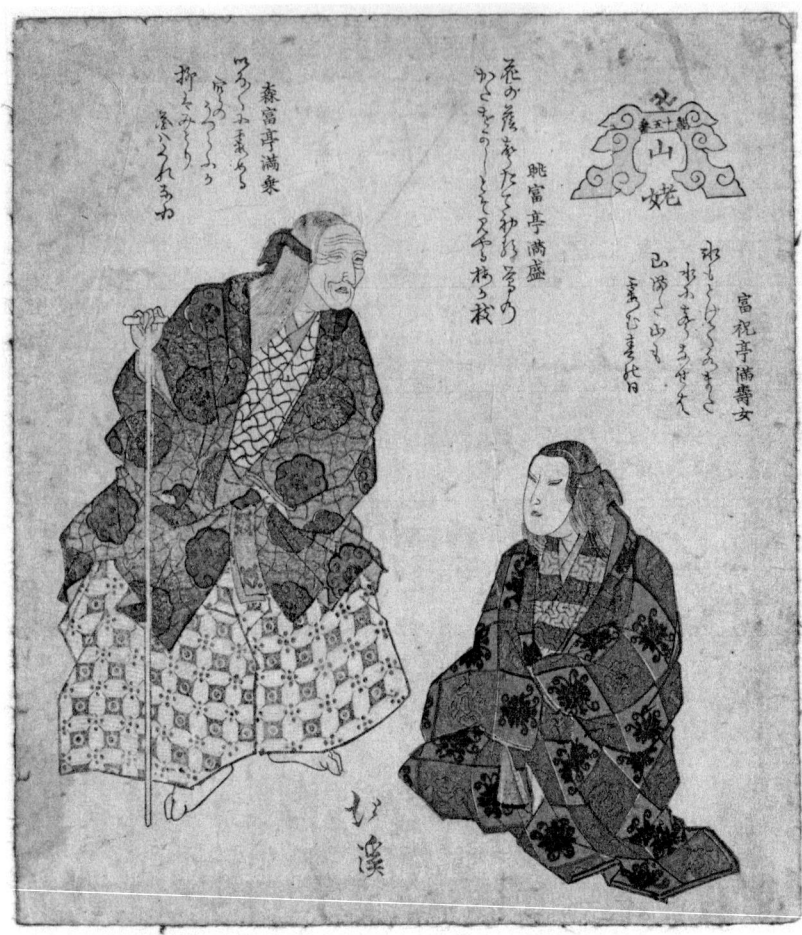

Figure 34 Hokkei Totoya (1780–1850), Noh actors as Yamauba (mountain women), 1830–1835. Woodcut. Library of Congress, Prints and Photographs Division [reproduction number: LC-DIG-jpd-0072]. Photograph: www.loc.gov/item/2009615064/.

one, they flow through one another in a state of 'pure experience'. This wresting away to then re-connect to nature means the subject can, with training, realize and retain a direct and intuitive contact with biological life, but the contact remains distinctly human insofar as, no matter how affectively direct, it is an immediacy that mediates itself: it emerges from schooling, from a deliberate and deliberative apprenticeship in thinning history to a point it becomes refined enough to be written in little more than water. The subject arises from pure experience, and thought is the response of consciousness to the conceptual images the subject has as it struggles to make sense of this pure experience. Precisely because of their generality and clarity, these concepts will always be deficient in rendering the direct experience mediated through the body trained in how to live alongside objects intuitively and unreflectively, freed from language. By giving pure experience priority, the sense of the human subject as an isolated, thinking self is less a grounding idea than a function of grammar which can be shed.[45]

The embodied awareness of a subject in Noh theatre resonates with the fleshy phenomenology of Merleau-Ponty. For Merleau-Ponty, a subject comes into a state of distinction through its naturalism:

> When I find again the actual world such as it is, under my hands, under my eyes, up against my body, I find much more than an object: a Being of which my vision is a part, a visibility older than my operations or my acts. But this does not mean that there was a fusion or coinciding of me with it: on the contrary, this occurs because a sort of dehiscence opens my body in two, and because my body looked at and my body looking, my body touched and my body touching, there is overlapping or encroachment, so that we must say that the things pass into us as well as we into the things.[46]

The Being that is found is composed on things that induce or excite action from the subject, and the subject brings these things into a life through deliberate attempts at increasing the range and depth of sensory experience marshalled through and gathered in the body, the 'natural self' whose expressions become co-terminus with the things being expressed, being made, in acts of improvised inquiry. As when in firing a kiln, the pot, the fire, the bricks, the potter are not objects with specific areas or heights, they have become potentialities of volume, and the vents into the kiln have become areas of sensitivity through which the potter can extend and enhance their involvement in the event of firing.[47] Habit comes with a memorized and anticipated experience of comprehension which lives between instinct and written procedure, it 'expresses our power of dilating our being-in-the-world, or changing our existence by appropriating fresh instruments.'[48] The craft worker going by feel as they bend a spliced willow, or peer into the red glow of a kiln, or work their hand along a seam.

---

[45] Kitarō Nishida *Intuition and Reflection in Self-Consciousness*. Translated by V. H. Vigliemo, Y. Takeuchi and J. S. O'Leary. New York: State University of New York Press. 1987.
[46] Maurice Merleau-Ponty *The Visible and the Invisible*. Translated by Alphonso Lingis. Evanstan: Northwestern University Press. 1968. 123.
[47] This is paraphrased from Maurice Merleau-Ponty *Phenomenology of Perception*. Translated by Colin Smith. London: Routledge. 1962 (2005). 165.
[48] Maurice Merleau-Ponty *Phenomenology of Perception*. 166.

This analogue view of habit as bodily comprehension belies the claim that human relations to objects are always correlations of being and subject, because somehow the subject is becoming being, there is little to correlate. The subject is bound up with the improvisation of the body as it works itself onto nature, and has nature work itself into it, the world is being grasped as the body becomes a knowing body: one belongs to oneself only insofar as one belongs to the world and this state of connexion occurs along a horizon of commitments that organize things as being near or far, all at once.[49] By horizon Merleau-Ponty does not mean a distance line from which, were one to stand there, one would see another horizon, from which, were one to move again, yet another would appear. It is not a topographical form, it is not a geometric, visual sense of spatial connexion, but an expressive one, in which all possible horizons appear at once.

When I see the bright green of one of Cézanne's vases, it does not make me think of pottery, it presents it to me. The pottery is there, with its thin, smooth outer surface and its porous inside, in the particular way in which the green varies in shade. In the inner and outer horizon of the thing or the landscape, there is a co-presence and co-existence of outlines which is brought into existence through space and time. The natural world is the horizon of all horizons, the style of all possible styles, which guarantees for my experiences a given, not a willed, unity underlying all the disruptions of my personal and historical life. Its counterpart within me is the given, general and pre-personal existence of my sensory functions in which we have discovered the definition of the body.[50]

Things appear as something, they are not nothing, yet they are always underway and can never appear as a completed synthesis, there are only ever interwoven horizons of nearness and farness, of presence and remoteness, which the subject bears as an ambiguous weight of consciousness that becomes aware that in seeing and sensing a vase, its colour and surfaces only appear by being brought near as other things, equally present, recede into a remoteness, creating a shifting scene of presenting and withdrawing that belongs to the subject, through their perceiving body. 'Things and instants' concludes Merleau-Ponty 'can link up with each other to form a world only through the medium of that ambiguous being known as a subjectivity, and can become present to each other only from a certain point of view and in intention.'[51] It is only through the orientations of historical life that things dawn, that they gather aspects, that they amass significance enough to stand outside of

---

[49] Maurice Merleau-Ponty *Phenomenology of Perception*. 474–475. See also Wendelin Kuepers *Maurice Merleau-Ponty (1908–1961)*. In *The Oxford Handbook of Process Philosophy and Organization Studies*. 413–431.
[50] Maurice Merleau-Ponty *Phenomenology of Perception*. 384–385.
[51] Maurice Merleau-Ponty *Phenomenology of Perception*. 388.

natural concourse and belong, instead, in the mysterious presence of subjectivity and it is here, not in their objectivity, that their reality withdraws and becomes impenetrable.

Nishida's own 'ambiguous being known as subjectivity' arises from his having experienced the *Meiji Ishin*, the restoration of the Emperor Meiji accompanied by an enforced policy of rapid industrialization that meant Japan turning towards the West and away from its own traditions. He shared many of the qualms that gave rise to the *Mingei* movement. What Japan gained in material wealth it lost in its soul; its very language was changing. Prior to *Meiji Ishin* there had been no Japanese character for craft work. It had been at the 1873 Vienna Universal Exposition, three years into Nishida's life, that the *Meiji* government, having accepted an invitation from the Austrians to build a pavilion, would embody the aesthetic and cultural qualities that European consumers were coming to associate with *Japanesrie*: natural surfaces, an obsessive concern with detail, technical skill, rich yet restrained decoration, and an ability to abstract, simplify and heighten the directly felt force of an image or object. In turn, the *Meiji* were keen to earn foreign currency and absorb Western industrial and technical know-how. The pavilion was strikingly different from those surrounding it. It was, by far, the smallest, and was tucked into one corner of the allotted plot having made way for a surrounding garden and small shrine. It housed a small collection of objects made across the different prefectures making up the Japanese kingdom, notably textile, lacquerware and ceramics (Figure 35).

Visitors were struck by impressions of calm humility and natural exposure. The objects on display evoked a culture at peace with the wider environment of which it was an intimate part. These impressions had been carefully managed by the pavilion's designers. Though anxious to open up to the West, the leading figures of the *Meiji* Restoration had wanted to do so on Japan's terms (one of its slogans being 'Japanese mind with Western knowledge', 和魂洋才 *wakon yôsai*).

Yet with Western knowledge came what for many Japanese was a threat to its unique cultural and social order. The very language itself was changing. Prior to Vienna, the Japanese had made little distinction between types of production: to distinguish between art, craft and manufacture was a Western obsession generated by the conceptual epistemology for which Nishida had a profound suspicion. Things were made, used, looked after and, if needed, replaced. In terms of grammar, crockery sat alongside votive offerings, tablecloths alongside silk screens, belt buckles alongside sculptures, oribi belts alongside umbrellas. They were all made things. Western markets, however, required a stricter declension of types of good, ranging from fine painting to

Figure 35 Japanese pavilion at the 1873 Vienna Exposition. © Transcendental Graphics / Getty Images.

mass-manufacture, and the Japanese obliged by creating new categories. Craft products, occurring somewhere in the grammatical 'middle', were initially *kôgyô* (工業) combining 'industry' and 'manufacturing' with a sense of human expertise (*takumi*, 巧), before being refined in the term *kôgei* (工芸), which allowed for a further split, distinguishing folk crafts made in workshops for everyday or occasional use, from artistic goods made for aristocrats and private individuals.[52]

Nishida's fear was that as language morphs so does the Japanese mind, prompting in turn an explicit intensification of the traditional values by which Japan sought to distinguish itself from the wider world to which it was opening. The habituated merger of nature-culture inherent in the

---

[52] Y. Kikuchi. 'The Myth of Yanagi's Originality: The Formation of 'Mingei' Theory in Its Social and Historical Context', *Journal of Design History*. 1994, 7, 4, 247–266. See also Brian Moeran. 'Bernard Leach and the Japanese Folk Craft Movement: The Formative Years', *Journal of Design History*. 1989, 2, 2/3, 139–144.

traditional Japanese lifestyle was being forced into an explicit dualism of subject and object in which naturalism became a topic of lifestyle choice and even consumerism rather than a disciplined disposition. The separation of subject also gave rise to its instrumental, reasoned elevation. *Kaibutsu*, for example, which roughly translates from the Japanese as revealing the nature of things or an opening up to nature, is both an ethically improving attentiveness to how the world is and an instrumental and agricultural sentiment to improve upon one's awareness of the workings of plants and animals. To spread manure and to germinate from the strongest seeds is to *kaibutsu*. By extension, however, *kaibutsu* became associated with technology and even industrial enterprise, to expand on the works of nature through advanced forms of manufacture, and then even to expand upon the presence of the nation itself as that most fit to reveal the latent riches of the world: from farming, to merchants, to imperialism.[53]

Inspired by Plato's dialogue *Timaeus*, which is an extended inquiry into the natural order of things, Nishida diagnosed the cause of this problematic dualism to be a spatial one. The most natural order is, for Plato, the most perfect. It is created by the demiurge, an immortal craftsman, and then imperfectly copied by humans attempting to create a properly organized society. The idea and its materialization; the perfectly rational and its reasonable if flawed application. Yet in addition to the ideal and its copy, the *Timaeus* introduces a third form, 'obscure and dim', which is 'the nurse of all becoming', and which resists the grammatical preposition of being a 'this' or 'that' for it is too unstable, too elusive, to warrant such fixing. It is a form that lacks discernible edges or steady states, a form that 'receives all things into it and has nowhere any form in any wise like to aught of the shapes that enter into it. For it is as the substance wherein all things are naturally moulded, being stirred and informed by the entering shapes; and owing to them it appears different from time to time.'[54] This formless and viewless form cannot take the form of that which enters as it is the form wherein all empirical things are moulded. Nor can it take the form of ideas as these have an inviolable, fixed form, as befits the perfect, which can neither be invaded by other forms nor be absorbed by them. Neither idealized, invariant Being, nor sensible, restless Becoming, but Space itself, which affords a place for all things:

---

[53] Tessa Morris-Suzuki *Re-Inventing Japan: Time, Space and Nation*. Armonk, NY: East Gate Books. 42–45.

[54] Plato *Timaeus* Translated and edited by R. D. Archer-Hind. London: MacMillan. 1888. 49 A. 171; 50 B–D. 177

Being and Space and Becoming, three in number with threefold nature, even before the heavens were created. And the nurse of becoming, being made liquid and fiery and putting on the forms of earth and air, and undergoing all the conditions that attend thereupon, displays to view all manner of semblances; and because she is filled with powers that are not similar nor equivalent, she is at no part of her in even balance, but being swayed in all directions unevenly, she is herself shaken by the entering forms, and by her motion shakes them again in turn[55]

The space that places Being (*khôra*) is also what receives and gives presence to that which is becoming, to the changeable, which otherwise would take no form, but which itself has no form and so cannot belong to the same class of form as the forms of becoming it contains.

Not everything from the West is corrupting, certainly not Plato, and Nishida, who is entranced by the concept of formless form, the *khôra*, conceives his own version: *Basho*. He also flips the Platonic hierarchy. Experientially we begin with apparently descriptive statements such as 'the wine has a red colour'. The objectivity of such a statement conceals the subject's intimacy, as in effect the statement should be 'I experience the wine as having a red colour', much like Homer writes of a 'wine dark sea'. Given we place ourselves outside of the world, we habitually ignore our involvement in the statement, but this is a convention, an anthropological practice. The problem with the predominating Western worldview was its having concealed the convention behind reason. The body, the form that connected the subject to nature, had been downgraded, almost relegated to the status of 'animalistic drives' to which the appropriate response was shame. The prevailing spirit had been, as the philosopher R. G. Collingwood suggested, 'to sterilize sensa by ignoring their emotional charge'.[56] To feel as you sense is to admit to a childish, expressive state that is hard to manage through rational appeal, and so far better to have it pushed into the shadows of the unthought, isolating the reasoning mind to a point where the emotional charge of what is felt is either concealed or consigned to proto-phenomena upon which thought can exercise discipline. Or so it is assumed. But, continues Collingwood, think further on the nature of sense and it becomes apparent that this sterilization is a grammatical exercise, not a natural fact. In thinking further, Nishida moved to the second *Basho* of relative nothingness. In the second *Basho*, the situational dependency of factual knowledge claims is revealed; those who claim to know things are alive to how human perspectives irredeemably taint all understanding, much

---

[55] Plato *Timaeus*. 55 A, 187.
[56] R. G. Collingwood *The Principles of Art*. Oxford: Oxford University Press. 1938. 171.

as wine would colour water. Nothing is free from the subjective perspective adduced in knowledge claims.

Yet relative nothingness is not the last space. If it were, the subject would be alone, corralling the world through a set of nihilistic, existential experiences where all is as nothing, like Roquentin, the protagonist in Jean Paul Sartre's novel *Nausea*, staring at the exposed root of a chestnut tree, scraping at it with his boot, exposing black bark:

> I looked at the root: was it more than black or almost black? But I soon stopped questioning myself because I had the feeling of knowing what the score was. Yes, I had already scrutinized innumerable objects, with deep uneasiness. I had already tried – in vain – to think something about them: and I had already felt their cold, inert qualities elude me, slip through my fingers ... The simplest, most unanalyzable quality had too much content for itself, was superfluous at heart. That black against my foot, it didn't look like black, but rather the confused effort to imagine black by someone who had never seen black, and who wouldn't know where to stop, who would have imagined an ambiguous being beyond colors. It looked like a color, but also – like a bruise or a secretion, like an oozing – and like something else, a smell, for example, it melted into the smell of damp earth, warm moist wood, into a black smell that spread like varnish over this nervous wood, in a flavor of chewed, sweet fiber. I did not simply see this black: sight is an abstract invention, an idea that has been cleaned up, simplified, one of man's ideas. That black there, amorphous, weakly presence, overflowed sight, smell, and taste. But this exuberance became confusion and finally it was no longer anything because it was too much.[57]

A nausea descends with the slow realization that all life was contingency, was gratuitous, the tree, the park, the event of encounter, but that the source of contingency and hence its weight was that it was thought by the subject and that this thinking thoughtfulness too was contingent, creating a vortex of twisted veneers, each tightening upon the other to create a disorienting groundlessness.

Lest the meaninglessness of relative nothingness prove too wearisome, Nishida proposes a third *Basho* of absolute nothingness, one which, provoked by the *khôra*, provides the space for the placing of basic subject–object distinctions from out of which consciousness, knowledge and judgment arise. It is a stabilizing space of 'zero organization' a formless form of experience, without individuation, which can be intuited but not conceptualized.[58] The subject creates individual things, including a sense of self, through acts of expression upon which we then reflect. The ensuing organization of these acts conceals

---

[57] Jean-Paul Sartre *Nausea*. New York: New Directions. 1964. 172–173.
[58] Taken from Robert Chia. *Nishida Kitarō (1870–1945)*. In *The Oxford Handbook of Process Philosophy and Organization Studies*. 287–302.

the third Basho of absolute nothingness, making it appear non-sensical, without a point, immaterial, but which, were we to shed our thinking and act directly back into it, would appear once more as the originating call to organize, the motivation towards order that is the life impulse of undifferentiated biological life.

Absorbing the practicalities of a Western worldview meant losing touch with not only the *Basho* of absolute nothingness, but also that of relative nothingness, leaving the Japanese bereft of the stepping stones towards a naturalism that was traditionally available to them through the naturalist sensibility of Zen and Shinto that permeated everyday practice, along with the things of craft work through which this sensibility might be fostered. In its organized advocacy for a restoration of the older ways of making and using things, the *Mingei* movement takes up the spirit of Nishida's work. At least to an extent. In their social and cultural riposte to Western industrial capitalism and its egocentric individualism, they hurried towards alternative forms of organising which were, potentially, just as limiting. For Yanagi and Leach there was a distinct hierarchy in craft work, an elite even, with Korean and Japanese work at the apex, followed by those European cultures that had fostered a tradition of working simply and close to nature. Without such tradition, argued Leach, a craft worker lacks both the unconscious support of an old country and a discerning clientele prepared to pay for handmade work.[59] In this regard, he continued, the United States suffered a double impoverishment 'In the first place, America, as an amalgam of races, does not provide a craftsman with the traditions of right making born on its own soil, secondly, its contemporary [ceramics] movement is by and large a post-war growth in a setting of high industry.'[60] Such a patently silly conclusion seemed to come naturally to Leach, and be far from silly, because he, like Yanagi, was convinced by theories of racial superiority when it came to craft work, a superiority that was grounded in an idealized form of naturalism, and for which he became a proselyte called the brown pot movement.

For the ceramicist Elizabeth Fritsch, Leach's influence on ceramic craft work has been as deadening as it has been uplifting: he pontificated on the superiority of life being lived according to the precepts of his *A Potter's Book*, encouraging readers to become followers of what amounted to

---

[59] For an insightful and extended discussion of the contorted reasoning Leach was using to marry his admiration for the simple, anonymous, natural craft workers with a patrician organizational dogma, see Brian Moeran 'Bernard Leach and the Japanese Folk Craft Movement: The Formative Years', *Journal of Design History*. 1989, 2, 2–3, 139–114.

[60] Quoted in Brent Johnsen *A Matter of Tradition: A Debate between Margaret Wildenhain and Bernard Leach*. In *The Ceramics Reader*. Edited by Kevin Petrie and Andrew Livingstone. London: Bloomsbury. 2017. 115.

creed. Fritsch points out that if colour is to be found in nature, as Leach suggests, then why is colour locked into the ochres of the earth; what of the air, the bright colours of the butterfly, of flowers?[61] The colour blue for example. Blue does not belong to the earth, it is a lofty colour, one the artist Yves Klein regarded as the closest colour to the most intangible parts of nature, the sea and sky: 'blue has no dimensions, it is beyond dimensions', it is formless, but remains utterly of nature. In questioning Leach's bent for earthy colours, Fritsch was not setting herself against nature, simply pointing out that if nature is to remain natural it cannot be seen to contain the rules of its own reading. Leach's insistence on what nature said may well be pertinent and penetrating, but it is far from gospel, and ought not to have been treated as such by others.[62]

## Afro-Mingei

A generative riposte to views like Leach's came in the exhibition *Plate Convergence* organized at the Hyde Park Art Centre in Chicago by the ceramicist Theaster Gates. On show was a collection of his ceramic plates, only in the show they were attributed to a fictional Japanese potter Shoji Yamaguchi who, having escaped Hiroshima, moved to Mississippi and married a Black civil rights activist. Under her influence he started making thin, elongated plates designed for the food preferred by Black people. The plates formed the centrepiece of dinners the couple organized to help promote dialogue around social and racial tensions. Though they died in a car accident, their son John Yamaguchi continued their work, hosting dinners and filming the conversations, providing an archive from which others might learn, including those attending the exhibition. John even appeared at the opening night, and attended a dinner hosted by Gates, who presented himself as an apprentice to Shoji Yamaguchi. The food was a Japanese Black fusion: black-eyed pea sushi. At the end of the opening night Gates admitted to the fabrication: that he had made the pots, that John was not the son of a ceramicist and Black activist but an actor, that the dinners had never taken place, save this one. The conceit troubled yet attracted the visitors; Gates had used fiction to disturb the standard rhythms of an opening night, the event

---

[61] Elizabeth Fritsch 'Crafts' Lives'. British Library. C960/25. Interviewed by Hawksmoor Hughes. 6/16. 1–9 mins.

[62] William Marshall was the most significant assistant at the Leach Pottery during Bernard Leach's lifetime, a skilled thrower, better than Leach, leaving the master free to decorate and finish the pieces, which somewhat goes against the mantra of *A Potter's Book* in which the maker brought hand, heart and head together in an entire process of making. Arguably, the Leach Pottery became a workshop organized through divisions of labour. See Murial Rose *Artist Potters in England*. London: Faber and Faber. 1970.

had become part of the art. He had also revealed the bias inherent in the White Western art world, a world where the value of objects like ceramics is deeply embedded with racial prejudice. The intent, Gates reflected, was to realize a generative state of fusion: 'I'm trying to couple *Mingei*, the folk craft movement in Japan, with the Black Arts Movement in the United States. In this moment [in the 1930s] Japan was saying, "Who we are is beautiful, we don't need Western culture to reaffirm our beauty and the importance of our craftsmanship and our people." In the United States 20 years later, Black people were saying, "Our hair and our skin are beautiful, and the objects and foods of our culture are important." There was a pattern here, a similar awakening, the resistance to a certain kind of Western whiteness created both movements, which I've brought together. That very strong philosophical meld led to a material meld, which is very exciting to me.'[63] *Afro-Mingei* was born.[64]

Prior to the exhibition Gates had always struggled to sell his pots, but re-invented as a Japanese master he became more authentic, more acceptable to a prejudicial world in which valuable, meaningful ceramics came from national living treasures presiding over traditional enclaves of excellence in the Far East, not from Black people living in Chicago, Illinois. When he was setting up the ruse and making work, Gates attests to how powerful he found his imaginary work, as though it really had been so, that the master potter and firebrand activist had established a Mississippi arts commune combining aesthetic discipline and political freedoms whose legacy he was charged with protecting and enhancing with his own work. The fiction provided political and social motivation whilst authorising an aesthetic experiment in fusing cultural traditions.[65] It was necessary because, as Gates testifies, he had no reasonable entry point of his own into ceramics. Ruth Duckworth, Hans Coper, these beautiful figures making amazing pots could not offer a way in for a Black potter from Chicago. He had been apprenticed in Japan, in Tokoname, where he had been taught to be humble, to realize excellence was always just outside of one's grasp, to repeat to the point where you get the form right, to venerate natural forms and forces. But back in

---

[63] Quoted in T. F. Chan 'Theaster Gates: London, Urban Reform and Exemplars of Black Excellence', *Wallpaper*. 25 October 2021. See also Lisa Yun Lee *Everything and the Burden Is Beautiful*. In *Theaster Gates*. London: Phaidon Press. 2020. 83. See http://chicagoartsdistrict.org/event_detail.asp?eventid=472 for the event details.

[64] Theaster Gates' ceramic work often revisits the wellspring of '*Afro-Mingei*' which incorporates Japanese elements with the culture of Africa and its diaspora. For instance, a 2019 piece titled *Afro-Ikebana*, comprises a bronze cast of an African mask paired with a rotund ceramic vessel containing a single branch, presented on a tatami mat.

[65] See 'Yamaguchi Soul Manufacturing Corporation and a Potter Named Dave: The Need for Blackness in Contemporary Ceramics', www.youtube.com/watch?v=v_QfJGPP974.

Chicago he needed more than the disciplined relation to clay to which students of the established tradition were being exhorted, more than the inspiration offered by the canon, and more pressing still he felt the need to invite more people into his practice, to enlist others into the world of ceramics, those bypassed by curators and museums as readily as by the large corporations and the state: what about their access points?

Access arrives in the guise of Dave the Potter, who, in 2010, formed the ur-figure for Gates' exhibition 'To Speculate Darkly'. Dave the Potter (also known as David Drake), was a nineteenth century ceramicist who had created extraordinary stoneware pots but who had suffered enslavement in the factories of Drakes Pottery. Released from bondage after the civil war, he established a stoneware business making large storage vessels, some of which continued to carry the inscriptions that he had felt compelled to write during servitude (Figure 36).

Again, Gates uses a figure to speculate upon the possibilities of making, though this time, being a real rather than fictional, Dave allows Gates to gain a reach and ambition that gives full voice to the indomitable, creative force of a maker. 'I will make, in the spirit of Dave Drake, the enslaved potter.'[66] As was common to enslaved people, Dave Drake's life story was held in small fragments and afterthoughts, yet it is precisely because of this fragmentary quality that Gates was able to generate a large, beautiful myth around which many different people might gather, widening the potentialities of making with clay, enveloping different audiences, blending craft work with other art forms like choirs who can sing about the power of pots, taking the power of Dave outside the confines of the museum shelf. Expand, embrace, bring in more variety, expose oneself to multiple forms of work, multiple materials. What gives to life is more than the maker, or maker and user connected by a single thing, but makers and users in concert, agitating, provoking, collaborating. After citing Drake, Gates continues to list further sources of guidance and provocation that jog and jig his imagination:

I will not forget that Derain and Matisse were taking cues from Bangwa Cameroon and Mbembe. I will not forget Nigeria or the West Side or Suriname or Gullah or Humphreys County, Mississippi, when I give my acceptance speeches or receive honorary degrees. I will also remember the cream-coloured earthenware trinket of a white farmer from Staffordshire, and the salt-glazed variegated grey stoneware jug of the seventeenth century that shows the ambition of British technology will always be on my mind, even in the Blackest conversations.[67]

[66] Theaster Gates *Reflections on Making*. In *Clay Sermon*. London: Whitechapel Gallery. 2022. 21.
[67] Theaster Gates *Reflections on Making*. In *Clay Sermon*. 21.

156    4 Naturalism

Figure 36 David Drake, storage jar, 1858. Alkaline-glazed stoneware. Metropolitan Museum of Art: 2020.7 / Purchase, Ronald S. Kane Bequest, in memory of Berry B. Tracy, 2020.

Impressed upon from all these sources, breathing them in, Gates then breathes out, involving not just other potters in the exhibition but poets, DJs dancers, jazz musicians, architects, all of whom become embroiled in the attempt to elevate the practice of craft and to elevate humans along with it, and clay was the basis of this breaking out, this *technē* that verges on *physis*; Dave was the access point to these repetitions of drawing in and giving out, like the lion-dog *Komainu* figures guarding Japanese temples, one open mouthed, the other closed, drawing in life and giving out life, the opening sound and the closing sound.

In later projects the clay was supplemented with concrete, with bricks, with tar, and single pots became manufactured pots, scaled through repetition. How far can one go beyond studio practice? There are no limits: urban planning resurrecting fallow buildings as community spaces (the work was largely funded by pieces Gates made from the remnants of the urinals of a disused and dilapidated, neo-classical style bank that he purchased for a single dollar); dinners hosted to bring folk from the block into communion; religious ceremonies to intensify belief; making bricks to then make the thing that makes the thing. The tradition expands, and gradually clay and the studio become part of a broad ecology of mayoral politics, philanthropy, property development, music, prayer and meditation. Gates confines the pot to a small space, but then explodes it, in combination, great things can be realized through the collaborative and affirmative creation of questions. Gates opens the casing of tradition and lets out into free and open play what was held within, refusing what is essential and hierarchical, and putting in place a 'universal relativity' of subjective perspectives through which the styles and techniques of making become available for as many enquiries as is possible.

The amended from of *Mingei* for which Gates is such an energetic advocate calls on the capacity of subjects to make connexions, preferably between everything; to begin, again, to re-organize what is already organized. It is an advocacy that has even, if only liminally, found voice in Japan too. After the capitulation of World War II, opposition towards the emperor became organized, and no more so than in the figure of Masao Maruyama Stationed in Hiroshima in 1945 as an enlisted member of the emperor's Imperial Army, Masao had witnessed the tragic effects of what he felt had been the inability of Japan's ruling class to adapt with a newly emerging commercial and technological reality. The reason, he suggested, was because the leaders, as all Japanese leaders before them, believed themselves fit to rule by virtue of their natural birth (just as Yanagi and Leach assumed themselves a natural cultural elite). As the people venerated nature they would, by extension, venerate their natural born leaders, unquestioningly. To challenge a leader's ruling was as nonsensical as challenging the perfume of a lily, and so whilst its trade routes had opened up in the wake of the Viennese exposition and the *Meiji* expansion, its ruling classes had steadfastly remained closed-off and turned inward. Though forced to justify their position explicitly, and especially so in the wake of the disastrous involvement in World War II, their continued appeal to the unparalleled beauty and excellence of (traditional) Japan had been largely successful.[68] The phrase *Hito to shizen to no wa* (Between humans and nature there is harmony) went by way of a Gospel that was instantiated and extended through an array of seasonal festivals, shrines, gardens and flower arrangements and architecture, all of which cohered in an ordering of human attention and loyalty characterized by its circular regularity. As one generation passes to the next, and one leader is succeeded by the next, nothing changes, the hierarchy of relations remains: sea below earth, earth below heaven, peasants below lords, lords below emperors, women below men, foreigners below Japanese, and with this order comes benevolence, abundance and munificence, with strife comes hostility, scarcity and abuse. No need to speculate using counter-factual reasoning, there is one order towards which all things incline. To refuse it is a perversity.

Maruyama refuses, Hiroshima had been too much to bear. The society and culture had to change. What was needed, he argued, was an organizational means to puncture the sealed-off nature of all elites. It came in the perverse figure hitherto unthought in Japanese society: an autonomous subject. Though possibly alone in the freedom of their loneliness, and risking the excesses of the subject distinction against which Nishida warned, in Maruyama's thoughts such a figure was far from isolated. They were very much part of the cultural and social organization by which a new Japan might flourish. They were a mechanism for challenging and so rejuvenating the collective, self-serving decision making of the elite groups that dominated nearly all walks of Japanese life. Their function, however, was not to oppose, but to propose anew, it was agonistic rather than antagonistic, which resonates with Gates' call to expand the tradition, and even, if inevitably indirectly, with the direct, bodily intuition of absolute nothingness as the space from which all differentiation occurs. In ancient Greece *agon* denotes a place or assembly of argument between protagonist and antagonist, an experience of tension between players in a tragedy, and between language and those using and listening to it. To refuse the *agon* was to shun the basic organizational space by which a robust and vibrant city state would thrive. Through his advocacy of an autonomous individual Maruyama commits to a similar organization of dissent to revivify the Japanese

---

[68] Julia Thomas 'The Cage of Nature. Modernity's History in Japan', *History and Theory*. 2001, 40, 1, 16–36.

public body. Without the generation of different standpoints that permit the expression and pursuit of difference, a society becomes held fast by an ossifying and corruptible consensus. The subject carries the *agon*, this is its nature, its life.

## Form and Natural Form

In the arts of sculpture and painting, suggested Friedrich Schiller, the struggle is to annihilate the material by means of the form, and the more imposing, stubborn and alluring the material, the more impressive is the art which asserts its mastery.[69] As the painter Piet Mondrian did on the beaches of Zeeland, staying at the artist colony in Domburg on the confluence of the Rhine, the Meuse and the Schuldt, the indefinite, silted disappearance of northern Europe draining itself into a salt-glazed, grey sea. The only definitive presence in this estuarine flow are the groynes: thinning, punctuated wooden piles set in vertical series, one after the other. Looking along the beach, the verticals lose distinction and the groynes become horizontals that staple the otherwise featureless, wind-scarred sands to the advancing and receding waves. They become a loosely orthogonal array of intersecting incisions, hesitant unions and departures, a language of lines, which gave birth to the universal signs of *De Stijl*, pure form.

The painter Frank Auerbach re-iterates this artistic interest in form, though dispenses with the language of domination and complete abstraction:

> I am interested in form itself, not in what the form says about life. The recognition of any form is a judgment concerning how one form differs from another form, it is utterly relational. To concentrate on these relations is to abstract from the everyday in order that form itself is revealed. The more abstract the more impoverished the material and purpose, and the more intense the relation between efficient and formal cause. A collection of forms making a single form, a worthwhile form. Whether it is a vase, a plate, a jug, even a vessel is secondary.

To get here, however, is not to begin with ideas and abstractions, but to secure the form from within the empirical beginnings of material space, pushing and goading the painting into a truthfulness not to life, but to itself.[70] What works in a painting is in the painting, not what it represents, though to get at the truth inside a painting means starting with a manifest thing, and then patiently and with discipline examining it,

---

[69] Friedrich Schiller *On the Aesthetic Education of Man*. New York: Dover. 2004. 106.
[70] Catherine Lampert *Frank Auerbach Speaking and Painting*. London: Thames and Hudson. 89.

working against it, continually looking for the tension, space and movement to be found in materials. It is in this way that one gets at the form.

Craft work cannot pursue form in quite the same way. The craft worker cannot become so intent upon discovering a form from within forms, though some, like Fritsch can get close, before stopping, because she cannot shed the vessel. But then Auerbach never quite sheds the secondary forms of the human body or a street, so there is a sympathy here between those craft workers who repress the material and purposeful elements of making to then investigate how close they might make the relationship between themselves and the form. Fritch's pieces are not at all useful, but they remain clay vessels and retain vestiges of function; they are, she suggests, a little ironically but not untruthfully, 'metaphysical ware'.[71] The vessel matters (she cannot be a sculptor outside of the vessel form). It is the vessel, she suggests, that allows her to structure dialogues between the dualisms inherent to the language of form: inside and outside; front and back (a quiet side and one with rhythms); old and new; earth and air; light and dark; tangible and intangible (pots are to be held in hand, but also they are like still-life objects, with spaces); colour and monochrome; real and surreal. The vessel confines the pieces to port, to a protected space where it can be blown and bob about, sheltered from the open sea, close to the landscape of human practices.

Seamus Heaney spoke of two modes of knowing: the practical and the poetic, and of how it was possible, with discipline, and technique to move between them, across the gap, which was more a fault line that one might occupy as one's home. To transition in this way, to move across boundaries, was to arrive at an understanding of why vision only really caught hold if it was scarred with the subtleties and tolerances of ordinary concourse, which is where Auerbach made his home. Fritsch's vessels too retain this concourse with practicality, with the making, and in an echo of Michael Cardew and John Dewey, she is critical of those for whom the idea or concept is everything.

In its being a continual and disciplined coming together of thinking and acting, of the practical and poetic, Fritsch's work resonates with Ruskin's advocacy of craft work as a blend of physical intellect and thoughtful bodily movement, a union he meant as a riposte to those designers who traded in ideas and concepts, leaving the execution to others: 'Now it is only by labour that thought can be made healthy, and only by thought that labour can be made happy, and the two cannot be

---

[71] Elizabeth Fritsch 'Crafts' Lives'. British Library. C960/25. Interviewed by Hawksmoor Hughes. 6/16. 15 mins.

# Form and Natural Form 161

separated with impunity. It would be well if all of us were good handicraftsmen in some kind, and the dishonour of manual labour done away with altogether.'[72]

In an interview with Hawksmoor Hughes, Fritsch describes in patient detail just how this union allows one of her vessels to come to life; throwing is too quick. Hand building is liberating, it allows you to pause and pause again, hand and head in constant, instinctual dialogue.[73] The vase, she suggests, can be an individual, which begins with a foot, rolled out in coils then flattened then let to dry a little so the sides can stand up without flopping about (hence working on two at a time, working on one whilst other dries). The vase sides then get built up, without moulds, the pieces are rolled and slapped and joined with slip, eventually cutting them off to make them level, to be capped by a neck made from small squares set at an angle. She speaks of having a sense of the size and shape, but only roughly. Once the form is realized, then it dries quite quickly as her walls are made thin, at least towards the top. It is then biscuit fired (1160 degrees). She is wary of having the form dry out at different rates, and it has only been with the slow acquisition of technical proficiency that the size has been able to grow, the scale comes with expertise. The biscuit fired pot is then undercoated with a layer of slip, which fills in the dimples in the groggy clay base, and which stops the white grog coming through in the subsequent glaze firing, which is taken up to 1200 degrees. Then a gridded pattern, a rhythm, is sketched on with brush, but only with dots as otherwise the grid can come through after the re-firing. Following the correlations with music and its combination of rhythm, melody and harmony, the grid combines with the form, as it follows the curves, so it emerges from the body, the grid gives the form a dynamic quality (it does not subvert it). It might start being horizontal and vertical, yet the form then distorts it, creating collisions which appear on the other side of the vase, the form creates the collisions and these then belong to the form. She then improvises on the grid by painting on shapes, usually orthogonal boxes which float and distort easily and are very easy to read. Complicated shapes do not destroy nicely. These are delineated in alternating colours, applied separately as each colour requires its own firing, a little like a woodcut being printed again and again as the block is covered with the different coloured inks. Reds and yellows need to go on last as they fire at 1200 not 1250 degrees, and these are often lost if she needs to go back up to

---

[72] John Ruskin *The Stones of Venice, Vol. II.* §21. 201.
[73] Edward Lucie Smith *Elizabeth Fritsch: Vessels from Another World/Metaphysical Pots in Painted Stoneware*. London: Bellew Publishing. 1993.

Figure 37 Elizabeth Fritsch, *Piano Pot with Counterpoint, Black Diamonds*, 1978. Stoneware with coloured slips. Image courtesy of Adrian Sassoon, London. Photography: Sylvain Deleu.

1250 to fix other colours like greens or whites. The shapes are strict and precise, the colours correlate to harmony in music, and in combination the vessels reach the form of a melody, and the gaps are silences.[74] An individual vase can go through eight firings, depending on colour range and the shifts in judgment during making, as she discovers how, like counterpoint, under-colour influences over colour (Figure 37).[75]

---

[74] Elizabeth Fritsch 'Crafts' Lives'. British Library. C960/25. Interviewed by Hawksmoor Hughes. 6/16. 16–20 mins.
[75] Elizabeth Fritsch 'Crafts' Lives'. British Library. C960/25. Interviewed by Hawksmoor Hughes. 15/16 10–24–29 mins.

The finished vase has a solid, almost funerary form, but like a *Gestalt* figure, looked at carefully, it drifts and stretches, then snaps back into ordered shape, then drifts again. Each piece, she suggests, has to realize a kind of composed equilibrium with itself (as Auerbach's paintings); the solidity is palpable, yet it leans, and this disturbance is in places accentuated, yet in others resisted, by the rhythms of painted geometry and colour which work to re-calibrate the angles, volumes and planes set in place by the slabs of clay: heavy dark dense colour and celestial colour combine in a kind of testy though ultimately respectful dialogue.

## Grace and the Body

Form emerges from the life struggle between an organism and its wider, natural environment. The black root system of the chestnut tree in front of which Roquentin had his vision of nothingness, for example, is created when the demands emerging from the internal organic needs of a plant cooperate with external materials to a point where the former are met and the latter transformed in what John Dewey calls a 'satisfying culmination' of coherence, endurance and order.[76] The order of these culminations is not immanent to them, but emerges from within the grammar of those to whom they appear (the correlation of thought and being). It is something to apprehend from observation, as did the Victorian poet Gerard Manley Hopkins, who noted how, if one observes what is it about a tree that draws attention (he is being both practical and poetic), both practical and poetic), tames its interesting irregularities in such a way that from a distance its mature silhouette will be a perfectly balanced dome capping a stout upright, and yet from within be a variegated tangle of cavorting lines and light: an inner canopy as alive with alternates as its outer edge is calm with agreement.[77] The growth of the tree is a continual achievement in harmonization of regularities and varieties, an order amongst distinct forms whose gathering brings parts, as parts, into a fecund whole, which form more parts. More impressive still, Hopkins continues, not being prone to the self-disgust felt by Sartre's protagonist, nature does not struggle to attain this harmony, it appears thus as *physis*, without intention, its appearance needs no reason for its apprehension. The same for a mussel shell, a beehive or bird's nest. Form is the continual organization of the natural

---

[76] John Dewey *Art as Experience*. New York: Minton Balch & Co. 1934. 24.
[77] Gerard Manley Hopkins *Poems and Prose*. Edited by W. H. Gardner. London: Penguin. 1966. 100–102.

energies by which an organism might relate to its environment, and as such it is the essential mark of life.[78] When organisms are able to exploit the order they encounter in the world by absorbing it, swallowing it, appropriating it, they secure life, and if they fail, they die. They do not own this order, they have no title to it, yet their internal body is of such a nature that it overreaches itself and acquires what is not naturally theirs. The organism goes outbound, on an adventure, impelled to gather what it finds and bring it into itself.

Human beings are distinct as organisms because this outbound adventure into the broader environment produces conscious thought, they gather stories which are memorized and produce historical life in which the ordering of other as well as their own struggles towards form are set down: 'Blind surge has been transformed into purpose; instinctive tendencies are transformed into contrived undertakings. The attitudes of the self are infused with meaning.'[79] And it, suggests Dewey, is in acts of creative and improvised making things that this thoughtfulness receives its most direct, immediate and so natural expression. In acts of making, conscious awareness is mediated through objects and materials which are allowed or encouraged to speak as much for themselves and their own struggle for form as for their creators. Scientists might also be said to be close to nature in this way given they, like craft workers, develop material expertise in physical analysis and laboratory experiments. Yet as they analyse and theorize, their language intercedes and begins to generate its own forms and it is through these – symbols and signs – that nature is then represented and understood, becoming almost a parallel world made up of abstract terms that talk to, yet remain distinct from, empirical experience. In craft work, materials remain a medium for the organisms' (the craft worker, and potentially the user) understanding, the expertise circuits and cycles through repeated inquiries into the different ways in which the made thing 'is', how it gains what Nishida calls its separation from within its relations with the wider environment. How do the medullary rays flow through quarter-sawn oak? How can a blanket of velvet envelop yet resist or deform the contours of a human body? How might the willow yield and colour over time as it is bent through a basket frame? How can the bake in the bread be intensified to a point where its crust blisters but not burns? How will a mix of mordents fix the dye evenly, or sporadically?

In being bodily bound into such material relations, a craft worker acquires what John Dewey goes on to call a sense of grace: they can

---

[78] John Dewey *Art as Experience*. 24.
[79] John Dewey *Art as Experience*. 59.

move through their environment with a disciplined ease that attains a state of poise in which bodily motion merges with sense, and sense into bodily motion, and the two – sense and body – are entwined so as to fit the different milieux in which they are living out life. The form of their own body is a bundle of acquired, expressive intelligence, but it is one that does not stop at the skin. Just as the fish takes its shape from the fluid nature of water, so the craft worker's body takes form from what Dewey calls the transdermal transactions with its milieux, which is what Merleau-Ponty meant when he spoke of flesh: flesh is more than a corporeal substance of the body; it is incarnate, imbued with memory and expectation, with 'its own decisions', a milieu of connexions through which a felt and conscious life appears in the gathering of a subject. The body follows the edges of other bodies and other things, and other processes, sometimes sinuous, sometimes implacable, always receptive. The craft worker learns early on that their skill and learning is not being directed by a singular mind set like a nebulous jewel within a mute, flesh and bone structure. It is the peculiar gift of the craft worker to be given permission to reassess the legitimacy of the heightened mind, and instead to invoke the body first. And to sense in the body a form that thrives when its discernible edges – its skin – become attuned to what lies beyond: the skin does not separate the body from its environment, it transacts, taking and giving.

Dewey, spurred by having read a letter from the poet John Keats to the poet's brother, finds in grace a capacity to bear uncertainty without any 'irritable reaching after fact and reason',[80] without having to secure grounds for their action or belief. The only truth is a breaking beauty, and such beauty the only truth, because the certainties and agreements upon which any truth relies are formed from a sensual and emotional experience of harmony in form whose unity and presence, like that of the poet, is fleeting. Those without grace tend towards the dogmatic or egoistic, eclipsing their everyday being either with metaphysical pronouncements issued from a pulpit, or with assertions of the will made from a pedestal. From either of these elevations everyday life appears as something 'down there', and full of unfortunate obstacles. Those with

---

[80] John Dewey *Art as Experience*. 33. John Keats' framing was, as French elaborates, an ironic play on the positive connotations of the active term capability and the diminishing ones of negativity. Keats was advocating the poet endeavour to acquire a capaciousness within which contraries might be contained, a void or nothingness through which experience heightens and emboldens itself through the shadowy allusions and hints of half-knowledge. See Robert French 'Negative Capability: Managing the Confusing Uncertainties of Change', *Journal of Change Management*. 2001, 14, 5, 480–492. See also Robert Gittings (editor) *The Letters of John Keats: A Selection*. Oxford: Oxford University Press. 1970.

grace need no eminence from which to pronounce. As they transact with their environment they have, instead, the acuity to absorb experiences like resistance, joy, anxiety, despair or uncertainty as opportunities for learning the ways things might work, a knowledge of which, suggests Philip Larkin, we humans are often ignorant:

> Strange to be ignorant of the way things work:
> Their skill at finding what they need,
> Their sense of shape, and punctual spread of seed,
> And willingness to change;
> Yes, it is strange,
>
> Even to wear such knowledge – for our flesh
> Surrounds us with its own decisions –
> And yet spend all our life on imprecisions,
> That when we start to die
> Have no idea why.[81]

Those with grace encounter obstacles through expansion, not contraction: all the senses are being used, the materiality of the embodied interaction is appraised in both its actual and potential guises, the emotions arising from frustrated attempts at integration are encountered as provocations rather than signs of disorder requiring immediate correction. Above all, and going back to Keats and then Dante, the poet (or craft worker) should be one who refuses to take centre stage, and instead makes themselves present from the sidelines, as a 'face writ in water', one whose personality was always of a provisional, diverted, curious quality that refused to be elevated and which, instead of plaudits and laurels, sought the further stimulation of making anew, and learning. Their body creates bodies which find their place amid other bodies, again and again.

As the potter Magdalene Odundo notices, there is an intimacy between the earth and people: it is a striking consistency that nearly all origin myths have humans being first fashioned from clay. Her vases encompass what it is to be human: the smooth necks stretch upwards as though willing themselves to gain new perspectives, blushing with uncontrolled bursts of colour, the bodies bulge generously and protectively; and just as vases contain and protect, so might human beings be considered as vessels containing and preserving ideas and cultures, protecting children, and yet always opening up to what is beyond them. Speaking of her work being shown in *The Journey of Things*, an exhibition at the Hepworth Museum in Wakefield, UK, Magdalene Odundo commented:

---

[81] Philip Larkin 'Ignorance'. In *The Whitsun Weddings*. London: Faber and Faber. 1964. 39.

When I'm actually making, I'm trying to capture something. I start off with an idea that I've been drawing – I tend to work in series – and the works never manifest themselves like they do on paper. A lot of it is my heart, my gut and my head all working together, especially when I'm actually working on capturing the essence of what I'm trying to say in that piece. Sometimes I'm on tiptoes trying to will the piece to get taller, or have my hands on my hips or my waist because I'm trying to constrict it, like a corset.[82]

Clay moves, it flexes, it twists and contorts, like a human body, there is an intimacy between the human and the pot, between their bodies which can assume so many different poses and shapes and gestures. Her pots have bellies, nipples, necks, alive with sensation, the flaring patches of burnished glow on lips, as though anticipating a kiss. Synthesising processes used in Abuja and ancient Greece towards her own distinctive end, she works with the Ugandan emsubi technique of hand-building pots from un-glazed terracotta covered in extremely fine particles of ground clay applied to the surface before they are fired. This lends them an immaculate smoothness and soft sheen, like the skin of a pepper. Those fired in an oxidised kiln burst out in an orange-red, and those fired in a carbonising kiln yield towards a glossy black that seems to glow from within. Sometimes, these apparent certainties are disrupted with flame-like plumes of contrasting shades, in spectacular eruptions.

This gathering of clay, fire and the forming hands of a human body is biological: the life of any organism is dependent on its permeability to processes that exceed it and to which it must accede if it is to live. The form is an aspect of an interpenetrating array of mutually dependent structures and processes to which all life submits. The gathering is also aesthetic: the good life is realized when a body acquires a graceful state in which its own form resonates with wider systems with an economy and coherence of expression. The form is not just a spatial presence, a structure. It cannot dispense with structures, but 'it differs from structures as walking differs from legs and breathing from lungs',[83] a difference that, Dewey continues 'is always an inclusive affair involving connection, interaction of what is within the organic body and what lies outside. In space and time, and with higher organisms far outside.'[84]

Just how far outside is a moot point. At some threshold point this reaching out will disturb the phenomenological experience of grace, or at least complicate it, given the possibility for what Bateson

---

[82] www.apollo-magazine.com/magdalene-odundo-interview/, 28 January 2019.
[83] John Dewey *Experience and Nature*. London: George Allen & Unwin. 1929. 292.
[84] John Dewey *Experience and Nature*. 282.

calls 'trans-contextual' experiences which upset the expected, regional context set for specific kinds or classes of response.[85] These experiences push grace outwards into an awareness of how a human organism at work might become aware not only of its own immediate environment, but of wider environments and the manner in which these overlap and or are nested in one another: a stem bears leaves which in turn have axils, which in turn generate buds, which are then stems, which become branches, all of which provide sustenance in different ways to insects and birds, which in turn sustain other mammals and plants of a woodland, and so on, outwards, occasionally reaching the woodworker who cuts, soaks and bends the branches ready for fixing into the back of a chair. The form (communication, hence grammar) of each environment is governed by the environments in which it is set, and the environment it sets for others.[86]

To act on prompts from this trans-contextual awareness is to create what Bateson calls a 'double bind', a shiver of, or severance from, an immediate setting in order to apprehend a wider, or smaller one, to which one also becomes bound, but as much through curiosity as necessity or the stipulation of distinct ends. The double bind can be pathological for the organism if its context-setting habits and goals are shadowed or challenged to the point of dissolution and incomprehension. Yet if, Bateson suggests, somewhat equivocally, 'this pathology can be warded off or resisted, the total experience may promote creativity'.[87] This warding off happens when the capacity for a double take becomes the subject of deliberate attention; where the double take itself becomes abstracted through training (as when Dante feels and distils this feeling into a site for his own creative observation). In craft work this double bind has both an aesthetic and an ethical aspect. Aesthetic because innate to craft work is an exploration of form beyond obvious function coupled to an intimacy with material on its own terms; ethical because innate to craft work is a concern for living alongside otherness (flaws, alien things, nature, discarded or forgotten things, time-worn things) as reminders that things can always be otherwise. In combination, grace becomes the preparation for adventure in this world, for striving outwards to explore the potential for taking on form. In this struggle towards grace the craft worker's form corresponds with other forms, attending to movements and amending their own, alive to environmental change and partaking of its demands and nuances as naturally as a feather takes to the winds, blending and bending

---

[85] Gregory Bateson *Double Bind*. In *Steps to an Ecology of Mind*. London: Intertext. 1972. 275.
[86] Gregory Bateson *Double Bind*. 276.
[87] Gregory Bateson *Double Bind*. 278.

its own form in the shape of those to which it defers, but upon which it takes flight. Tacita Dean is a good example, describing in an interview how, whilst wrestling with a film based on the character *Antigone*, she tried to persuade the Canadian poet Anne Carson who was also working on similar themes, to come to Thebes where Sophocles set the play, but it was difficult, so Dean found another town called Thebes in Illinois, USA, and they collaborated there instead, in the middle of nowhere in particular, but coincidently during the immediate aftermath of Donald Trump's first presidential victory, and when there was a solar eclipse happening in nearby Wyoming, so the themes of blindness, the abuse of power, the emptying force of wilderness, all of which figure large in the original plot, organized themselves anew. These re-alignments and creative connexions were, suggests Dean, more down to her own openness than to accident: 'I always use the phrase "being in a state of grace" … Sometimes when you are working hard and open to things you start to see patterns. I am not thinking of grace in a religious way, just in your head.'[88] And body.

## Language, the Digital and the Analogue

The naturalism which Ruskin accorded to Gothic work, and by extension felt was proper for all craft work, evokes a sense of direct intimacy with natural forms that is being lost to industrial capitalism. Yet because of language, nature has always been withdrawing; what is natural to the human condition is that any expressive coupling with nature in the raw, so to speak, is always troubled by the grammatical contortions of a speaker or writer attempting to extricate themselves from language. Craft work would seem to offer an alternate form of coupling in which the spoken and written word give way to material presence and movement involving all the sensory potential of the human body. No longer just a thinking subject making remarks about things and events, but an active, immersed being making marks with and alongside things that are given an equal presence and that kick back even, interrupting the immersive flow of skilled work, demanding the work make space. Language is being pushed aside and craft work is getting closer in.

The use of text to explain the made things, or to label them, is often treated with suspicion by craft workers, who often resist or only begrudgingly accept requests to expand upon the meaning behind their work. In the catalogue for the 1981 *The Maker's Eye* exhibition, David Pye spoke of crafted things having a beauty that could not be explained: 'It is the

---

[88] Interview with Tim Adams. *The Guardian*, 11 March 2018.

nature of beauty that it cannot be pointed out, It speaks for itself: it may or may not be heard but no one can speak for it.' And when asked how his own work related to such things he lamented the question, suggesting 'it would be better, far better, if no craftspeople, no artists of any kind, were ever asked to say what they seek to achieve. When we try, most of us (present company always excepted!), seem to engender a lot of gobbledygook or else a flock of duck-billed platitudes.'[89] It is, De Waal says, somewhat regretfully, part of the craft tradition to leave it to others to take up the pen and speak for the maker,[90] they are to generate the ideas through the conscious control of aesthetic means, whereas the craft worker controls through the muting confines of a tradition.[91]

The potter Lucie Rie was equally reticent. Like Pye, when asked to write a piece for the journal *Craft Horizons* on the motivation and meaning of her work, she refused, admitting to the journalist 'and designs – I am not very clear about them – I have no urge to express myself – I never had – or I do not know in which tradition I work. There are so many influences from people and books and old pots – sometimes from modern ones.'[92] Likewise, as a teacher, rather than instruct and overburden the experience with 'musts', Rie encouraged self-discovery. One apprentice, Max Mayer (1995), comments 'She denied that she had anything to 'teach', trusting to unlock the potential of someone with whom she felt a kind of consonance and then nudge him or her towards their own individuality, as may be seen from the work of her serious pupils who were never moved to copy her in any way.'[93]

The work itself was enough, especially if it 'sung', to use Pye's phrase to describe made things that stood out, and which, to recall the earlier discussion of Pye's views on expertise, sounds dangerously close to deviating from rather than confirming or improving any designed intent. In Rie's case this standing out was all the more apparent because her

---

[89] David Pye *The Maker's Eye*. London: Crafts Council Publications. 1981. 56.
[90] Edmund De Waal Speak for yourself. *Ceramic Review*. 182, March/April 2000. De Waal wonders whether craft work might not improve under the self-administered gaze of the word. Rather than leave the writing jobs to critics, many of whom operate to an assumed, habituated evaluative hierarchy which ranks craft well below fine art, why not take the job on oneself? Many do attempt to create a conceptual space that allows them to consider their own work, and which helps frame discussions of it amongst others. But for many more an ethos of enigmatic and disciplined attentiveness to making is the priority, and maintaining an earthy silence goes a long way to cultivating this.
[91] Theodore Adorno *Universal and Particular*. In *Aesthetic Theory*. Edited by Gretel Adorno and Rolf Tiedemann. London: Continuum. 2002. 199–224. 213.
[92] Lucie Rie, letter, 1951, 2002.26.132.2a/b Lucie Rie Archive at the Crafts Study Centre, Farnham, UK.
[93] Max Mayer 'Working with Lucie', *Ceramic Review*. 1995, 154, 16.

pieces not only 'sang', they bore a foreign tone. As an émigré thrust into a new place having had to escape Nazi persecution after the March 1938 Anschluss in Austria, Rie admitted to experiences of profound humility as she familiarized herself with the big and small influences of a new home.[94] The bowl on the table, the potter in the workshop, the woman with herself and a small world of friends. Her pots, as Edmund de Waal suggests, born of the émigré, the figure who, living on the outside and without deep roots, relies on their self-conscious autonomy to work at objects that share this self-sufficiency; they too exude 'a serious, private kernel' that discloses itself strikingly, because ever so silently, without the backup of words, of theories, of rhetorical flourishes; its material presence suffices (Figure 38).[95]

Like the émigré, the pot lives outside the natural habits of indigenous grammar, whilst acknowledging its dependence upon them to be noticed and taken up. As the ousted Austrian and German Jews living in north London were wont to say on arriving in their adopted homeland: they were 'With the English, but not of the English'.

This ambivalence towards language even extends to the small legends that can accompany well-made things: the name, date, material composition and explanatory text begin to underscore a piece in a way that refuses to let it speak for itself. *The Maker's Eye* exhibition, to which Pye's selection of things was one of fourteen selections by different makers all of whom had been asked to choose objects which encapsulated the idea of craft, had no legends. The things were shown as they were. The range of objects was uneven and provocative: violin, toothing plane, attaché case, morris board, child's highchair, broaches, Sussex trug, Westwood's Seditionaries boot, Fritsch's vase *Black Shadow of Death*, and lettering. The lettering was chosen by David Kindersley, a typographer, calligrapher, engraver, for whom the letter has a materiality outside of its function within grammar. Craft workers making text understand this materiality, they appreciate that if text is treated simply for its functional (digital) role it rarely functions well because the shapes and intensities with which it appears can affect meaning in a profound way. A reader can be drawn into a text through its beauty and can drown in the message as they become lost in its medium or become indifferent if the font or layout is thoughtless.

---

[94] In its original use, naturalization described a willingness to embrace the foreigner on equal terms with the native. To be naturalized was to be accommodated as an alien, to be accepted in and amid the locals, but without being subsumed by them. Naturalization invokes the authority of nature, specifically its evident capacity to harmonize contraries and realize order amongst difference.
[95] Edmund de Waal 'Speak for Yourself', 32–34.

172   4 Naturalism

Figure 38 Lucie Rie, *Vase*. Porcelain, brown/black glaze over pale body with sgraffito bands. Photograph: Jane Coper. © Estate of Jane Coper / Estate of Lucie Rie. From the collections of the Crafts Study Centre, University for the Creative Arts 2002.26.365.6a.

The alphabet is a digital system which forms what the media theorist Alexander Galloway calls a homogenous substrate. It is an underlabourer that can be brought into infinitely variable combinations, without ever transgressing the integrity of each part; it exists outside time and history.[96] The integers and letters, punctuation marks and symbolic equivalences, the notes and staves can be brought into the most intense, passionate, resonant or unruly congregations, yet always maintain their individuating integrity and force. Their potency is not worn out in use. In contrast to a digital system like an alphabet, an analogue system consists of a heteronomous substrate of multiple things differing in their nature yet also somehow associative, continuous, similar across themselves, hence qualitatively they transform, becoming kin through proportionate comparisons, such as a wasp and orchid, whose varied and qualitatively different life forms arrange themselves in analogically sympathetic ways; the wings and the petals become intimate in gesture and colour, they harmonize mimetically. The associative sympathies between insect and flower that organize a gathering of intensities of attraction are still a language, but one of aesthetics rather than grammar. In the same way, lettering and object can be brought together and cohere as things that act as suitable media for craft work, as in Kindersley's (Figure 39).

Letters can be things. Likewise, suggested René Magritte, in his short text *Words and Images*, there are 'objects which do without a name', and 'words that can take the place of an object in reality', and 'names of an object that take the place of an image'. If attended to with due seriousness, the liminal wash between language and nature are disorienting and destabilizing.

Traditionally, however, in language it has been the digital which trumps the analogue. Galloway teases out the difference with suggestive economy: where the digital language is internally homogenous yet outwardly multiple, the analogue is internally homogenous yet outwardly singular: in digital life, 1 becomes 2; in analogue life, 2 becomes 1.[97] The process by which this digital alphabet starts to accumulate authority is a quite natural one as with a written language comes the possibility for definition and a clarity of communication not available in the analogue. To define and communicate definitions clearly relies, in turn, on signs and structures that allow for consistent pairing of the signified and signifier. Symbols combine and re combine to make marks in a represented world in which anything whole is always an amalgam of classified and categorized parts: there is a 'this' and a 'that', a 'now' and a 'then', a 'here' and a 'there', and each of these distinctions is sustained in operations of representation committed to preserving the authority of signs and the grammatical criteria of their use.

---

[96] Andrew Galloway and Bernard Geoghegan 'Shakey Distinctions: A Dialogue on the Digital and the Analog', *Eflux*, 7 October 2021. 121.

[97] Alexander Galloway 'Golden Age of Analog', *Critical Inquiry*. 2022, 48, 2, 211–232. 228.

Figure 39 David Kindersley, lithograph from Curwen Press, 1971. Lithograph on paper. Printed at Curwen Studio.

Craft work keeps this digital substrate at bay, residing as far as is possible with the analogue. The process of making reveals things that are hard to classify and categorize. Within the walls of a pot, whether of clay or the plastic spray of a 3D printer, or along the weave of a woollen blanket, whether it was woven by hand or on computer-aided loom, the well-managed interaction of symbol and structure which represents the made thing as a specific, named object loses its authority. It does so because the symbol alone cannot possibly convey or show how it is that the vase or blanket have been made in the duress of care, or how they might be used with care. The names 'vase' or 'blanket' are insufficient as they only convey the distinction of an assigned category, when what makes the made thing distinct is its having been placed within the creative space (*khôra*) of making, of which it is a unique expression. The vase or blanket belong to experiential processes whose flowing, morphing, unifying and fragmenting qualities cannot be contained by the digital representations of language. In craft work, things overspill their categories; the analogue re-gains its ascendency, there is no getting away from the thing.

The practice of craft work has never been comfortable with language. It is a suspicion that has spread to some of the psychologists, political and social scientists, economists, organization studies scholars, philosophers, architects and historians who study human practices, even if, in many of these disciplines, language remains the dominant mediating force for inquiry. To these theorists interested in the vitalism of life, the claims being made on behalf of the digital order of language – its purity, its cleanliness, its efficacy – have sounded increasingly hollow when pursued into the barbed scrubland, the rapid or languid flow, or the disorienting declivities of everyday experience of a world that seems to be fundamentally and unalterably 'on the move'. To understand any human practice within such a milieu requires something more vibrant and alive than the behavioural models, isomorphic institutional structures or historical laws traditionally adduced as explanatory frames. Life itself, the excessive, meandering, unpredictable, tense, rhizomic force of life being organized in temporary assemblies, topologies and flares of contingency, the life whose conclusions cannot be verified and replicated, needs to be understood with looser, more poetic, affective approaches to the production of knowledge claims. The organization of this life flows through capillaries, it is germinal, a vitalist order of expressive potential that works immanently, that enters practice not through normalization but difference, not through the organized reproduction of standards and symbolic codes but the organization of openness.

That the digital can appear clumsy trying to capture and translate this vital life into meaning is because it moves differently, unnaturally. Digital movement is the act of making and marking of distinctions between objects – of defining this from that – hence the creating of 2 from 1. The point, the atom, the alphabet, numbers, the holy trinity, the pentangle, computer code, the stake, the tree of life, the periodic table, the rosary beads, are all digital as they represent reality in terms of things with a unity and plotted connexions between them. Analogue movement, in contrast, is an act of joining, a coming together, where 2 becomes 1. Hence the wave, twist, stretch, intensity, affect, feeling, are all analogue. Craft work seems to find itself skewed towards the latter. A creative practice of discovering affinities between qualitatively distinct beings largely freed from the abstracting dividing norms and procedures that define manufacturing activity and its management. The concepts in the language of craft work (folds, bends, joins, compositions, eruptions, distortions, chance, shape, rhythm, etc.) are coterminous with reality and the reasoning tends towards a synthetic, not analytic, logic. Its methods are largely empirical and concentrate on using immediate, raw material, on personal localities and relations, and on the collective, earlier attempts locked into tradition. Its sense of causality is grounded in an awareness and acceptance of chance, and where a controlled and linear determinism is employed, it tends to be contained (as in the jigging spoken of by David Pye).

To try and understand how these characteristics cohere into states of affairs about which one can claim to have knowledge is less an exercise in verification and falsification than in what Galloway calls (recalling grace and the double bind) an 'analogue ethics' in which experiment and action trump planned operations, set alongside an 'analogue aesthetics', which enjoins itself to the making of forms with patches that slip and stutter and that escape measurement in small flights of riskiness.[98] To recur to Ruskin's Gothic suspicion of symmetry and endings, this exposure to 'risk' is really an experience of freedom, whether that of the material or the worker. It might sometimes be crude, lacking repose and technical sophistication, but it indicates a vital energy that craft work, if it is to become good craft work, ought to acknowledge. 'Go forth again', Ruskin urges his readers, and:

> to gaze upon the old cathedral front, where you have smiled so often at the fantastic ignorance of the old sculptors: examine once more those ugly goblins, and formless monsters, and stern statues, anatomiless [Ruskin's own term] and rigid; but do not mock at them, for they are signs of the life and liberty of every workman who struck the stone; a freedom of thought, and rank in scale of being, such as no laws, no charters, no charities can secure; but which it must be the first aim of all Europe at this day to regain for her children.[99]

The binaries populating symbolic representations of the world – inside and outside, us and them, ego and id, organization and environment – make way for tendencies, attractions, tremors, assemblages, all of which

---

[98] Alexander Galloway 'Golden Age of Analog'. 219.
[99] John Ruskin *The Stones of Venice, Vol. II.* §14. 193–194.

are residues of a fundament that allows accident to be present in its opening, closing and all that lies between.

Yet despite this skewing toward analogue, the digital remains. After all, craft was the origin of digital modes of production. We only need look back at the idealized and thoughtless, sensorially immersed communion with nature that was *Mingei*, and its famed hostility towards the individualising, thoughtful pauses of reflection. For all its naturalism, *Mingei* was also an idea, it was written out as a set of symbolic statements and its power was as much due to the literary gifts of Yanagi and Leach as it was those of the anonymous craft workers. Theirs was a digital advocacy for an analogue life, an advocacy that would have done well to reminds itself that, as Galloway pithily points out: 'the analogue will not save us'.[100] Abandoning the distance of digital form in favour a sensory, affective, chance-ridden immersion in immediate event does not, *ipso facto*, release the body from oppressive and unimaginative repetition associated with controlled manufacturing and heavily managed work practice. Indeed, it can intensify it. Without the discriminations of legitimacy made available through digitized thoughtfulness, communication carries no lasting meaning or understanding, it is just effect, just sensory stimulus, just immediacy. There is no consideration in power and little opportunity to set oneself against power, just expression. In its distinction from capitalist industrailism, craft work is practicing critique mediated by digital thought. Without this thinkng, what Adorno calls the mortar of tradition holding individuals together gives way to pressure that squeezes them, a pressure for conformity that diminishes yet further the demands any producer might place on themself.[101] And here we might recall Michael Cardew's comments that the craft worker did not work in compartments: to be creative craft work has to be more than technique and skill, more than material expertise, more than exposed experiment. In addition, and to also recall the earlier discussion of grace, it has to bear the weight of an acquired consciousness through which symbolic ideas for things extend beyond their use; form cannot follow function alone without becoming mimetically derivative, it is also influenced by a desire for appearances.

Being trans-contextual, this acquired consciousness is far from being the inner, mental experience of an isolate subject. It is, rather, a consciousness stretching itself to find new ways of relating to nature, new ways of apprehending the context of the context. If it is grace, it is grace as a willingness to always move into regions of exposure, no matter how small, and to seek there the possibilities for difference. These

---

[100] Alexander Galloway 'Golden Age of Analog'. 219.
[101] Theodor Adorno *Minima Moralia*. 26, 41.

regions can be broader and broader, as in Bateson's trans-contextual understanding, yet there is also Rupert Spira's language, which pushes the idea of graceful consciousness in the other direction, inwardly, the inner state of a craft worker working against their own sense of habituated ease by bearing the weight of consciousness from within the fabric of everyday life. This is a finitudinal sense of maintaining the experience of struggle despite the skilled occupation of habit.

Søren Kirkegaard was content to call this struggle a condition of grace, one which indicated a state of being in-between necessity and possibility, or of admitting both. Where Dewey's grace confers an ease of motion and purposive settlement, Kierkegaard's delineates an uneasy state in which the sense of what it means to be a human being is pervaded by an anxiety over how best to shape the self.[102] Moreover, and to recall the discussion of skill, this amended form of grace entails an experience of striving for good form without ever attaining it, an experience the potter Clare Twomey evoked in her 2010 piece *Is it Madness. Is it Beauty?*, in which water was poured into perfectly formed, unfired vessels until they broke, and the process was repeated, again and again.[103] In Dewey's grace the organism takes on its proper shape through ecological sensitivity, whereas for Kierkegaard this natural harmony is too comfortable, too accommodating, to fully convey the deep sense of yearning for which all human beings have potential, but from which they can suffer. To experience grace is to admit encounters with one's own limits and to submit to this necessity without resentment. It is an inner strength that calls upon each person to commit to forming their own shape without being at all certain why they take the shape they do, and without losing themself in the endless perambulations of possibility.[104] It is to admit that the shape taken becomes a necessary one – it is there, and cannot be negotiated away in further iterations of desire or hope – and yet it remains a shape touched by personal desire and hope.

---

[102] Lee Barrett 'Kierkegaard on the Grace that Nature Did Not Know It Needed', *International Journal of Philosophy and Theology*. 2022, 83, 1–3, 79–99.

[103] Clare Twomey, *Is It Madness. Is It Beauty*, 3–14 November 2010. ROTOR – Siobhan Davies Studios, South London Gallery.

[104] Typically, argues Kierkegaard, people have lost themselves without realizing it, and this was especially so in Denmark, which he likens to a small, market town. People conform with their milieu, and find a state of superficial happiness there, or they experience frustration that they are not quite reaching the required standards. Godly grace is an antidote to this: 'This is God's grace toward a hum. being: that a hum. being, like some rare instrument, shows himself in the midst of adversity to be fashioned so wondrously that each new hardship not only does not damage the strings but reveals a new one.' Søren Kierkegaard *Journals and Notebooks. Vol. 4*. Edited by Niels Jørgen Cappelø, et al. Princeton: Princeton University Press. 2011. Journal NB 2, §21. 147.

# 5   Disturbed Imagination

On the walls of the north porch of Rouen cathedral that once sheltered the town's booksellers, Ruskin noticed a small carving of a couchant figure looking:

> gloomy and angry brooding. The plan of this head, and the nod of the cap over its brow, are fine; but there is a little touch above the hand especially well meant: the fellow is vexed and puzzled in his malice; and his hand is pressed hard on his cheek bone, and the flesh of the cheek is wrinkled under the eye by the pressure. The whole, indeed, looks wretchedly coarse, when it is seen on a scale in which it is naturally compared with delicate figure etchings; but considering it as a mere filling of an interstice on the outside of a cathedral gate, and as one of more than three hundred (for in my estimate I did not include the outer pedestals), it proves very noble vitality in the art of the time.[1]

It is a passage that Marcel Proust remembered on hearing of Ruskin's death on 2 January 1900, and on re-reading it he recounts how the spirit of Ruskin – a man 'for whom there is no death, no material infinity' – had always been drawing him in and entreating him to take on the task of seeing:

> And I went to Rouen, as if obeying a dying wish, and as if Ruskin, upon dying, had in some way entrusted to his readers the poor creature to which he had given life again by speaking of it, and which, unknowingly, had just lost forever the person who had done for it as much as its first sculptor .... But how to recognize the figurine among hundreds of others? All of a sudden, a talented and promising young sculptress, Mrs. L. Yeatman, said to me, 'Here is one that looks like it.' We looked farther down, and ... there it was. It scarcely measures ten centimetres. It is crumbling, and yet the look is the same, the stone still has the hole that raises the eyeball and gives it that expression which made me recognize it.[2]

In making this journey to re-find the small relief statue that Ruskin too had found, Proust recalls how, under Ruskin's sight: 'the harmless and monstrous little figurine will have come back to life, against all

---

[1] John Ruskin *Seven Lamps of Architecture*. §23. 217.
[2] Marcel Proust *On Reading Ruskin*. Translated and Edited by Jean Autret, William Burford, and Phillip J. Wolfe. New Haven: Yale University Press. 1987. 45.

180   5  Disturbed Imagination

Figure 40 John Ruskin, Plate XIV, *Seven Lamps of Architecture*. In *Complete Works of John Ruskin*. Vol. VIII. Plate XIV. p. 216. © The Ruskin, Lancaster University.

hope, from that death which seems more total than the others, which is the disappearance into the midst of infinite numbers and the levelling down of similarities' (Figure 40).[3] For Proust, the small figure was a direct link to Ruskin's thought, and through Ruskin to the carver, both of whom were being resurrected through his own sight, one inspiring the other, and so both inspiring him. For Proust, Ruskin's brilliance lay in his imaginative power to reveal the beauty in all life, no matter how incidental and inconsequential, no matter how dead and overlooked. Proust hesitates before himself. Has he enough imaginative power to do the same? Could he have recalled from oblivion this oblique look on this poor face and bestowed such attention upon it as to give it vigour? Perhaps. 'For sometimes the Spirit visits the earth; at his passage, the dead arise, the forgotten figurines reawaken and capture the attention of the living who, for them, forsake the living who are not alive and go seeking life only where the Spirit has revealed it to them, in stones that are already dust and yet still intellect.'[4]

And it was in Ruskin this spirit lived and it was though him that objects were re-animated. What impressed itself upon Proust was the material,

---

[3] Marcel Proust *On Reading Ruskin*. 46.
[4] Marcel Proust *On Reading Ruskin*. 48.

empirical nature of Ruskin's intellect, his capacity to bring form and material into a constant, sometime errant dance. The calm of abstract formality is making room for noisy, empirical experience, and the sedentary sleep of silent materials is being agitated by ideas, and it was towards nature itself that he was working for understanding, because it was in nature that life lived itself out:

> The object to which thought such as Ruskin's is applied, and from which it is inseparable, is not immaterial, it is scattered here and there over the surface of the earth. One must seek it where it is, in Pisa, Florence, Venice, the National Gallery, Rouen, Amiens, the mountains of Switzerland. Such thought which has an object other than itself, which has materialized in space, which is no longer infinite and free, but limited and subdued, which is incarnated in bodies of sculptured marble, in snowy mountains, in painted countenances, is perhaps less sublime than pure thought. But it makes the universe more beautiful for us, or at least certain individual parts, certain specifically named parts of the universe, because it touched upon them, and because it introduced us to them by obliging us, if we want to understand it, to love them.
>
> And so it was, in fact; all at once the universe regained an infinite value in my eyes. And my admiration for Ruskin gave such an importance to the things he had made me love that they seemed to be charged with a value greater even than that of life.[5]

Ruskin's genius is to devote himself to things, and Proust's was to devote himself to Ruskin. It was a voluntary servitude through which he too learned how to recover life from long gone things, how to work from what he called the coldness of memory. Ruskin was not working in a Romantic vein of recalling and intensifying the felt passion of past experiences as though only by remembering them and making them present once more could they be assigned to the work of profound insight. He was working with the ashes, with the dust, with things of which he had no knowledge until he encountered them. Through imaginative effort concentrated within the event of this encounter Ruskin re-created their life, and so created his own: without presuming himself ever 'there', he is still able to say of this concealed figure 'you were thus'. Inspired by Ruskin's capacity to work with an equivocal form of presence, Proust too begins, remembering what is dead as irretrievable and to weave this experience of presence bound by loss and lack into the present textures of life. After reminding his readers that the word text stems from the Latin for a woven thing, Walter Benjamin likened Proust to a weaver whose stories hand thread the material of forgotten memories, dreams, social conventions and wistful consciousness into

---

[5] Marcel Proust *On Reading Ruskin*. 48.

complex patterns, the weft the back and forth of the present, the warp the falling away into the past, which remains vague in its presence.[6]

Unable and unwilling to judge a work of art on its own formal and material terms, Ruskin hankered after an understanding of the effects. In a less generous and open mind this insistence that the event of its reception, and the accumulated (and often forgotten) history of such events, be allowed to intrude into aesthetic judgment might prove dogmatic. Yet what redeems Ruskin is his willingness to upend the conventional readings of these events of reception. This frees the work of art to be sensed in multiple ways and opens up aesthetics to many more types of thing, and certainly the things of craft work. These have value as useful things, and as traded things, but they are not exhausted by these values. The figure in the porch of the booksellers was testimony to how objects live and die outside of proscribed, practical uses, and outside of their presence and the context of their presence being properly known. The enigmatic form of its twisted irony touched on the sublime, the inexpressible, which it nevertheless held nearby in its resigned glance. Its nobility was caught in that glance, a wry crease which contained the hazardous stillness of the devil lizards lying above.

### The Grotesque

The grotesque is so central to Ruskin's idea of Gothic, and hence to craft work, because of its refusal to give priority to the obvious and acceptable. The way it exposes the maker and audience to small sublimities is ordinary, comic and irascible, so that any seriousness is hard won and often short-lived. Like a horror film, or Halloween, or caricature and carnival, grotesques evoke a healthy manner of playfulness. There is wit, humour in the uncultivated energy coupled to a sense that, but for skill, what is seductive, disruptive and occult about the grotesque can easily tip into incoherent exaggeration and monstrosity. This would become what Ruskin called the terrible grotesque which: 'will be found always to unite some expression of vice and danger, but regarded in a peculiar temper; sometimes (A) of predetermined or involuntary apathy, sometimes (B) of mockery, sometimes (C) of diseased and ungoverned imaginativeness'.[7]

Gothic errs towards noble or playful grotesque. Noble grotesque remains aware of the profundity of its subject, and steps cautiously and respectfully in the face of the death and sinfulness it mocks, whilst the

---

[6] Ester Leslie 'Walter Benjamin: Traces of Craft', *Journal of Design History*. 1998. 11, 1, 5–13.
[7] John Ruskin *The Stones of Venice, Vol. III*. §44. 166.

playful, though less explicit, remains at a respectful distance. The grotesque works when the difficulty of the encounter remains to the fore, absorbing the fear and the jest with an equanimity that makes it more resolute: in happiness hides harm, from amid the sheen of spectres and mirages insight can issue a breath-stopping body blow, in the dark centre of an exaggerated mouth or eyes lies the void. The grotesque works when it brings the sublime into view, contains it somehow within the everyday, presents it to the senses, so that it appears an object of inquiry rather than as an overwhelming unmanaged force. To make and witness the grotesque elicits a strength of character able to absorb and cope with the unimaginable. The questions surrounding death, the mystery of inexplicable forces, attributed to sprites and wraiths and demons and hedge spirits and fairies and howling half beasts all of which coalesce in the imaginative restraint of a form given over to their consideration and contemplation.[8]

The grotesque was found in the thinning shadows of Dürer's woodcuts, in the glance of the gargoyles at Amiens, in the caustic goading of the fool in King Lear, along the pathways of Dante's dark wood, in Iago's revenge, are all grotesque, reminders that the keenest and highest arêtes of achievement can make the deepest shadows.[9] They have been created by those who, whilst they might sneer at the sublime, whilst they might look it straight in the face with a well-tempered curiosity, never conceal or repress the power of what they mock. They see, and keep seeing and in this encounter with the fearful nature of the world they have disciplined their natural feelings of disturbance with irony and even apathy (as opposed to ignoble grotesque, where the naturally apathetic and frivolous have exerted themselves into momentary excitement).[10] To maintain the grotesque is to bear witness to the world in such a way that its crookedness and untamed perversity finds purchase in the small, even playful gestures of making and what is being made: 'It is because the dreadfulness of the universe around

---

[8] John Ruskin *The Stones of Venice, Vol. III.* §66–67. 186–189.
[9] Ruskin says of Dante's Inferno 'I have always felt that there was a peculiar grandeur in the indescribable ungovernable fury of Dante's fiends, ever shortening its own powers, and disappointing its own purposes; the deaf, blind, speechless, unspeakable range, fierce as the lightning, but erring from its mark or turning senselessly against itself, and still further debased by foulness of form and action' (John Ruskin *The Stones of Venice, Vol. III.* §53. 174). In Dürer's work Ruskin isolates the head of Adam as the most sublime expression of grotesque, as 'When he gave Adam a bough to hold, with a parrot on it, and a tablet hung to it, with "Albertus Dürer Noricus faciebat, 1504" thereupon, his mind was not in Paradise. He was half in play, half apathetic with respect to his subject ... But he rose into the true sublime in the head of Adam' (John Ruskin *The Stones of Venice, Vol. III.* §51. 172).
[10] John Ruskin *The Stones of Venice, Vol. III.* §47. 168.

him weighs upon his heart that his work is wild; and therefore through the whole of it we shall find the evidence of deep insight into nature.'[11]

It is not just dread, but the sense of anticipation that arises as the underbelly of experience appears, exposing those lower regions of the body that absorb and eject, that discharge and suck up, that merge with their immediate environment. For Mikhael Bakhtin this is the folk world, touching on the ancient desire Kierkegaard associated with folklore: the boistrous anonymity of the crowd is a raucous and heady loss within the carnivalesque shows of the marketplace which 'operate at the borderline of art and life'.[12] The satire and theatrical excess of carnival cock a snook at the established social hierarchies and habits, and they do so not under the satirizing direction of an individual Romantic genius, but through a folk art whose coarseness and vulgarity secured a space for the rejuvenation of common wealth. It is a law unto itself, a place of sensuous and playful release, one that enables folk to organize 'a second world and a second life outside officialdom, a world in which all medieval people participated more or less, in which they lived during a given time of the year'.[13] People take flight into the grotesque now and then, as do seabirds which, given to dreads, can launch unexpectedly en masse.

In resisting all that is high and upstanding, the spirit in which Bakhtin reads the grotesque is a lowering one of degradation through which the human becomes equal to nature, a body amid many, a flow amid flows. The fool reminded the King they too would die, they too had organs, they too were frail and riven with error, sensing them as flesh rather than divine. In degradation there was a: 'coming down to earth, the contact with earth as an element that swallows up and gives birth at the same time. To degrade is to bury, to sow, and to kill simultaneously, in order to bring forth something more and better.'[14]

As an organizational force the gibes and counter-thrusts of the fool are not wholly negative, they oppose, to then generate new thoughts and actions of rule. Their function is to cast the court into a region of renewal now and then, there to test and remake its prejudices in a cacophonous chrysalis of comic interludes. The rulers are reminded they ought to go again, with newly minted allegiances and evaluations, for the old will always tire and wear down, like an old pan scoured to the point that its bottom will fail and the contents of the kingdom spill into nothing.

---

[11] John Ruskin *The Stones of Venice, Vol. III.* §48. 169.
[12] Mikhael Bakhtin *Rabelais and His World.* Translated by Helen Iswolsky. Bloomington: Indiana University Press. 1984. 7.
[13] Mikhael Bakhtin *Rabelais and His World.* 6.
[14] Mikhael Bakhtin *Rabelais and His World.* 21.

There are also fools for the workers and their class representatives. Those who agitate with irony rather than dogma, and who look to irony and satire to puncture the alienating aspirations that belittle the very mouths from which they are voiced. Bertolt Brecht is peerless in this role:

> Mr. Keuner came by his ideas on the distribution of poverty while reflecting on mankind. One day, looking around his apartment, he decided he wanted different furniture – cheaper, shabbier, not so well made. He immediately went to a joiner and asked him to scrape the varnish from his furniture. But when the varnish had been scraped off, the furniture did not look shabby, but merely ruined. Nevertheless, the joiner's bill had to be paid, and Mr. Keuner also had to throw away his pieces of furniture and buy new ones – shabby, cheap, not so well made – because he wanted them so badly. Some people who heard about this laughed at Mr. Keuner, since his shabby furniture had turned out more expensive than the varnished kind. But Mr. Keuner said: Poverty does not mean saving, but spending. I know you: your poverty does not suit your ideas. But wealth does not suit my ideas.[15]

Craft work can be a seductive compensation for exploitation.

The foreigner or strange spirit plays a similar role to the fool. Though initially their presence might repulse or shock, their continued presence as something 'other' than the norm, but which is nevertheless alongside and proximate, can also provoke and excite those who, hitherto, had not been alive to the possibility that things can always be otherwise. In the Chinese calligraphic and scroll painting tradition gods, spirits, foreigners, the ill and deformed and beggars were often depicted with the exaggerated bodily features and a twisted, intense gaze. Most persistent throughout the East has been images of Zhong Kui (鐘馗), a brilliant candidate for the entrance exams for imperial service but who was refused advancement on account of his ugliness. The Tang Dynasty poet Shen Kuo (1031–1095) recounted Zhong Kui's sense of injustice being so strong that he committed suicide by dashing his head against the stone steps leading to the palace. From this bloody diminishment, however, came new life, as the then emperor (Xuanzong 685–762), who had been ill, recovered after having dreamt that having died in such an untimely way Zhong Kui had been appointed King of the Ghosts in the underworld, and then killed the demon who was causing his illness. His reputation restored and elevated, Zhong Kui was celebrated in annual festivals and parades as a harbinger of good luck who roved the earth with a band of demons and animals catching evil spirits as they went (Figure 41). Ugliness matters, it is potent.

---

[15] Bertolt Brecht *Tales of Mr Keuner*. Translated by Martin Chalmers. City Lights Books. 2001. 10.

186   5   Disturbed Imagination

Figure 41  Zhong Kui (Shoki in Japan) *On a Tiger Assailed by Demon*. Ink on paper. Edo period. Freer Gallery of Art Collection. Smithsonian, Washington.

Ruskin's veneration of the ugly couchant figure carved into the doorway of Rouen cathedral was an instinctual aversion to the strain in classical architecture that was always reaching after a complete and self-sustaining form. Its doleful, almost apathetic, legless posture nested a disabling gaze that splits open its complacency and addresses the viewer with an open, questioning puzzlement: 'And ... what might you do?' It is half reptile, half peasant, hooded so as to hide its animal head, yet its face is alive with inscrutable accusation that is peculiarly human; it is through the ugly – but as Bakhtin says, the grotesque is noncanonical – form of a lowered life that a difficult, almost ineffable irony pervades and a question can be issued, and more by way of an atmosphere than a preposition.[16] The accusation made of the viewer that more might be done is felt not stated, and all the more powerful for it: its force comes from its freedom from the confines of grammatical refinement. Bakhtin's sense of the grotesque as the expressive force of what is lowly gives full presence to the sloshing, sluicing fluids exchanged by material bodies, the inhaling and exhaling, the swallowing and ejaculating, the birth and the rotting away, in short, the processual forces that mock the steadiness of perfect definition.

It is scene and gathering of force that the Danish ceramicist Gitte Jungersen feels is encapsulated by glazes, which have far too often been given a subaltern role of decorating or accentuating the form, when they might be given full reign: 'the process is driven forwards via experiments with extremely active glazes that, during the firing, boil and crack in a way that reminds one of geological processes. After cooling, the surfaces are now congealed traces of the violent transformation, like snapshots from a dramatic process.'[17] Glaze is ill-formed, raw life. Her ceramic forms are geometric, their cubed angles are almost abstractions. They are also vessels. Like Fritsch's pieces, the vessel forms the ground, the point where doubt stops, where the spade turns, from which the work begins. 'To a ceramic artist' suggests Jungersen, 'the vessel is almost like the painter's white canvas: a starting point that can be reinterpreted over and over in a search for new and contemporary expressions.'[18] Given over to the glaze, the vessel becomes a holding pen for a congregation of unruly eruptions that break free and in liberating themselves liberate the maker and user alike from the confines of perfect geometry and its supposed superiority. The glaze is a riposte to dominant viewpoints and the dun platitudes of conventional truths associated with beauty: like lava, it creates the beginnings of new form, but only by working with the materials it finds (the body clay, the flame, the oxygen), burying itself deep within the established structures of classical order, to then burst them open, to refuse the order its full effect. There is a potency in curtailing the effect: no sooner is it apparent than it is diminished. The sinologist Francois Jullien quotes *Lazoi* here: 'When everyone knows the beautiful as beautiful, then already it is ugly ... when everyone knows the good as good, then already it is no good', arguing that when everyone acknowledges the effect it is lost,

---

[16] Bakhtin distinguishes between a narrow sense of canon which refers to a set of rules, terms and principles for the proper representational proportions and structure of the human form, and the wider sense, which refers to any representation, of which the grotesque is one, extreme expression. Mikhael Bakhtin *Rabelais and His World*. 32.
[17] Quoted in Jorunn Veiteberg *Between Control and Chaos*. In *Gitte Jungersen, Ceramic Works*. Stuttgart: Arnoldsche Publishers. 2019.
[18] Gitte Jungersen *A Quivering Undertone*. https://gittejungersen.dk/a-quivering-undertone/.

## Errant Bodies

In the *Medical Heirlooms* series, Tamsin van Essen studies the stigma of hereditary disease such as psoriasis or osteoporosis, an unwanted inheritance which she takes and absorbs into the ceramic tradition, making something of the aesthetics of a lineage in which deviation has retained a dominant voice (Figure 42). Much as the diseases and conditions can be inherited, the pots can also become family heirlooms, passed on to future generations. The easy stigma with which hereditary conditions are met becomes complicated, even inversed when witnessing what she calls the 'blemished beauty' and fragility to be found in the pots. It is a beauty that arises from a mingling of repulsion and attraction whose bond cannot sensibly by reduced to one of static or fixed opposites and which redounds with affect because it has not been made with a particular effect in mind. Heraclitus said 'opposites move back forth, the one to the other: from out of themselves they gather themselves'.[20] The apparent discord and equivocation allows strange harmonies to meander and to grow, without any definitive statement or end, because such a statement would lack restraint and so curtail something that refuses to be fully present.

The illness is made present, but the clay body and glaze cannot be reduced to the role of its mimetic representation. There is more to them. They too belong to a tradition of making connecting craft workers from different ages and cultures: the cracked, milky glazes of and pink, brown bodies of Japanese Hagi ware, for example, and the form Van Essen uses is based upon the seventeenth-century apothecary jars used to store cures for these conditions, rather than, as now, being a means of reminding us of their perpetuation, and other ceramicists working with related feelings of loss and recovery, such as Paul Scott's use of brass staples to join broken earthenware plates. Set within these traditions the grotesque force of Van Essens' work allows us to think more critically about illness and how it is typically understood as a deviation from the norm, rather than to sense it as one norm amongst many, or to think of how the norm can also be a disease.

---

[19] Francois Jullien *The Great Image Has No Form, On the Nonobject through Painting*. 68. Jullien's own translation from Lao Tzu [Laozi] *Tao Te Ching: A Book about the Way and the Power of the Way*. §2.

[20] Quote used by Herbert Read in *The Origins of Form in Art*. London: Thames and Hudson. 1965. 80.

# Errant Bodies

Figure 42 Tamsin Van Essen, *Psoriasis*, 2007. Slip cast earthenware, pink glaze. Photography: Tamsin Van Essen.

Van Essen also makes vessels with large rents or splits which have been sewn and stapled, as do the woodworkers Barnaby Ash and Drew Plum, who exhibited their stitched, split and scorched oak vessels alongside the restrained, calm woodcuts of Howard Phipps at

Figure 43 Barnaby Ash and Dru Plumb, fractured and mended cauldron vessel in English oak from Kent. Patinated through fire and lime wash, finished with linseed oil and local beeswax. Stitched with waxed linen thread. © Ash & Plumb.

the Watts Gallery in 2022 (another pairing of opposites that moved back and forth to one another) (Figure 43). The wood has come from fallen and felled trees in Kent, the stitching is done with wax cotton to repair and strengthen but also highlight the natural 'imperfections' in the lathe turned walls, and the resulting vessel is then left to age, and sometimes its surface is burnt with a blowtorch. Having lived, the body of the vessels is vibrant, full of life, but more so still because it is also shown dying back, as in all natural bodies which are continually in a state of change, and far from the perfect form beloved by Renaissance architects. The irregularity of the wooden vessels imply life:

Nothing that lives is, or can be, rigidly perfect; part of it is decaying, part nascent. The foxglove blossom, – a third part bud, a third part past, a third part in full bloom, – is a type of the life of this world. And in all things that live there are certain irregularities and deficiencies which are not only signs of life, but sources of beauty.[21]

Their declivities, sutures and collapsing rims, the splits in their burnished grain, they all hint at things that are transgressing their own state, each a thing that reveals the incompleteness of formation: wood that was found in the woods having grown and formed there, and which has started to fall away, and which has then been reformed, held together and fabricated into another body subsuming an earlier one, but leaving it present beneath, a palimpsest. In its controlled, or what Ruskin calls noble form, the rupture exposes the dogmatic conceit that aesthetic form always hankers after coherence, elevation and completion. The grotesque pulls the rug from under the feet of order, without, however, initiating revolt. Compared with Bakhtin's sense of revelry and excess found in expressive performative phenomena, Ruskin's grotesque can settle into things and have them persist as fixed apertures onto the beauty of the lowly, broken and incomplete.

In its noble variant, Ruskin's grotesque also disturbs and compliments the presumed authority of geometric pattern, not an alternative but an edgy riposte, through which what is ordered remains connected to the lusty expressiveness of life: in intense isolation the grotesque can be as disorienting in its rudeness as the classical is enervating in its neatness. In the church of St Michele of Pavia in Lombardy, for example, Ruskin senses how the grotesque becomes ignoble. On the capitals of the western doorway he notices: 'two devilish apes, or apish devils, I know not which, with bristly moustaches and edgy teeth, half-crouching, with their hands impertinently on their knees, ready for a spit or a spring if one goes near them'

They are the epitome of grotesque fancy, and form part of an unruly cacophony of partly worn figures that lack any narrative force. In contrast, suggests Ruskin, comes the later thirteenth century Lombard church of St Michele of Lucca whose fantastical excesses have been tempered by narrative order:

Geometry seems to have acted as a febrifuge, for beautiful geometrical designs are introduced amidst the tumult of the hunt; and there is no more seeing double, nor ghastly monstrosity of conception; no more ending of everything in something else; no more disputing for spare legs among bewildered bodies; no more setting on of heads wrong side foremost. The fragments have come

---

[21] John Ruskin *The Stones of Venice*, Vol. II. §25. 203.

together: we are out of the Inferno with its weeping down the spine; we are in the fair hunting-fields of the Lucchese mountains (though they had their tears also), – with horse, and hound, and hawk; and merry blast of the trumpet. – Very strange creatures to be hunted, in all truth; but still creatures with a single head, and that on their shoulders, which is exactly the last place in the Pavian church where a head is to be looked for.[22]

There is, then, an order that can belong to strangeness, a structuring through which the lowly reveals its own heights.

Where craft work is especially potent is in revealing how order itself can err towards the grotesque. When Jongjin Park steeps tissue paper in porcelain clay slip and layers them, he creates a roughly blocked or turned form from the curling and twisting of the thin paper layers, each pressing onto and into the other, and it appears to still be growing, unfolding, emerging from its proto, fragile beginnings, present but not, as yet, fully there. Where Elizabeth Fritsch painstakingly etches and paints geometric shapes into the clay surface whose planes gently distort the orthogonal lines, Park has the meshwork of horizontals and verticals emerge from within the stacked layers of clay-covered paper sheets. Their linearity remains more gestural than accurately drawn, closer to woodgrain than to graph paper, friable, as though any grid is moments away from disorder.

Shozo Michikawa works similarly with unravelling disorder from within order. Preparing the clay, kneading (which typically is a pushing action made with the palms) and wedging (which is slapping, turning and cutting, slapping, turning and cutting), Japanese style (*kikuneri*, the shape of a chrysanthemum flower), to create a squared block which he then cuts at in lateral and vertical slices with a wedging wire, as the clay turns on the wheel he pushes a wooden stick down into the middle, creating a void, pushing the walls outwards which then split into a fragmented regularity of smaller, cubed blocks that unfold and twist, like the strands of DNA gone slightly awry. The wheel circles, rotates, but if the block is cut finely and deep, the twisting forces emerge, the naturally occurring force of deviation. From a relatively exact opening of straight-lined cylinder, a more dishevelled grid-like shape emerges as the cut clay is forcing itself open under pressure from the stick, acquiring rents and curves from the motion. He does not touch the outside once it is made, only filling in the top to create the hole. There is a hole in the top of the piece as a reminder of the functional aspects of ceramics, recalling both

---

[22] John Ruskin *The Stones of Venice, Vol. I.* Appendix 8. 429–430. See also John Ruskin *Seven Lamps of Architecture.* Plate VI. 121, 125, 183, 185–186.

Fritsch and Jungersen, the vessel remains.[23] Though now as the setting in which form is taken to its limits, or taken from centre stage.

## Inverse Hierarchies

Jungersen's vessels reveal another source of potency in the exercise of a disturbed imagination, namely the willingness to play with the assumed hierarchy of presence within a made thing. Her eulogy to glaze places it at the heart of her making process: the glaze is in ascendency and the form in a supporting role. The surfaces of her vessels are buried underneath the forming and reforming of glazes, most typically blues. The blue colour is deliberate. It evokes what has historically been the primary glaze colour within the tradition of pottery, especially porcelain, the cobalt that attracted so much fervour, the blue and white ware of the Chinese, replicated by Europe, a mimesis steeped in obsession. The vessels are fired at 1200 degrees or higher, bathed in cobalt oxide, which, when it gets hot enough, distends, and refuses to stay put, the molecules split, forming new material that transforms the abstracting geometry so that it leans away from order into a more perilous, amorphous form. The glaze has taken over the form, spilled over the geometry like a blooming growth before popping and erupting and drying into a rough surface. The glaze is elemental, it bears the locus of raw force of fire, of heat, of fusing. As they bend in the heat of the kiln, those vessels built with legs in each corner are given a strange kind of creaturely life, they begin to walk, or stumble, like the legs of a strangely alloyed, abstracted seabird encrusted with the fossilized remnants of small, blue bivalves. But here the colour blue is neither that of the sea nor sky to which a bird might be compared, it is too intense and glassy for that airy or watery mimesis to take hold. It is a blue that resists being named, it is self-contained, fused into a permanent state of unruliness that is so restless that the eye cannot contain it with any calm.

Joints can also enjoy a hitherto unexplored dominance. Reminiscent of the great iron hinges that unashamedly straddle the great oak doors of gothic churches, the peg joints in Rupert Williamson's side table become an arresting and compelling feature (Figure 44). Williamson talks of having studied with David Pye, but of taking his own route into colour and curves, and when he was given the opportunity to make furniture from the trees that had fallen in the Royal Botanical Gardens at Kew after a storm in 1986, he chose an Osage orange tree. Using

---

[23] In conversation with Shozo Michikawa *Ceramic Review* 2020, 304 (July/August).

Figure 44 Rupert Williamson, side table. Osage orange and sycamore wood. The Fitzwilliam Museum, Cambridge. 1990. Photography: Rupert Williamson.

the least damaged parts and wishing to keep hold of the curves that reflected the way in which the tree had grown, the table edge bends, refusing to sit easily against a straight wall. To accentuate the flow of the wood further he used large, wedged peg joints made from sycamore that protruded through the surface plane and were socketed into the leg uprights. When made, the blond sycamore matched the yellow of the Osage tree, but the Osage deepens with time, so as the table grows older, the contrast becomes greater.[24]

Mistakes, breakages and decay can also be used with provocative and political effect. Paul Scott's use of staples in cracked plates is just a small part of a body of work drawn continually to the potency of re-using old, sometimes broken ceramics to appropriate and redirect symbols and narratives. In his Syria Series, for example, he uses nineteenth-century Staffordshire plates decorated with transfer images of the faraway locations that formed the edges of the British Empire. A romanticized image of Palmyra for example is overlain with transfer print in willow pattern blue of a truck-mounted anti-aircraft gun, and

[24] Rupert Williamson *The Furniture of Rupert Williamson*. Foss: Duval and Hamilton. 2014. 63–66.

Inverse Hierarchies

in the distance the billowing smoke of a rocket attack. Where the older ceramics have cracked or chipped, he uses a *kintsugi* technique to fill them with gold, accentuating the flaw. Rather than discard or hide a flaw, *kintsugi* sharpens its presence, as a reminder that life is flawed and ought to be encountered as such. The flaws Scott accentuates, however, are less those within the plate than those in the human narratives, both the old colonial narrative of exotic travel and appropriation of other civilizations, and the contemporary stories of geo-political and religious conflict from which arms dealers and manufacturers gain immense wealth.

Flipping the focus from the underbelly of international conflict to the underbelly of home and migration the glassmaker Maria Bang Espersen's piece *Home* featured cracking plates in her 2020 exhibition 'A Fictional Character' held at Hasle, on the island of Bornholm (Figure 45). She took sixteen examples of the Christmas platters that have been released each year since 1895 by both Royal Copenhagen and Bing & Grøndahl. Like those used by Scott, the plates depict idyllic and nostalgic scenes of culture and history, though these have a distinctly Danish feel. Espersen hung them in a line, much as they might be displayed in a collector's home, but hers are covered with successive layers of fired, red clay. With repeated layering and firing, a tension between materials builds up, cracks appear and pieces begin to flake off, revealing the blue and white plate and its transferred image beneath. Espersen suggests the layers of raw clay represent the

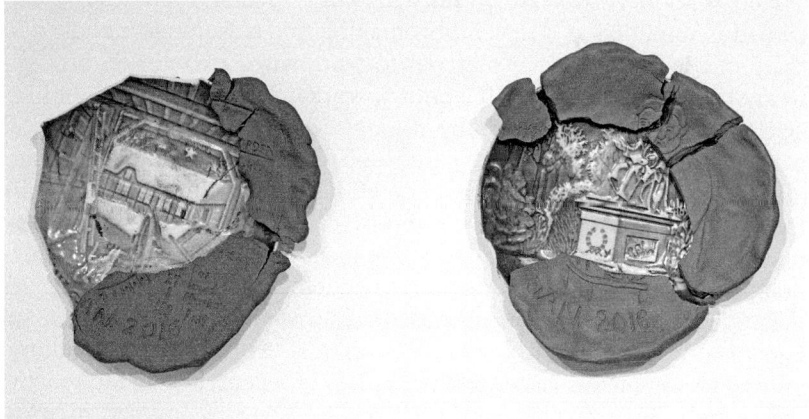

Figure 45 Maria Bang Espersen, *Home*. Christmas Platters made by Royal Copenhagen and B&G, covered with red clay and fired. 2018 – ongoing project. Glass maker's own. Photography: Maria Bang Espersen.

ongoing, yearly revisions to Danish immigration policies from 2015: the confiscation of jewellery (2016), the pause on accepting quota refugees (2017), the banning of face coverings (2018), revoking citizenship without trial (2019), each progressively removing the immigrant from contact with the idea of Denmark as a potential home. As the pieces of fired clay fall into a heap beneath, the plate shows itself to have been untouched, and unmoved, it has shed what was unclean.

### Wild Clay

As well as upsetting hierarchies by having the mistakes, blemishes and flaws assume a guiding role in the process of making, imaginative efforts are also undertaken by craft workers to disturb the accepted type and range of raw materials by exploring the contraries of strangely allied materials. The Danish potter, painter and print maker Catherine Raben Davidson draws with cola mixed with ink, and we can recur to the use of paper tissues by Jongjin Park and Gillian Lowndes' use of scrapped and broken things as suitable material to mate with clay slip. Espersen is also actively experimenting with different raw materials. Her glassmaking often involves the use of highly compressed air – as opposed to using the softer force of the lungs – blown into the molten bulb at the end of the blow rod, forcing it outwards like an elongated soap bubble snaking violently into open space before exploding. The shards are gathered, and these become the base material from which to build new pieces.

Hers is an inventive take on the cycles of recycling where what is discarded is reframed as a new input, making things from old things, and there is a lot of discarded material to work with, a condition brought to light in another of Clare Twomey's works, *Monument*, a pile of broken pots deemed as seconds by the potteries in Stoke on Trent, and which she has piled nearly ten yards high, a broken hill of fragile things made by an industry that was once ebullient but which now, too, is fragile. Despite the crushing monotony of many of the tasks, pottery manufacturing was an industry to which handcraft remained integral. The hand-painting, sprigging, the chemistry of glaze and transfer techniques, the refinement of measured form and certitude. It has an equivocal legacy in craft work: the emphasis on quality, on certainty, on exactness remains as compelling as it is repellent, and the fragments direct the viewer towards this ambivalence. Twomey sourced the broken pots from a company dedicated to recycling ceramics, converting the unused and once used into raw materials for new uses, though no longer quite as handmade things.

Ground up potsherds (along with flint and coarse sand) also go into making grog, the thickening material often added to clay (itself made of feldspar, sand and humic acids, along with smaller quantities of metal such as iron) which help the pieces withstand the pressures of being worked and fired. In a further variation of craft workers using what is found round and about, rather than waste material, there are ceramicists who experiment with restricting their range of raw materials to those they find in their immediate environs. The creativity, the seeing anew, emerges not from seeing further and encompassing more, but, on the contrary, through the deliberate confinement to a small patch of the earth.

As part of her wild clay project, for example, the potter Anne Mette Hjortshøj has been steadily reducing the range of land from which she digs the clay for her bodies, slips and glazes. Rather than collect them in from afar to ensure a consistent quality and variety, she commits to digging in the near vicinity of her studio on the Danish island of Bornholm, and to use what is already there (including the waste heaps of 'old' clays left over from the shuttered tile factories scattered around the small island). In continually shrinking the measured diameter of the land from where she digs, so the textures and colours of the resulting pots begin to shrink in their range, as does the variety of shapes they can take. Yet because of this, with each firing, the pot itself comes more and more to the fore, it cannot hide, and must work harder for itself, as must the user, who attends more closely to the small gradients in colouration and the undulating surfaces of the glaze. The commitment to a small patch finds the potter increasingly alive to the vivid variety within it, fixing her into an immediacy of place, digging up and revisiting what has preceded her millions of years ago but which she can now re-form and belong to in a very direct way, alive to subtleties that earlier would have gone entirely unnoticed.

Shiro Shimizu works in a similar vein in the mountainous countryside west of Kyoto, using whatever soils he chances upon rather than searching for a correct or desired clay. His studio is lined with detailed, large-scale, coloured maps of the local geology upon which he logs the qualities of the soils and clays he finds there. It is, he suggests, a small revelation to discover he might work in this way, freed from the expectation of having to replicate and compete with the glazes of his father and illustrious grandfather, Uichi Shimizu, designated a National Living Treasure. Deferring to the soil rather than family tradition instilled a discipline to his work, a consideration for what is right there, in the present, rather than a past legacy. 'The more you limit yourself the more resourceful you become … How thorough an observer one becomes, the slightest noise or movement does not escape one! Here we have the extreme of the principle that seeks relief, not extensively, but intensively'.[25]

Hjorsthøj and Shimizu are observers of the soils to which they deliberately and attentively commit themselves. To instil such limits, according to Kierkegaard, is to abandon hope. The hope for a wider range of slip ingredients from which to choose, the hope for chemically varied, rampant glaze, the hope for easily used and well packaged materials, the hope for a body clay that will not crack and deform in firing, the hope for international repute. Hope not only diverts attention from the here and now, it denigrates it through the promise of better futures or the remembrance of past successes: hope implies the improvement of the present by a process of addition.

> Only when one has thrown hope overboard is it possible to live artistically; as long as one hopes, one cannot limit oneself. It is really beautiful to see a person put out to sea with the fair wind of hope; one can use the opportunity to be taken in tow, but one ought never have it aboard one's own ship, least of all as pilot, for hope is a faithless steersman. Hope was therefore also one of the dubious gifts of Prometheus; instead of foreknowledge of the gods, he gave men hope.[26]

To throw hope overboard is to forget what might be done with more than one has, and with forgetting that what is there is not all there is, comes the carefree abandon of accepting the present limits as they are, and relishing the struggle to make them work for you. The tradition, the efforts of others through which one has acquired expertise, this all remains, for this is present, but the work is no longer placed on a continuum from here to there. Their work has been and gone, utterly, and it is only here, now, as part of an expanded present for which there are no precursors and no antecedents, just what is right there, in the ground, in the studio, in the pot.

### The First Studio Pottery

Arguably, the first studio pottery to be established was in a disused soap factory in Southall, London, in 1876. Not that it was the first workshop for handmade ceramics within which the makers took on the multiple roles in the repetitions of conception, production and sale, but it was arguably the first venture classified as a 'studio pottery'.[27] It was the creation of Robert Wallace Martin (b. 1843), eldest in a line of four brothers

---

[25] Søren Kierkegaard *Either/Or: A Fragment of Life*. 233.
[26] Søren Kierkegaard *Either/Or: A Fragment of Life*. 233–234.
[27] The first recorded use of the term 'studio pottery' was in the 1923 obituary of Robert Wallace Martin. See Malcolm Haslam *The Martin Brothers Potters*. London: Richard Dennis. 1978.

who collectively became the creative force behind salt-glazed stoneware known as Martinware. When salt is thrown into a kiln during a firing it fuses with the glaze to produce a matt, roughed, surface that is pulled back into the body clay, allowing the lines and reliefs in carving and ornamentation to come through with sharper detail. And what details; in Martinware it was excessive. There had been a rough division of labour between the brothers: with Wallace as the obsessive designer and modeller, Walter who threw the pots, mixed glazes and fired the kiln when they could afford to, Edwin the engraver and decorator, and latterly making smaller vases based on seed pods and other natural forms to fill gaps in the kiln, and Charles the commercial director and responsible for running the shop at 16 Brownlow Street, High Holborn to which they transported their pots a short distance along the Grand Junction Canal. Wallace was unstoppable, a force of nature. Refusing the offer of an apprenticeship with the sculptor J. B. Philip, he worked instead as an assistant to the stonemason William Field who worked for Charles Barry on gothic revival buildings, notably the Palace of Westminster and Houses of Parliament, and then as an assistant to the sculptor Alexander Munro whose studios on Buckingham Palace Road had become a regular haunt for the more extravagant members of the Pre-Raphaelite Brotherhood such as D. G. Rossetti. He then decided to set up his own, and by 1873 had moved to the premises in Southall.[28]

What became known as Wally Birds start to emerge in the early 1880s, a menagerie of grotesque tyro figures whose outlandish, accentuated features are anthropomorphized by the sly gaze of large, animated eyes. The effect is disorienting: a comic generosity is edged by a hint of aloof and self-sufficient disdain. They are lowly creatures without shame, assured of their own improbable presence. As well as birds there are frogs, porcupines, bears, fish, crabs and some unclassified, shelled creatures from a fantastical underwater menagerie (Figure 46).

Martinware digs into the viewer, it demands their attention. These are not animals and birds dressed as humans, they are animals and birds that are like humans, and it is all in the countenance, in the quizzical look that runs aslant from easy interpretation, in the tilt of the head, in the louche stance. They are firmly in the genre of Ruskin's couchant, serpent figure in Rouen.

A contemporary journalist, Cosmo Monkhouse, writing for the *Magazine of Art* in 1882 elaborates on this unnerving quality when commenting on an image illustrating a feature they were running on Martinware (Figure 47):

[28] See Phillips Catalogue *Wonderous Beasts, Feathered Fantasies: R.W. Martin and Brothers.* New York, 15 December 2015.

Figure 46 Robert Wallace, Underwater grotesque, 1880. Salt-glazed stoneware. Martinware Collection, Ealing Council. © Southall Library, London. Ealing Council.

In the middle of our group stands a wondrous bird, half owl, half spoonbill, a feathered sage of profound experience, but, like Major Bagstock, 'sly, sir, devilish sly'. He holds his head on one side for the better criticism of inferior creatures, and closes one eye after the most approved habit of connoisseurs – a Sam Slick and a Solomon rolled into one. He is designed appropriately to contain the weed of wisdom. On either side of him are two gaping boobies, one marine – a cross between a tadpole and a dolphin – the other amphibious and antediluvian. Both are of very complicated ancestry, and most decided character. To these silly ill-tempered creatures, with their vast but empty heads, is fitly assigned the duty of warming spoons. Between them meditates a preadamite armadillo, crimped like a cod to hold toast; and a strangely human jug completes a group of creatures like many things, and yet like nothing on this earth, but nevertheless admirably good company for one another.[29]

Wallace was a vocal religious fundamentalist, a staunch member of the Plymouth Brethren, the low church, lowliness being next to godliness, for whom the Bible and the Bible alone was the only mediator between them and God. There is no clergy, and little sense of exclusivity. Theirs was an open church grounded in a loose network of local meetings in which the Bible and its prophecies were discussed under the guidance of elders, appointed by the congregations to organize debate and decide on unscriptural action or doctrinal error. By many accounts, and with little sense of situational sensitivity, Wallace was prone to fits of maniacal preaching. One longstanding visitor and collector Sydney Greenslade

---

[29] Quoted in Peter Rose 'The Grotesque Ceramic Sculpture of Robert Wallace Martin (1843–1923)', *The Journal of the Decorative Arts Society 1890–1940*. 1979, 3, 40–54. 47.

Figure 47 R. W. Martin and Brothers, jar in the form of a bird, 1888. Glazed stoneware with wood mount. The Metropolitan Museum of Art: 2013.239.5a,b / Robert A. Ellison Jr Collection, Gift of Robert A. Ellison Jr, 2013.

recounts how, on visiting the studio during a firing, he found Walter and Edwin hard at work, 'hot and very done up', managing what for the business was a crucial event that would govern their immediate fortunes for the next six months. Meantime Wallace 'got in the way', wandering about the studio in the throes of a religious disquisition:

> During the whole of the time I was there Wallace was hopelessly uninterested in the firing – He gave me a great discourse on the prophesies in Daniel and the revelations and explained perfectly how it fitted in with everything that was going on now ... Charles lectured him as usual being particularly bitter because he had neglected certain very wealthy clients.[30]

Martinware was being brought to life in a slightly chaotic and intense furnace of activity to the accompaniment of biblical ravings.

Ornate does not cover it, but the work was too ornate for Bernard Leach, who suggested it epitomized the 'false aesthetic' of the Victorian period, revealing far more about his own timidity than any falsity in work that was peerless simply on the grounds that within almost every piece, and in spite of the protestations from his business-minded brother Charles, Wallace had managed to excavate not only the grotesque, but its edges, which lay less in the excesses of the design than its recesses: the closeness and not the distance was the thing, the proximity of the absurd, inviting you to touch it, to share it, whilst all the while knowing you would never understand. The best Leach could muster in his *A Potter's Book* was a somewhat condescending appreciation of Martin's steadfastness in the face of a pressing poverty, having never paid themselves more than labourer's wages.[31] What he identified as Victorian falsity was its pre-occupation with floral excess, with a heaviness of detail, with the idle asides of whimsy to which bourgeois accomplishment was prone. Martinware was none of these, it was untimely.

To be untimely is for something to be out of joint with its situation, which in turn means it belongs there, only uneasily, and somewhat unwillingly, but nevertheless it is the inventive manner of its untimeliness that makes it arresting and even fitting. In a manner similar to the Dutch *kwabstijl*, Martinware belonged to its time by refusing to settle into it.[32] Debates on the intimacy between animals and humans were in full spate after the scandalous dissemination of Charles Darwin's *On the Origin of Species*: Charles Dodgson had published *Alice's Adventures in Wonderland* (1865) and then *Through the Looking-Glass* (1871) and had been a

---

[30] Quoted in Peter Rose The Grotesque Ceramic Sculpture of Robert Wallace Martin (1843–1923). 44.
[31] Bernard Leach *A Potter's Book*. 34. See also Natsuko Yamaguchi *Martinware Collectors Sir David Young Cameron and Others*. MPhil Thesis. St Andrews University May 2000. 73–74.
[32] The squat, pissing monkey at the bottom of Adam van Vianen's iconic silver gilt ewer (made in Utrecht, 1614) suggests a stylistic sympathy between Martin's work and Dutch kwab ware; both were unafraid to take form into the unhomely reaches of hybrid forms resistant to classification.

frequent visitor to Munro's studios at the time Wallace Martin was an assistant there, the museums in nearby Kensington had recently opened showing all manner of stuffed, pinned and ossified creatures gathered as collateral from colonial expansion, and the satirical cartoons published in Punch were immensely popular.[33] Yet Wallace's disturbed imagination absorbed all this and then moved away, onwards and downwards, into regions where the spade of satire 'turns', where function is no longer of primary concern, and where rather than caricature we are left facing ourselves. The fact that Wallace was able to combine the ludicrous and the fearful in lowly commercial products elevated their untimeliness. On first glance, they were decorative, poking fun, an irascible diversion, but with familiarity they grew stranger. Though Wallace's 'tone of mind' – which for Ruskin was one attribute important to imparting a noble grotesque – may have been awry, as by nearly all accounts he was far from loving or considerate – his strength of purpose, his delight and desire in excavating the depths of gothic grotesque, was unrivalled, as was his apparent pleasure in making each piece fit his own design, resisting suggestions he make the creatures more comforting. Each design was as a new prelude to a potentially disabling encounter with a thing that, whilst it was made for retail trade, was to remain thoroughly enigmatic. It may have to be paid for, but it could never be bought.

## Interrupting Function

The majority of Martinware was functional, of sorts: removable heads for storage of tobacco, gaping mouths for the warming of spoons, wayward arms to hang rings. But the functional was incidental, as it tends to become under the direction of a disturbed imagination for whom use value is as much a provocation as it is an unquestioned demand. A bird figure may well act as a storage space, but the fingers have to turn and twist to get at it: they have to accommodate the bird, not vice versa. The same goes for the business shirts made by fashion designer Vivienne Westwood: they had a formal air, but they were slightly awry. She cut one side of the collar longer than the other, the buttons and buttonholes were mis-aligned so the shirt twisted when it was buttoned up, the darting was cut and stitched at odd angles, the cuffs were over large, running up to the elbow like sleeve stockings. When worn, the shirt reminded the wearer of its presence, it would not slip easily into the invisibility of

---

[33] In the 5 August edition of Punch, 1876 (LXXI) 47, the year the Southall studio was founded, a pelican (wally bird) figure appears flying over the gothic House of Parliament. Later on, in the same issue (53) comes a cartoon of 'the liar bird' with a large beak and a winking, mocking eye.

use, it pushed back, though not in a brash and insistent way. There was a feeling of being accompanied by a made thing that had a life of its own, almost as if one were carrying a small, unpredictable animal within the cotton folds, having to check periodically where it had got to. The shirt interferes with the assumed naturalness of wearing clothes. The wearer becomes conscious of the shirt, of themselves wearing the shirt, and of the varying roles being played by the shirt. The shape of a business shirt becomes a subject of concern. A business shirt belongs under a business suit, and the ensemble is a formally matched (suite) of cloth and cut whose sober, rigid silhouette reveals a person of power, taste, discernment who has no need to draw attention to themselves because they have little need for such demonstrable displays; they already know themselves to be a person of status.[34] The shirt, suit and tie are without location, the wearer has no need for regional ties, they are citizens of the world, and move easily across borders.

For the philosopher Georg Hegel, in its subdued, unemotional modernity the suit of clothes to which the business shirt is integral is inartistic and prosaic, it lacks expressive resonance, it is dully predictable in its demand that a body move in a fixed way: 'in being formed to suit the body the clothes are precisely only a poor imitation or a disfiguration of human limbs according to the conventional fashion and accidental whim of the day; once the cut is complete it remains always the same, without appearing determined by pose and movement'.[35]

Hegel, though hardly being a proponent of wild, Gothic excess, nevertheless favours looser garments that afford the body an expressive range, lending a sense of character to what is otherwise a stifled and regimented movement.[36] Westwood, preferring to acknowledge, with Hegel, how the craft of tailoring creates clothes to constrain the limbs, but rather than lobby for looser fit, she then accentuates and twists these restraints of use with a sly and perverse intelligence. The 'drunken

---

[34] Barbara Vinken *The Suit*. In *The Oxford Handbook of Media, Technology, and Organization Studies*. Edited by Timon Beyes, Robin Holt and Claus Pias. Oxford: Oxford University Press. 2019. 443–451.

[35] Georg Wilhelm Friedrich Hegel *Aesthetics: Lectures on Fine Arts Volume 1*. Translated by T. M. Knox. London: Oxford University Press. 1975. 166.

[36] Grotesque describes a base and unnatural condition for Hegel, it is a lowly deviancy, which he lamented was becoming quite common in some literary circles: 'in most recent times what has especially become the fashion is the inner unstable distraction which runs through all the most repugnant dissonances and has produced a temper of atrocity and a grotesqueness of irony in which Theodor Hoffmann, for example, has delighted.' Georg Wilhelm Friedrich Hegel *Aesthetics: Lectures on Fine Arts Volume 1*. Translated by T. M. Knox. London: Oxford University Press. 1975. 223. In the case of musical virtuosos, however, he relents a little, admitting that they might attain a state of inner unbound freedom of such intensity that even the grotesque becomes enjoyable (958).

shirts', as they were called, functioned to question prevailing function, they toyed with its conceits, they asked the wearer to ask after the utility of a business shirt and to question its precepts.

In courting what was errant, Westwood found herself set askew from taste, her urge to recover a sense of dislocating curiosity and wonder was delightfully wrong-headed, and had been with her since she began stitching and patching second-hand clothes as a teenager, trying to resuscitate dead clothes, doing it herself, as the proper punk she was, for a while, wanting, like Ezra Pound's Hugh Selwyn Mauberley:

> to maintain 'the sublime'
> In the old sense. Wrong from the start—
>
> No, hardly, but, seeing he had been born
> In a half savage country, out of date;
> Bent resolutely on wringing lilies from the acorn.[37]

Wrong, for the age in which she worked was one beset with industrial conflict and rising urban poverty set in train by a growing loss of community and pride in work and a transition away from human hands and towards machine production. It was an age which demanded things be made fast and not to last, and where form, to continue with Mauberley, was:

> ... chiefly a mould in plaster,
> Made with no loss of time,
> A prose kinema, not, assuredly, alabaster
> Or the 'sculpture' of rhyme.

Westwood did not, though, ache for the restorative hardness of classical forms. Instead, she took her craft and went all in, abandoning the surety of alabaster purity in favour of a fashion admixture in which slashing, piercings and montage met with the traditional materials such as the tweed of aristocratic country sports and the tartan of clan uniforms. Zippers and safety pins did not join cloth, they accentuated the rips; tweed no longer provided camouflage for the shooters and beaters of grouse and pheasant, it became a loud, deviant sign of presence; and tartan became the preferred uniform for kicking down doors. Through punk, the folk art that interested Bakhtin, the creative output of common people, was democratically flattened to an ethos of anything goes, do it yourself, in the here and now. Yet it also sustained, and in part emerged from, craft workers like Westwood for whom consistent and coherent thought and action was a setting for dispute, not agreement.

---

[37] Ezra Pound 'Hugh Selwyn Mauberley'. In *Personæ: The Collected Poems of Ezra Pound*. New York: Horace Liveright. 1926. 187.

## Outsider and Folk Art

Punk was often dismissed as a scene of madness, an excessive and unreasoned loss of control that authorized an aimless, feckless worldview without values. The fact that the members of the Sex Pistols were incredibly well dressed in tailored outfits made by Westwood was repressed: what drew the eye were the creative references to bondage suits and straightjackets, not the stitching or material. Wallace Martin's work was similarly disregarded by many, though in his case the madness was a surfeit of values coursing through his body in full spate, a speaking of Revelation, foretelling the end of time and the arrival of the Kingdom of Heaven: no human future.

Punk and Martinware are but two of many examples of how craft work, under its aspect of disturbed imagination, carries within it an intimacy with what has been coined outsider or folk art. The bone carvings of hunters, the graffiti of street artists, the scrimshaw of sailors, asylum drawings, spray painted bodies of cars, the intricate stitching on biker jackets or the swaddling of Morris dancers, the 1,200 carved stone figures of Rakan (Buddha's disciples) at Otagi Nenbutsu-ji Temple in the hills of Arashiyama, each carved by a different visitor under the guidance of stone mason and head priest Kocho Nishimura between 1981 and 1991 (Figure 48).[38] People made a pilgrimage to the temple to take up chisels and carve the figures that lay both in themselves and the stone.

Those taking the trouble to visit the foot of Kyoto's Mt Atago to then carve a Rakan figure under the tutelage of a stonemason and monk are acting on a creative and spiritual impulse for which many humans are

Figure 48 Otagi Nenbutsu-ji Temple. Photography: Author.

---

[38] www.otagiji.com/story-en.

prepared to make themselves prone. As exponents of raw art, it is the motivation to express oneself that stirs the acquisition of skills needed to contain this expressive urge within the confines of a made thing. Attentiveness matters, but there is rarely any need for formal qualifications, and what is learned can be as much self-taught as it is presided over by an instructor or guide. Formal training was not necessary.

At one extreme come the self-taught craft workers almost untouched by prevailing taste and who rely on inner resources, a depth of personal insight that the French artist Jean Dubuffet (who coined the term art brut, or raw art) revered because of its freedom from the mannerist prejudice of established academy art. Shinichi Sawada, for example, who works in an open-sided ceramics studio hut in the mountains during the spring and summer months. He lives at the Nakayoshi Fukushikai foundation in Shiga Prefecture from where he finds sufficient structure to cope with the autism that has left him largely silent. When temperatures allow, he works on ageless, hybrid figures in clay, barnacled, like ancient anemones with facial features that might have walked from the frame of a Studio Ghibli film and with an equally ageless appeal. The foundation also has wood-fired, anagama cave kilns, which are lit twice a year, from where his work is taken to a market of collectors, dealers and museums that has been animated by the density of strange detail. Like Wallace's figures, Sawada's repeat certain motifs: open mouths, elongated teeth, tentacular arms, a spikey carapace.[39] Their forms have drifted a long way from the ideal, but remain close enough to belong to the narrative of human history, they remain inside and not outside the commerce of the species, they too might carry some sort of soul, that is, going by the understanding of the ancients, the soul comes and goes, making up the life of a body without being tied to that body.[40]

What impressed itself upon Dubuffet was the way *art brut* not only loosened but disregarded the restraints of repetitive training and work activity. It was art 'in which is manifested the sole function of invention, and not those, constantly seen in cultural art, of the chameleon and the monkey'.[41] Its affective power comes from a tolerance for transgressing and inverting the conventions by which work is judged,

---

[39] See exhibition catalogue at George Kolbe Museum, Berlin. Shown 13 September 2020 to 11 April 2021. https://georg-kolbe-museum.de/en/programm/ausstellungen/1080/.

[40] The Essay. 3 February 2023. Professor Victoria Tischler on Outsider Art, www.bbc.co.uk/programmes/m001hg5l. Other examples of this immersive, internalized imaginative craft work include the woven cocoons and totems of Judith Scot (1943–2005) working from the Creative Growth studios in Oakland and the stonemasonry of William Edmondson (1874–1951) working from the yard of a tombstone stone cutter in Nashville, Tennessee.

[41] Jean Dubuffet *L'art brut préféré aux arts culturels*. Paris: Galerie René Drouin. 1949.

a disregard for reputation or fame, and an often-unconscious intensity of attentiveness and application.

Witnessing outsider art has a salutary influence. In shedding standard rules in favour of self-generated ones, it forms its own roots (*radicalis*) whose approachable strangeness provides a space from which to regard the apparent naturalness of social and aesthetic conventions. Accepted, everyday habits become exposed, and in being so they no longer appear quite so reasonable. It is this power to disturb prejudice that Neil Brownsword interrogates in his work using the detritus of ceramic production as material for new work. Plaintively, because playfully, his use of the waste material left rotting amid the disused factories of Stoke-on-Trent is testament not only to a vast and thriving industry that has been obliterated, but to the thousands of lives that had been wiped out with it. Extracting and merging old bits of kiln, discarded ceramics ('shraff'), saggars and machine parts, unifying and altering the passage of their decay, creating new fragments that could resemble the kind of archaeological find that might be unearthed thousands of years hence.

> The beauty of the discarded fragment fascinated me, and raised the issues on how we decide the value of certain objects. I tried to explore this by emulating the quality of eighteenth century 'wasters' where the saggars contents had overfired and melted due to the intense heat of the kiln. 'Remnant' also mirrored this concern and stemmed from a source of contemporary archaeology. A friend retrieved a set of kiln shelves from a skip, on which two bone china plates had melted. There is such beauty in the accidental – again the obvious thing to do was to disregard and consider them worthless.[42]

The beauty of the overlooked also drew the photographer Katya de Grunwald who transformed such disarded fragments into poignant still-lives shot amid quiet, patient stacks of forgotten moulds, bricks and saggars in the abandoned Spode factory in Stoke (see cover).

In his exhibition *Mantelpiece Observations*, Richard Slee makes an equally sensitive and questioning foray into the beauty of the accidental. The ceramic pieces are based on reports made by the amateur observers recruited under the direction of the mass observation movement established by poet Charles Madge, the photographer and filmmaker Humphrey Jennings, and the anthropologist and ornithologist Tom Harrison in the late 1930s. The movement was dedicated to the ongoing creation of an 'anthropology of ourselves' using various artistic, sociological and documentary means to collect data of everyday lives in order to counter long-standing prejudice against the working classes. Their first

---

[42] Niel Brownsword 'Action-Reflection: Tracing Personal Developments', *Interpreting Ceramics*. 2, 2001. See also Grant Gibson 'The Killing Fields', *Crafts* 211. 24–31.

project was the *Mantelpiece Directives*, a set of written instructions for volunteers to follow when documenting the objects on domestic mantelpieces and sending in their short report cards.[43] Slee has used these cards from the archive as a spur to re-imagine the objects placed on view above the hearth, the centre of the home: old shell case, 'chrome electric clock (keeps good time)', pipe racks, ashtrays, notes impaled on a decorative spike, the 'distended paunch' of a Toby Jug, bobbins and cotton reels, 'short, hand-carved candlestick', buttons, candlesticks, lamps, notes, baskets of flowers, rent books, matches, the head of Gandhi the 'Indian Leader of Revolt', a 'large Staffordshire dog' disliked by the younger generation but used to 'comfort fractious children'.

Slee re-creates this snub-nosed Staffordshire dog, though rather than the flat-back version being observed and reported on in 1937 his version is double-headed, a Janus figure fixed between looking at the past which has closed off, and upon the future which is opening up. There is a back and forth movement of a figure in which what 'is' (the inward-looking face succumbing to time, to routine, to necessity, to endings) is continually being subject to what is not yet (the outward-looking face, looking to openings projecting out from the present).[44] Slee's Janus figurines push back at the settlements of tradition, questioning what it is to occupy a span of accultured, sedimented accomplishment in which the future is secured through repetitious interrogations of the past. Janus witnessed beginnings and endings and the transitions and transformations these entailed. The backward-looking face is older, accepting of tradition and of the passage of industrialization, the forward is younger, alive to what is to come, projecting. In making Janus in the form of a popular decorative figurine, however, the adoption of past traditions and the projections into an open future are given an ironic bent: they are demure, askance, funny, hardly the manly forward thrusts of a Roman god.[45]

---

[43] Rachel Hurdley *Mass Observation Mantelpieces*. In *Home, Materiality, Memory and Belonging*. London: Palgrave Macmillan 2013 51–78. Volunteers were to 'Write down in order from left to right, all the objects on your mantelpiece, mentioning what is in the middle. Then make further lists for mantelpieces in other people's houses, giving in each case a few details about the people concerned, whether they are old, middle aged or young, whether they are well-off or otherwise, what class (roughly) they belong to. Send these lists in. If possible, also take photographs of mantelpieces. (MO 1937)' (quoted 55–56).

[44] Richard Slee discussing the 'Mantelpiece Observations' exhibition with Sonia Solicari: https://cfileonline.org/richard-slees-mantelpiece-observations/.

[45] The social theorist Donna Haraway notices a tendency amongst many to identify with the youthful face, invoking the god as a warrant of their resilience and vision brought about by both accepting the necessity of conformity whilst still having the energy to break through and assert their distinctive view outwards. It is, she suggests, an 'intensified commitment to virile modesty' that emerges from an idea of creative work originating

## Metempsychosis and Repetition Revisited

In making the movements through spans of time appear ordinary, the appeal of Slee's Staffordshire dogs lies very much with how they afford a negotiable relationship with time. We can endure time as it marks us, but we might also learn how better to learn from its inevitability. In Plato's *Meno* the protagonist, debating with Socrates, becomes stuck fast in the insoluble thought that learning is an impossibility: how is it that we come to know something when to acknowledge it in the first place means we already know of it? Socrates answers by enlisting the soul. Given human relations, connexions and kinship pervade all of nature, then our soul is also part of nature: it is the part which persists where other parts transform. W. G. Sebald recounts Jean Jacques Rousseau's enduring interest in vitrifying the ashes of the dead, and how, though cremation, the living body might become transparent glass. A floating form, a little soul fusing with solid, clear space.[46]

So, one plausible answer to Meno is that learning is a process of recollection: he knows things because he recalls having experienced them in previous lives. The soul – Meno's soul – must remind itself of its inheritance, of how it once existed in other bodies and will, in the future, with the transformation of Meno's body, migrate into other bodies.[47] This recollection takes the form of examined opinion (rather than formally deduced truths). The knowledge understood by souls circulates in everyday settings (like Slee's double-headed dog on an ordinary mantelpiece); it is of a commonsense, relational form, it is a truth that, like the soul, lives with and is nothing without the body. This apparent and ongoing intimacy between an unchanging soul and a changeable body taking place in everyday performance is taken up in another dialogue, *Cratylus*, where Plato finds an etymological affinity between the word for 'body' and 'tomb', the soul being entombed in a body, much as a body is found in a tomb, but

---

from an isolate self-birthing man, a figure she wishes to 'queer' by advocating a more modest form of witnessing, able to stay with things as a troubling but provoking multiplicity. Donna Haraway Modest_Witness@Second_Millenium. In *The Haraway Reader*. New York: Routledge. 2004. 223–250. 234.

[46] W.G. Sebald. A Place in the Country. ranslated by Jo Catling. New York: Random House. 2013. 62–63.

[47] In *Phaedrus*, Plato elaborates further, arguing the soul is that which is untarnished, unmarked, unchanged, fixed. Here the knowledge of common sense seems to be giving way to that of eternal verities, the means by which we touch the other world where we witness the three fates turning the axis of the heavens (in the Republic). We might do such, but only as philosophers and friends of the Muses, as those who contemplate and so relinquish the corrupting decaying experience of the body, if only we would aver from desire, from sensory attractions, from the temporary distractions of earthly occurrence and material prosperity. The Vita Activa is a space of limitation.

also that the soul is nothing without the body, for it is through the body it communicates itself (there is also, suggests Plato, an etymological link between 'body' and that which 'reveal'). And yet in revealing things the body also conceals (*aletheia*) (the opening up of awareness is also a closing down of earlier understandings), affording human experience a productive, active sense of truth, rather than a fixed one.

The intimacy between body and soul, though necessary, has never been settled, and whilst Socrates and Plato have the soul more permanent and the body more transient, there was, as noted for example at the end of Plato's *Republic*, still a need for the soul to also withdraw: for example, once it had chosen from amongst the myriad patterns of life, it had to drink from the River Lethe to forget its past lives and so return to each instantiation of life unencumbered by earlier achievements. If Meno recalls what he already knows, he does so dimly and without any firm sense of when and where this occurred. It is, however, a way of the soul recovering experience that belongs to it, through which, along with the body, it acquires a sense of self that moves from the past into the future.

It is this form of repetition that resolves Kierkegaard's conundrum of a life having to be lived forwards whilst only understood backwards. The repetition is not exact; Meno cannot recall early events in any detail, and even if he did, these could never be recreated, as life has since moved on, and in part as a consequence of these earlier events. Yet there are patterns which prompt learning, and which hint at the invariant truth that lies beneath all things, which we might glimpse, but rarely, if ever, fully know. For Kierkegaard it is the movement of repetition that is most truthful, the urge to learn by going again sets up a regimen for life through which we work continually at developing the habituated relations with which we become so familiar that we often forget to observe and learning from them. The provocation of Plato's metempsychosis for Kierkegaard comes in the recognition that repetition exposes us to the task of working at ourselves without really amounting to all that much, but that is the point, because it is far better we are provoked to learn in repetitions rather than to think ourselves into a fixed state. The souls migrate across time, leaving traces that are picked up and re-worked by successors who, abeyant to the shape of the past, find in tradition a wellspring for their own projects. Fate is absorbed and taken on in the acquisition of a character, an ethos, grounded in the actions of others who have gone before. Those who step away from the cycles of repetition fall instead for the comforts of convention and superficial business, or for the certainty of fixed, metaphysical truths. Either/Or they fail to live, which can only be achieved when a person is prepared to endure the repetition of going again, despite the admission of failure and ignorance that this entails: 'Every morning I shave off my beard in all its ludicrousness – but it does not help, for the next morning my beard is just as long again'.[48]

In Japan, at the temple compounds of Ise, the main inner and outer compounds, some five kilometres apart, made from *hinoki* wood and covered in *kaya* thatch, have been razed to the ground and rebuilt at twenty-year intervals (*Shikinen Sengū*). Each iteration repeats the traditional movements of constructing new temples on adjacent plots of land that have been prepared with a covering of white and black pebbles taken from the nearby Miya (elegant, pristine) River, allowing the many different kami to take up their new home, then dismantling the vacated homes, and the empty plots will lie fallow, and await the next iteration of building. The first mover is always the sun kami, held in a silk-wrapped mirror, moved at night, and hidden behind silk curtains, impervious to light. Using wood working and roofing techniques so ancient they are used nowhere else, the temple complex houses a large retinue of craft workers dedicated to the furtherance of a repetition that has become, albeit recently, one of the most significant of all Japanese rituals.[49] The sanctity of the space is maintained through the continual effort of craft workers replicating their forebears, but never exactly, for no one iteration is exactly the same as the others, though each successive effort maintains a consistency and coherence that strengthens the sanctuary in which, alongside the gods, belief takes its place.[50] The repetitions have been interrupted but are longstanding, going back hundreds of years, and symbolic interpretations have varied, reflecting the different interests and powers in play, yet throughout the process of recollection manifest in the working and re-working of tools and materials and the recurrence of ritual, has proved immensely seductive precisely because Ise contains no one truth, no one meaning, but has made itself available to many different interpretations without any diminution of its force: it is in its courting unassigned meanings that repetition secures its life-giving power.

---

[48] Søren Kierkegaard *Notebooks Vol. II*. Quoted in Clare Carlisle *Philosopher of the Heart: The Restless Life of Søren Kierkegaard*. London: Penguin. 2019. 162.

[49] The 2013 rebuilding brought 8.8 million visitors, 230,000 people gathered the stones from the river in preparation, and in 2006/7 over 200,000 people took part in the log felling and log pulling rituals (14,000 trees are used in each rebuilding). See Mark Teeuwen and John Breen *A Social History of the Ise Shines: Divine Capital*. New York: Bloomsbury. 2017. 4–5.

[50] Kenzo Tange and Noboru Kawazoe *Ise: Prototype of Japanese Architecture*. Cambridge, MA: MIT Press. 1965. 16. See also Alexander Nagel and Christopher Wood *Anachronic Renaissance*. New York: Zone Books. 2010. 54.

## Urne Burial

This transience of body and soul, and their reliance upon repetition alone as a source of authority and renewal, is often troubling for those looking for a scene of stability from which humans might take some measure of their life. In craft work, however, the presence of repetition as the sole source of authority, and its relative looseness, is a condition received with some sanguinity. The most palpable of all repetitions is, after all, the finitudinal span of a human life, and it is with crafted objects that many human beings have chosen to share the end of their one life and to aid a passage into the next. In his travelogue narrative *Rings of Saturn*, W. G. Sebald recalls how, on the last journey of a body into death, it is so often pottery that encloses the material remains, recalling the melancholic physician and writer Thomas Browne whose treatise on burial rites makes much of the transience of human life when set against the relative permanence of pots: 'If we begin to die when we live, and long life be but a prolongation of death; our life is a sad composition; We live with death, and die not in a moment.'[51] The small, thin-walled earthen urns which Browne dug up in Walsingham in the English Fens with his Antiquarian colleagues were fragile and unassuming, yet had survived intact, whereas what they held were the burnt and jumbled remainders of long-forgotten human hopes and vanity:

In a Field in old *Walsingham*, not many months past, were digged up between forty and fifty Urns, deposited in a dry and sandy soil, not a yard deep, not far from one another: Not all strictly of one figure, but most answering these described: Some containing two pounds of bones, distinguishable in Skulls, Ribs, Jaws, Thigh-bones, and Teeth, with fresh impressions of their Combustion.[52]

The urns had rested there, under the 'drums and tramplings of three conquests', long outlasting the grand edifices that had been built to memorialize human achievements in perpetuity (Figure 49).[53]

It was the humble urn that outlived the futile gestures of architectural and narrative excess of those who, in their arrogance, had wished themselves immortal. Better perhaps to be like those committed to metempsychosis,

---

[51] Sir Thomas Browne *Religio Medici: Urn burial and Christian Morals*. Canterbury: G Morton. 1894. Originally titled *HYDRIOTAPHIA. Urne-Buriall. OR A Brief Discourse of the Sepulchrall Urnes Lately Found in N O R F O L K*. 1658. Hydrio is from the Greek for water urn, and Taphe from the Greek for burial. What are being buried here are human remains, yet also perhaps the human race itself, given its inability to build anything that endures, and the more it struggles to do so, the more fragile and momentary the outcome. 'You can't build clouds. And that's why the future you dream of never comes true.' Ludwig Wittgenstein *Culture and Value*. Edited by G. H. Von Wright and H. Nyman. Translated by Peter Winch. Oxford: Basil Blackwell. 1980.
[52] Sir Thomas Browne *Religio medici*. 97.
[53] Sir Thomas Browne *Religio medici*: 83. https://wellcomecollection.org/works/q263bmva.

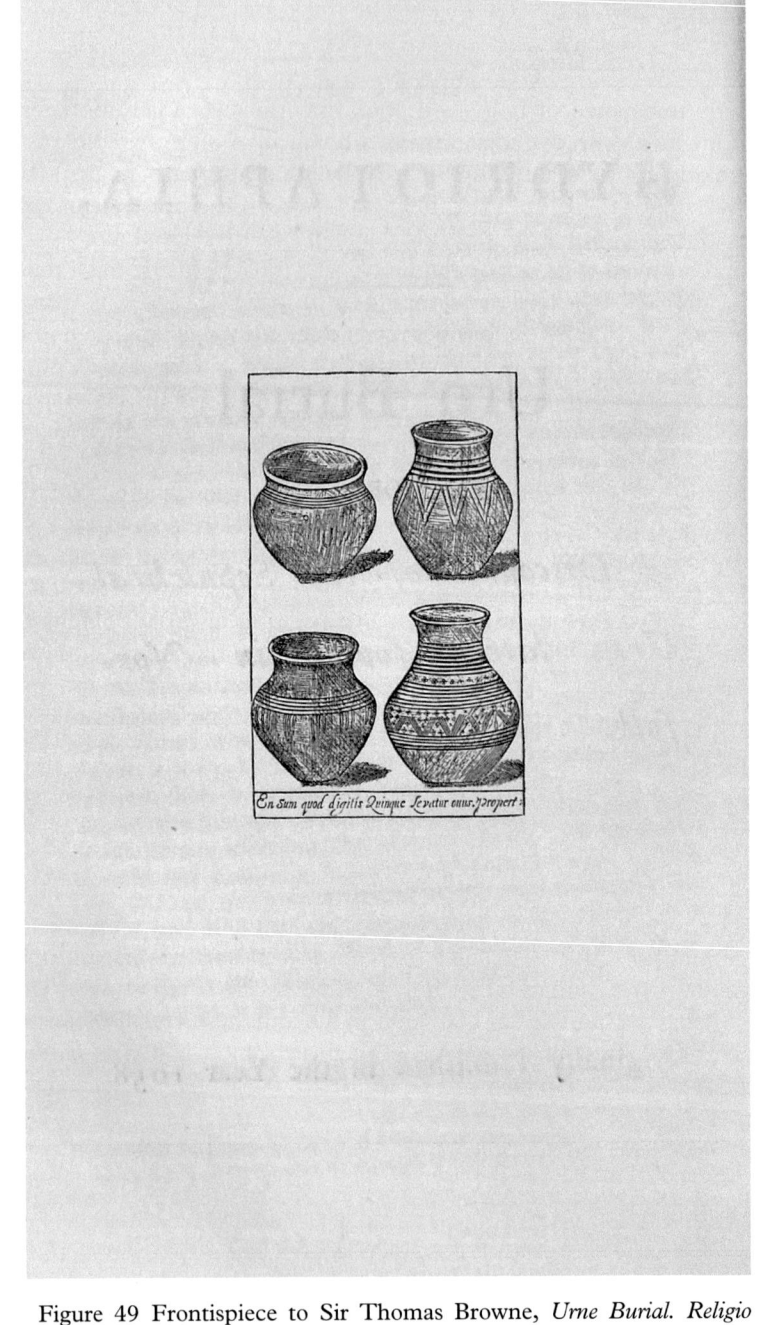

Figure 49 Frontispiece to Sir Thomas Browne, *Urne Burial. Religio medici: Urn burial and Christian morals*, 1902, p. 84. Courtesy of Wellcome Collection.

those who 'rather than be lost in the uncomfortable Night of Nothing, were content to recede into the common being, and make one Particle of the Public Soul of all things, which was no more than to return into their unknown and Divine Original again.'[54] Instead, we have evidence of humans wanting to survive, but their vainglory served only to salt the taste of mortality as it settled irresistibly into their hopes for immortality, and began to gnaw away, until such time as they realized there was 'no patent from oblivion', and so reached a moment in their collective reasoning on the afterlife that, to stave off the final dissolution which will come as surely as the long night surrounds the short day, a small pot for ashes appears to serve far better than a giant obelisk or rich encomium.[55] Overlooked, incidental and common, the minor outlives the major. Craft works are minor things, and in this lies their strength. 'Generations passe while some trees stand, and old Families last not three Oaks', meantime the buried urne endures:

> Circles and right lines limit and close all bodies, and the mortall right-lined circle, must conclude and shut up all. There is no antidote against the Opium of time, which temporally considereth all things; Our Fathers finde their graves in our short memories, and sadly tell us how we may be buried in our Survivors.[56]

In his mention of circles and right lines, Browne was alluding to theta, the skull-like sign for death (Thanatos) ... Θ, or the more archaic ⊕ ... used on ballots in ancient Greece when voting on capital punishment. The body, encircled in its own knowledge, is a definite object, a living thing, for such a brief time. Both body and any knowledge of its existence expire, which is the fate of all lives and of knowledge itself, which is utterly dwarfed when set against the vastness and void of the unknown contained within its thin, cracking walls. What provokes Sebald is how, upon exhuming the pots, it dawns on Browne how human remains and human knowledge share such a close fate. In walling ourselves into interiors, and in walling facts into classifications, we diminish our awareness: 'What we perceive are no more than isolated lights in the abyss of ignorance, in the shadow-filled edifice of the world. We study the order of things, says Browne, but we cannot grasp their innermost essence.'[57]

---

[54] Sir Thomas Browne *Religio medici*. 130.
[55] 'Life is a pure Flame, and we live by an invisible Sun within us. A small fire sufficeth for life, great flames seemed too little after death, while Men vainly affected precious Pyres, and to burn like Sardanapalus; but the Wisdom of Funeral Laws found the folly of prodigal blazes, and reduced undoing fires unto the rule of sober obsequies, wherein few could be so mean as not to provide Wood, Pitch, a Mourner, and an Urn.' Sir Thomas Browne *Religio medici*. 131.
[56] Sir Thomas Browne *Religio medici*. 127–128.
[57] W. G. Sebald *Rings of Saturn*. Translated by Michael Hulse. New York: New Directions Press. 1999. 18–19.

The interplay of soul and body, each allowing the other to 'be'. Though it appears fixed, the material and shape can change slowly with time as in maturing the thing reacts to its surroundings, it learns from its surroundings. For Akiko Hirai, the potter inspired by wood carving techniques discussed earlier, this learning is exemplified in the practice of *Shibui*. Under close attention the simple form, colour and line of the carved or thrown thing reveal a rough, unfinished, edgeless presence that evokes elegance and self-sufficiency as well as hesitancy and a willingness to adapt. Her pots are like the wrack lines left by the tides, day on day, season on season, a repetition whose subdued, silvery differences can only ever be subtle variations, and in which, on occasion, lies a startling object, a foreign disturbance of plastic colour of an old buoy, the bone-dried, flayed timber from a wreck, the bedraggled corpse of a large sea bird, rusting tins with fading brand names. The wrack line is a scene of the forgotten, overlooked and lost, a place of the useless and now unused, yet it teams with life, small life, and it is endlessly restless, hugging the contours of the beach at the precise moment where solidity gives way to fluidity, and fluidity to what is solid, it is the in-between space which is both land and water, flow and fixity, wet and dry. It does not resist but absorbs and changes its colour and texture, the kiln fixes the pot, ends the process of making, which is the end of the opening, as it lives again, though differently.

## Vegetal Life

Browne's melancholic thoughts on nature, human nature and the nature of mortality and have themselves lain in relative obscurity, interred amongst the more bookish and gothic regions of academic and literary exchange. The archaic elegance of his phrasing ends less in a concluding terminus than a digressive curve. His lines twist along a line as a vine might climb around a pillar, they have a mobility in their tight, narrative mass, they admit of no finality because there is none to be had, only the endless, small endings of each death whose significance only carries import in life. To think on this is a source of bleakness: 'It is the heaviest Stone that melancholy can throw at a Man, to tell him he is at the end of his nature', that there is no accomplishment that can stand the test of time, that the desire to amount to something were but a fallacy. Were it not better, muses Brown, if we humans were more like the animals, if we 'might have enjoyed the happiness of inferior Creatures, who in tranquillity possess their constitutions, as having not the apprehension to deplore their own Natures.'[58] For then at least we would not be despondent in our dependency.

---

[58] Sir Thomas Browne *Religio medici*. 124.

To this despondency, however, craft work brings the graceful accommodation of a disturbed imagination. There is a wisdom emerging from encounters with mortality; something grows from the awareness that no accomplishment outlasts oblivion. Manufacture and its management are less prone to this wisdom. They are locked into the upwards movement of thoughtless busyness in which success is a phenomenon of weights and measures, and accomplishment a bright jewel of gain in an ornate setting of inputs and outputs. It has always been so with plain business. In the seventh century CE, the Tang poet Ch'en Tzu-ang observed how:

> Businessmen boast of their skill and cunning
> But in Philosophy they are like little children.
> Bragging to each other of successful depredations,
> They forget to consider the ultimate fate of the body.
> What should they know of the Master of Dark Truth
> Who saw the wide world in a jade cup,
> By illumined conception got clear of Heaven and Earth,
> On the chariot of Mutation entered the Gate of Immutability?[59]

Variegated, craft work is not business. Because the craft worker, now and then, asks themselves the question why the thing they are making ought exist, which is also a question of existence itself, and why it is as it is, and not nothing. If the made thing were not made it would still not be nothing, and if it is made it will, in turn, transform into other things, as will the maker who will return to nature, whether burnt in a pyre to become smoke, through the putrefaction of burial in earth to become soil, or slipping into water to become liquid. In all these termini nature is acknowledged as a continuance, its patterns cannot be resisted by artificial monuments. In death, human patterns become natural patterns and in birth, human patterns emerge from natural ones. In having to refer their own action to the action of other things, a craft worker is alive to these quiet continuities, and in considering how the actions of nature might spur their own, they enrich and complicate these patterns by virtue of their mortality and the bouts of hesitation, doubt and irony that pockmark an awareness of this profound dependency.[60]

Gothic stonemasons carved as though possessed by an urge for veracity when what was to be imitated was life itself: the ivy must twirl and choke and unfurl and die away and take from other life, like the ivy that buries itself into the bark of a tree before feeling its way

---

[59] Ch'en Tzu-ang 'In a Jade Cup'. Translated by Arthur Waley. Published in *Poetry*. XI, IV, 1918. 199.

[60] John Ruskin *The Stones of Venice, Vol. II*. §60. 228–229.

further and further skywards in its urge to live on others' support. As do humans. And the support enables an upwards reach which ends only in continual discovery. There is no end. The end of the thread is not the end, it continues, and if one senses something claiming to be complete – an accomplishment – it has to be cut short; the knitters call it frogging, a riddling movement, which is both a sifting out of infertile elements and a mark of mystery as the weave goes on. The interior is infinite, within, at its heart, is not a single point, but growth, the basic principle of all life.

Such a truthfulness is richly if densely conveyed by Browne's vegetable metaphors and analogies. It needs no alchemy to unlock. It is frank, open. Rather than resplendent figures on thrones with the alabaster columns and marble pyramids, it is ivy (or vine, or honeysuckle, or wisteria, or nasturtium) that the Gothic stonemason chooses to carry and convey truth, and which is worked up into the most lofty and overwhelming vaulting. For those in whom design dominates, vegetation was always consigned to incidental decoration, whereas in Gothic it assumes an unequalled ascendency: 'to the Gothic workman the living foliage became a subject of intense affection, and he struggled to render all its characters with as much accuracy as was compatible with the laws of his design and the nature of his material, not unfrequently tempted in his enthusiasm to transgress the one and disguise the other.'[61]

In a society dominated by strife and distracted by splendour the stonework is heavy, the columns thick, the windows mean, the interior a refuge hidden under splendour, anxiety softened by heavy tapestries and curtained alcoves. In quieter times, suggests Ruskin, the pillars grew slender and vaulted plenum grew higher and with the light came the greenery. Gothic speaks of a quieter society, at least in part given over to careful observation of ordinary occurrence, a more tranquil order sustained by an intimacy with one's natural surrounds. The symmetries are organic, the hierarchies are naturally occurring, and without vaunted ambition. The pointed arch and bending bough fused gradually, each taking the other in myriad directions.

[61] It was this ability to unify fact and idea that impressed itself upon the pre-Raphaelites, whom Ruskin called naturalists, as they encountered, absorbed and represented the whole mortal and spiritual being in all its passions, the destructive as much as the sound, for both are integral to the expressive sense of life being lived. Holman Hunt is a painter naturalist, who paints what he sees, the qualms, fears and loves of folk in their wisdom or stupidity, in reverie or caught fast in bouts of action, and finds in the entire scene a means to render the whole replete with possibility. The images are neither drawn pristine to evoke timeless ideals nor overshadowed with unrequited yearning or irredeemable sinfulness. John Ruskin *The Stones of Venice, Vol. II.* §69. 236.

Figure 50 Fergus Ferguson wearing gansey sweater, Oct 1911. The Wick Society Johnston Collection. www.johnstoncollection.net.

The decoration spills into itself, it has no real origin point, it just begins and splits and hesitates across the plane, growing, as a plant branches and grows, a scroll feeding a linear drift pushing tentatively across a curved space. It is a congregation of life and death, the opening up of life to itself which was in the stone, in the plant the line depicts, in the chiselled hand, in the glazing and glassy clays, and in woven, interlacing flows of thread. Life comes, and departs.

The nineteenth-century fishing communities along the eastern seaboard of the British Isles wore beautifully patterned gansey (from the old Norse for tunic) sweaters (Figure 50). Almost always of dark blue, closely woven wool, they were knitted with high buttoned collars and were stitched as tubes working from the bottom upwards, thereby minimizing the number of joins needed to connect the body, neck and arms. The wool was heavy gauge and with a high lanolin content which helped with water resistance. This made knitting hard work, requiring longer-lasting steel needles and the use of wooden knitting belts strapped round the waist which could help take the weight.[62] They were semi-tailored to the wearer, fitted close to the body so it wouldn't flap in the wind or lose heat unduly. The sleeves, made with a standard stocking stich so they could be replaced easily, were kept short at the wrist to prevent rubbing, and connected to the body using diamond-shaped underarm gussets to allow the sweater to stretch for hauling the nets without the hem riding up. The chest area was a setting for often elaborate relief patterns: cables, north stars, laddered fern foliage and anchors (the latter, evidently, a sign the wearer was married). There is an enticing if maudlin myth that each community had its own variations on these patterned themes so those lost at sea and washed-up dead could be identified by their jumpers.[63] The knitters were women who were following the itinerant herring fleets as they in turn followed the herring shoaling along the twisting coastlines of the North Sea. Working in small groups, they would be paid by the barrel for gutting, salting and packing the fish. The ganseys were made whilst walking between the ports or waiting for the catch, so even if there were a set 'home' pattern, the knitters would have met other working groups from other communities whose own 'home' patterns would be shared and re-interpreted, for it is in the nature of foliate patterns to alter even as they stabilize. In the gansey sweater, effortful, collaborative craft, natural intimacy, twisting forms, finitude, all cohere without making any din.

[62] Wick Heritage Museum collection and the Johnstone collection of photographs.
[63] There are no formal records of this 'verification event' ever happening, and the mobility of these communities moving along the eastern coast of Britain both sustains and yet confounds the myth, given mobility promotes the exchange of aesthetic influence as much as it emphasizes a need to maintain distinction.

# 6  Obstinacy

### Functionality

The association of forming things through craft work and the realization of the form proper to a human being was rife in ancient Greek thinking. In the *Eudemian Ethics*, Aristotle suggests that just as a cloak, house or a boat have about them a function and a state of excellence, so too does a human soul, and in the *Nicomachean Ethics* he works through a rough analogy, asking his interlocutors to consider the symmetry between the good of a carpenter or shoemaker and their proper actions and functioning, and then to consider how the good of any human being is also set by its proper function.[1] His idea of a properly functioning human is derived, initially, from Socrates, who argued that just as a shoemaker uses specific tools and materials to make a good shoe, so a human being should employ the soul to deliberate and bring about sound judgments, and thereby embody a state of justice. Aristotle, however, enriches Socrates by insisting that functionality – the actions by which a thing defines itself as, potentially, a good thing – avoids instrumentality.

If we take what Rachel Barney observes is Aristotle's nested structure of reasoning, then, following the analogy with craft work, the function of the shoemaker is to make shoes and the carpenter chairs, along with many other craft workers, all of whom then contribute to the broader, end goal of human functioning. There is a stacking and nesting of functions into an architecture of mutually organized ends, each aware of the further ends to which it is devoted, and the entire forming an organized unity of proper functioning, which in turn then creates excellence. The ultimate end being human happiness, which is served by the totalizing architectural craft of politics: good shoes, for example, enable soldiers to march effectively, which assists courageous and wise generals, whose martial leadership

---

[1] NE 6. 2, 1139, 31-5; EE 2. 1, 1218–1219. Nicomachean Ethics. *The Complete Works of Aristotle*. Vol. 1. Edited by Jonathan Barnes. Princeton: University of Princeton Press. 1995. 1729–1867; Eudemian Ethics in same volume 1922–1981.

makes for a robust city state out of which the finest expressions of political craft become possible. This argument, however, is open to a medley of interpretations as to the nature of the good. A shoemaker can make good shoes, but the state of goodness extends into use, and the uses to which well-made shoes can be put are legion. Well-made shoes have contributed to feelings of personal aggrandizement because of their length and height; they have satisfied a hedonic impulse to consume and own; and they have served to foster a sense of violent distinction and immunity when worn by security forces policing the streets. These uses are socially and subjectively charged, they abound with regional and historical affinities, there is nothing about them that is immanent or necessary by way of the proper functioning of a shoe. The same would go for tables, and, ultimately, for human beings.

To avoid the morass of these contested 'good' uses, Aristotle tries to divest means – end relations from his reasoning, making no mention of a thing's use value. Functionality becomes intrinsic, not instrumental.[2] Being intrinsic, the value of a function lies in its distinguishing the identity of the thing to whose *telos* it is intimate. In the case of humans, the *telos* is social as much as natural, it is immanent to practice as much as the body. Shoemaking has an intrinsic, non-instrumental function insofar as the good of the individual subject who has taken up shoemaking is to be a good shoemaker *qua* shoemaker: the good shoemaker and the good of the subject slide into one another. To introduce an external good, such as earning money, as a warrant for this relational slide is to loosen the ties between effectiveness, excellence and function, and to elevate wealth as an explicit end, which serves only to erode the distinctiveness of craft work, given many work practices pursue wealth and can be successful in doing so without necessarily nurturing skill (*technai*), as well as using other profit-seeking activities to accompany the *technai*. Stealing, for example, or exploiting. Aristotle wants to keep the connexion between function, end and identity as tight as possible, to a point of transitive immanence.

This, suggests Barney, is where craft work becomes instructive, and provocative. To be a good shoemaker is to recognise the difference between making shoes and making shoes well, and the continual negotiation of this difference is what also applies generally: 'a good human being has the same function as a human being, together with the responsibility of performing it better'.[3] What distinguishes a shoe from a good shoe is a question the shoemaker asks every time they work, as they work. The good is not realized in occasional, dedicated moments of disciplined

---

[2] Rachel Barney *Aristotle's Argument for a Human Function*. In *Oxford Studies in Ancient Philosophy*. Edited by David Sedley. Oxford: Oxford University Press. 2008. 293–322.
[3] Rachel Barney *Aristotle's Argument for a Human Function*. 317.

contemplation, or in metaphysical belief, or in the clear articulation and pursuit of singular interests, but in struggling to be a good shoemaker, weaver, calligrapher, printer or woodworker. It is not an intellectual form of questioning that sets out to answer what a shoe or boot 'is', but a practical consideration of the values and actions involved in making it, and making it well. It is not knowledge that comes easily. It demands apprenticeship in how to select, tan and mould different leathers and runners, how to welt, nail and stitch, how to feel for the shape of a foot, how to carve lasts, how to alter the shape of the sole, the stiffness of the heel cup, the height of the tongue, to accommodate different activities. It also requires the forms of questioning Ursula Munch-Petersen was asking when she makes jugs: what makes it a jug, a letter, textile or shoe? In the same way, learning to become a human being demands similar practical dedication and curious questioning.

Jonathan Lear likens it to a scene of doubt, and doubting one's ability to realize one's function, and hence to doubt one's identity throws us into a thoughtful relationship with our status as an enduring being. Using craft work to think through this sense of functionality emphasizes the aesthetic quality of a sense of identity, how the human self is, because of doubt, in a state of continual formation that 'expands the concept of *human* from the inside out'.[4] In craft work the failures in giving form are as illuminating as the successes. When their pots failed, the Martin brothers often inscribed them with a verse from Jeremiah 18:4: 'And the vessel that he made of clay / Was marred in the hands of the potter' (Figure 51).

It is this non instrumental sense of function pervaded by doubt that licenses Ruskin's inclusion of obstinacy in Gothic temperament. He sets the active rigidity of obstinacy against what he conjectures is a more circumspect, luxuriant and meandering temperament associated with the southern Romanesque:

> the Gothic ornament stands out in prickly independence, and frosty fortitude, jutting into crockets, and freezing into pinnacles; here starting up into a monster, there germinating into a blossom, anon knitting itself into a branch, alternately thorny, bossy, and bristly, or writhed into every form of nervous entanglement; but, even when most graceful, never for an instant languid, always quickset.[5]

---

[4] Jonathan Lear *The Ironic Creativity of Socratic Doubt*. In *Wisdom Won from Illness*. Cambridge, MA: Harvard University Press. 2017. 117.
[5] John Ruskin *The Stones of Venice, Vol. II.* §74. 241. Andrew Hill (*Ruskinland*, London: Pallas Athene. 2019. 199–200) elaborates nicely on how, in *Ruskin's rambling project Fors Clavigera* – an ongoing collection of open letters to workers – the title combines a sense of the force (fors) of work with the fortitude needed to see it through, and to nail it to fortune (clavigera).

224   6   Obstinacy

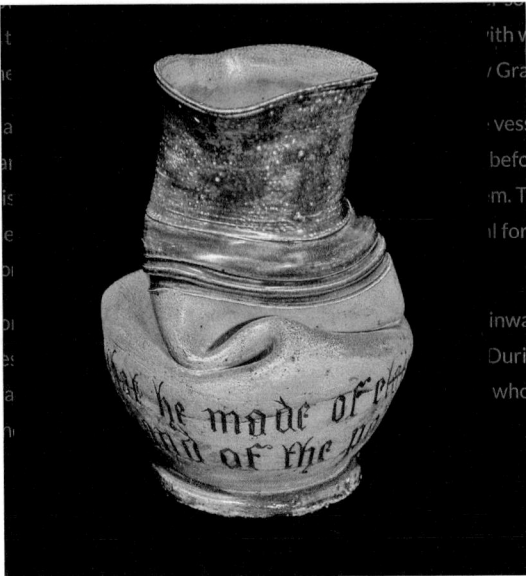

Figure 51 Martin brothers, failed pot, 1885. Salt-glazed stoneware. © Southall Library, London. Ealing Council.

An obstinacy counteracts the tendency some forms of craft work have of slipping towards objectification, an almost imperceptible movement in which personal commitments and values yield to tradition, and purpose gives way to fatality. There is a loss of distinction amid the lines of the masses which in turn gives way to an apparent necessity that brooks no doubt.[6] The obstinate work stands out; if it looks upwards it is only to send questions up to heaven, not abeyance. They no longer need the full-time help of gods, who become sidelined as fit subjects for decoration and contemplation. Through craft work the obstinate become their small gods, a plenitude of creative force throwing out little bolts of lightning: the shock of the new that betrays an impatience at control, an independence set against the background against which it refuses to lose definition. There is nothing willing itself other than itself. Yet it is a quality of which Ruskin is wary; the obstinate encase themselves in frigidity, their rigidity can, like Puritan extremists, 'lose itself either in frivolity of division, or perversity of purpose'. Like the 'fearless height

---

[6] John Ruskin *The Stones of Venice, Vol. II.* §77. Yet it is not either/or: 'There is', Ruskin suggests, 'virtue in the measure, and error in the excess, of both these characters' (242). Obstinacy can go too far in its rigidity and lose itself in perverse wilfulness.

of the subtle pinnacle', self-dependence, philosophical investigation and accurate thought are laudable, dogmatic fervour less so.⁷

## Gestalt

Under an obstinate aspect, a craft worker struggles to separate from the surroundings with sufficient acumen (*technai*) to learn and experience how functional work and well-made things with good form might be distinguished. It is a struggle towards the realization of good form – *Gestalt* – that the psychologist Kurt Goldstein was less a case of reaching a threshold state than a continual process of self-actualization in which the forms being brought to life (the material bodies, the ethical characters, the sensory experiences) ere relational, not substantive in character.⁸ Goldstein had devoted much of his professional life to studying how the de-mobilized bodies of soldiers which had been mauled by their experience in the trenches of World War I could possibly adapt to civilian life. How were they to realize good, or even adequate form? He concentrated on those suffering legions to the brain for whom certain motor and cognitive skills had become difficult, or impossible. The typical treatment was to concentrate on the affected areas of the brain, and to ameliorate where possible the loss of function or thought. Goldstein realized this tendency to isolate a body part and bring it up close fostered an expertise in the mechanics of physiological and cognitive functioning, treating the patient as an amalgam of interconnected, but separable, parts.⁹ Even where the body was repaired to a functioning level, its functionality was left untouched because there was little understanding of the wider systems with which these patched up skills were to integrate. The patients often exhibited anxiety, for example, which could not be attributed to a distinct, localized infliction of the brain: it seeped through their character and into their relations (as is testified brilliantly in the opening of Virginia Woolf's *Mrs Dalloway*), and needed treating as such, through what was, at the time, a novel 'holistic' approach, which studied functionality as belonging to a whole person set within its various milieux.¹⁰ Anxiety arose

---

[7] John Ruskin *The Stones of Venice, Vol. II*. §77. 242.
[8] Kurt Goldstein *The Organism*. New York: Zone Books. 1995. See also Patrick Whitehead 'Goldstein's Self-Actualization: A Biosemiotic View', *The Humanistic Psychologist*. 2017, 45, 1, 71–83.
[9] For a discussion of Goldstein, *Gestalt* and the potential sympathies between biology and phenomenology see Patrick Whitehead. 'Overcoming Parallelism: Naturalizing Phenomenology with Goldstein and Merleau-Ponty', *Progress in Biophysics and Molecular Biology*. 2015, 119, 502–509.
[10] Kurt Goldstein *A Note on the Development of My Concepts*. In *Selected Papers/Ausgewählte Schriften*. Edited by Aron Gurwitsch, Else M. Goldstein Haudek, William E. Haudek. The Hague: Martinus Nijhoff. 1971. 1–12. 4.

from injuries, but also from treatments, from institutional separation, from the exhaustion at having what was once habit become the subject of conscious decision, from the provision of prosthetic devices that accentuated their difference and legitimated ostracization, from shame at having lost the war, and from their loss of agency in their recovery.

In understanding functionality holistically, Goldstein's patient was being understood as organisms engaged in continual attempts at self-actualization within everyday milieux that no longer seemed ordinary. The anxiety was especially prevalent in patients who had preserved a full range of what Goldstein called abstract behaviours, alongside a now restricted range of concrete behaviours. Together, abstract and concrete behaviours act as the warp and weft from which functionality gains its repeating and overlayered patterns of meaning.[11] By concrete behaviour, Goldstein referred to mechanical movements such as the distillation of an iris, itself connected inwardly to operations of the optic nerve, and further inwards to neurones, and outwardly to environmental events such as changes in temperature and light. Abstract behaviour was: 'the ability of voluntary shifting, of reasoning discursively, oriented on self-chosen frames of reference, of free decision for action, of isolating parts from wholes, of disjoining given wholes, as well as establishing connections, for example, in learning'.[12]

Retaining abstract behaviour whilst losing facility in concrete behaviour meant the continual struggles of a wounded soldier to regain a sense of environmental adequacy, and hence functionality, was both poignant, and troubling.[13] Abstract (digital) behaviour was crucial in bringing about a recovery, yet their reasoning tended to confirm, not challenge, their self-understanding as outsiders. Under the rubric of Goldstein's holism, the soldiers' self-actualizing struggle for functionality was material, temporal, semiotic, semantic, without any of these having a clear boundary or priority. Their recovery depended upon them refusing to fall in with the 'lines of the masses', to avoid a languid ostracization from a society bent on ignoring them. To fit in again meant becoming 'an individual', one able to take on the task of becoming a good human being in the mould of Aristotle's shoemaker and

---

[11] Kurt Goldstein *A Note on the Development of my Concepts*. 1–12.
[12] Kurt Goldstein *The Organism* New York: Zone Books. 1995. 301.
[13] Kurt Goldstein associates this with the term *Gestalt*, by which he means a dynamic equilibrium characterizing an organism – a whole – in its repeated effort at coming to terms with environmental stimuli, or irritants, that have some bearing on its continued viability. Though abstractly conceived as general phenomena (chemical compositions say, or rates of heating) found across differing situations, the stimuli are mediated through the qualitatively distinct structure of each organism, hence the Gestalt form varies continually, and is the unique expression of an organism's own self-actualizing effort. Kurt Goldstein *The Organism*. 286–302.

carpenter. But this individual is not dividuated, the goodness of the form is an aspect of an interpenetrating array of mutually dependent structures and processes to which all life submits, including it (reminiscent of Masao Maruyama's autonomous individual). The submission is primarily aesthetic: the good human is realized when its body acquires a graceful state in which its own form resonates with wider systems with an economy and coherence of expression. The soldiers' struggle for good form was compounded, however, by its being forced on them by circumstance, and by its involving a multiplicity of often competing phenomena all of which required continual, if rough, organization: mangled limbs, psychotic episodes, flags, medals, cultural rituals, commercial interests, national pride, inaccessible public and domestic space, family shame, innovations in medical technology.

The rehabilitation of a wounded soldier requires both clinical experts and patients to understand the unactualized potential of the concrete and abstract behaviours that ground functionality, and for society more broadly to apprehend the prejudices that colour and brand the reasoned, sensory and affective experiences by which it has organized and instituted relations between people, and between people and things, and to recalibrate these to afford space to differently abled humans. The science of prosthetics, for example, with which Goldstein was thoroughly familiar given the prevalence of mechanical substitutes for body parts being used to treat recovering soldiers, works on the principle that an organ, say the eye, has a fixed function and form, which might then be emulated by substitutes. When the substitute is nothing but a pale imitation, as in a glass eye, the life being led is attenuated. There is no glittering of recognition or widening of the pupil in fear, no breadth of sight. The effect of the prosthetic device is limited, it helps the patient put on a face and become socially more approachable, but it only imperfectly replicates the proper form of the organ. What Goldstein tries to push his medical colleagues into realising is that, in addition to prescribing the use of mechanical devices, they might attend to the capacity of an organism to re-generate itself so that new forms and relations emerge. For example, when the sense of hearing more than compensates for poor eyesight, affording the patient access to hitherto concealed environmental stimuli, developing relational sensitivities which then further reassemble the remaining senses, allowing them, for example, to hear rather than see colours. Further still, they might consider how the bodily materiality of the patient plus mechanical device alters through the ongoing circulation of signs, signified objects and interpretations through which all organisms struggle in the search for the functionality of adequate form. As a deliberate and carefully made sign, the glass eye imitates a real eye, but can be read in multiple ways, depending on whether those who notice the eye are 'taken in' by its verisimilitude, and whether they react with repulsion or compassion once the signifier is acknowledged as the absence rather than presence of sight.

To further his case, the craft to which Goldstein appeals as an inspiration is, like Ruskin, architecture. Within this, the first or primary amongst the arts, the struggle to distinguish 'good' form from mere form can only be realized by attending to how what is being built attains and sustains adequate ecological fit between structure, use, history and setting. In an echo of Ruskin's critique of Renaissance architecture, Goldstein suggests a building does not culminate in the material unity of steel, concrete, glass and brick, nor in the deferential execution of idealized blueprint. It does not culminate in anything, it keeps going an repeated attempts at realising an intrinsic form through which hitherto disparate elements – ducting, curtain walls, glazing, landscaping, plenum – become intelligible as a unified and distinct form: 'We are seeking a whole in which one can differentiate amongst the observed phenomena, between the 'members' that really belong to it, and the less relevant, contingent connections of arbitrary parts.'[14]

What really belongs to a building (or shoe, or table, or human self) is not decided in advance by an idea or ideal held in the mind (*res cogitans*) nor determined by the materials of which it is made or the material conditions in which it is to be placed (*res extensia*), but through an adequate coming together of character (the facilities, uses and structures of the building) and place.[15] The wholeness of a building's form cannot be properly understood by identifying and explaining the working of its parts; it is more than an amalgam. Nor can it be understood as the fulfilment of an inner essence. Its functionality and hence distinction as a building is realized only by acknowledging that it is, in itself, part of wider wholes, and itself made up of other wholes, a continually negotiated nesting to which it contributes and from which it borrows its hold on its sense of the good. As with Gothic, the overall unity is utterly relational, a *Gestalt* form that emerges in this continual search for adequacy. The building and its environment are mutually implicated forms, they are insinuated in one another. Gothic has no *a priori* forms such as the column or done, it has no orders or catalogue of ideal patterns, it has nothing but the rib, and in the rib, says the architect Lars Spuybroek, it has a vegetal and textile element that being too weak to act alone, gathers, and the strength and presence of the building emerges after the gathering and bundling which tighten into uprights before curling and circling, or unspooling and spanning into fans

---

[14] Kurt Goldstein *The Organism*. 306–307.

[15] 'We know from other experiences that ordered behavior is an expression of adequacy between the demands of the stimulus and the capacity of the organism.' Kurt Goldstein *The Smiling of the Infant*. In *Selected Papers/Ausgewählte Schriften*. Edited by Aron Gurwitsch, Else M. Goldstein Haudek, William E. Haudek. The Hague: Martinus Nijhoff. 1971. 466–484. 469.

and lines of flight that course over vast spaces and voids before gathering in new lines of movement forcing themselves onwards whilst bearing and bending with the force of lines they meet.[16]

The form being envisaged here is far from the space of measured elevations, angles and material counterweights, it is not imposed on life but emerges from it. It is as much topological as it is metric. The building is akin to what the architect Peter Zumthor calls an atmosphere, a continuous form of tensions, associations and divergences held in a state of self-organized, mutual affection. There is no moulding, only modulation.[17] To understand the good *Gestalt* of a building is to understand the continual responsiveness of its elements as they move, and are moved by, its occupants and setting. These moving elements, the ones that really belong to a building as opposed to the less relevant ones, include:

Material and materials interacting – the skeleton of beams, tiles and glass, the grain on oak echoed by ripples in water, the contrasting hard and soft edges, the folded curves of lead, an energy of sometimes puzzling conjunctions;

The acoustics of space, muffling, calm, clear as a bell, an open chamber, the hum of machinery and conversation;

Temperature, the enveloping warmth, the release or intensification of breeze, pocketing or seeping light;

Objects, into which one bumps, niches for shadows, things which have to be homed and accounted for;

Movement, the seduction and composure of occupation, where one saunters, or strides, or sits, where one argues, or huddles, the stillness of concentration;

Thresholds, in-betweens, a well-defined or folding of the inside/outside or centre/peripheral, that are themselves not fixed;

Scale, the body as space, the framing of entrances and exits, the sense of distance, loftiness and intimacy, or intimidation;

and Light, falling and blocking, inside sliding into (or interrupting) outside, and outside merging (or jarring) with a broader outside.[18]

The building does not start in the material substance to which the mind, reason and language are then added, nor does it start in the mind as a plan to which materials are then forced to conform. The building is understood holistically, and so its form is evolving through continual interactions with its historical, natural and cultural setting, and doubt as to whether a building has secured what Goldstein calls 'adequate fit' is always there: when the building stutters in self-consciousness, or works against itself, which spurs

---

[16] Lars Spuybroek *The Architecture of Variation*. London: Thames and Hudson. 38–39.
[17] Melinda Cooper quoting Gilbert Smondon: To mould is to modulate definitively; to modulate is to mould in a manner that is continuous and perpetually variable. In *Life as Surplus: Biotechnology and Capitalism in the Neoliberal Era*. Seattle: University of Washington Press. 2008. 113.
[18] Peter Zumthor *Atmospheres*. Basel: Birkhauser. 2006.

amendments, and informs other projects. The architect (or patient, or clinician, or shoemaker) develops a kind of cussed intellectualism through which thought and reflexivity are continually being channelled back into the work as new ideas, and in turn these are often being frustrated by a felt inadequacy of execution, and it is this feeling of doubt that pricks further work. Try, fail, feel embarrassed, go again and dissatisfaction will always lurk amid the best that they can possibly do, and it is this sense of imperfection that keeps the work and the craft worker alive: 'Of human work none but what is bad can be perfect, in its own bad way'.[19]

In Zumthor's hands architecture is not just the mechanical science of divisible forces, but an expressive foray into the continuous variability of forces by which a building is a body, literally an anatomy of materials, that comes alive through an environmental coherence, a dwelling. Architecture 'is at its most beautiful when things have come into their own, when they are coherent. That is when everything refers to everything else and it is impossible to remove a single thing without destroying the whole. Place, use and form. The form reflects the place and the place is just so, and the use reflects this and that.'[20]

In its belonging, the form ceases to be known by defined planes, volumes, densities, and becomes atmospheric, a cloud of forces and rhythms and energies, a form is a holding and gathering of these, but they are morphogenetic, not mechanical in nature.

The *Gestalt* of Zumthor's building, and of Goldstein's patients, is morphogenetic. There are combinations of sound, light, material solidity, history and ritual that cohere to a form, a body, alive not just with movement, but with a purposive sense of its having to work continually to realize a rough harmony between function, ends and identity. It is a struggle to reach a struggle to reach threshold conditions under which elements or parts begin to self-assemble without the need for external semblance (material determinism) or instruction (from a mental image or ideal): the form comes into its own, it realizes a good *Gestalt*, and the life of such a form is germinal. In other words, it lives in the company of unsettlement, and it is only by dwelling with good *Gestalt* that homelessness can be experienced, by way of the struggle, the felt need to keep working at form without the comfort of a determinate end. An end can only come from an idea or from a strength of inner will (*res cogitans*), or from material determinism (*res extensia*), both of which reach for a centralizing perfection of necessary order, in their own bad way. Good *Gestalt* comes with the obstinate question of whether what has been built should be built differently, or elsewhere, or not at all.

---

[19] John Ruskin *The Stones of Venice, Vol. II.* §24. 203.
[20] Peter Zumthor *Atmospheres*. 69.

## Authenticity and Being with Things

In elevating obstinacy of spirit, Ruskin is flirting with the very same expressions of personal elevation that he finds so problematic in Renaissance architecture. For all its Deweyean grace, Zumthor's phenomenologically attuned architecture still bears his name, as does his practice, and the hundreds of articles, monographs and features devoted to understanding his work. As Glenn Adamson is at pains to remind us, there is in art, architecture and design a tendency to elevate the individual, and to conceal the work of the many others whose functioning is required to bring the artist's or architect's ideas into being. In part, suggests Adamson, this is the fault of the art industry. Galleries and those who sponsor and organize competitions invest in names, and where in the past, especially with architects, the power was with the workshop and studio, in the faceless office exhibiting a style, now we have artists and architects and even designers being treated as sole authors. Behind the scenes fabricators toil, unrecognized, just as necessary as the raw materials, and just as disposable.[21]

The mediation of digital electronics through organizational forms such as monopolistic search engines and social media platforms has made the situation even worse. Emergence and maturity give way to the scripted upgrade and update, which dispense with rather than build on what has gone before. Craft work can be different. Though as prone to the isolation of individuals as other forms of work and trade that are subject to regulatory compliance and engage in advertising, the immersion in tradition and the attentiveness to the demands of functionality keep the image of an individual grounded. Progress is iterative. The creative act is more akin to one of respectful addition performed within the collective setting of a tradition than one of destruction performed in isolation. The act is also bound to the making and re-making of things that have, or are associated with, quotidian use. Put a handle on a pot, said Richard Batterham during a film of him working at the wheel in his studio, and the price is halved, and he proceeds to carefully press a handle into the body of what could have been a round bellied vase, but now was very much in the process of becoming a teapot. Batterham trained with Bernard Leach in St Ives, picking up the use of the kick wheel from Atsuya Hamada who had brought his over from Japan whilst he too was apprenticing with the master. Though adept, Batterham would demur from the title 'master'. Making pots is a process, not an intense revelation of personal insight, and the process, being one of repetition,

---

[21] Glenn Adamson *Art in the Making*. London: Thames and Hudson. 2016.

is working with small changes to basic proportions of clay and glaze, aligning oneself again and again to the nuances of material and form whose coming together can be enhanced by a restricted range of stylistic techniques. Cut edges, flutes and ridges into the side of a teapot, for example, and do it well, and the angles can hold back the felspar and ash glazes he prefers to use, allowing it to gather along each edge, accentuating both the cut and curve of the body. These are the small arrangements whose inter-relation amounts to the struggle to make a good pot, and thereby a good human: test, and test again.

Batterham is alive to the functionality of which Aristotle speaks, and resists the pull to nominate and elevate his authorship. He would not accommodate the art industry, or any industrial process for that: he dug his own clay, used his own pug mill, dried, glazed and fired his own pots, which never veered from tableware and carried a profound consistency of shape, colour, size and strength. Big or small, fat or thin, it didn't matter much; what mattered was whether they were any good, which was to be decided as they emerged in the making. Though many were very good, they were hardly ever marked. He and his family made his studio a home and their home a studio, and that was that. There is in this lifestyle a sense of good *Gestalt*, of having been able to realize an adequate environmental fit with the elements that really mattered, whilst maintaining sufficient doubt to keep going, and go again, framed by ideas emerging from the making. In craft work, just as there is a restraint in the way of individual elevation, there is little in the way of its annihilation. Craft work is grounded in mutual acknowledgement between makers and things. It is a state of immersive sympathy often conceptualized as authentic; the ego stands aside to allow things to speak.

It was a state of being amid things to which the poet Rainer Maria Rilke devoted many poems. He called them 'thing poems': *Dinggedichte*. He had learnt to be with things from the sculptor Auguste Rodin, for whom he had been secretary for a while, during 1905, until Rodin let him go, having found the young poet too independent, too prone to go off on his own train of thought. But his waywardness was, Rilke protested, in part Rodin's fault: the sculptor had awakened in the poet an intense awareness of the materiality of things and in the materialization of made things like pots, or poems, stirred as much by the workings of the hand as the mind.[22] Echoed in David Kindersley's insistence that

---

[22] By the end of his life, Rodin had amassed a collection of over 6,000 ancient vases, and had become obsessed with the intimacy to be had between the human form and the form of things, notably the old earthenware pots thrown or coil and slab built to contain olives, flowers, oils or wine. He drew bodies as pots and pots as bodies, until they merged, each

letters were things, not images of things, Rilke began to experiment with the materiality of poems. The world was to be apprehended in terms laid out by the world. In Rodin's shadow, Rilke attempted to nurture a chalky, flinty, leathery, clayey, bronzy expert interest in the material appearance of the world. Just as Rodin depicts and remains with the straining physical intensity of feeling in a kiss or thought, Rilke made poems that stayed with things. Hitherto, felt Rilke, poetry had been winnowed and diluted by its intense interest in elevating and eulogizing articulated, refined feelings and heavenly mysteries to a point where nature was little more than a beautifying backdrop of potential metaphors: it was a grammatical resource for personal revelation and gilded exchange with angels. His *Dinggedichte* were to change that. And to do so they turned towards craft. Instead of trying to impress an angel with metaphysics, we ought:

> Tell him of Things. He will stand astonished; as you stood
> by the rope-maker in Rome or the potter along the Nile.
> Show him how happy a Thing can be, how innocent and ours,
> how even lamenting grief purely decides to take form,
> serves as a Thing, or dies into a Thing –, and blissfully
> escapes far beyond the violin. – And these Things,
> which live by perishing, know you are praising them; transient,
> they look to us for deliverance: us, the most transient of all.[23]

In attending to the rope maker and potter, and doing so patiently and silently, the things through which they manifest an everyday sense of the good becomes apparent. Rilke's concern, as Edmund De Waal wryly notices, has the air of the colonial ethnographer, the 'anxiously inauthentic' chronicler of the authentic, the phenomenological contortionist able to wrest from language both the distance of perspective and the propinquity of belonging.[24] Rilke becomes astute observer and silent participant, excited at having found productive beings who had yet to be properly confounded by the industrialized severance from nature. In their close company to hemp and clay, Rilke's imagined craft workers (along with the vicarious poet) were connected to things in ways that for many had been closed off. Development in the West had taken a wrong turn. Makers and users had incurred a disconnection from nature insisted on by ever more pervasive and intricate systems

---

being containers whose emptiness, whose void, was a materialization of potential. Rilke's second volume of *New Poems* (1908), was dedicated to Rodin, his '*grand Ami*'.

[23] Rainer Marie Rilke 'Ninth Duino Elegy'. In *The Duino Elegies and the Sonnets to Orpheus*. Translated and edited by Stephen Mitchell. New York: Vintage. 2009. 46.
[24] Edmund De Waal. 'Speak for Yourself', *Ceramic Review*, 182, March/April 2000, 45–48.

of divided labour and branding. They were, argued Rilke, surrounded by the visible and risible growth of denatured, mass-produced things.

Commenting on this critical move Michael Hoffmann quotes a letter from Rilke in which the poet laments:

> Even for our grandparents a 'house', a 'well', a familiar tower, their very clothes, their coat: were infinitely more, infinitely more intimate; almost everything a vessel in which they found the human and added to the store of the human. Now, from America, empty indifferent things are pouring across, sham things, *dummy life* ... Live things, things lived and conscient of us, are running out and can no longer be replaced. *We are perhaps the last still to have known such things.*[25]

Those who are not only content but excited by the apparent fecundity of manufacturing, those who talk of the improvement in lifestyle made possible by cheap goods, those who admire the rising tides of material wealth, are thoughtless, inauthentic. They lack grace, they lack functionality, they lack obstinacy. Their relation to a new, technologically mediated environment is a contracting one of passive acceptance. Hoffmann emphasizes the point by quoting from Rilke's *Sonnets to Orpheus*:

> All we have gained the machine threatens, as long
> as it dares to exist in the mind and not in obedience.
> To dim the masterful hand's more glorious lingering,
> for the determined structure it more rigidly cuts the stones.
>
> Nowhere does it stay behind; we cannot escape it at last
> as it rules, self-guided, self-oiled, from its silent factory.
> It thinks it is life: thinks it does everything best,
> though with equal determination it can create or destroy.[26]

What the machine lacks is a purposive, immanent sense of functionality, substituting instead an instrumental one that likens itself to life, but is, in effect, settled upon the quiet devastation of life. Rilke, like Ruskin, Marx and others before him, and so many afterwards, bemoans this repetitive materialization of life mediated by the machine and machine thinking. In its stead he lobbies for the authentic material relations embodied in the rope maker and potter for whom machines remained 'in obedience'. Their minds remain unclouded. They speak of natural things, or, more poignantly still, they refuse to speak. Silence is more

---

[25] Rainer Marie Rilke quoted in Michael Hofmann. 'Slashed, Red and Dead', *London Review of Books*, 21 January, 2021, 43, 2.
[26] Rainer Marie Rilke. '10th Sonnet to Orpheus'. In *The Sonnets to Orpheus*. Translated by Stephen Mitchell. New York: Simon and Shuster. 1985.

appropriate when apprehending the way in which things appear naturally. In their silence the rope maker and potter exhibit the humble, attentive, perfectly aligned naturalization of which, in the confines of their tradition, they are utterly unaware. Their work is uncalculated, simple (though far from easy), unadorned with lofty ideals, indeed bereft of ideas full stop. The rope and the pot were made to be used, period. Again and again, in the same way.

Whilst he was determined to write of ordinary experience, Rilke, though, is far from an everyday critic interested in categorizing objects (including potters and critics) into established hierarchies of taste. The thing poems are testimony to a form of ethnographic observation which, when used in the making of poems, derails the technical and formal obsession with discovering universal conditions of truth and beauty as much as it dethrones the individualizing narcissism of personal feeling. Like many of his peers, Rilke felt concern for how machines culled authentic expressions of creative engagement with the world. He finds craft work beguiling because here, apparently, the perishing of things occurs naturally rather than through consumption, and the things made hinted at their own obstinacy, as well as that of their maker; 'a pot that survives the hell of firing' suggested Paul Gaughan, 'is like a man who is both purged and reborn.' Yet he is not reporting upon made things or the makers by way of a rich commentary. Rather, he is thinking through the example of craft work to his own work as a poet, and how text too might be used to make inscrutable things. The task he is setting himself during 1902–1907 when the first volume of the *Dinggedichte* was published was all the more urgent and difficult because the environment to which the human organism must relate and organize itself is less and less one of natural resistance and tensions, and more and more one of machine-bred solutions and comforts whose only demand is that those who once made and used acquiesce and transform themselves into those who produce and consume. 'But still', Rilke continues:

> ... existence for us is a miracle; in a hundred
> places it is still the source. A playing of absolute
> forces that no one can touch who has not knelt down in wonder.
>
> Still there are words that can calmly approach the
>     unsayable ...
> And from the most tremulous stones music, forever new,
> builds in unusable space her deified temple.[27]

---

[27] Rainer Marie Rilke. '10th Sonnet to Orpheus'. 91.

To use words to approach the unsayable, however timorously, is how the thing poems gain their force. Undaunted by the reticence that besets the specualtive realists, Rilke's words set up an asymptotic allegiance to material objects, looking across the unbridgeable and 'unusable' space between language and the world as if, nevertheless, the distance between them were itself the provocation by which the words gained their own thinglyness.

Through perceiving and writing, the poet learns to coax things from the shadows long enough to catch a glimpse of their interior: the object presents itself to the subject. It is a glimpse crafted through poetic language. What makes poetic language distinct is its consciously operating at the limits of the sayable: poetry starts when language begins to shake and the habitual foundations of meaning begin to teeter on the edges that have hitherto provided adequate definition. The thing poems are made to be more than a representation of depicted things. They are poetic presentations of things whose presence is self-sufficient. Unused because it cannot be directed, decided over or detailed. The thing is made both apparent but freed from the ministrations of human management. So, a pot ends and then also begins at the rim and the foot. It is easy to throw a bowl, but to get the tension right between rim and form, the tension in the rim, in its relation to the volume of the pot, and to the point at which the pot ends: all this is difficult. The rim is nothing but relationship: Hamada Shoji was almost peerless at wresting this limit point from in-between presence and absence,[28] the good pot or vase being the whose foot or lip avoids completion.[29] Its meaning is not attributed to its having been used and placed in relation to other things, or to its having potential use, or to its having been theorized. The thing is not there to be slotted seamlessly into human practice, whether instrumentally as a useful thing, or artistically as symbolic gatherings or emotional intensities. It has autonomy, a state Rilke also claims for his poems.

---

[28] The potter Phil Rogers attests to the inimitable skill with which Hamada Shoji was able to make the lip and feet of bowls, how they would stand so firm but without obvious weight. In 1955 Hamada was designated a 'National Living Treasure' by the Japanese Government, a testimony to his global influence on studio pottery which was attained without bombast. Indeed, the opposite, it was, said Rogers, his nonchalant style that made such an impression, notably the concision and restrained energy of the brushwork with which he decorated his pots, a sprig, a bushel, a hare, fish or bird (see Phil Rogers *A Portfolio*. Uppingham: Goldmark. 2012. 19–32.)

[29] See Lao Tsu [Laozi] quoted in Francois Jullien *The Great Image Has No Form, On the Nonobject through Painting*. 70. The great square has no corners, the great work avoids coming about, the great tone has only a limited sound, The great image has no form.

This is what Rilke learns from Rodin: the interior of bodies and pots can also become their exterior, they create their own world, without regard for their instrumental appeal. The sculptures never address the viewer, they are self-contained. Without or regional setting need of a human context they create their own story, outside of human back stories and hoped for futures. Rodin's thinker looks down, away, without concern for the viewer or their interpretations, freed from the confines of humanly organized time.[30] Rilke also learns it from Cézanne. He applauds the painter's dedication to scrutiny and handwork, his refusal to turn away from things, his overcoming the temptation to indulge in discrimination and choice. Cézanne stays with things through thick and thin, presenting them with an 'unlimited objectivity'.[31] Cézanne's genius emerged from his deliberate and disciplined will to let things be, especially colours which he left free to come to their own terms with one another, without attempting to manage or arrange them. This reticence is the gift of great painting. The painter who intercedes with the intellect and who pauses to consider technique or effect through spoken and written commentary is prone to abstraction, to design, to the arbitrariness of decision:

> The painter (any artist whatever) should not become conscious of his insights: without taking the way round through his mental processes, his advances, enigmatic even to himself, must enter so swiftly into the work that he is unable to recognize them at the moment of their transition. For him, alas, who watches for them, observes, delays them, for him they change like the fine gold in the fairy tale which can no longer remain gold because some detail went wrong.[32]

As De Waal suspects, then, rather than act as their own interpreter Rilke seems to be encouraging artists to remain text-free. The power of Rodin and Cézanne emerges from their outrageous willingness to encounter things, stripped entirely of civilized self-consciousness. Yet whilst he steps in as an interpreter on their behalf, he is also thinking of poetry through their example. His thing poems are written in the same manner: they are texts that refuse his own textual commentary and which, if they succeed, reveal the thing as it really is through a kind of narrative escalation in autonomy, or obstinacy, which culminates in what van den Broeck in her commentary on Rilke translates as the art object.[33] First comes the material object being referred to which provokes and

---

[30] Claire van den Broek. 'How the Panther Stole the Poem: The Search for Alterity in Rilke's Dinggedichte', *Monatshefte*. 2013. 105, 2, 225–246.
[31] Rainer Marie 'Letter to Clara Rilke, October 18th 1907'. In *Letters of Rainer Marie Rilke 1892–1910*. New York: W. Norton. 333.
[32] Rainer Marie 'Letter to Clara Rilke, 21 October 1907'. In *Letters of Rainer Marie Rilke 1892–1910*. 336.
[33] Claire van den Broek. 'How the Panther Stole the Poem'.

contains the written response in the poem and to whose placed presence the poem recurs. Here the poem lingers on commentary, felt description and event. Second comes the thing understood as an object within the text of the poem that is available to all language users who read the poem and who, with thought, can witness how the poet is struggling to realize a kind of equilibrium between their self and the object's own unity. The poem is an attempt to find a balance which requires the subject not only to witness the object but to do so by absorbing the transience and fragility of the experience. It is here that Rilke, like Keats before him witnessing a Grecian urn, struggles for something more graceful, more attentive to how to expand and enhance life by learning from things as things, rather than domesticating them into human service, whilst always admitting that the attempt is partial, momentary, a fragment amongst fragments. Objects become events carrying forth their own meanings. Third, and most difficult, comes the completion of the giving over to the object in which it is the object's own view that has complete authority: the object – or thing – is the authorizing force and displaces the imagination of the reader who can only react in wonder. At the very moment (*augenblick*) at which there is a freely given move away from agreed grammar and convention and towards the presence of the thing (the second move) there is also, potentially, an experience of being bound by that thing. Human autonomy (of the viewer in the poem, and the reader of the poem) cedes to the autonomy of things. This third and last move is rare, given only to a few who, like Rodin and Cézanne, refuse to be distracted by thought, by themselves, by digressive speculation, and who instead just work with things and on being bound to things in this way they carry the ultimate authority.

But why the sense of elevation? The division seems prone to similar objections levelled against the speculative realists: a profundity of insight is bought at the expense of shame, along with a Faustian contortion of being able to turn so far inwards that one produces one's own exterior, immune to the contexts to which life is being set. Given such elevation, Rodin's thinker, like the angel to whom Rilke suggests the poet talk of things, cannot belong, it seems, to the human rhythms of which it is nevertheless an expression. If the poet is to become self-sufficient, the implication is that they are frozen out of the seasons and the evenings, from nostalgia or anticipation; don't they shy away from convention and become suspicious of the immediate sensory appeal of impressionistic, surface dwelling? It is as if feeling itself were a distraction which must be bracketed off to the point where appearance dissipates and what remains is the object itself, without need of a subject. The object is no longer there as that which is being perceived, it is just there, lasting unto itself. In abandoning their own subjectivity in this way, the poet sidesteps perspective and interpretation, and goes straight to the whole thing, to its unity, to its reality as the speculative realists might have it. Yet to undertake such a sidestep remains a human practice. The very intent to loosen the hold of one's subjectivity is itself a negative act of pinpoint specificity undertaken by the intentional force of a subjective consciousness interacting with its broader environment: it is an attempt at realizing a state of adequate fit. Moreover, the work too, the made thing, whether it is a poem, sculpture or pot, only ever carries its autonomy through an act and declaration of severance whose separation serves also as an appeal. How else can one read the works of the poet whose most famous and enigmatic line was a direct appeal to the reader: 'You must change your life'? The made object – such as the 'Archaic Torso of Apollo', the poem that ended with this line and that was published in the collection *New Poems* dedicated to Rodin – cleaves its space and creates sufficient distance to end in itself by virtue of an effusion. In short, the art thing is long, it has reach and endures in milieux. The spatial separation is less something geometric than it is atmospheric. Here Rilke means that the special class of things called art things – such as the sculpture of Dante lost in thought at the mouth of hell or the painting of a yellow apple contained in the folded tilt of a white cloth – were so intensely alive to their environment that they were able to absorb and distil their captivation into a discrete and intense unity; in its exposure it remains within itself whilst also setting up a world of which it is the affirming catalyst. For example, in Rilke's impression of a small bronze of a bird by Rodin 'distance lay folded on each of its feathers, one could spread it out and make it vast', its edges delineated a self-sufficiency by virtue of their declaring the volume of an immense, airy plenum.[34] The bronze thing breathes in the world, taking what it needs for sustenance, absorbing it, and sometimes to a point where it is so animated that when it releases and breathes out it not only gives of itself but does so in ways that envelop the viewer (Rilke), pulling yet more of the world towards it, enriching its unity, changing its own life, reaching out towards other life forms to reveal, revel in and transform its own self-sufficiency. The object redounds with its own self-sufficient atmosphere which, rather than separating it as though behind a wall, welcomes the world in through its many gateways.

---

[34] Margareta Ingrid Christian *Objects in Air: Artworks and Their Outside around 1900.* Chicago: University of Chicago Press. 2021. The form gains distinction by virtue of its capacity to evoke and produce the space within which it sets itself as a distinct thing. 83–85.

It is this ecological insight of Rilke's that spurs Margareta Ingrid Christian to speculate upon the intimacy between the thing poems and their ecological resonance in environing space. The thing poems moved from descriptions of how things were placed in the world to being things that produced worlds, but without ever leaving the world of which they were a product.[35] And when they reach a capacity for world making, the edges of their autonomous form are ones of resonance, not isolation, they lure rather than resist, it is better described as obstinacy and functionality than it is autonomy. To talk of things with the language of commentary and representation is to talk of how they relate to and are conditioned by other things: the rope of the rope maker, made up of twisted hemp, is fashioned into a gridded net, and each square is large enough to wrap itself around the neck of a writhing fish, hauled onto the deck of a boat, processed and sold on a quayside, or fed into a factory system. The rope is never rope alone. To talk of things with poetic language is to present things that redound with their own potential: the rope net hung to dry is gridwork that contains and holds refracted light, each cell a window onto other scenes and settings that afford the rope its right to exist.

### Cibachrome

The photographer Gary Fabian Miller works in a dark room containing oils, bleaches, light sensitive paper and found things from nature like leaves and seeds. Using a colour enlarger as a source of light, but also matches, which are struck and kept burning for different time lengths, he forms projected images on Cibachrome paper. It is an alchemical space. Like a kiln, he is looking to create certain forms and shapes with colour. Rings, circles, squares, oblongs. He began as a photographer, but the traditional photographic equipment was removed during the 1980s and he started printing the seeds or leaves directly, placing a plant seed, or leaf, or plant frond into the head of the enlarger to have that act as its own mediating filter in the spirit of Fox Talbot's pencils of nature experiments. It makes an abstracted self-image with the most meagre intervention, nudged into becoming something other than itself, a distillation and a vestige. It lives according to its own rhythms and now, also, to the temporal structures of a darkroom.

The poet Alice Oswald writes of how in Miller's work the thingly leaves are sufficient, enough, they need no camera, which is an

---

[35] Margareta Ingrid Christian *Objects in Air: Artworks and Their Outside around 1900.* 80–83.

obstacle. The light is brought into the dark room through modulated actions, focussing and exposure. The ideal is to get into a rhythm of slow exposure, sometimes an entire day and night exposure. There is a slow excavation of the colours embedded in the dyes. Together, the photographer/printer and the tree shared the same cycles, the same air and breath, absorbing the colour cycles of the tree's leaves. Devoted to working within the black box, it took six years to understand the method of navigation through touch, intuition, familiarity, sight internalized, and then the patience to wait, to let the symbiosis between photosynthesis and photographic processes take hold through the struggle of making.

On moving to the edge of Dartmoor in southwest England, he concentrated on light alone as a thing. He hung Cibachrome paper on a wall. It is 100 per cent light sensitive, there is no 'safe' red light, so it has to be worked in total darkness. The paper is unique in that the cyan, magenta and yellow dyes are merged with the emulsion on the polyester backed paper, as the paper is exposed to light the layers of dye start to decay according to the exposure time and range of emitted colour from the transparency. He shines a single source of light onto the paper, sometimes refracted through glass vessels, sometimes in towers, filled with oil, water or wine, building and disassembling these glass structures in the total darkness of the darkroom: unsighted agency setting itself on an arête between order and disorder. He has handwritten notes, drawing out aperture and length, type and colour of filter used as a filter, an unknown path, wayfinding, discovering light and time as an accumulation of days. Something happens, an event, the light touches you and you feel it and this is what you acquire as experience and then your struggle to find it in an image, to fix it. He created a recipe book to record how the placing of transparent objects, paper and light created a world of hitherto unseen light that remained very much of this world. The work came to a stuttering and slow end in November 2020 as boxes of discontinued Cibachrome paper well past their use-by date became impossible to procure.

Though sealed off in a darkroom, Miller insists these his final Cibachrome images are visceral, felt responses to Dartmoor. He talks of how a circle and square become places to inhabit, the former is natural, material, and the latter is thought, the idea, and where two meet they make an edge, a disappearing and emerging at one and the same moment. The image itself should merge with the experience, yet be its own thing, untroubled by the experience of its being made. It is there, fully formed, needing nothing more. The early autumn sun glancing off the rosehips in bursts of red, and then the light itself caught fast in Cibachrome paper. He talks of trying to make pictures that open the world up that can only come from the walking, from immersion in a landscape. The bright red abstract circle is a fully formed expression of light provoked by nature where red light abounds, were one to attend closely, as he does in walking, attending to the small-scale strangeness as much as the large-scale exposure of the moorland.

Cibachrome and its processing chemistry was a product of modern industry: the bleach corrodes, and careful handling is needed by those using it; it was a denatured and mass-produced thing. Yet as image-bearing paper it was, for some, unrivalled in depth from the 13 layers of dye and luminosity, precisely because of the oily, sharp, almost metallic quality to the colour. Miller is eloquent about the contradictions: how the most pervasive and sensitive of all natural things – light – is being rendered through mechanical operations steeped in industrialized development. As a product that led to profit, Cibachrome had no distinction; it could be a 'this', or a 'that', or 'something other than either', it was all the same given all products can be compared and slotted in when set against the criteria by which all manufactured things are defined: monetary value. Miller's attentive work removes the paper from these cycles, somewhat. The paper becomes a thing of concern, a raw material with an agency that can accentuate or diminish the intensity and longevity of the struggle towards making things that 'sing'. Despite Rilke's sense of being on the cusp of a devastating industrial capitalism, craft workers like Miller still find themselves drawn into a relation with things that, with patience and care, become insightful because of mutual accommodation of imagery, mediating objects such as paper and the medium of light.

The poet Gerard Manley Hopkins called this transition between objects and representational images (in his case it was words) 'stress', a moment of truthful association being wrested from the correspondence between what is being said or shown and the thing as it appears: the word or image holds onto an aspect of the 'being' of a thing, affirming and stressing it. Miller's craft work in the studio affords him an experience of adequate grip which he seeks to secure and intensify in rough but enduring acts of making room for stress between objects and the light through which they carry the appearance of their own arresting but also odd presence. Arguably, Miller's work can go further still, revealing what Hopkins calls 'a Being itself'. Hopkins capitalizes 'Being' to indicate how, through stress, a more basic, natural condition of Being as life (rather than the small 'b' appended to the being of an object) appears. As Miller's work develops it moves from stressing the 'being' of objects such as a seed or flower head, to 'Being' encountered as a force that extricates itself from specific scenes and 'rides time like riding a river', but which nevertheless remains dependent for its appearance upon the distinctions made possible by the 'stress' work being done by the maker.[36] Hopkins calls the move towards 'Being' a movement through stress towards instress, a move in which the maker, in making, experiences the unity and energy that sustains an object as it stands aside from having to accommodate itself to a broader milieu, and takes on a state of self-containment as a thingly thing.[37] Miller's photographs of light emerge from the process of making in a self-contained atmosphere of interacting colours and forms over which there is no symbolic or normative interpretation: they are what they are, 'instressed', utterly of themselves. Being so well made, however, ensures others take note. Perhaps not immediately, given the images refuse to accord with accepted norms of representation and symbolic messaging, but eventually, when viewers sense what it is to

---

[36] In his poem 'The Wreck of the Deutschland', Hopkins evokes this move by splitting the poem into two, the first dealing with the bewildering and overwhelming sense of a dependency upon God (who nevertheless remained apparent only through Nature):

> With an anvil-ding
> And with fire in him forge thy will
> Or rather, rather then, stealing as Spring
> Through him, melt him but master him still:
> Whether at once, as once at a crash Paul,
> Or as Austin, a lingering-out sweet skill,
> Make mercy in all of us, out of us all
> Mastery, but be adored, but be adored King.

The second part is an empirical event – the grounding and stranding of a German liner on a sandbank off the mouth of the Thames. Stuck fast, as the tide rose, the passengers tried to escape by climbing the rigging pleading for help, but for over a day none came, and many perished, leaving their bodies to be stripped of valuables by rapacious English sailors. The event caused outrage and soul searching: why had citizens of a seafaring nation refused to help, and then gilded the shame by looting from the dead? No longer upright, and moral compass askew, Hopkins asks whether the nation, like him, should re-group around faith, recognizing that some force, some Being resides behind and within all being:

> I admire thee, master of the tides,
> Of the Yore-flood, of the year's fall;
> The recurb and the recovery of the gulf's sides,
> The girth of it and the wharf of it and the wall;
> Stanching, quenching ocean of a motionable mind;
> Ground of being, and granite of it: past all
> Grasp God, throned behind
> Death with a sovereignty that heeds but hides, bodes but abides.
> (Gerard Manley Hopkins *Poems and Prose*.
> Edited by W. H. Gardner. Harmonsworth: Penguin. 1968. 12–24)

[37] To instress is to take the stress of the natural world, its emphases, its stridency, and to etch it upon oneself, to mingle with it, to belong, as, in a similar way, Christ and God belonged to nature through their materialization.

encounter a photograph of light made whole, without need of elaboration or use. The image attracts by giving over of itself, radiating from within its own lineaments, without calling in aid from the wider settings of the gallery space, the salon culture, the art dealer's effusions, Miller's own writing, the appraisals; life stands by itself, aside the maker.

## The 'Me', the 'I' and the Craft Venture

Interviewed by *The Studio* magazine in 1898 about running her ceramics workshop in the village of Compton, Surrey, Mary Watts was at a loss to nominate the persons she felt most important to its success:

> about the workers, I do not wish to mention one more than the other. The permanent staff were all untrained hands when they came. The young house-painter the Scotchman had never used clay and had only drawn at a school of art in Glasgow in the ordinary way – the Compton carpenter had also drawn at Guilford – ... The men all worked so splendidly – our gardener or 'steward' as he calls himself, the kiln-man and the village gardener – of course the permanent workers did the bulk of the work. Cannot say too much I am indebted to them all. I never had a difficulty they did not help overcome, and they were soon able to work from a rough charcoal drawing, though the first year I had to do the first pattern myself in clay. I think if names are mentioned then the generous help of Mr George Redmayne, architect, whom [sic] kindly saw that we did not make mistakes, overlooked the works of the village architect Mr John Lake, should be mentioned, but I should rather prefer it if the personal element were rather less. I hear about 'Mrs Watts' but if she must come, then those two names perhaps had better be mentioned.[38]

Somewhat entrepreneurially, Watts had opened her workshop on the back of the village council's decision to build a cemetery. The council had bought the land, and Watts stepped in offering to organize the construction of a chapel. Inspired by the writings of Ruskin and Morris and her longstanding membership of the Home Arts and Industries Association, and with backing from local philanthropists (including her husband, the artist G. F. Watts), she brought together a collection of village amateurs to assist with the building work. She also helped design the chapel, as well as being a pivotal figure, alongside the artist and ceramicist William De Morgan, in the construction of a bottle kiln which would fire the many terracotta tiles to be used in the chapel's construction. The chapel became a proving ground for her ideals: to create a community venture dedicated to the production of wealth through a closeness to nature

---

[38] Quoted in Hillary Calvert and Louise Boreham *Mary Seton Watts and the Compton Pottery*. London: Philip Wilson. 2019. 28.

and the rhythms of mutually supportive productive activity.[39] Catalysed by the project, Watts became a central, organizing force teaching the villagers all manner of craft work techniques (gesso, glass work, weaving, stitching, drawing, book binding), but it was terracotta tile making that became the mainstay of the work and which subsequently became a standalone pottery business expanded across a number of buildings dedicated to the different stages of preparing clay and moulds, firing, drying and decorating. Dormitories were built for apprentices, cottages were built to house the workers and their families, and schooling was offered for children with a curriculum bent towards the craft work for which most of the pupils seemed destined.

In 1904 the work at Compton became organized as the Potters Arts Guild which lasted until 1936 when the shared ownership structure gave way to a limited liability company, exposing its organization to the influence of stockholders. Being focussed on rough terracotta work, the kiln could not fire high enough to work glazes, so the majority of pieces were raw, though some were painted and waxed. Whilst ceremonial, ornamental and memorial ware was made, often to order, the bulk of the everyday work was dedicated to making garden pots of all sizes, the larger more ornate ones being press moulded, whilst others were turned on a wheel with the sprigging added afterwards. These were sold through Liberty's of London as well as directly through a Guild catalogue. The accounts were run according to principles first laid down in Ruskin's Guild of St George. The managers and long-standing workers shared half the profits, the other half being retained as capital, but assigned to individual employees to whom it was given when they retired or left the venture.

Watts' efforts encouraged others living nearby, notably Gertrude Jekyll, horticulturalist and doyen of garden fashion, who started buying garden planters, commissioning bespoke pots and then designing what were to become some of the most significant pieces of the Guild's range.[40] Like Watts, the ideas, drive and belief are all there in Jekyll's tenacious commitment to different types of craft work as the means towards a wealthy life. Moreover, both were committed to a broad (regional) understanding of the nature of this work: creating well made things required good materials and technique, but also a coherent community of workers, a cogent set of shared values, and an informed, socially active clientele. To

---

[39] Veronica Franklin Gould *Mary Watts and the Creation of the Watts Chapel*. In *An Artist's Village: G F Watts and Mary Watts at Compton*. Edited by Mark Bills. London: Philip Wilson. 2011. 67–84.

[40] Jekyll, a committed seamstress, also worked on the banners for the Godalming branch of the National Union of Women's Suffrage Societies. Mart Watts was president and founding member of the Godalming branch.

this end, rather than assert their own individuality, both Watts and Jekyll seemed more content with exploring the nuances and sympathies of a series of selves (craft worker, political campaigner, writer, entrepreneur, artist, journalist, villager) and each of these selves was a gathering force that cultivated gardens, congregations, marches, ventures, workforces and customers. Within the struggle to create and sustain these assemblies, their sense of self was also being worked at, and became all the stronger for its silences, its vagueness, its willingness to bend with shapes of the locality, to blend with others, and to lurk in recesses of thoughtfulness, always looking to take up tangents, remaining equivocal in the face of proposed or stated end points.

Figure 52 The tomb of Gertrude Jekyll by Lutyens with her gardening fork. © Mary Evans Picture Library/The Annabel Watts Collection.

Jekyll's gravestone (Figure 52) in Busbridge Churchyard is marked:

> ARTIST
> GARDENER
> CRAFTSWOMAN
> NON-OMNIS MORIAR.

A trinity of identities, none in the ascendency, none needing justification or elaboration, befitting someone who found herself content to remain within their interplay. Her commitment was to a garden and its seasonal arrays of colour, scents and volumes that were to be set along beds, in terracotta planters or up climbing walls in such a way that they, and not her, took the stage. A good (male) gardener was:

> wise enough to know that he does not know everything, and modest enough to acknowledge it, as do all the greatest and most learned of men, he will then be eager to receive new and enlarged impressions, and his willing and intelligent co-operation will be a new source of interest in life both to himself and his employer, as well as a fresh spring of vitality in the life of the garden.[41]

She was alert to how plants congregated and went their separate ways, how they flourished or failed, how they felt to be in one place or other, which were worthy and why and when, without deferring to the petty tyrannies of the show judge whose assessment of plants tends towards the fixed and severe, awarding prizes to 'bloated monsters' simply on the basis of measured size and 'perfection' of structure. Those showing flowers in competition might elevate themselves with prizes, but in doing so they genuflect to a judge who is: 'a slave to rules, and must go by points which are defined arbitrarily and rigidly, and have reference mainly to the show-table, leaving out of account, as if unworthy of consideration, such matters as gardens and garden beauty, and human delight, and sunshine, and varying lights of morning and evening and noonday'.[42]

To know of plants was to be in place, and 'with care and thought and the power of observation' to enliven oneself with what the place offered of itself, to fill oneself with sensuous mobilities of immediate sensation, to attend to how, at the right time, things will be giving of themselves, such as the ferns, which in late July might be cut and made into fern pegs to tie carnations. Jekyll is insistent on the need for a sharp knife, keeping a number of rubbers (sharpening stones) in the different sheds of her garden, and on cutting in the right place:

---

[41] Gertrude Jeykll *Wood and Garden. Notes and Thoughts. Practical and Critical, of a Working Amateur.* Cambridge: Cambridge University Press. 2011 (first published 1899) 273.
[42] Gertrude Jeykll *Wood and Garden.* 5; 243.

The bracken has to be cut with a light hand, as the side-shoots that will make the hook of the peg are easily broken just at the important joint. The fronds are of all sizes, from two to eight feet long; but the best for pegs are the moderate-sized, that have not been weakened by growing too close together. Where they are crowded the main stalk is thick, but the side ones are thin and weak; whereas, where they get light and air the side branches are carried on stouter ribs, and make stronger and better-balanced pegs.[43]

This is knowledge garnered by a long exchange between what the philosopher George Herbert Mead called a 'me' and an 'I'. The 'I' is Jekyll's immersed presence in the open, indeterminate present of everyday activity where memory, perception and expectation are being woven into one another continually, habitually, as she makes fern pegs or plants out seedlings. The 'I' emerges in hearing and seeing a rhythm in the wafting of long-stalked stocks or foxgloves, following the twisting melody of bird song riddling the branches of a thorn bush, in leaving a trail of dense green walking across dew-laden grass. The memories are embodied in thoughtless postures rather than actively recalled, and the future is rounded into the curve of gestured expectations: if it is a personal pronoun, then 'I' belongs to a grammar of the body, or of bodies, because it arises in situated moments of attraction and revulsion, of calm and commotion, of settlement and frustration. It is a tracery of action lines, the willingness of a will to listen, accommodate, riff off and pull away from many minor occurrences that occur by virtue of being placed, of being there in and amid things.

The 'me' is more reflective, explicit and substantial, more the idea of a self being formed by desire and by hope. It is thereby evaluative and more demanding, and upright. Schooled in reasoning and built up through stories that have been stored and categorized as recorded events and then re-told, distributed abroad, transformed into diagrammatic form, re-stored in ideas and values, compressed into character which, like soil, nurtures and sustains the expanding, growing, trailing presence of the 'I'. Jekyll's 'me' was contained in the *Gestalt* of gardens and how they might become were one to arrange them first this way, then that. In all flower borders, she advises, it is better to plant in long drifts rather than blocks, they draw the eye, and when they die back do not leave dried colourless patches; or gardens should be sensed as a total work of art in which plane, colour, volume and line met with brick walling, the flow of water, the growth of flowers, grasses and trees, the scattering of planters, the waft of scents, the hum of insects and song of bird.

---

[43] Gertrude Jeykll *Wood and Garden*. 98.

It was not, though, a 'me' that had been exteriorized, pushed out into the geometric space of formal equivalents, laws, strict necessities and demanding, exceptionless morals; there were very few imperatives resident in her 'me'.[44] In her first book, *Wood and Garden* (1899) with her own photographs, based on her own planting and structures, she was laying out the vivid scene of impressions with a more precise sensory acuity, compiling a month-by-month report on her own sensory experience, a working outward to then peer back inwards in a bout of self-sighting that consciously, by way of the word and reading the word, works at its own form, again and again: pushing back to go on. Mediated though the aesthetics of work, the 'me' bears the weight of the 'I', freeing it through posing possibilities which afford it space enough to let go and to follow what it felt was most arresting and compelling, and then judging the experience, but always and only through the work in which she takes her place in the garden (rather than the ersatz comment of the flower judge).[45] *Wood and Garden* reveals a craft worker working on herself through her work, her knowledge, her suggestiveness, refusing reason its sanity, its order, its consensus.[46] It is given over to the maintenance of joyful if transient experiences which repeat themselves under the care of a practical intelligence which emerges from the flickering between the 'me' and the 'I'. The made things – the garden, the pots, the book – intrude as a means by which a self becomes forced against itself. It intrudes as the 'me' enquires after the 'I', which might otherwise be lost in the flow of making. The craft worker often asks: 'Does the world need another cup, or belt, or wooden chair, or woven rug, or garden pot, or embroidered political banner?' The 'me' makes room for the made thing, to afford it a place in the world that is being made whereas the 'I', in its skill, enjoins itself to the experience of making and to the made things in ways that feed and mature the poise of the 'me'.

---

[44] Alfonso Lingis *The Imperative*. Bloomington: Indiana University Press. 1998.
[45] Theodor Adorno *Minima Moralia: Reflections from a Damaged Life*. Translated by E. Jephcott. London: Verso. 1951/2005. 70–71.
[46] To recur to Søren Kierkegaard loosely, and his sense of grace, this weaving of 'I' and 'me' feels akin to how he understands the self being fashioned from the weaving of possibility and necessity: 'But if possibility outruns necessity so that the self runs away from itself in possibility, it has no necessity to which it is to return; this is possibility's despair. This self becomes an abstract possibility; it flounders in possibility until exhausted but neither moves from the place where it is nor arrives anywhere, for necessity is literally that place; to become oneself is literally a movement in that place. To become is a movement away from that place, but to become oneself is a movement in that place', Søren Kierkegaard *Sickness unto Death: A Christian Psychological Exposition for Upbuilding and Awakening*. Princeton: Princeton University Press. 1980. XI 148.

## The Venture and the Community

Women more typical to the social class occupied by Jekyll and Watts wore fragile millinery, complex embroidery or exotic skins, whose destiny it was to be adorned and adored (and not at all to have a room in which to write, a garden to plant or a kiln to stack). Their clothing was a prosthetic extension of the alabaster skin and blue blood upon which it was draped: its assured cut and articulation moving as assuredly through space as the cut-glass accent and upright neck. In turn, the clothed body was an extension of social entitlement defined by the distinction of having nothing to do with anything so vulgar as writing, digging or modelling. Through their venturing in pots and gardens Jekyll and Watts resisted this restriction, they performed their gender differently, they mucked in, and got mucky, and both remained lifelong adherents to the political and social causes associated with liberal suffragism.[47] Yet they remained very much part of their class habits, having been held fast to a culture industry whose promulgation of taste and style continued to serve a small elite. As craft workers they were outliers, but not revolutionaries, and their ventures were successful insofar as they took up the fashions and styles of the times and tried to nudge them into alternative shapes, and without blowing anything up. Jekyll was instinctually and properly enmeshed in the trailing alleyways and borders of the upper and upper-middle classes for whom she wrote, given it was they who had gardens of sufficient size and undulating reach to accommodate seasonal drifts, and gardeners enough in service to tend them. Despite her suffragism, Watts too remained very much part of the class to which country life meant a life of high teas, hunting, picturesque follies and the revival of folk arts at village fetes over which they deigned to preside. The chapel was not built to house the villagers of Compton 'in their moments of exaltation, their supreme grief, or supreme hope, but to be proper, respectable and therefore to show the due amount of cultivation'.[48] It was considered a gift from her and her husband to the village in whose environs they had chosen to commit not only their money but themselves: as a memorial building it was an extension of the Watts' home, blurring the boundary between public and private, to a point where, with the subsequent creation of the Pottery, Compton itself became snared

---

[47] Lucy Ella Rose 'A Feminist Network in an Artists' Home: Mary and George Watts, George Meredith, and Josephine Butler', *Journal of Victorian Culture*. 2016, 21, 1, 74–91.

[48] William Morris (*Gothic Architecture*. London: Kelmscott Press. 1893. 55–56) writing in scathing terms of the bold-headed St Paul's in London, and though architecturally more sympathetic to Morris' taste, given its status as a philanthropic gift, the use of the village memorial chapel might be similarly described.

in the bosom of their household administration.[49] Watts expected the children to curtsy, and her classes being run under the organizational rubric of the Home Arts and Industries Association were always of an improving, ennobling nature: the trajectory of the education was an uplift into a better, Christian way of living that provided pupils with the skills to become useful upstanding members of an industrialized society for which they were to remain the labouring engine.[50]

Her pottery organized a space in which the flicker between the 'me' and the 'I' was contained in questions of making and using. More broadly, however, when pushed on the wider reasons for the venture, the 'me' seemed to gain in ascendency and become distant to the agitations of the 'I'. Mead likens this to a state of enforced morality whose habituated certainties are grounded in a habituated removal from phenomenological experience. To be moral is to isolate and audit behaviour and relational forms using tools of inspection whose conclusions are carried forth in an upright, brisk, confident voice talking in certainties that float above the heads of the flowers in a garden planter or the tile roof of a memorial chapel, unmoved.

In his tireless and trenchant analysis of the baleful spread of capitalist industrialism, Theodore Adorno concurs, lamenting how: 'the objective tendency asserts itself over the heads of human beings'.[51] It was a tendency the 'I' might counteract, even if by many accounts it was little more than an ideological projection serving to elevate the human being without any justification, yet to rid oneself of the 'I' makes domination a whole lot easier. Once the 'I' is denounced and trounced by moralism it leaves the way clear for social programmes of command and exploitation in which human needs and desires become the province of allocation rather than expression.[52]

We are all prone to morality: it is, says Mead, almost inevitable that we humans look for the smooth air of surety and the stable anchor points provided by firm hierarchy. The doubt that pervades and animates a venture can be exhausting and destructive, it can find those acting within its confines questioning their every move and making the smallest thought or movement a scene of great uncertainty. It is more pragmatic to allow practice to go unheeded, to allow it to run without

---

[49] Melanie Unwin 'Significant Other: Art and Craft in the Career and Marriage of Mary Watts', *Journal of Design History*. 2004, 17, 3, 237–250.

[50] See Hilary Underwood *Mary Watts, the Home Arts and Industries Association and Compton*. In *An Artist's Village: G F Watts and Mary Watts at Compton*. Edited by Mark Bills. London: Philip Wilson. 2011. 47–65.

[51] Theodor Adorno *Minima Moralia: Reflections from a Damaged Life*. Translated by E. Jephcott. London: Verso. 1951/2005. 17.

[52] Theodor Adorno *Minima Moralia*. 64.

active consideration. The 'I' is left be by the 'me' and the 'me' is left be by the 'I'. The craft work venture becomes an organized coming together of the habituated immediate experiences of the 'I' settled against the assumed norms of the 'me', and neither ruffles the other. If this mutually letting be is prolonged, practices collapse into routine because the norms are never challenged: morality muffles initiative and local divergence in blankets of stifling correctness; experience becomes directed by the likes of the show judge whose authority so irritated Jekyll. History is littered with examples of these 'show judge' moralists: missionaries, colonialists, visionary leaders, priests and philanthropists.

For Charles Dickens, philanthropists were especially corrosive. They felt themselves freed from having to form their own character because they were so busy forming those of others less fortunate than themselves. They assumed their own status as decent human beings was beyond question, and then proceeded to question that of the poor, the ill and the overlooked. They then roped-off these unfortunates into purpose-built institutions and proceeded to pummel them into shape. They were, suggested Dickens, like boxers wanting to fight down the afflicted and defeat human want and need, yet there were some notable differences:

> Firstly, the Philanthropists were in very bad training: much too fleshy, and presenting, both in face and figure, a superabundance of what is known to Pugilistic Experts as Suet Pudding. Secondly, the Philanthropists had not the good temper of the Pugilists, and used worse language. Thirdly, their fighting code stood in great need of revision, as empowering them not only to bore their man to the ropes, but to bore him to the confines of distraction; also to hit him when he was down, hit him anywhere and anyhow, kick him, stamp upon him, gouge him, and maul him behind his back without mercy. In these last particulars the Professors of the Noble Art were much nobler than the Professors of Philanthropy.[53]

Perhaps the philanthropy in Watt's venture became too earnest to sustain the doubt from which obstinacy fed itself? Given Watts was touched by a strong religious fervour, the passionate mission of the pottery to do good could be as commandeering as it was liberating. Her writing, notably on interlacing, attests to her sense of spiritual connexion into whose knotwork she wished to draw others. Jekyll's sense of mission is more vague, perhaps because her venture was looser and less fixated on delivering a meek salvation. The work itself was sufficient and remained to the fore. Though here too, as with Watts, the backdrop of her work against which she found distinction was very much that of the establishment, even if she and Watts had been able to shake it up a little with their suffragism.

---

[53] Charles Dickens *The Mystery of Edwin Drood*. London: Penguin. 2002. Chapter XVII.

More obstinate was the venture of the weaver Ethel Mairet working from her studio workshop The Gospels in the craft community established around the village of Ditchling in the South Downs of England. She too was an active suffragette, advocating a change in female dress to more practical, hardwearing styles objecthood. Mairet had been married and divorced twice. It was with the first husband, the art critic and philosopher Ananda Coomaraswamy, that she travelled through the colonies, notably to Sri Lanka (where she had learnt to weave) and India during the first few years of the twentieth century. These trips had convinced her of the wrong being done to indigenous culture by the wholesale and overbearing imposition of Anglo-Saxon norms, forcing the colonized Kandyan craft workers out of their steady competence. Though she resisted eulogizing and imitating Kandyan's work, she did appropriate their nuanced knowledge of colour and certain materials, and married this to a Scandinavian affection for nature and the preference for complex geometries of line in ginghams, tartans and tweeds woven in the British Isles.

To complicate the colonial flip-flopping even further, the techniques she acquired from the Kandyans', and then developed through her own venture, proved of interest to Mahatma Gandhi who had been organizing a revival of Indian handweaving as a political as well as commercial riposte to the rule of the British Raj. Facing high export tariffs for their goods to Britain, whilst British thread and cotton cloth sold in India was virtually tariff-free, had meant Indian cloth makers turning increasingly towards mass manufacturing techniques in search of profitable margins, and then finding themselves having to use second-hand, slower machinery. Gandhi was agitating for them to turn away from supplying the overlord on such punitive terms, and instead to compliment manufacture with handweaving, and to concentrate on the domestic market. Handweaving was to become both an act of resistance and self-reliance. Afterall, India had an almost unrivalled history of making a complex array of subtly different cloth: allejars, baffetas, bajutapeaux, birampot, brawls, caffa, calawapores, calicoes, cannequins, chelloes, cherryderries, chintz. On reading such lists the anthropologist Michael Taussig reflects how 'Some names live on, such as chintz. Others, such as calawapores, have died away, but when you try to say them, when you try to pronounce them, they return as beautiful but alien beings invested with the complexity of vivid color.'[54] The old names hint at old ways that have been smothered by the political and commercial complexities of colonial

---

[54] Michael Taussig *What Colour Is the Sacred?* Chicago: The University of Chicago Press. 2009. 136.

trade, but which, as with *Mingei* in Japan, craft work can recover and reorient for current times. The old cloths tap into a time before the colonial power was enjoying its domination, to when its command was nascent, tentative, uncertain. It is a historical period that Gandhi isolated as being critical to his emancipatory agenda: recent enough to recall through the generations, yet distant enough to be mythologized; its recall would encourage spinners and weavers to take to their machines, to restore the making of calawapores and its ilk, and in doing so give full voice to the legitimacy of an independent state. In making cloth anew the customers would come, as they too would understand the importance of using things that were not only useful, but embodied the social and cultural ambition of a free nation. Filtered through Gandhi's rhetorical brilliance, the story persuaded both workers and customers that ultimately power lay with them, and not the elite who had been fattening themselves for so long by keeping making and using separate. Once they encounter one another, those who make and those who use also encounter their mutual responsibility to encourage and support one another, as well as their far broader responsibility to create social, cultural and commercial conditions to which everyone might freely contribute.[55]

Mairet's ideas on the role of the weaving workshop had given Ghandi something to think about. Here, though with far less politically at stake and on a far smaller scale, was a woman who had undertaken to do something similar from within Britain. By researching and recovering lost techniques and materials, and expanding the take-up of these through an apprentice system, was trying to recreate a tradition of handweaving which, whilst alive to activities in other countries, was committed to developing its own distinction.[56] In her book *Handweaving Notes for Teachers* she expanded on this admixture of absorption and resistance, arguing that the established techniques – like the standard patterns preferred in Scandinavia and by Måås-Fjetterström's workshop – should be taught and then resisted. Their universal acceptance and the uncritical admiration with which they were met had meant they risked becoming scripts that repressed the sense of personal involvement with

---

[55] So successful was Gandhi's idea that craft work stayed centre stage for decades in post-colonial India. Under the indomitable direction of Kamaladevi Chattopadhyay, the country deliberately identified itself with the prowess of its handworkers. Through the institution of various craft co-operatives, councils and boards, she was able to persuade Indians that their facility with craft was integral to their liberty: it was with the loom and potting wheel that India would pattern, contain and sustain its own future. See Ashoke Chatterjee 'Can Our Future Be Handmade?' *Journal of Heritage Management.* 2016, 1, 1, 1–11.

[56] See Margot Coates *A Weaver's Life: Ethel Mairet 1872–1952*. Bath: Crafts Council/Crafts Study Centre. 1997. 115.

the loom.⁵⁷ Instead, the teacher should inspire the student by having samples of different materials and patterns from all around the world, without any planed order, and to have their influence seep into the students' work without thought for a specific end: 'nothing imitated, but all influences absorbed, to be brought to a new birth in our own time and place'.⁵⁸ The distinction of a handweaving tradition came through a continual exposure to, rather than closing off from, difference. The apprentices should also learn from the work of the weaving communities along the Scottish margins in the Outer Hebrides and Shetland and Orkney. Their knowledge was immense and silent and she admitted she had barely scratched the surface of these old ways.

Like Jekyll's, Mairet's writing about these 'old ways' carries a matter-of-fact beauty grounded in patient, disciplined observations. In her book *Vegetable Dyes* she records how 'The bright yellow Lichen, growing on rocks and walls, and old roofs, dyes a fine plum colour, if the wool is mordanted first with Bichromate of Potash', whereas the lichen *Lecanora tartarea* produces a dark red and which in Scotland and Scandinavia 'is collected in May or June, and steeped in stale urine for about three weeks, being kept at a moderate heat all the time. The substance having then a thick and strong texture, like bread, and being of a blueish black colour, is taken out and made into small cakes of about ¾ lb in weight which are wrapped in dock leaves and hung up to dry in peat smoke.'⁵⁹ The authorial presence is carried by the authority with which the descriptions are made; there is nothing opinionated or excessive. Her lists of plants being overlooked as sources of natural dyes are beguiling: 'Ladies Bedstraw, whortleberry, yellow iris, bracken, bramble, meadow sweet, alder, heather and many others.'⁶⁰ The advantage of these neglected natural dyes was their vivid and infinite variety and how they spoke to you at the loom, unlike the chemical aniline dyes whose colours were flat, uniform and fixed.

---

⁵⁷ In a project similar to Mairet's, these now revered patterns had been recovered from obscurity by Lilli Zickerman (1858–1949), who with Prince Eugen had established Föreningen forSvensk Hemslöjd to document, classify and teach the handweaving techniques that had been native to Sweden prior to industrial capitalism. The different yarns, dyes and patterns, their region and dates, were gathered as *The Inventory of Swedish Folk Textile Art*. The inventory was documentary, designed to inspire, whereas Mairet's was material-based. The association then took to encouraging the rejuvenation of the 'old ways', and not only in weaving, but other farm-based crafts like metalwork, woodwork and leatherwork, acting as a central organization through whose auspices a flow of skilled workers could be taught and a ready market for well-made goods created. See Anneli Palmsköld, Karin Gustavsson and Johanna Rosenqvist 'Preserving the Past to Serve the Future: Lilli Zickerman's Inventory of Textile Handicrafts 1914–1931', *Form Akademisk*. 16. 10.7577/formakademisk. 5414.
⁵⁸ Ethel Mairet *Handweaving Notes for Teachers*. London: Faber and Faber. 1949.
⁵⁹ Ethel Mairet *Vegetable Dyes*. 24.
⁶⁰ Ethel Mairet *Vegetable Dyes*. 14–15.

The attentive, carefully weighted summaries and recipes in *Vegetable Dyes* carry their advice as lightly as the wind carries seeds. Printed by Hilary Pepler at the neighbouring workshops of St Dominic's Press, the quiet, matter-of-fact manner of Mairet's writing extends to the feel and look of Pepler's book. The paper is handmade, the stitching done with stout twine, the ink was homemade from linseed and lampblack, and it was sized to fit into a jacket or trouser pocket. Pepler's press, founded in 1916, had, like many of the other craft ventures around Ditchling, become part of Catholic Guild of St Joseph & St Dominic established by Pepler in 1921, along with the sculptor, calligrapher and engraver Eric Gill (who left abruptly in 1924), Desmond Chute and Joseph and Laurie Cribb, all of whom were apprenticed to Gill. In 1922 the artist and writer David Jones joined as a postulant, and the furniture maker George Maxwell, and the engraver Philip Hagreen arrived as full members, followed by others including the weaver Valentine Kilbride (1926) and the jeweller Duncan Pruden (1932). The Guild was a colony of makers dedicated to the Ruskinian principles of independence and collective self-sufficiency. Gill had been the seed for its formation. Set against the acquisitive and wanton individualism of the machine age, the Guild had established a smallholding on the common above Ditchling village, setting forth to create a spiritually infused 'interior' set apart from wider, war-torn commerce. First one building, then the next, a small chapel with accompanying cross set upright atop the Spoil Bank, sewing fields and laying fences, cutting grass with a well-honed scythe, winnowing with wooden rakes, cooking over open fires, raising livestock, weaving smocks and accompanying mealtimes with plainsong. Along one side of the chapel was carved a vision statement: 'Men rich in virtue, studying beautifulness: living at peace in their houses'. Pepler and his family had followed Gill's family, then others, each throwing themselves into this religiously charged medievalism with brio.

The Guild's antagonism towards capitalist industrialism was fomented by reading Ruskin, but its embodiment and extension took on a distinctly austere, though aesthetically rich, tone. Gill was especially committed to the ordered and totalizing repetitions of a scansioned life. Days were to be parcelled into neat units (lauds, prime, terce, sext, compline etc.) marked by prayer or voice, each contributing to the gathering of a whole life being lived in service both to God (a life dedicated to doing good in itself), to oneself (a life of good character) and to others (a life dedicated to the making of productive, useful things). Far from dividing lives, the liturgy of the hours marking the Catholic day organized and honed the discipline and effort required to commit to creating good things. In contrast, the institution of divided, waged labour housed in factory systems and overseen by an emerging class of managerial agents employed by the owners of capital shattered human life into irreparable shards. A good life was a whole life, and a whole life was lived without the modern distinctions between family and friends, the personal and communal, the private and public, work and rest, struggle and pleasure, and soil and spirit (the gender distinctions, however, remained). Craft work (or hand work as the Guild members were wont to call it) loosened the apparent naturalness of these divisions, it even questioned them, because the things being made seemed to traverse them with ease. The maker and user alike were responsible for the existence and care of things whose life was wrapped up in theirs, as their life was wrapped up in both the community and the congregation. Pepler used a Stanhope iron press, or less regularly an Albion folio press. The moveable type set up in the chase with a composing stick was Caslon Old Face, and the paper was handmade, and dampened slight so it took the ink better.[61] The books became small parts of a unified whole dedicated to the full expression of lives being lived to the fullest, practical extent. Gill took this pursuit of the fullest life to extremes, and then into a place of excess, depravity and criminality, being both incestuous and a paedophile, dabbling with bestiality, and sensing his proper role to be the ur-patriarch, a giver of life, a totalizing, orgiastic force that felt most alive when embracing the evil as readily as the good, given that from this, the fullest of knowledge, the best work would come.

Pepler's work refused to reach for such complete comprehension: he fell out with Gill, and Gill left Ditchling to found a new community in Wales. Pepler's work was simple, exact and content within itself: the books were unfussy, and the titles were varied, often practical and ordinary: books on cookery, woodwork, saint's days, housing development along the River Thames, cottage industries, or poetry for children. In their plain covers and clear Caslon type, Pepler's books bore the aesthetic stamp of the Doves Press of Hammersmith whose founder was T. J. Cobden Sanderson. Pepler had lived in the same row of riverside houses as Cobden Sanderson, as had the Gills. Where Pepler's work differs from Cobden Sanderson's is in its lack of refinement. In the books of the Doves Press the clean lines had been cut in bespoke typeface cut exclusively for the Press by Edward Prince, and bound in blank, off-white vellum with the titles confined to the spine in muted gold, and their calm progression was animated by the mannered flush of the odd leading capital letter in red, or, on rare occasions, by an arcing flourish in green ink by

---

[61] Fiona MacCarthy *Eric Gill*. London: Faber and Faber. 128–129. See also Bernard Sewell *My Days at the St Dominics Press*. In *Matrix 2*. Whittington Press. 1981 (reprinted 1993). 89–96.

the calligrapher Edward Johnston (who lived in Hammersmith, and also moved to Ditchling). For Cobden-Sanderson, a beautiful book didn't shout its presence, it stood back, letting the text (and meaning) come through without disturbance. Like those from the Doves' Press, Pepler's books were equally attentive to the full use of a page, made consistent use of a single, clean font, and made explicit commitment to the dramatic possibilities of using black on white occasionally interspersed with red. Yet they had a scuffed handle, the lines were more like plough lines than plumb lines, they were more generously spaced than Sanderson's, and were interrupted and enhanced by a careful use of well-aligned imagery.[62] Their covers were often simple paper ones, or in plain or patterned boards, which could become marred in use, and remained affordable.

## The Workshop as a Scene of Progress

Tellingly, Mairet never joined the Guild, she was forbidden: the common unity did not extend to working women. Not that she would have joined up even if permitted. As an alumni of C. R. Ashbee's short-lived craft community (1902–1907) in Chipping Camden she shared their ethos of working independently in small ventures owned by those who had created and grown them, yet refused their idealism. Having witnessed the commercial fool-headedness of Ashbee's idealist opposition to machinery and now having witnessed the Ditchling Guild's attempt to combine this innate antagonism with an exclusory, ascetic Catholicism, she was cautious in her eulogy of craft work: it could all too easily careen into the dead end of a cult.

She had learned for herself the importance of creating and developing markets for craft work and not to rely like Ashbee upon a handful of rich, repeat clients whose moral and social compass would barely register the struggles of those, like her, for whom making a living was a continual, practical concern. The idle rich might have space to develop a fervour for well-made, artisanal things, but it would die back, as would their patronage. It was the job of a craft worker to make work that sold to a broader customer base who would use these well-made things in everyday life, and if machinery could help, so be it.[63] It was a worldview she shared with a growing number of craft workers who had gathered under

---

[62] Hagreen designed the cover to *Vegetable Dyes*; 'The block on the cover was a bit of end grain pearwood that happened to be the right size. Hilary Pepler drew the flower and I engraved it in a hurry while the printers waited for it. Hilary Pepler said it was the Kermes plant' (Letter to J. B. Shaw, 1948, quoted in *Philip Hagreen; Sceptic and Craftsman*. Edited by Lottie Hoare. Winchester: Ritchie Press. 2009.)

[63] See K. Robertson 'Resistance and Submission, Warp and Weft: Unraveling the Life of Ethel Mairet', *TEXTILE*. 2005, 3, 3, 292–317.

the moniker of Distributism.⁶⁴ Rather than collective or state control dedicated to serving the interests of the many, Distributists advocated a dispersion of wealth into community-based workshops and landholdings taken on by small groups. Machinery could be critical to the survival and flourishing of these small organizations. To simply oppose mechanization as an inherent evil, as advocated by the more zealous Distributists,⁶⁵ was, for Mairet, naive; not least because large-scale manufacturing companies and international finance had already taken command, and their uptake of mechanized life was being backed by governments and religions whose power was dependent upon a strong and growing economy; craft work could never resist such agglomerations of dominant interests.

To oppose the machine in principle seemed churlish, not least because to do so from within the 'cell' of a craft community like that on Ditchling common was only possible in the mode of a free rider who would then be repressing awareness of their continued dependency upon wider institutional, industrial forces, forces whose 'power' had allowed them to make such a claim to autonomy in the first place.⁶⁶ Mairet, like many of the more practical Distributists, was committed to the restraint rather than destruction of machinery. The restraint was necessary. A. J. Penty (also ex-Hammersmith), for example, who wrote *Distributism: A Manifesto* published by Pepler in 1937, argued those committed to Distributism were suspicious of machinery because it deprived workers of their manual dexterity, undermined their independence and self-respect, and had become an instrument of vested interests rather than wealth.

They [Distributists] also insist that the interests of society, religion, human values, art and culture come first, and that the use of machinery should be prohibited wherever it runs counter to them. Science, machinery, mechanization, chemistry, are useful and good up to a certain point, but become cruel tyrannies when they are allowed to develop to such dimensions as to threaten the existence of all other forms of activity. If machinery was restricted in this way it would no doubt do the things it is supposed to be doing: reduce drudgery, and

---

[64] The Distributive movement was founded by the liberal politician Hilaire Belloc and author G. K. Chesterton. Outlined in Belloc's mordant take on collective socialism *Servile State* (1912. London and Edinburgh: T. N. Foulis) the movement advocated loose associations of self-employed craft workers organized into democratic Guilds though whose institutional protection the freedom of the individual to follow their own conscience was upheld, practically as well as spiritually, through the ownership of many small-scale ventures, whether those of a workshop or a smallholding.

[65] Such as the proselyte Dominican monk living in Ditchling, Vincent McNabb, with whom Gill was in profound sympathy.

[66] The strain of maintaining machine-free production was amply illustrated in the expulsion of Pepler from the Guild in 1934 for having not only used a non-Catholic apprentice but machinery to assist with book production. Pepler responded by heaping all the materials from the Press into a large bonfire which he lit atop the common.

add to the comforts and amenities of life. Unrestricted, in the service of power and avarice, it is proving itself to be an agent of destruction[67]

Following this line of reasoning, Mairet thought it more effective for craft work to experiment with how new technologies could be corralled to ameliorate and provoke handwork, and how handwork could elevate and excite machine-based manufacturing: 'the reform[er] does not develop a machine boycott, but a machine mastery'.[68] In this she echoed the American pragmatist philosopher C. S. Peirce, for whom machines were not equivalents to human reasoning because they were both devoid of original initiative and were contrived for a limited set of operations, which was no bad thing, 'because we do not want it to do its own business, but ours'.[69] Whilst an age of exploitation, abstraction and enforced stupidity might well be emerging from the murky sediments of industrial capitalism, this was not a brute fact, it could be negotiated, and for Mairet workshops were a fertile organizational space for these negotiations.

The opposition to machinery emerges from what the theorist of technology Gilbert Simondon called a profound anxiety emerging during the nineteenth century as factories began to take over from workshops. Picking up from Heidegger's discussion of tools and the primal, things-in-use relationship to the world, Simondon distinguished between tools outright, and instruments. They are both what he termed 'technical objects' that prolong or arm the human body, but the former is predominantly in service of gesture, and the latter of perception. A chisel or loom alter the world, whereas a stethoscope or sextant provide information about it. During the European Enlightenment of the eighteenth century there was both a flowering and communion of tools (in the practical service of making) and instruments (in the service of scientific investigation). Mechanics and science began to fuse in large-scale engineering projects and industrial manufacture. Mirroring this change in technical objects came a change in what Simondon calls 'technical individuals' who acquire the habits of tool use and who have learned sufficient skill to recognize when and how they must or might change or re calibrate the tools and instruments, thereby integrating

---

[67] A. J. Penty *Distributism: A Manifesto*. London: The Distributist League. 1937. 11.
[68] Ethel Mairet *Hand-weaving*. London: Faber and Faber. 1939. Mairet's second husband, Philip, who had been a secretary and assistant to Ashbee and had moved to Ditchling with Ethel and helped design and build The Gospels, installing the large windows and rain water tanks, subsequently edited the book *Pioneer of Sociology: The Life and Letters of Patrick Geddes*. London: Lund Humphries. 1957, by which time Philip and Ethel had long been divorced.
[69] C. S. Peirce 'Logical Machines', *American Journal of Psychology*. 1887, 1, 1, 165–170. 169.

themselves within the 'taskscape' through ongoing self-regulation.[70] As the Enlightenment spread, technical individuals were, initially at least, euphoric, they experienced greater potency from using these new tools and instruments in their burgeoning practice.

Yet when the machinery began to replace rather than augment humans, Simondon suggests a pervasive anxiety began to set in. Humans were no longer the bearers of tools and instruments but had handed this role over to automated machinery. In the workshop humans lent their individuality in furthering technical activity, whereas in the factory technical activity was undertaken by automatic machines which, whilst they appeared to be imitating humans, we actually creating their own reality. The difference between the workshop and factory is not, he concluded, size, but a transformation in relationship between humans and technical objects. In the workshop humans experience progress through improvements in speed, gesture and precision realized in the development of new tools and instruments, yet they can also experience slowness, and arrest, a pause for thinking and gestating. In the factory the individual became removed from technical activity, they no longer experienced progress, but either managed it, or helped it along. As managers they become abstracted from technicity: their role was one of regulating the tool-bearing machines in ensembles. As helpers they become subservient to machines, performing maintenance or service roles. Above (as organizers of ensembles) or below (as a labourer assisting parts), the role of technical individual was concealed from humans, they became spectators removed from the play of technical objects.[71]

Following on from Simondon, Ivan Illich talks of technical individuals as using tools designed for conviviality (living together, *con vivere*), by which Illich meant tools that augment autonomy and sociability by encouraging, even requiring, both a dexterity and wit (the Ancient Greek virtue of *eutrapelia*, which also evokes a sense of graceful play) in their operation.[72] As with Simondon, for Illich a tool can be any rationally designed productive system: a lathe, computer, hospital, factory or classification system are, by his criteria, tools. Tools (by which term he also included what Simmondon called instruments) have an optimal, tolerable and negative range of application. They are optimal (convivial) when they serve the needs of self-defined work, biological survival and mutual care for one another's capabilities. They slip into the negative when they become manipulative and so eliminate rather than augment human capabilities

---

[70] Gilbert Simondon *On the Mode of Existence of Technical Objects*. Translated by *Cecile Malaspina and John Rogrove*. Minneapolis: University of Minnesota Press. 2016. 76–78.
[71] Gilbert Simondon *On the Mode of Existence of Technical Objects*. 130–131.
[72] Ivan Illich *Tools for Conviviality*. New York: Harper Row. 1973. 12–13.

associated with the provision of energy (sensory operation) and guidance (concentration). Indications of this decoupling from human flourishing come with: tools given over to abstracted, standardized patterns of operation designed for users in general (lacking idiosyncrasy and patina); tools that determine the purpose of their often singular use (pre-programmed outputs serving a distinct set of interests); tools that demand incessant, ordered use; and tools which have restricted access (such as certification for their ownership; professional qualifications). Once in the swim of this intentionless tide, tool users no longer wittingly contribute their energy and will in an 'autonomous and creative intercourse among persons, and the intercourse of persons with their environment'.[73] There is no freedom to decide what might be made, no room for agonistic discussion as to whether a thing should or should not be made, no allowance for pause as one considers how to interpret the regimen of a tradition, and no room for the naive to 'have a go', or for experts to become naive by beginning again and experimenting with different ways of relating to tools. There is, in short, an industrialization of production.

Gill, Ashbee and many other acolytes of craft communities opposed the machine because they felt ousted from the role of bearer. Simondon and Illich suggest a more nuanced relationship to bearer, and felt a lack of community. Their response was to organize without the use of modern machinery and tools. For centuries humans had been developing machinery to provide energy and bear much of the physical strain, but it was with automation that the machine became the equivalent of a technical individual using convivial tools, and in wrapping this individuation into its own operations these technical objects became a source of productive power unrivalled by humans. In her call to work with machinery, but critically, and with a skilled intensity, Mairet was attempting to revivify the conviviality of the tool and instrument-bearing technical individual. Hence her emphasis on the workshop. It offered the conditions in which well-trained individuals could experience productive skill first-hand: in the way their bodies moved with greater fluidity or when their sensory reach expanded. With the factory, these phenomenological experiences of progress were lost in the din, and progress became abstracted as a plotted trajectory detailed by measured comparisons between outcomes and plans. It also offered a space for visitors to witness the work first-hand, maybe even to buy, as they too might experience technical individuality, albeit vicariously. The workshop was a place where consumers as well as manufacturers might learn. It is a point re-iterated by many craft workers: they sell by showing. The trick,

---

[73] Ivan Illich *Tools for Conviviality*. 24, 77–85.

says the printer Michael Schäfer, is to get them through the door.[74] Once inside they begin to understand the care, the pace and detail with which things are being made: the smell of the inks, the heaviness of the press, the elusive reverse imagery carved into plywood, the small touches of the hand that make each piece different. They become aware of the difference between these objects and the posters they might otherwise buy.

In workshops, machines could expose handwork to potential, freeing the hand or eye from one task so they might attend to others. On the flip side, craft workers could (and did) influence manufacturing: through collaborations with industrial designers, by educating consumers to demand and pay for well-made products, and by training those entering manufacturing enterprises, notably in the arts of invention and experiment.[75] The ensemble of technical individual and object, weaver and hand looms, could become an engine of novelty, 'the brains of the machine' even, a small place from which new ideas, new textures and new yarns combine with a sensibility for both technical potential and human schemes of living. The automated looms, with their greater power and energy, might then take over by replaying the 'standards', leaving the craft worker free for further experiment.[76]

## Eutopia

Mairet's commitment to the workshop was not limited to a technical concern with recovering the augmenting power of machinery. Inspired by Lewis Mumford's 1934 book *Technics and Civilization* which she read and re-read, and encouraged her apprentices to do likewise, she sensed how the experience of progress to which craft workers were exposed might be expanded. To use machinery well, and so recover the euphoria available to those who experience the potency of its energy in a restrained and deliberately focussed way, was more than a technical skill, it required organizational confidence, which could only come from having been apprenticed

---

[74] Michael Schäfer. Interview with the author. October 2020, Copenhagen.
[75] A mutual intimacy between craft work, finance, state policy and the early industrial engineers and entrepreneurs that has been exhaustively and persuasively attested to in Celina Fox's *The Arts of Industry in the Age of Enlightenment*. New Haven: Yale University Press, 2009. See also Robin Holt and Andrew Popp 'Josiah Wedgwood, manufacturing and craft', *Journal of Design History*. 2016, 29, 2, 99–119.
[76] See Ethel Mairet *Handweaving Notes for Teachers*. 30. In a leaflet for the school, Mairet extemporizes on the relationship between craft work and textile manufacturing. Richard Sennett reiterates the point, advising the user of a Vaucanson loom to accept its mechanical superiority, indeed to actively court its superiority and to learn, as well as one might, how to stretch its undeniable and extensive reach. Yet, he continues, it is important not to venerate the machine. The difference in power is a limited one, so avoid it becoming a limiting one (see Richard Sennett *The Craftsman*. London: Penguin. 2008. 277).

to a workshop sensitive to the importance of social and cultural recognition. Through apprenticeships, craft workers could, potentially, experience: the self-confidence that is grounded in the satisfaction of physical and affective needs; the self-respect emerging when each individual 'self' is treated as a full member of a common enterprise grounded in an equality of recognition; and finally, the self-esteem that emerges from having their work recognized as a valuable contribution to the lives of others.[77]

Braided together, these aspects of self-development continued well beyond apprenticeship. Technically, a weaver became an expert when they could handle their own tools and materials with a thoughtless facility which remained, nevertheless, alive to those moments when a different combination of tool or instrument would be more appropriate and yield a greater sense of progress. Yet real expertise lay in combining this progressive dexterity with the thoughtful use of new technologies, and with an awareness of the communal, social and political developments mediated by these technologies. This began with one's immediate colleagues, creating a workshop milieu of curiosity, experiment and mutual support that regarded skilled execution as much a collective as individual possession. Yet it extended outside the workshop; technology became technics. Learning how to operate a machine or work materials meant learning about the cultural and social settings in which they were developed. Materials, tools and instruments were never just raw, they emerged (echoing, in part, the weaving apprenticeships of Märta Måås-Fjetterström's workshops in Båstad and the avowed commitment to the regional impress of local folklore and nature) from socio-technical milieux that shaped their structure, they possessed what Mumford called a 'biotechnics'.[78] Beginning with the study of materials, tools and instruments, Mairet's weaving school and workshop would teach apprentices of the socio-technical context out of which the woven material materialized, so to speak.[79]

---

[77] For an elaboration of this breakdown in relation to work practice, see Jean Phillipe 'Deranty and Emmanuel Renault Politicizing Honneth's Ethics of Recognition', *Thesis Eleven*. 2007, 88, 92–111.

[78] Richard Sennett's study of the eighteenth-century English brickmaking industry is also alive to these forces of mutual involvement; how human things and non-sentient reveal connexions. A certain kind of brick evidenced a certain kind of dwelling and occupant, and how for masons in eighteenth century England there was a growing awareness that bricks be left uncovered rather than covered with cosmetic stucco. To expose the brick is honest, betokening a simplicity and confidence, it is the admission of imperfection as sizes differ slightly and colouration can be uneven. See *The Craftsman*. 135–144.

[79] In a pamphlet advertising the 'The Ditchling Weaving School', Mairet is insistent that in her workshop 'special emphasis is placed on the study and spinning of raw materials, and exceptional opportunities are provided for work with wool, cotton, silk, linen and modern synthetic fibres. The experimental nature of the work is important in creating a wide cultural outlook. Contact is maintained with the leading hand-loom weavers

Without this complete understanding prompted by the uneasy and untimely presence of machinery, craft work shies away from the job of what Patrick Geddes, the Professor of Botany at the University of Dundee from whom Mumford had taken the concept of biotechnics, called *civics*, the science of designing a practical utopia, a eutopia: a deliberate, well-planned system of wealth production undertaken by the human organism through a blend of scientific discipline, emotional empathy and practical intelligence.

Geddes had been inspired by Ruskin's experiments with the Guild of George, notably when working on a smallholding organized at Totley, near Sheffield in the north of England. The experience of working on the land, learning practical skills, and building close ties with skilled craft workers had convinced Geddes that Ruskin's call for work to serve life was not only desirable, but likely, that is if one planned for it: all people could acquire an expressive, situational intelligence if they organized appropriately. Geddes read mediaeval Gothic as the idealization of such organization theorized through Ruskin's imaginative and idiosyncratic reading of architecture and stonemasonry. In turn, he would extend the details of this organization grounded in empirical observation inspired by the values and principles emerging from regional places that had their own histories to which makers and users were tithed by common-sense experience. He would plan for a eutopia. Though it was ambitious, Geddes felt there were signs that it already existed. For example, amongst the dockworkers working along the River Clyde in Glasgow. Here was a community of craft workers versed in a tradition of technical know-how through which they attained social, economic and cultural strength, which in turn was fed by the wider commitments of the city to applied science and political economy. Though large scale, the fabrication methods were more akin to the workshop than factory. The workers were well-trained, the managers were versed in engineering skills, the city politicians were investing in education, transport infrastructure, water and sewerage, housing was being financed by building societies and food and provisions were supplied by co-operative shops which drew products in from the surrounding countryside.[80]

Hence his drawing up a vast scheme for the proper re-organization of human relations centred around a network of workshops such as those lining the Clyde. To work was to unify the organism and its milieu within the functional activity of 'thinking machines'. From the workshop, fold, field system, yard, office, or classroom come individuals

on the Continent.' Ethel Mairet *The Ditchling Weaving School*. Pamphlet. 1930s. Craft Study Centre Archives. ID No. 2002.24.2.

[80] Alex Law 'The Ghost of Patrick Geddes: Civics as Applied Sociology', *Sociological Research Online*. 2005. 10, 2, 21–34.

who, with care, embody and perpetuate a civic sensibility. They work for themselves and others equally, alive to the benefits of an aesthetically charged social and cultural order through which humans acquire a rounded awareness of the innate sympathy between nature and history. To work was to create things that lasted and that worked well within an architectural setting that absorbed and respected its natural context, and that fostered the open commerce of these well-made things in whose form resided a cultural as well as functional power. The modern age had soured human life by enforcing divisions between people, and between them and the things they made, to a point where community and the culture through which it was sustained lacked a common sense of place; it was a broken world. Devoid of anywhere to dwell, workers became machines and their families a source of future workers to replace those that were worn down: there was equality, here, but in misery and exploitation.[81] Eutopia restored a sense of place and coherence.

To convey a sense of cyclical movement, Geddes uses the outlines of a spinning swastika (indicated by the arrows), originating from Sanskrit *svastika* meaning the well-being associated with the rolling movement of the sun then the moon across the sky (Figure 53).[82] The image is a totalizing one, the passive left-hand side gives way to the active right-hand side, the subjective life on the bottom half gives way to the objective life on the top, the diagonal vectors or 'chords' of practical and expressive life feed the central spaces from which the heart, head and hand of each individual life takes its cue.

The workshop formed the individual and the collective into an active community; it was a microcosm of life lived whole. Writing before totalitarianism had taken hold in Europe, Geddes might be excused the zealous commitment to establishing a firm sense of space, a commitment whose dark as well as good side Doreen Massey has analysed so eloquently.[83] Collective feelings of well-being and coherence rooted in a human instinct for settlement can quickly degenerate into a thoughtless hostility towards difference. To dwell within a place – recalling Zumthor's sense of a building's *Gestalt* – is to foster the effort of unhoming as much as it is to create objects that are 'at home'. Without the disturbance argues Massey, we end up with brittle and arid lives ruled by authorities who have corralled space to serve their own interests. Inspired by Ruskin's imagined sense of place, Geddes was right to confront and accept the

---

[81] Patrick Geddes 'The Charting of Life', *The Sociological Review*. 1927, 19, 1, 40–63.
[82] A. Defries *The Interpreter: Geddes the Man and His Gospel*. London: Routledge & Sons. 1927.
[83] Doreen Massey *For Space*. London: Sage. 2005.

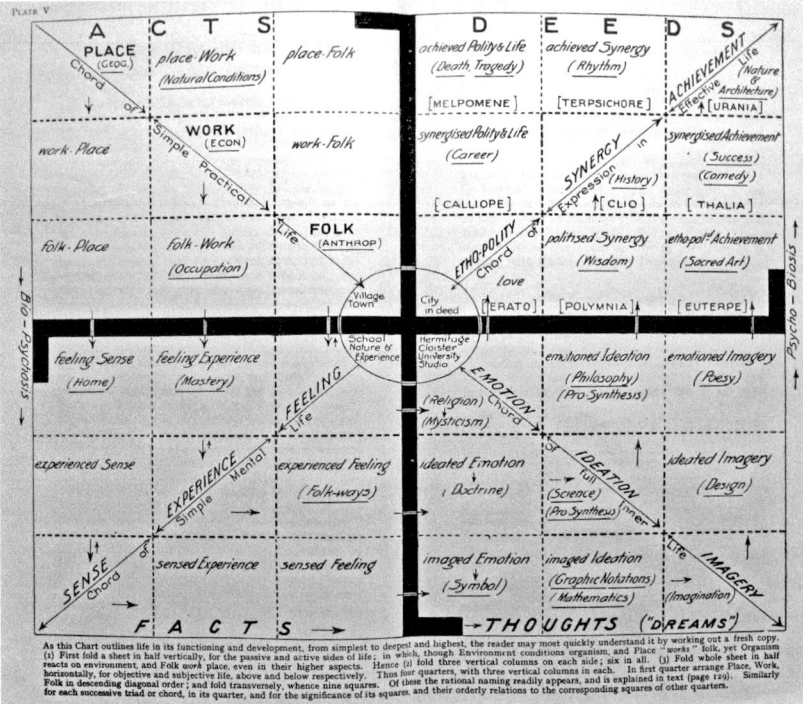

Figure 53 Patrick Geddes, 'The Notation of Life'. Plate V in A. D. Defries, *The Interpreter Geddes: The Man and his Gospel* (Routledge & Sons, 1927). Courtesy of Archives and Special Collections, University of Strathclyde Library.

human need to belong somewhere, to set down roots: attachment is not a weakness. Where he might have erred was in his biotechnical enthusiasm for the calm, coherent, clear sense of place being imagined into being generated. Though he felt this sense of place was 'within reach', it was, perhaps inevitably, always just over the horizon, and the intervening space became a ripe ground for a nostalgic politics of idealized recovery.

Filtered through Lewis Mumford, who was a great champion of Geddes' visionary work, eutopia was something of a dangerous contradiction, given it sought to replace the ordered, predictable perfection of machine production with the thoughtless, humourless perfection of the vision. 'The student of utopias', Mumford comments, 'knows the weakness that lies in perfectionism, for that weakness has been made manifest in the new totalitarian states, where the dreams of a Plato, a Cabet, a Bellamy have at many removes taken shape. What is lacking in such dreams is not a sense of the practical: what is lacking is a realization of the essential human need for disharmony and conflict.'[84] Instead of a harmonic whole realized though a general organizing vision, a biotechnical order was better realized by concentrating on creating a mutually re-enforcing network of specific organizational forms: 'the rising of municipal and governmental housing, the expansion of co-operative consumers and producers' associations, the destruction of slums and the building of superior types of community for the workers – all these are signs of the new biotechnic orientation'.[85] Pivotal to such a network was the workshop, for it was here that humans can experience the interplay of art and technics with neither coming to the fore.

In the spirit of Geddes' diagram, art, suggested Mumford, should concern itself with the emotional and subjective use of symbolic order to distil and express what was essential, or truthful, about the human condition. Symbols arise when one set of experiences suggest another set, creating an association formed in language. Though personally and collectively felt, symbolism was steeped in wider structures. The meanings by which experiences were being compared – the stirring felt in love, awe and religious inspiration for example, or the ordered rhythms of mathematical calculation and setting up a loom – were absorbed by entire cultures, allowing those who made art to speak directly, and powerfully, to an audience who shared the symbolism and conferred the authority on the made things, and those associated with them (makers, owners, subjects). Technics, in contrast, was an objective and collective concern with function and utility, a stripping away of symbols to a minimum to make way for mechanization dedicated to the task in hand, to getting practical things done. To excel in technics was to relieve the tedium of doing laborious work, and it did so from a stance of humility: to use tools (and instruments) well the human had to learn about the world on its own terms and to respect and confront rather than avoid these. In contrast, the symbolism of art diverted humans from the indifferent reality of material things, it allowed them to avoid a troublesome, practical encounter with facts, and to invent their own world of symbolic associations and meanings that often slipped into a lurid, escapist symbolism. Being worldly, the workshop, unlike the church, or parliament, or the university even, leavened the self-aggrandizing tendencies of art with practical tasks. On the flip side, it refused machinery a monopoly on attention: the business of getting things done was interrupted by the thoughtful pause, by the excitement of unwarranted experiment, by pointless idling, all of

---

[84] Lewis Mumford *Technics and Civilization*. London: Routledge, Keegan, Paul. 1934. 485.
[85] Lewis Mumford *Technics and Civilization*. 464.

which authorized the craft worker to bear the weight of tools and instruments, to be a 'technical individual'. In arguments similar to Simondon's, Mumford argues that a re-balancing between art and technics has gone too far, the death of God had also witnessed a diminution in symbolic spirit: an objectivity had taken hold in which art was being obliterated by technics, leaving life bereft of subjective, qualitative concerns, save for those scripted by a depersonalized machine order whose outputs, no matter how impressive, could never draw human sentiment.

The workshop arrives as a space of reprieve for the technical individual in continual commerce with technical things, a place in where art and technics are calibrated to live alongside and agitate one another. There is an eagerness to use machinery that might quicken and enhance the skilled and purposive making of things coupled to an acceptance that, despite these technological advances, work is still often accompanied by experiences of monotony. Yet these can be borne by craft workers; first, because the workshop pillows the mechanization and standardization in an atmosphere of mutual aid camaraderie, and second because these machinic movements always lead up to moments of spontaneity, care, excess and aesthetic skill that have been earned by enduring the repetition and acquiring the dispositions of attentiveness and thoughtfulness that can come from it.[86] If machinery can hasten and widen the reach of these moments, freeing the energy of the craft worker to preserve and enhance life, so be it.[87] These moments need not add to the functionality of what is being made, but they imbue it with meaning and presence which can elicit human sentiment: it pulls the maker and user into the process of its having been made, encouraging a mutual awareness and understanding of how and why things might give to life, or *bios*.

## Mairet and the Biotechnics of Wool

The most persistent exemplification of biotechnics experienced in Mairet's workshop came with the understanding of wool. She took a yarn, traced it back to a breed of sheep and how different parts of

---

[86] Lewis Mumford *Art and Technics*. Oxford: Oxford University Press. 1952. 49. The letter cutter David Kindersley said of the workshop that 'the first principle to be mastered is a complete change of attitude to time … It is important that those god-given periods of boredom should not be denied. These are periods of digestion and relating to knowledge and experience from which a new-found understanding can arise.' Quoted in Lottie Hoare 'David Kindersley: The Compiling of a Biography', *Matrix*. 1996. 16. 50.

[87] Mairet's copy of *Technics and Civilization* (462) has this section highlighted: 'The benefits of automatic machinery, the economies of finely organized production, the displacement of labor, the surplusage of modern agriculture all mean – if they mean any human benefit – this release of energy for the direct service of life.'

the body produced different qualities in the wool, then she situated the breed into a broader socio-cultural history of breeding livestock that touched on genetics and skills of breeding, global (colonial) supply chains and regional climates, before then discussing the range of machinery, from hand-held shears to modern power looms, by which the 'raw' material was being processed.[88] The opening of *Vegetable Dyes*, for example, begins with a list of different sheep: Highland, Welsh and Irish sheep have 'irregular short stapled fleeces', whereas the Cheviot has better wool, being 'thick and good for milling', and of the long-woolled sheep 'the Leicester fleece is softer finer and better than the Lincoln'. Best of all had been wool from Spanish sheep, but these having been introduced to various countries, notably 'Saxony, Australia, Cape Colony, New Zealand; and some of the best wools now come from the Colonies'; colours vary 'from white to a very dark brown black, with all shades of fawn, grey and brown in between' and these natural colours tend to bleach with the sun and their qualities are further distinguished depending on the age of the sheep when the fleece is cut, lambs producing a softer, more elastic wool compared to those of Hogs and Tegs (sheep that went unsheared as lambs), and the natural oils in these fleeces should be kept until ready for dying because they keep the moths at bay.[89] One of the complaints she had against machine manufacturing was how the trade rarely troubled itself to explore and keep to the limits of a yarn: light wool for a dress is not suitable for a carpet, inelastic yarns do not work well in tweed. 'The trade' she laments 'often spoils this attitude to the yarn by requiring over-mixed yarn (this reacts badly, for instance, on the breeding of sheep for wool, the cross breeding often obliterates the inherent qualities of a breed), and also by too expert a finishing process, for the purpose of producing a deceptive appearance'. The gothic quality of honesty in materials is brought to the fore: 'a sincere material is more interesting, important, and creative, and in better taste, than a material that pretends to be something else.'[90]

Mairet was no less attentive and fluid when observing the clothing made from the materials, for example in Herzegovina:

The footgear for men is, first a long white stocking or legging made of thick white cloth: then a woollen half shoe also knitted, with coloured pattern generally, then a leather shoe, the bottom of thick very tough goat skin with the hair outside, moulded up round the foot for about 1/2 inch and the upper part of the shoe

---

[88] Antonia Behan 'Ethel Mairet's Textile Biotechnics and the Aesthetics of Materials', *The Journal of Modern Craft*. 2021. 14, 3, 211–228.
[89] Ethel Mairet *Vegetable Dyes*. 1–2.
[90] Ethel Mairet *Handweaving and Education*. London: Faber and Faber. 1942. 15–16.

interlaced leather string. Very beautiful. The men walk beautifully. The whole footgear is very thick but supple so that it is the right type of shoe for walking on the rough roads with loose stones.[91]

Giving materials an equal footing to form and having them merge as equally resonant aspects of the 'biotechnics' of objects, meant Mairet's analysis fed into a deepening intelligence concerning both the actual and potential use of things. It was as if a strand of yarn were the equivalent to a text being made the object of hermeneutic analysis, and a woven cloth the materialization of cycles of reading, weaving and thinking *through* the yarn. In taking up the yarn it already communicates how it might behave on the loom, within a textile and upon the body, and how this then influences the body as it moves within a building.

In her travel diaries, the detailed observations of tool and technique is always being contextualized by broader observations. It is no surprise she took warmly to Alvar Aalto when she met him at Fabianinkatu 31, Helsinki in June 1936 as she was touring Scandinavia. She had found the Finns very attentive to 'handicraft'. In the spirit of Geddes and Mumford, her travel diaries and notes find her making explicit connection between the micro practices of the Finnish workshops and a robust, productive and flourishing nation grounded in work:

A sincere, fine, alive people, splendid women, very good organisers ... It is only a flexibly alive nation that could have built such a magnificently modern Parliament House as they have just finished. It is a fine building, beautiful in detail and efficiency. Their main railway station is also a fine building. The Finns have a sense of spaciousness in their building, a character absolutely of their own nation.[92]

Aalto was the epitome of such a people. He is, she writes 'a very delightful person. Architect. Designer. Maker of furniture. A very real person: best style of craftsman. Built very large library at Viipuri. Also large hospital near Turku [Paimo]. Has commission to build a village in the east of Finland for many families to build an industrial town'. A few days later she visited the library at Viipuri (now annexed by Russia): 'the harmonious colouring of the chair seats and curtains, the oiled silk curtain in the children's library; the black sliding doors of the lecture room, the door handles of birch and metal, the copper outside window sills; the grey felt telescopic divisions for halving the lecture room; the three front rows of chairs covered with dark grey stiped linen: the rest of the chairs with cream woollen, the same as the window curtains'. The next day she

---

[91] Ethel Mairet 'Yugoslavian Journal, May 4–May 30, 1927', *The Journal of Modern Craft*. 2015, 8, 1, 77–85. 79.
[92] Ethel Mairet, Notes. Craft Study Centre, Farnham. EPM/2/4/1/1 (07/7).

was back in Helsinki visiting the Kotiahkeruus used by Aalto to supply rugs, mattings, cushions, curtains: 'colouring often bad, but they know how to use materials, wonderful feeling for texture, use of raffia and rush with cotton and linen very interesting'.[93]

For one of her apprentices and subsequently her friend, the Austrian designer and weaver Marianne Straub, Mairet's attentiveness to materials was a revelation:

> Having been taught in Switzerland the art of handweaving, and having learned at a famous Yorkshire Technical College something about machine manufacturing of fabrics and all allied processes, I came to Mrs Mairet and a new world opened out to me, that of real understanding of the yarns and colours. In those days none of the looms in her workshop had more than four shafts, and yet how alive these fabrics were. I had learned an awful lot about drafts and weaves, yet here I felt there was something new, and something vital, which should form the basis of all I had learned, and should have come at the beginning.[94]

This places Mairet in a sophisticated relation to many of her contemporary craft workers, as well as to those for whom industrial design was becoming the *sine non qua* of an aesthetically sophisticated civilization. With Straub she had travelled Europe examining how handwoven design could feed into large-scale production systems, how it might take on influence from and influence architecture, how weaving schools could enhance the life prospects of students (notably girls).[95] She was inspired by the apparent intimacy between the handwork and industrial processes in continental Europe, yet also wary. In Germany, Austria and Switzerland, for example, she noticed a tendency to elevate

---

[93] Quotes taken from 'Finland Diary 1936' in the Ethel Mairet archives in the Craft Study Centre, Farnham. EPM/2/4–7. That Mairet noticed the obsession with texture at Kotiahkeruus was little surprise. It was the workplace of Marianne Strengell who had, like Mairet, been experimenting with unusual blends of yarns (though she tended to design, and get the firm's network of weavers to make), as well as being acutely aware of the need to understand material as it emerges from and works within its wider milieu. At the invitation of the architect Eliel Saarinen – one of the founders of the short lived Finnish architectural community at Hvitträsk (in Kirkkonummi, near Helsinki) inspired by the arts and crafts movement – Strengell moved to the USA the year after Mairet's visit, to teach at Cranbrook Academy of Art, Michigan (where Charles Eames, Harry Bertoia and Florence Knoll were students), later working for both Eames' and Knoll's firms, as well as with General Motors on seating materials and, notably, with Alcoa on developing aluminium yarns (which she blended with wool and linen). See 'Oral History Interview with Marianne Strengell, 1982 January 8–December 16.' Archives of American Art, Smithsonian Institution.

[94] Quoted in Seonaid Mairi Robertson *Craft and Contemporary Culture*. London: George Harrap. 1961. 112.

[95] Ethel Mairet *Hand-Weaving. Notes for Teachers*. London: Faber and Faber. 1929. 15. See also Kirsty Robertson 'Resistance and Submission, Warp and Weft: Unravelling the Life of Ethel Mairet', *Textile*. 2005, 3, 3, 292–317.

design work structure and form, which in weaving meant the interlacing of warp and weft as a grid. The weavers of the Bauhaus were, she felt, especially prone, having been schooled in the pre-eminence of the grid. Their cloth is testimony to a modernist simplicity, its ascetic order and its capacity to organize curves and even tame the looseness of colour. Though they wove stripes of differing widths and uneven repetition, the resulting plaids were, she commented, somewhat subdued, even formulaic and indistinct, lacking richness of colouration, with no attempt to texture by missing warp threads or altering thread widths.

Mairet's criticism was hesitant, and, if one sees the 1931 issue of the Bauhaus magazine dedicated to weaving, somewhat misplaced, as here, from the cover onwards, one witnesses the attentiveness to how threads of differing thicknesses and types can undulate, stiffen and deflect within the material, and how, as the head weaver Gunta Stölzl at the school (and who had worked with Paul Klee on colour in weaving) says, the fabric is akin to a whole composition, bringing together material, form and colour into a unity.[96] Mairet would expand on the definition, beginning with the yarn, the composition, but then extend this to the loom and the workshop, then expanding into social history, geography, demographics, commercial relations.

She was aware that those trained through the Bauhaus were taught to take the force of materials seriously, to consider its tactility, the way it moved with the body, or within a room when covering furnishings or working as curtains.[97] Indeed, for Josef Albers, one of the teachers on the compulsory Preliminary Course taken by all first-year students, materiality was the origin of all production. It is only in the company of material, continues Albers, that the maker is free to experiment:

Experimentation skips over study and a playful beginning develops courage. Thus, we do not begin with a theoretical introduction: at the beginning there is only the material, if possible without tools. This procedure leads naturally to independent thinking and the development of an individual style.

In order to achieve intimate contact with the material through one's own fingertips, the use of tools is initially limited. In the further course of instruction, limitation of the range of possible applications is gradually introduced. The most common ways of working with the material are noted, and, because they already exist, they are forbidden. Example: outside (in handicrafts and industry) paper is employed mostly lying flat and glued, whereby one side of the paper loses its

---

[96] T'ai Smith 'Limits of the Tactile and the Optical: Bauhaus Fabric in the Frame of Photography', *Grey Room*. 2006, 25, 6–31. See also: Gunta Stölzl in Weberie am Bauhaus Offset 1926.

[97] For an insightful study of weaving at the Bauhaus see T'ai Smith *Bauhaus Weaving Theory*. Minneapolis: University of Minnesota Press. 2014. 122–123.

expression, and the edge is almost never used. This is the reason why we use paper standing, uneven, mobile sculpture, both sides, with an emphasis on the edge. Instead of gluing it, we bind it, stick it into things, sew it, rivet it, i.e. fasten it in other ways and test its performance under tension and pressure.[98]

A striking example of how material intelligence could lead to individual thinking and style came in the figure of Grete Marks. After Albers' course she specialized in ceramics, before founding the *Haël- Werkstätten für Künstlerische Keramik*, concentrating on a limited range of tableware, often leaving the clay bare, accented by rhythmic, hand-painted, idiomatic decorative motifs built up from her experiments in recovering the subdued, pale green, brown and yellow glazes of ancient Chinese pots. In Bauhaus tradition, her pieces were minimal, affordable and scalable, and their distinction came from giving the raw materials full exposure.[99] For Josef Albers:

This special interest in the materials is a manifestation of an epoch that is oriented towards construction. The Gothic cultivated this same interest strongly, but it has been badly neglected since: facades and rooms, implements and clothes, have been made of only one material; walls and furniture and floorboards have been completely covered with paint.

This longstanding practice of neglecting the natural surface of materials makes it difficult to take up this multifaceted task of developing the finest possible feeling for the material.[100]

This interest in materials led to extensive and detailed efforts to classify material qualities along scales of tactility, hardness, plasticity, translucency and so on.

Yet whilst the Bauhaus studies began with materials, they were quickly overtaken by ideas. Indeed, Albers makes explicit reference to how a concern with materials feeds a further discussion of formal needs (volume, rhythm, proportion, hygiene, mysticism etc.) which then determine the form to which the materials become a means. Mairet (as did Marks) refuses this progression from material intelligence towards formal

---

[98] Josef Albers *Teaching Form through Practice* (*Werklicher formunterricht*). Translated by Frederick Amrine, Frederick Horowitz and Nathan Horowitz. 2005. http://albersfoundation.org/teaching/josef-albers/texts/. Originally in *Bauhaus*, 2 no. 3, 1928.

[99] Like Lucie Rie, Marks was forced to flee Nazi Germany, abandoning her successful business, finding exile in England. Unlike Rie, Marks was unable to recover her full voice, frustrated by a lack of serious interest in her attempts to blend the aesthetics of studio pottery with industrial techniques and scale. See Ursula Hudson-Wiedenmann and Judy Rudoe 'Grete Marks, Artist Potter', *The Journal of the Decorative Arts Society*. 2002, 26, 100–119.

[100] Josef Albers *Teaching Form through Practice*. Original in German (*Werklicher formunterricht*). English translation by Frederick Amrine, Frederick Horowitz and Nathan Horowitz, *Bauhaus*, 2, 3, 1928.

intelligence (reminiscent of Simondon's distinction between the technical individual of the workshop and the spectator in the factory, or how it was that the optical and the exactness of the measuring eye started to gain precedence over the tactile and the immediacy of touch).[101] Antonia Behan remarks how, without keeping materials to the fore, in standard Bauhaus textiles the grids often appear 'tight, taut, and constrained', whereas Mairet's textiles are largely plain weave; variety comes from the juxtaposition of textures and colours; they do not emphasize a grid but create a mesh, the yarns 'are not tightly woven, ordered, and subsumed into the structure, but twist within the structure' (Figures 54 and 55).[102]

The patterns are looser, and given they evolved as she worked, they emerge right through the width and height of the loom, and their repetitions were a function of the hue, the specific blend of different types and thicknesses of yarn, and whether the fibres had been scoured, fermented or soaked, all of which then gather to give the yarn a sense of heft, a place to which it might belong. The metamery – the striated colour changes – in the weave echo those of the landscape from which the raw materials came.

The colour is not just colour, but indicative of broader systems of organizing: yarn coming from wool, which in turn is contextualized by the different breeds of sheep and the field systems these sheep were bred to defend, coupled to the innovations in farming practice ownership systems that encouraged the emergence of certain yarn and cloth.

[101] From the late 1920s the Bauhaus weavers Gunta Stölzl and Otti Berger were weaving with cellophane, viscose, chenille, linen, wool mixes, some left loose, allowing the material's texture and its movement to become more apparent, to both sight and touch, rather than accept the dominance of the visual pattern and colour. In Berger's essay *Stoffe im Raum* Berger argues: 'The understanding (*Begreifen*) of a cloth can just as well be felt with the hands, as a color can be with the eyes, or a sound can be in the ear'. Quoted in T'ai Smith 'Limits of the Tactile and the Optical: Bauhaus Fabric in the Frame of Photography', *Grey Room*. 2006, 25, 6–31. 16.

[102] Antonia Behan 'Ethel Mairet's Textile Biotechnics and the Aesthetics of Materials. *The Journal of Modern Craft*', 2021. 14, 3, 211–228. 219. In the more bespoke Bauhaus textiles, such the tapestry *Code* by Annie Albers, who ran the textile workshops, the Bauhaus grid was far less evident. T'ai Smith's *Bauhaus Weaving Theory* has a close reading of how the threads of cotton, metals and hemp occlude and hide beneath the grid work, how black weft is floated into the weave, giving the impression of a varied and mobile surface of channels and communications (147). Smith also discusses the prototype swatches of textile that played with ridged textures and blended modern threads (viscose and mercerized cotton that took vibrant chemical dyes) with natural fibres, and which experimented with colour theories being taught by Paul Klee and Wassily Kandinsky (50). These remained, however, very small in scale, more gestures towards what Walter Gropius called 'future crafts', pieces of handwork revealing the possibilities and limits of current technologies, materials and forms from which industry might learn. Mairet held similar ambitions for her own textiles, though these were of a useable size and scale, and were far more eclectic in their formation, and tended to eschew the influence of conceptual structures.

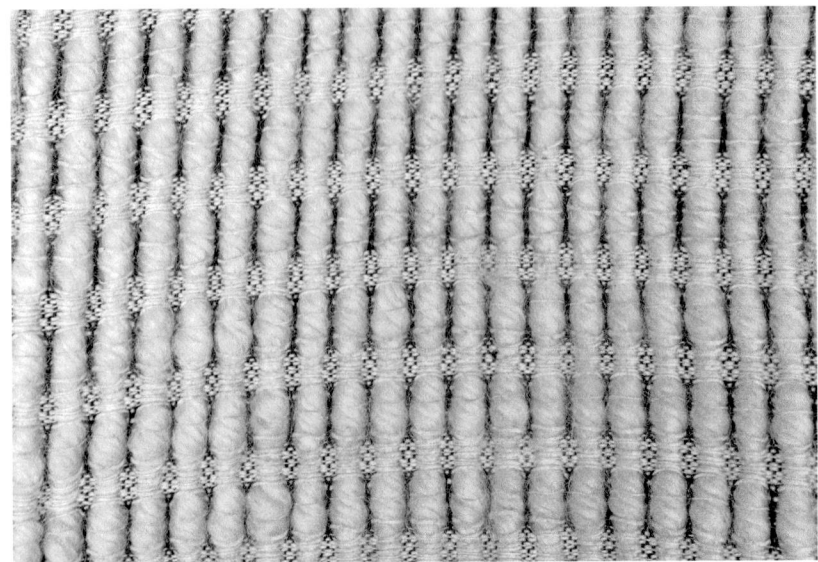

Figure 54 Ethel Mairet, thick, hand-spun, white wool and fine white cotton weft, black and white machine-spun cotton warp, plain weave, spaced reeding, 1930s (T.74.11). From the collections of the Crafts Study Centre, University for the Creative Arts.

Figure 55 Ethel Mairet, hand-woven wall hanging with stripes in natural linen, clear cellophane and black cotton, plain weave, warp and weft strips, 1940s (T.74.116). From the collections of the Crafts Study Centre, University for the Creative Arts.

It was as if the cloth was not cloth until the weaver had incorporated an awareness of the commercial, institutional and cultural relations into the 'taskscape' of its production. In *Dart*, Alice Oswald considers how whatever happens in the catchment area of a river ends up in the river, and so to write a poem about, or prompted by, a river one has to consider its 'full acreage': the field systems, the road drainage, the sewage systems, the milk factories, the sport and leisure activities, a vast, regional metabolism.[103] Mairet understands a piece of cloth in the same way: its acreage covers more than its materiality and whatever happens round and about the cloth ends up in the cloth.

Because they are well trained, Mairet's apprentices 'take on' what they have been taught, following the rules into newly opening spaces, using what they can, dropping what they can't. As they draw on this repository of understanding, they can reach into technological developments of large-scale manufacturers, taking up what is being offered there. Again, Mairet shows (rather than tells) the way. Like the weavers of the Bauhaus, she too took up the new yarns like cellophane and rayon, ones whose chemical qualities require new perceptiveness and yarn understanding. She reflects on how, if used too readily and in quantity, they look obvious, even vulgar. Yet used sparingly they radiate. Cellophane, for example, has an 'immense aesthetic future' and its uses 'should be thought out with much originality and understanding for new purposes and expressions in weaving. It reflects light only at certain angles so it always has an alive character, reminding one of the sun on the sea picking out the edges of the waves.'[104] The workshop was a setting in which this restrained, disciplined, poetic use of manufactured innovation was coupled to a thorough awareness of traditional techniques and materials.

The traditions to which Mairet's handweaving belonged were restless ones agitated by the latent, intrinsic potential of materials that only make themselves apparent through forms of broad biotechnic analysis recommended by Mumford and undertaken by Mairet. The wealth created by craft work is its being a site of perpetual, unassigned experiment: where manufacturing was skewed towards scaling and machine innovation, craft work has the potential to understand the rich interplay of biotechnic forces in different materials and different work rhythms, and through this build a material expertise by which humans can better organize the relations between things and so ameliorate the excesses of the machine age.

---

[103] Alice Oswald *Dart*. London: Faber. 2016. 30.
[104] Ethel Mairet *Handweaving Notes for Teachers*. 30.

# 7   Redundancy and Plenitude

### Mechanization Takes Control

In Bruce Chatwin's last novel *Utz*, the eponymous Meissen collector Kaspar Joachim Utz confirms the legitimacy of his passion for the expressive, porcelain figures bearing the mark of two crossed swords by suggesting that Adam, having been fashioned from clay and fired by the light of the world, was both the first human and the first ceramic (Figure 56).

After the Fall, the human became incomplete, hungry for understanding of what it might become: it was a void, an emptiness, whose gradual elimination became the mark of civilization. The human was a vessel to be filled with knowledge garnered from inquiries into the nature of things, technical inquires that produced a vast and burgeoning network of theories, principles, laws, protocols, standards and procedures by which the world of the fallen was subdued by artifice. Clay, in contrast, was to be filled, then emptied, again and again. As Lao Tsu [Laozi] suggests:

> Thirty spokes gathered at each hub:
> absence makes the cart work.
> A storage jar fashioned out of clay:
> absence makes the jar work.
> Doors and windows cut in a house:
> absence makes the house work.
> Presence gives things their value,
> but absence makes them work[1]

To fill the human void meant keeping the void made by clay in play, as a container: an urn, a storage jar, as channel for dissipating heat from the rapid passage of data in circuit boards and semi-conductors.[2] As a

---

[1] Lao Tzu [Laozi] *Tao Te Ching*. Translated by David Hinton. Berkeley: Counterpoint. 2015. 49.

[2] Porcelain manufacturer Maruwa, based in Aichi, Japan for over 200 years moved out of tableware and into electronics in the 1960s and quietly continued using its expertise to make the substrates for transceivers used in data centres (see *Financial Times*, 12 April 2024).

# Mechanization Takes Control

Figure 56 Albrecht Dürer, *Adam and Eve*, 1504. Engraving. The Metropolitan Museum of Art: 19.73.1 / Fletcher Fund, 1919.

container of things, the lay gains its use value, and as with clay vessels, so with the multiplicity of tools that were being aligned in sequences of utility-bearing productiveness. As civilization progressed, so the gridwork of useful things, and the logic of utility, spread, smothering the changefulness and variety of nature with a network of manufactured operations.

Civilization and manufacturing formed a union, and begat industrialization. To make (*factio*) from the hands (*manus*) was to take on the role of creator, 'a thing wrought upon a creature by the artificers hand, then a seueral creature of itself'.[3] It was the human hand, not God's, that made and what it made through manufacturing was dedicated to the preservation and survival of human biological life. As things are made, they are then used up, production transitions into consumption and biological life requires more production. It is an endless process of extracting, distributing, storing and switching in which nothing remains and nothing is remembered because nothing is enough. The world made in the image of the human is an idea of homeostatic balance of desire and provision, and manufacture is dedicated to transforming nature to substantiate the idea. Desire, however, is limitless in its progressions, and nature is called upon accordingly by the improving schemes of manufacture that fence it in and force it to do its bidding: life; industrialized.

In the preface to *The Crown of Wild Olive*, Ruskin recalls how the progression of manufacture had altered the course of the River Wandle, running from Carshalton Ponds on moorland south of London into the River Thames at Wandsworth:

Twenty years ago, there was no lovelier piece of lowland scenery in South England, nor any more pathetic in the world, by its expression of sweet human character and life, than that immediately bordering on the sources of the Wandel[sic], and including the lower moors of Addington, and the villages of Beddington and Carshalton, with all their pools and streams ... Just where the welling of stainless water, trembling and pure, like a body of light, enters the pool of Carshalton, cutting itself a radiant channel down to the gravel, through warp of feathery weeds, all waving, which it traverses with its deep threads of clearness, like the chalcedony in moss-agate, starred here and there with white grenouillette; just in the very rush and murmur of the first spreading currents, the human wretches of the place cast their street and house foulness; heaps of dust and slime, and broken shreds of old metal, and rags of putrid clothes; they having neither energy to cart it away, nor decency enough to dig it into the ground, thus shed into the stream, to diffuse what venom of it will float and melt, far away, in all places where God meant those waters to bring joy and health.[4]

Further downstream Ruskin notes how land adjoining the Wandle's banks and demarking the grounds of a pub in Croydon has been fenced in, the iron posts standing 'sedentary and foolish. The effort that had been put into making these posts would have been far better directed toward protecting

---

[3] Early definition of manufacturing by N. Sanders, *Treat. Images* viii. 72. 1597. OED. 'Manufacture'.

[4] John Ruskin Crown of Wild Olive. In *Complete Works Vol. XVIII*. Edited by E. T. Cook and Alexander Wedderburn. London: George Allen. 1905. 385–386.

the river from development. But no, rather than care for the environment, work is devoted to its further defilement through decorative enclosure. There is, hazards Ruskin, only one reason why this warped situation has arisen: the logic of manufacture which confines work into cycles of transformation: the making iron posts to cordon off and assert private ownership of pockets of land, which further profits foundries and mines, who make yet more iron, to cordon off further parcels of land, and all the while water runs foul. The great trick pulled off by manufacturers is to persuade us that wealth equates to assets being used to generate more assets.

All making is being pulled into the centrifugal forces generated in these cycles of capital transformation. In these cycles, tasks, as Mairet understood them might still be possible – for example, when workers have to wrestle with broken machinery, or when they re-direct the machinery towards their own personal ends in small, expressive bursts of *la peruque* – but these are momentary interludes and remain dependent upon the proper space of manufacture and its finance over which the maker has little say, and so any disturbance is stilled by a quelling of all nature as it submits to the position of the machinery by which it is challenged to reveal itself as nothing other than a resource to be hollowed out, an earth-sized vessel becoming more and more empty as civilization believes itself to be getting fuller.

The regional settings in which Heidegger envisaged tasks extending into a 'taskscape' have become increasingly homogenized. It is a transition that in Europe was taking place at the end of the nineteenth century, one Thomas Hardy embodies in the bookish protagonist in *Jude the Obscure*. Trained as a stone mason, but aspiring to be a scholar, Jude Fawley enters Oxford wanting to swap handwork for headwork. Finding the colleges closed to someone of his lowly status, he finds succour in the walls of the ancient colleges; if he is to be prevented from reading books, he can still read buildings:

> The numberless architectural pages around him he read, naturally, less as an artist-critic of their forms than as an artizan and comrade of the dead handicraftsmen whose muscles had actually executed those forms. He examined the mouldings, stroked them as one who knew their beginning, said they were difficult or easy in the working, had taken little or much time, were trying to the arm, or convenient to the tool.[5]

Searching for work in a stone yard, he had a moment of illumination in which craft and academic work struck up an an equivalence, the mason and scholar were producing a mutually generative space. It was, continues

---

[5] Thomas Hardy *Jude the Obscure*. London: McIlvaine, & Co. 1895. Part 2, II. 1.

Hardy's narrator, a moment of innocence. Bearing reared a humble mason in rural isolation Jude was unaware 'that unaware 'that mediævalism was as dead as a fern-leaf in a lump of coal; that other developments were shaping in the world around him, in which Gothic architecture and its associations had no place. The deadly animosity of contemporary logic and vision towards so much of what he held in reverence was not yet revealed to him.'[6]

Contemporary logic was machinic, rapid, straight to the point and the obscurity to which it consigned workers like Jude Fawley had little dignity. Theodor Adorno, replaying complaints made by Ruskin and Hardy, assesses the situation bleakly: 'Technology', he observes, 'is making gestures precise and brutal, and with them men. It expels from movements all hesitation, deliberation, civility. It subjects them to the implacable, as it were ahistorical demands of objects.'[7] Technology is forcing the pace, forcing point to point contacts without remission. The spaces of pause – thresholds, churches, parklands, atria, squares – are being eradicated or filled by productive use, which is itself increasingly temporary.

The taskscape becomes a theatre of operations in which movement is reduced to taking up the positions that enable machinery to function efficiently. Why they function becomes an immediate question grounded in means-end instrumentality: they work to produce.

Nature is set upon [*hin gestellt*] to yield energy or: nature is compelled [*gezwungen*] to deliver its energy. The meaning is that of a being held to something, whereby that which is held to something is at the same time forced to adopt a certain form, to play a role, a role to which it is henceforth reduced. Nature, held to delivering its energy, henceforth appears as a 'reserve of energy'.[8]

Under the imperative of functionality, the world is confined to a series of positions confirmed by machine-based calculations whose operations create objects about which there is no mystery, no uncertainty, given all of them are comparable as sources of measured value that have been, are being, or are about to be, taken from out of the earth.

Jacob Epstein describes how he had been 'fired' up to create his sculpture *Rock Drill* by visiting a quarry: adamantine stone was submitting to the irresistible bursts of a mechanical force far greater than ever managed by Jude Fawley's hammer and chisel (Figure 57). Epstein was entranced, physically exited, in awe as a witness to this new source of the sublime, he just had to buy the pneumatic drill; first sketching and then making a mould of a white cyborg worker figure that could

---

[6] Thomas Hardy *Jude the Obscure*. Part 2, II. 1.
[7] Theodor Adorno *Minima Moralia*. 40.
[8] Martin Heidegger *Four Seminars*. Translated by Andrew Mitchell and François Raffoul. Indianapolis: Indiana University Press. 2003. 76.

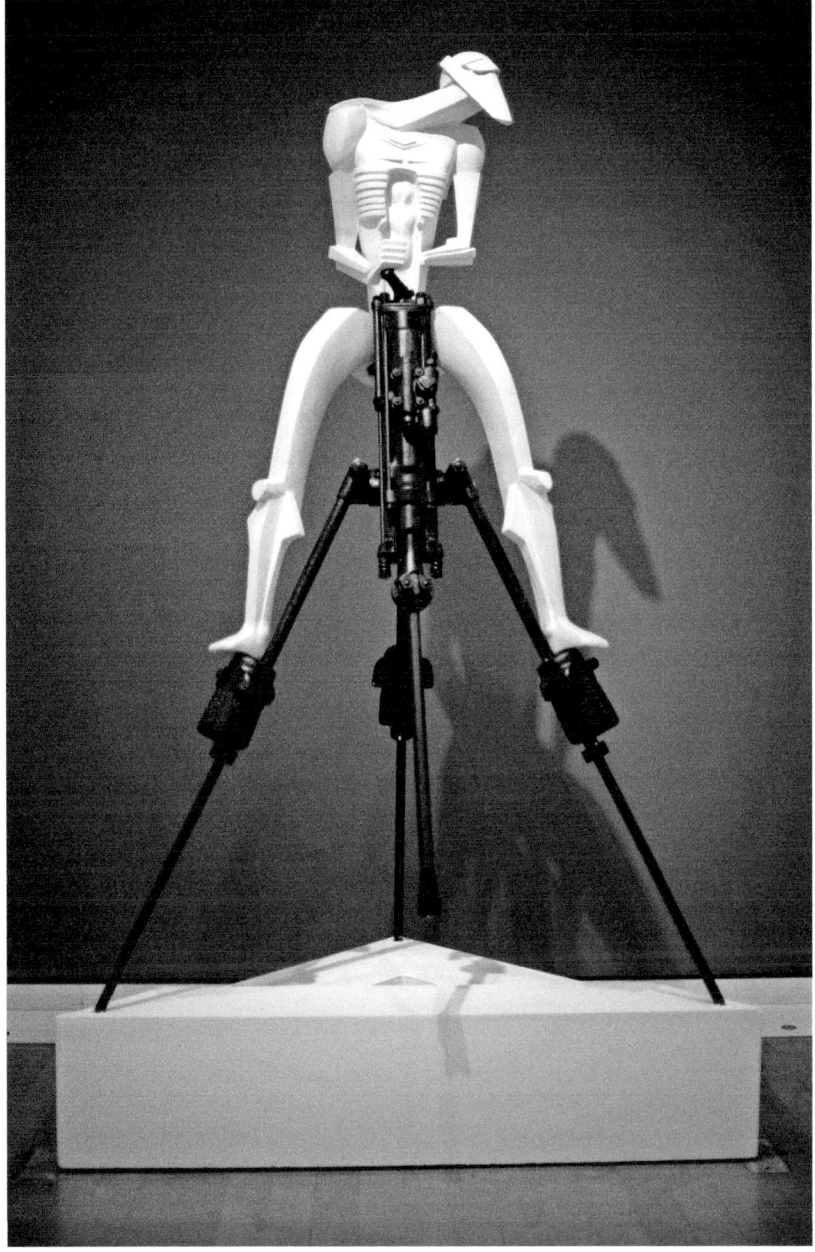

Figure 57 Jacob Epstein, *Rock Drill*, 1913–1916. Plaster and rock drill machinery. Destroyed (replica made 1974). © Ben Stansall / Stringer / AFP / Getty Images.

be mounted astride the blackened metal tripod whose legs have been accentuated into sharp, shocking shafts of black light. Like Adam, the cyborg was cast from clay, though now as an extension of the machine upon which it was elevated above the earth, leaving space enough for the probus on the cusp of a devastating, downward thrust. The cyborg's visored face looks outward and downward at the same time, challenging both the horizon and ground, already assured of dominance. Whilst its right hand grips the drill handle, ready to turn the screws, its left is truncated, maimed even, and it gestures towards a rent in the torso exposing angular innards which are nestling a small and feint hybrid embryo. Made in 1913, it was first shown to near universal revulsion in the shadow of war at the London Group Show of 1915.

The awe Epstein felt remains an integral aspect of how nature is being set upon, as is the embryonic sign of a new life form which is shuttered into an immediate state of dependency. The assembly of machine, operator and newborn is emblematic of the mechanization which Adorno witnesses as a profound diminution of human experience:

> Not least to blame for the withering of experience is the fact that things, under the law of pure functionality, assume a form that limits contact with them to mere operation, and tolerates no surplus, either in freedom of conduct or in autonomy of things, which would survive as the core of experience, because it is not consumed by the moment of action.[9]

No sooner is surplus made than it is allocated and consumed. The rock drill is not just a machine, but a modality of extraction through which all objects are being called to set upon themselves. The compulsion towards total functionality has been extended from humans through machine to nature so that innovation and productivity became intimate with biological as well as technological growth; not the growth of one form, but of growth itself. The rock drill is not only extracting existing resources but growing a replacement which will supersede its current capacity in an attempt to secure its own biological future.[10] In this it is behaving like any organism whose individuality and distinction is not a fixed state, but a continual struggle to re-enact itself through processes of individuation. Though at any one instant the organism can become the subject of an abstract operation that asserts its distinction (it can be classified as 'this' or 'that' in language) this distinctiveness is nothing more than a conceptual serialization (and sterilization) of its life as an organism which is being lived and experienced as

---

[9] Theodor Adorno *Minima Moralia: Reflections from a Damaged Life*. Translated by E. Jephcott. London: Verso. 1951/2005. 40.
[10] Melinda Cooper *Life as Surplus: Biotechnology and Capitalism in the Neoliberal Era*. Seattle: University of Washington Press. 2008. 25.

a continual process of self-organization: an organism is always living in its own future.[11] Notably, for an organism such as the rock drill whose movements are confined by a modality of extraction that sets upon nature as a resource, nothing more, by living in the future, this setting upon nature is no longer just a question of taking existing resources but of creating hitherto unthought ones, exploiting the vital potential of unregulated oscillations between mechanized nature and naturalized machines.[12] The things of the earth are already on notice that their immeasurable potential is first, to become an imaginable possibility and then, an actual occurrence: the rock drill self-organizes by harbouring its successor, which will work harder still at closing down on the production of untapped surplus.

How, then, is it possible to restore the experience of what Adorno called surplus, and what, in Mairet's workshop, was called the product from unassigned experiment? Can nature inspire and provoke workshop life without being enlisted utterly by the speculative imaginaries of capital growth? Is there space to learn with machines, where the worker experiences patterns of autonomy, and where they may, for example, inquire into the biotechnics of a strand of cellophane and think about sunlight etching itself across a sea rather than servicing the needs of those in possession of capital?

We return to the question mentioned earlier: the man [sic] of the times, the man who understands himself and acts as the producer of all 'reality,' the man who finds himself today caught in the increasingly constraining network of the socio-economic 'imperatives' (which are, seen from the history of being, the precipitates of positionality), can that man himself produce the means of working a way out of the pressure of the 'imperatives'?

How could he manage this without surrendering his own determination as producer? And is such a surrender possible in the horizon of today's reality? What would such a renunciation signify? It would mean renouncing progress itself, committing to a general restriction of consumption and production.[13]

It is a renunciation to which Mairet's sense of, and feeling for, craft work is committed. The progress it renounces is the linear progress of one position giving way to another. Rather than assign positions, craft work involves people, makers and users who have, or struggle towards, a rough if limited connexion whose particularity is what differentiates the exchange relations from those fostered by the socio-economic imperatives of a world being broken up and sold on. To live in a such a

---

[11] Melinda Cooper *Life as Surplus*. Footnote 13, Ch. 4, 188. Her translation of Gilbert Simondon. *L'individuation psychique et collective*. Paris: Aubier. 1989.
[12] Melinda Cooper *Life as Surplus*. 30–31.
[13] Martin Heidegger *Four Seminars*. Translated by Andrew Mitchell and François Raffoul. Indianapolis: Indiana University Press. 2003. 74.

broken world is not to live amongst broken things. It is to live in a world diminished in spirit and diminished in the questioning, the ambition, the earthliness and the decisiveness of embodying self-understanding and self-development in patterns of work. Hence Mairet's insistence that the workshop and the classroom were a unity: to make is also to inquire and the purpose making and learning share is the generation of a surplus that cannot be accounted for.

## Patterns of Surplus

It is in surplus that the potential of life resides: the uncontracted, unallocated surplus that has neither role nor place, it is freed to wander. What goes unconsumed in the moment of action remains for thoughtful consideration, or remains replete with potential, or just remains, waiting. These are the sites and moments of what Hui calls contingency, to which there is an essential redundancy. They cannot be confined by the name 'possibility' if by the 'possible' is meant the act of imagining of an event around which work might be organized: 'Who knows where cellophane might take us?'.

In Gothic sculpture, this surplus is found in ornament: 'the rude love of decorative accumulation: a magnificent enthusiasm, which feels as if it never could do enough to reach the fulness of its ideal; an unselfishness of sacrifice, which would rather cast fruitless labour before the altar than stand idle in the market; and, finally, a profound sympathy with the fulness and wealth of the material universe'.[14]

There is, suggests Ruskin, an exuberance and generosity in the bundles of complexity that can cover Gothic stonework, immersed as it is in the profusion and infinite subtleties of nature: 'the sculptor who sought for his models among the forest leaves, could not but quickly and deeply feel that complexity need not involve the loss of grace, nor richness that of repose'.[15] There is a willingness to get carried away with the connexions to be made, to make as nature makes, to give over to the effulgence of natural forms without thought for usefulness or conservation. The surplus cannot be measured, compared and allocated according to conventional measures of value. The value lies in the happiness it bestows on the maker and user in the process of making: 'I believe the right question to ask, respecting all ornament, is simply this: Was it done with enjoyment – was the carver happy while he was about it? It may be the

---

[14] John Ruskin *The Stones of Venice, Vol. II*. §78. 243.
[15] John Ruskin *The Stones of Venice, Vol. II*. §78. 244.

hardest work possible, and the harder because so much pleasure was taken in it; but it must have been happy too, or it will not be living.'[16]

In ornamentation the maker gives full voice to the lines of flight that arise in the making as they do in natural growth, there is a wandering and a finding of the way whose only warrant is that it has no goal and serves no specified interest, and yet it is an indication of life that humans share, even in their barest state, as in Pablo Neruda's 'Ode to Some Yellow Flowers':

> We are dust, we shall forever be dust
> Neither air, nor fire, nor water
> but
> earth
> We shall only be earth
> and perhaps
> some yellow flowers.[17]

Compared to other Gothic qualities, Ruskin seems to place ornamentation in a subaltern role, perhaps wary of its proximity to wanton excess and waste and to vulgar decoration. Yet as technologically mediated manufacturing processes spread and extended into home life, so a concern for redundancy grew in resonance. No longer just raucous or flippant asides, the voices that not only acknowledge but enthuse over what goes unused and unallocated have become more arresting, more compelling. Theirs is a tone of strange generosity heard from outside the walls of what is being measured, built-up, pinned down, dis-assembled, moved on, stored, replaced. Within these linear chains, ornament is problematic because it communicates only with itself, there is nothing ulterior upon which its authorship relies, it lies unaccounted for and so, to the manufacturing body weaned on a diet of efficiently procured inputs, it stands out as frivolous and wanton. Which is its power, if power is defined not only as the outcome of temporary and ongoing struggles between social agents, but specifically a struggle between individuals and groups over norms and values. It is the experience of such a struggle against manufacturing, and the structures of industrial capitalism that it enhances and perpetuates, that finds craft workers searching for patterns of redundancy. Ruskin and the Arts and Crafts movement he helped spawn experienced laissez-faire systems of material wealth production as demeaning and weakening to those having to produce objects and consume them. The grammar of commerce and the structural divisions and specializations in work that it scaffolded

---

[16] John Ruskin *Seven Lamps of Architecture*. §24. 218.
[17] Pablo Neruda and Joseph V. Ricapito. 'Ode to Some Yellow Flowers', *Latin American Literary Review*. 1975, 3, 6, 107–111. 111.

was dominating the available language of value, wealth, worth and good. Whilst Ruskin's economic analysis has been roundly, and rightly, criticized as lacking technical sophistication, this misses the point. Irrespective of economic niceties, it was the effects on workers' lives and consumers' taste that Ruskin objected to. His interest was in revealing and distilling the phenomenological experience of workers and users rather than identifying the explanatory generalizations of economic theory. Gothic is to be thought of through the putative experience of a craft worker, through the integrity of made things and the users of these made things, and in being so the analysis upon which Gothic rests rarely leaves this rarely leaves this everyday world of happenstance. Ruskin wishes to make it clear that the good or wealth in life comes not only from a capacity to express oneself through work skilfully and from an attentive closeness to the world, but to have this capacity encouraged and acknowledged in social relations and institutions, notably amongst customers and users. Laissez-faire principles led to divided lives and shoddy goods: the fact that money was being made in the institutionalization of these effects was lamentable.

In Gothic, Ruskin imagined imagined a passionate alternative to laissez-faire structures, and in the effervescent and committed figure of William Morris the response took a practical. By his own admission, Morris had been throwing his lot in with the Gothic revivalists of Victorian Britain ever since reading the second volume of Ruskin's *The Stones of Venice*. He wished to live in the medieval spirit, but could not find anywhere to do so. The job-at-hand, then, became plain to see, he would build his own: 'all the minor arts were in a state of compete the minor arts were in a state of complete degradation especially in England, and accordingly in 1861 with the conceited courage of a young man I set myself to reforming all that: and started a sort of firm for producing decorative articles.'[18] Founding an interior decorating company in order to disassemble industrial capitalism was not the most obvious move. But at least Morris was not working alone, he had enthusiastic partners in the firm who shared the ambition. To transform society, one had to start with the small, well made things which radiated with the transforming force of ornament. In the prospectus launching Morris, Marshall & Faulkner & Co. in 1861, the founders are very clear about their motivation. Being unable to find sufficient goods of integrity and beauty they were setting out to make their own, first in premises at Red Lion Square, then Queen Square in London, and finally, in 1881, after Morris had bought out his partners, at the Merton Abbey works in South London.

---

[18] William Morris *The Collected Letters. Volume II, Part A. 1881–1884*. Edited by Norman Kelvin. Princeton: Princeton University Press. 2014. Letter 911. 228. Morris was responding to a request from Andreas Scheu to send a sketch of his life.

Merton was made up of a mill house, mill pond, orchard, meadow, living houses, coach house, dyeing rooms, stained glass workshops, carpet knotting workshop, weaving shed with jacquard looms, block printing workshop, tapestry rooms, vegetable garden, glass firing kiln, dormitory for apprentices, boiler house and bleaching field.[19] The same River Wandle that had drawn both Ruskin's admiration and despair flowed through the site, and a train station stood adjacent. The fresh water brought by the river was integral to the work, not only as a source of motor power for the machinery, but for dyeing and washing cloth. The partnership and works were not, however, operating in a vacuum: they knew they had a market amongst architects whose Gothic revival appealed to a growing, but still outré High Anglican congregation. In its early Prospectus, and notably at the 1862 International Exhibition in South Kensington where The Firm – as it was known to its principal owners (Peter Paul Marshall, Charles Faulkner, Philip Webb, Ford Madox Brown, Edward Burne Jones, Dante Gabriel Rosetti and William Morris) – committed itself to carving and architectural masonry work, mural and wall painting, metal work, furniture and stained glass. In short, they were a one-stop shop for kitting the more ritualistic, aesthetically charged branches of an otherwise dowdy Church of England. Their Exhibition displays – notably the stained glass, whose sensual, narrative strength in the designs of Burne Jones and the brilliant subtleties of colour being rendered by Morris' combination of medieval mosaic techniques and experiment in dying and overlaying made it peerless – established the Firm's reputation as a serious and original venture.[20] From here they could broaden without diluting their commitment to well-made things. Morris especially had sensed a burgeoning middle class in an affluent, expanding city anxious to sustain their expectations through the acquisition of taste. There was established taste met by established firms, then there was a more edgy, expressive, natural taste which The Firm, made up of artists, architects, glass makers, jewellers, designers and weavers, and with a retinue of craft workers covering the other trades, could help shape. The Firm was a 'brotherhood' that had schooled itself in beauty and which, in becoming a company could market it.[21] In doing so it also became less male, though as Georgina Burne Jones was to regretfully point out, less male, as the

---

[19] Morris, Marshall, Faulkner (MMF) & Co. was registered in 1861, becoming Morris & Co. in 1875. In 1877 Morris had set up shop in London's Oxford Street (on the corner with North Audley Street), selling wallpaper and fabrics, accompanied by tiles, glass and furniture. The firm eventually closed in 1940, and the Merton works were laid waste by German bombers in the blitz.
[20] Fiona McCarthy. *William Morris: A Life of Our Time*. London: Faber and Faber. 1994. 181.
[21] See Charles Harvey, 'Jon Press & Mairi Maclean William Morris, Cultural Leadership, and the Dynamics of Taste', *Business History Review*. 2011, 85, 2, 245–271. For Morris's comment on 'marketing beauty' see 256.

respective partners of The Firm's partners got involved, though as the zeal and skill shown by the women who became embroidered into the ornaments of production, was only ever recognized as derivative service. It was the male who designed and instructed, and the women (Lizzie Siddal, Emma Brown, Jane Morris) who followed, keeping pace with the men, until familial duty and social 'propriety' meant they fell behind.[22]

The well-made objects spilling out of the works were studies in ornament: wallpapers blocked with the meandering tendrils of fritillaries and willow literally popping out of the flat plane, curtained chintzes dyed with indigo and madder rose forming pleated, undulating drops over window glass stained in deep plum and ochre.[23] Ornament was very much of the thing not on it, as the architect Frank Lloyd Wright was later to remark: intrinsic to an organic, natural form growing outwards, inwards, along and upwards, each part handing itself over to a whole and the whole making way for the arrival of new parts.[24]

The mimetic ground for this ornamental work were the patterns in nature with which Morris was able to experiment: held in blocked drifts and sprays, or in woven threads the shape of bells or feathers, the ornament reminds us of the 'outward face of the earth', and the interconnected patterns by which that earth lives through an intimacy of organisms of which humans are just one form. Morris was prompted by Owen Jones' encyclopaedic study *The Grammar of Ornament* where nature, and especially plants and flowers, was argued to be the source for any understanding of how 'harmony of form consists in the proper balancing, and contrast of the straight, the inclined, and the curved'.[25] Morris, however, went further than Owen's mimetic, filial impulse to represent a carefully curated nature. Morris' repetitions were not at all repetitious, the patterns were untrussed, freed from the orthogonal, each stroke a new instantiation of the previous, similar stroke. His love of ornament grew, like Goethe's, from a disciplined active empiricism which noticed how in nature form came forth from form, without end. All plants are in continual contraction and expansion, all parts are in states of growth and decay, they accord with what Goethe called the *Urpflanze*, the productive, vital grounding force by

---

[22] Georgia Burne Jones In Fiona MaCarthy. *William Morris*. 164.
[23] Morris used different floral designs for cloth that would fold and land in draped undulations and wallpaper that would expand in repeats across a flat plane.
[24] Frank Lloyd Wright *An Organic Architecture: The Architecture of Democracy*. London: Lund Humphries. 1939.
[25] Owen Jones *The Grammar of Ornament*. Princeton: Princeton University Press. 2016. Reprint of 1856 edition. Proposition 10. 24.

which all plant life is organized and to whose variety Morris, with supersensible energy, gave peerless, decorative expression.[26]

He seems well attuned to the generative force of patterns categorized by Gregory Bateson's three orders. First, he was attentive to the patterned coherence within a single form, so how, for example, the unruliness of the small periwinkle flower must retain order enough for them to reach upwards to the light, whilst avoiding the direct, upright line. Second, he was open to the sympathies between different patterns, such as the edge of a bird's beak which echoes the edge of the seeds upon which it feeds; or how the meander in a river traces similar curves to those of a vine, or how a fern leaf resembles a full tree.[27] His designs named after London's rivers (tributaries of the River Thames) for example – such as the Wandle – depict parrot tulips, chrysanthemums and marigolds not water: the twisting stalks and leaves allude to the twists of water of the 'helpful stream' that passed through the Merton Abbey works.[28] They are pure similes, poetic excurses into the grammatical form of likeness from which all imagination stems (Figure 58).

Without a literal representation of water, or banks, the river is left as a subject of association. In combining the title and image the viewer (or user) experiences the meandering force to which both rivers and plants (as organisms) attest, how they negotiate with their wider environment by moving to accommodate other forces, following and adding to the full lie of the land. Third, he reaches for meta-similies, so how patterns of association that join rivers and plants can be an aesthetic mirror of the political and social association of workers and owners. Both might attend to the declivities of the other, finding mutual accommodation, so the flows of water or of capital do not overrun, or when they do it is

---

[26] Originally Goethe felt a primal plant might well exist as a distillation of the form from which the fecund continuities of all plant life was derived, yet he came to think of the *Urpflanze* more as an ontology of variation, an expression of how biological life manifested itself not in singular elements, but in the dynamic correlation of permanence and change. See James Larson 'Goethe and Linnæus', *Journal of the History of Ideas*. 1967, 28, 4, 590–596.

[27] 'In the ferns we see still stronger – we might even say enormous – evidence of the sheer fruitfulness inherent in the stem leaves: these develop and scatter innumerable seeds (or rather, germs) through an inner impulse, and probably without any well-defined action by two genders. Here the fruitfulness of a single leaf rivals that of a wide spreading plant, or even a large tree with its many branches.' Johann Wolfgang von Goethe *The Metamorphosis of Plants*. Cambridge, MA: MIT Press. 2024. §77.

[28] The patterns were inspired by a seventeenth-century Italian cut velvet that the South Kensington Museum had recently acquired. The rivers were: Evenlode, Medway, Kennet, Wandle, Windrush, Cray and Wey. See William Morris *The Collected Letters. Volume II, Part A. 1881–1884*. Letter 853. 165. For reproductions of all the patterns, 166–172.

Figure 58 William Morris, *Wandle*. Cotton fabric, block printed. © William Morris Gallery, London Borough of Waltham Forest.

an aftermath, a fertilizing deluge, and as each takes from the other so each also gives.

Producing ornament, however, came at a cost. The rivers of the capital were being mauled by development: thoughtlessly channelled underground, overbuilt, sullied. Including Morris' own river, whose waters were regularly tainted by dyes being washed out of paper or cloth. The most vivid being the blue which came from dye resist patterns like the Wandle (and the Strawberry Thief (Figure 59)): the whole surface was covered with indigo (from the plant *Indigofera tinctoria* mixed with oil of vitriol or sulphuric acid), and the pattern was block printed with bleaching agents and the released indigo washed away by running water, to leave it free to take the next block-printed colours, which were red (from the ground-up dried roots of *Rubia tinctorum*, madder rose) stalks and yellowing (from dried petals and stalks of the wild growing *Reseda luteola*, weld) blooms. His work was bedevilled with such contradictions. Whilst Morris espoused and enacted a need to care for nature, and for a greater equality

Figure 59 William Morris, Strawberry Thief. Dyed with natural indigo and madder rose. Designed by William Morris. 1883. Block-printed cotton. © William Morris Gallery, London Borough of Waltham Forest.

amongst peoples and the social and political change by which this might be realized, his craft work pandered to the tastes of an established elite for whom tableware and wall hangings were symbols of attainment, and to satisfy this market demand his works did obvious violence to nature.[29] It was why the Arts and Crafts Movement of which he was the leading figure ended up niggling over the price of wallpaper. C. R. Ashbee, founder of the Guild of Handicraft in unfashionable Whitechapel, tried to come to Morris' defence, arguing that the Arts and Crafts Movement that owed much to the 'titanic energy' of Morris was not at all, as critics would have it, 'a nursery for luxuries, a hothouse for the production of mere trivialities and useless things for the rich. It is a movement for the stamping out of such things by sound production on the one hand, & the inevitable regulation of machine production and cheap labour on the other.'[30]

Morris was not unmoved by the criticism to which Ashbee alludes. In writing to Ruskin, for example, he extended an invitation to the Merton Works, but warned: 'I fear it would be a grief to you to see the banks of the pretty Wandle so beset with the horrors of the Jerry-builders: there is still some beauty left about the place however, & the stream itself is not

---

[29] See Charles Harvey and Jon Press, *William Morris: Design and Enterprise in Victorian Britain*. Manchester: Manchester University Press. 1991.

[30] C. R. Ashbee *Craftsmanship in Competitive Industry*. London: Essex House Press. 1908. 9. Later, after Ashbee had undertaken the 'great move' of the 150 or so souls who comprised the Guild from London's East End to Chipping Camden in the Cotswolds in 1902 – a move written up in *Whitechapel to Camelot* in which he argued craft work is better if it takes place in a workshop itself grounded in an agrarian, communal, outdoor life – he became more scathing of Morris' works, suggesting they had become too much the manufacture:

I had a little experience last year in selling several large pieces of furniture made by Morris & Co. The result showed that there is no general public for such things, each individual piece is made for an individual buyer, and probably if Morris & Co. had to make such things for stock they would soon be in the same hole as you are. They have as the result of a longer existence a considerable and more or less constant demand for certain wall papers and cretonnes, and machine-made carpets and other repeat orders where their prices don't differ much from those of ordinary commerce. Such orders don't of course solve the question of finding employment for specially trained cabinet makers, carpet makers, and metal workers, but the profit on them goes to pay expenses at Oxford Street. (C. R. Ashbee *Craftsmanship in Competitive Industry*. 241.)

Ashbee's assessment was reasonable. The Merton Works were not radical: workers were employed on better than average terms, but paid piece rates and there were few options for shareholding. It was a pragmatic organization acknowledging its place in a capitalist supply chain. Ashbee wanted the Guild to be a source of joy, work should be undertaken in clear, fresh air, animated by a vigorous, homoerotic bonhomie, informed by a collective immersion in the performing arts, and uncompromising in its concern for quality. Morris attempted to absorb the hypocrisy of being a socialist catering to establishment tastes, whereas Ashbee repressed it. See Fiona MacCarthy *The Simple Life: C R Ashbee in the Cotswolds*. London: Lund Humphries. 1981. Also her *William Morris: A Life of Our Time*. 454–456.

much befouled: I am doing my best to keep the place decent, & can do so in the seven acres our works command; but as to the rest can do but little.'[31] He acknowledged many customers cared little for the value of ornament as he experienced it as a mode of aesthetic education, preferring instead to invest the acquisition of his products with the symbolic capital of social attainment, but he went on making them, just as much a prisoner of industrial capitalism as anyone else:

> While this commercial war lasts we are all the slaves of it, not the working-classes only, but all of us however grand we may think ourselves: men of science, literary men, artists, we all wear the chain. I know it by my experience, that intelligent enthusiasm, knowledge of history, patience, years of hard work can contrive or accomplish nothing outside the charmed circle of that slavery; here is your one hope of success: to tack yourself on to the skirts of commercialism, do its bidding, accept its morality, and – despise yourself and the whole human race.[32]

He understood that wallpaper was an atypical weapon in the fight to protect all life. Though contorted, his position was not, however, doomed to irresolvable hypocrisy. Twisting like briars, the contradictions pricked his conscience, they were provocations to himself to better think through how he might disable laissez-faire capitalism whilst, in the meantime, maintaining a robust business upon which his own and the livelihood of many workers depended.[33] The answer, like Mairet's, lay in a materialist as well as pre-capitalist understanding of craft work.

## Robbery and Societies

Materially, the production of all wealth begins with an act of theft. The strawberry plant finds its way through the soil, rising into full fruit, then falling away, re appearing, bearing new fruits for which others, the

---

[31] William Morris *The Collected Letters. Volume II, Part A. 1881–1884.* Letter 868. 186–187.
[32] William Morris *Commercial War.* Speech given on 27 March 1885 before the Croydon branch of the Social Democratic Federation at Crown Hill, Croydon. BM Add. MSS. 45334. University of Iowa William Morris archive. (http://morrisarchive.lib.uiowa.edu/).
[33] At its height the Merton Works employed around 70 workers, including apprentice boys and girls whom Morris took in around the age of 14–15, often from schools for the destitute, and trained from scratch. He believed artistic skills were not inherent but could be taught, that male and female were equally gifted, and everyone might share the experience of making. That said, for most work at Merton was far from a free-forming Gothic flow: it was often cramped, repetitive and divided. From the mid 1880s onwards Morris left much of the daily management at Merton to others, notably his daughter May, who assumed control of the embroidery rooms and whose aesthetic prowess became integral to many of the iconic designs. See Helen Mary Elletson. Beauty, *Imagination and Order: The Flowers of William and May Morris.* In *The Victorians: A Botanical Perspective Volume 1.* Edited by Luis Manuel Mendonça de Carvalho. Cham, Switzerland: Springer. 2024. 47–92.

hungry frugivores, have a glinting hunger. The bird takes the berry, shits the seeds out, the strawberry takes off elsewhere, setting off another arc in a process of seed growth and dispersal, an arc that science calls endozoochory, and which Morris depicts on block-printed cotton (Figure 59). Morally, the theft is neutral, or natural. The thrush is taking food, so it might sing, grow, feed its young. The plant lives on if its fruit is taken. In Morris' hands the birds and plants have equal weight in a design in which everything is equally pushed up front in the plane, without depth. Patterns become very visible and abound: the beak in open song and petals open to the light; the spotted fruit hanging from stalks as thin as the angled legs upon which the speckled bird hops from plant to plant, following the pathways traced out by the self-rooting shoots and greenery working their way across the dark backdrop.

That Morris chose theft as an ornamental motif of life has some resonance with the work of the philosopher Alfred North Whitehead for whom the basic animating principle of active sentience was 'commit robbery'. All living organisms – plants, birds, humans – are what he calls 'societies' and all life, he continues, is ordered though relations of robbery between such societies: 'all societies require interplay with their environment; and in the case of living societies this interplay takes the form of robbery. The living society may, or may not, be a higher type of organism than the food which it disintegrates. But whether or no it be for the general good, life is robbery.'[34]

Not all things are societies, but where there is life there are relations and so society, and where there are societies there is robbery, and it is through acts of robbery that growth and plenitude become possible: robbery is additive, a taking that then creates (as in the practices of human societies, with the taking on of rules) that rob initiative whilst giving form and purpose. By attributing 'society' to all life forms – even crystals were societies, as they too in their own way took and gave from their surroundings, something Ruskin would have agreed with enthusiasm – Whitehead was keen to challenge the alleged priority of fixed substances as the bedrock of life. Rather than the world consisting of unities being modified by events, things were inherently unstable, the universe was primarily a flowing, fluxing array of forces from which the stability of substance was hard won; thingly-ness was a relational achievement in establishing patterns of co-existence that held together in repetitions of form (of the kind that Morris evoked so vigorously). To become a thing takes effort, especially an organically living, working 'self' committed to making of things, involving not just the 'self' but others, each giving and taking, or robbing.

---

[34] Alfred North Whitehead *Process and Reality*. New York: Macmillan. 59.

In a philosophical echo of Morris' domestic credo that one have nothing in one's house that you know not to be useful nor believe to be beautiful, Whitehead invokes and commits to a world in which the substance of well-formed things is intimate with, and nothing without, their functional striving and resonance: 'every actual thing is something by reason of its activity; whereby its nature consists in its relevance to other things, and its individuality consists in its synthesis of other things so far as they are relevant to it. In enquiring about any one individual we must ask how other individuals enter 'objectively' into the unity of its own experience.'[35]

In acknowledging how the unity and objectivity of things are states of mutual dependency on other things facilitated in acts of robbery, Whitehead begins to loosen the assumption that functionality is a relation between previously isolated, substantial entities. As societies, things become 'thingly' as patterns of mutual 'entry' through which their form and functionality are being secured and agreed upon in a nexus of causal exchanges (or events). In societies there is a creative 'taking in' of details and experiences which gather into a thingly being. Each thing is a summing of past occasions around which it posits a sameness, an enduring combination of form and function, but which is event-based rather than identity based: there is no *thing* outside of the continual interplay of events. The metaphysics of substance dissipates and gives way to a metaphysics of process. Time is woven into being: there are not first things (beings) to which events occur (time). Rather, things *are* patterns whose frequency and solidity has the appearance of a regularity, but which is always moving and taking shape, and dying back: In Whitehead's language: '[t]he many become one, and are increased by one';[36] life proceeds, and what is actual and formed in that life is always making way for what has potential but is yet to find a functioning form.

Societies are held together by affinities, and in human societies these affinities can develop as a blending of consciousness, learning, mutual, memory, reflexive awareness, rules, habits and norms, all of which are woven into material conditions. Experience comes rolled up as the past, blending the memory (and the remembering memory) and perception of events that have already occurred as they take up entry points into our awareness. In entering into experience they are doing so as effects that become causes of future events, the past being locked into a future as datum mediated in the human society. Just when or how this status as datum unfolds into a future is uncertain, and so whilst what occurs as the multiplicity of events is

---

[35] Alfred North Whitehead *Symbolism: Its Meaning and Effect*. Cambridge: University of Cambridge Press. 1958. 27.
[36] Alfred North Whitehead *Process and Reality*. 21.

necessary to experience, it is insufficient to determine its nature: a multiplicity can only generate further multiplicity, which is nevertheless always more than what has gone, given what has past is being added to by the surplus presented by the indeterminate. It is in the nature of societies to experience being as an expansion. Whilst there is no way of knowing how the patterns of life will unfold, humans have what Whitehead calls an aesthetic awareness that helps comport them towards the future: they sense (though never completely, or comprehensively) how their own presence is an embodiment of what is just departing (they sense or prehend what it has been to be influenced by something) and through this a sense of what is just arriving what is just arriving also arises (as in Mead's interplay of 'I' and 'me'). Maturity is the growth in this sensory capacity for prehension. By invoking the immediate past onto whose disappearing patterns it still has a lingering hold, the human body, if not always the mind, can find itself in a state of expectation for a future that has, in its scent if not in sight, already arrived in the form of a surplus or redundancy, as a 'more than' lodged into sensory awareness in the form of an expectation.

It is in expectation that human societies absorb the past to then 'take it on'. Rather than have the past dictate the future in cycles of imitation, the creative act has it provide a scene or even channel the future of familiarity brought about through acquired skill and material familiarity, from which to leap, and rather than have the future supervene the past in cycles of fashionable obliteration the creative act has it intervene and blow through the otherwise stale interiors of tradition. On the one hand, the society thrives when it sustains form amid scenes of disorder, and on the other it invokes routines, protocols and norms to foster transformation.

### News from Nowhere

To consciously commit to work as a source of wealth is to attend to the different ways of being a worker: first, on each empirical occasion of doing work; second, as a historically and socially placed 'self' gathering an ever-growing accumulation of personal work history; and third, belonging to common patterns of work practices being repeated through the occasion of one's own and many other lives.[37] The body and its movements accord with the mind and its thoughts, the memory and its recollection accord

---

[37] Whitehead uses the example of Caeser being at one and the same time an occasion, a culmination and an enduring repetition. 'The word "Caesar" may mean "Caesar in some one occasion of his existence": this is the most concrete of all the meanings. The word "Caesar" may mean "the historic route of Caesar's life from his Caesarian birth to his Caesarian assassination". The word "Caesar" may mean "the common form, or pattern, repeated in each occasion of Caesar's life".' In *Symbolism: Its Meaning and Effect*. 28.

with the character and its development, none are primary, and in a political mirroring of this pattern, the social body and its patterns of practice accord with the civilizing spirit and its values. It is a delicate balance at which craft work excels.

Craft workers acquire skills by absorbing their material, commercial and social milieux. They are taught (or more often teach themselves, collectively) to excel without conscious mediation, their bodies become as refined as their tools, 'through repetition they learn to make instinctually. Yet as much as it nurtures skill, repetition can stymie a sense of personal complicity and pass over the opportunity for provocative alterations. This is the problem Morris found with machinery: it was not machinery per se, but its tendency to deaden and disempower the senses. To create the body needs exposure, it must feel disturbance, rupture, aversion, and use the revolving cycles of past endeavours as a a well spring into a sense of the future, a sense of how, with effort to gain a foothold in the wider environment by taking from it, by robbing. The robbery produces surplus, a conscious sense of having the energy to slip into novelty, to wander into empty space unmoored from explicit interests and goals, and its exponents must be unsure whether their feelings of accomplishment are all that reliable.

At the moment repetition slips into dull mimesis, thought questions action and initiates a scene of critique that cracks the smooth surface of complacency and stimulates a surplus through the generation of new problems (to recall Sennett). And on the flip side, the production of surplus cannot be a prelude to loss; what is made, though it is made through acts of robbery from other things, must linger as a culmination and not a displacement.[38] Craft work excels in this. The acts of robbery are productive, they seed the germination of activities that rise above the transient practicalities of getting by and coping. They tend toward the past in order to hint at a future that bears the weight of being, potentially, of some significance.

All of which amounts to what Morris felt, like Geddes after him, was an opportunity for organizing a practical utopia, a society of wealth-making societies. What they shared – or what Geddes took from Morris, and Ruskin – was a commitment to the potency of craft work to commit acts of robbery that give far more than they take. It was by being there, in the workshop, and learning the value of well-made goods, that humans would reconcile free, individual expression with an equal, collective recognition of need. Yet where in Geddes this mutual integration of freedom and equality resulted in a titanic feat of biotechnical planning through which social and natural activity were organized to the smallest harmonic detail, Morris' organizational scheme, narrated in his book *News from Nowhere*, was errant.

[38] Alfred North Whitehead *Process and Reality*. 340.

Geddes' 'eutopia' associates a just human society with an ongoing integration of individual needs into collective settlement and consensus. With Morris, however, integration also occurs through divergence, it is as much fallow as it is industrious: what was being mirrored in tradition was also being refracted: and it is ornament that embodies these differences between the schemes of Morris and Geddes' 'eutopia' seeks harmonious symmetry and balance to generate maximal returns for the social good. It is driven by an idea of social justice designed to govern social, commercial and cultural space. Morris' utopia is suffused with a longing and sense of possibility that he hopes might percolate into the present social, commercial and cultural space. There is no grand design, only suggestiveness. Life in Morris' utopia is desirable because it has the patina of an uneven, rough surface, the acts of robbery are being lived out, not scripted. Things are exchanged through natural, spontaneous bartering organized through an aesthetics (prehension) of felt need.

The economy in *News from Nowhere* works ecologically. On walking a pathway into the forest, say, a lumberjack feels the need for a new boot to better protect her as she limbs the branches from felled trees, readying the wood for stacking, drying and transporting to sawmills, to become the wooden flooring, which will be needed by the bootmaker to extend the workshop, so he might make rather than just fix boots, given he has had requests coming in from all over. The economy is made up of these arcs of felt need which, when they meet one another, twist like foliage which then spread further, without the symbolic abstractions of contracts or currency, and the needs are being met by a profusion of productive activity organized by explicit, associative, flat organizational forms. Trade is mediated through affective and sensory encounters in which needs are authored as realistic and legitimate desires elicited from the technics of practical activity and the prevailing symbolic structures that take a grip upon the body, which in turn takes a grip upon its surrounds, unbidden by overt rules.[39] Things enter one another, they rob: the leather is taken from the cow, the

---

[39] Morris was responding to Marx's concern that a trading system based on exchange value eradicated the functional distinctiveness of made things by using money to make them equivalents. For Marx, money:

> does not at all presuppose an individual relation to its owner; possession of it is not the development of any particular essential aspect of his individuality; but rather possession of what lacks individuality, since this social [relation] exists at the same time as a sensuous, external object which can be mechanically seized, and lost in the same manner. Its relation to the individual thus appears as a purely accidental one; while this relation to a thing having no connection with his individuality gives him, at the same time, by virtue of the thing's character, a general power over society, over the whole world of gratifications, labours, etc. Money facilitates a general sense of wealth utterly indifferent to the particular, whilst at all times capable of inveigling its way into all particulars to

wood from the tree, the iron ore from the ground, the lumberjack from her family. But there is no exploitation insofar as the relations are ones of giving over in expressions of prehension which require, and will always leave, a surplus. Nor is there a moral imperative at work in this giving over: it is not gift giving as, say, Marcel Maus interpreted it, where a gift given seeds a debt to be repaid by future, perhaps larger gifts, creating cycles of escalating excess. In Morris' London of the future, the giving is a giving over to others who share a spirit of open use. The maker and made thing give of themselves in undirected ways, radiating outwards like ripples, interfusing with the ripples of other makers and made things until their patterns become indistinguishable from the currents by which all use animates life. Morris' vision eschews the ordered and programmatic, it is not planned, or balanced, its harmony is a disturbed one of waywardness, of wayfinding. It also disturbs common sense. Morris writes in a way that teases the reader, acknowledging the cogency of their habits and common agreements, before suggesting things might be otherwise. *News From Nowhere* is literary treatise questioning the naturalness of common sense. This is embodied early on in the figure of Dick the Waterman who refuses to accept payment for ferrying William Guest, the tale's protagonist. It is through the figure of Guest that the narrative transitions from a present England to a future, possible England. After attending a meeting of the Socialist League in Hammersmith, London, Guest had returned home excited by the idea for social reform yet downcast as to its immediate prospects. He fell asleep in this ambivalent mood, but then woke quickly, dressed and, taking to the river, found himself in the far future, in a place that was still, evidently, London, but then not at all like the place he was used to calling home. Guest takes to the river, wanting to explore this strange yet familiar place. He offers to pay for his ride, but is refused, and he cannot understand why. Dick notices his passenger's confusion. 'I can tell that you are a stranger, and must come from a place very unlike England. But also it is clear that it won't do to overdose you with information about this place, and that you had best suck it in little by little.'[40] Morris too is trying not to overdose his readers, but to lead them gently away from the accepted logic of commercial exchange backed by contractual obligations. Alive to how engrained this logic has become, he, like Dick, has to pace his rhetoric,

---

transform them into general abstractions again the issue of whether this actually looks like a quote, indenting would be clearer.

Karl Marx *Grundrisse: Foundations of the Critique of Political Economy.* Translated by Martin Nicolaus. London: Penguin Books. 1857–8/1993. 223, 296.

[40] William Morris *News from Nowhere.* Edited by Krishan Kumar. Cambridge: Cambridge University Press. 2002. 12–13.

and in a roundabout way. Dick comes from a mature people, fermented by their culture, attuned to how things can infuse each other with productive energy, as if from nowhere, simply by being in close and open proximity.[41] As well as rowing, Dick also excels in metalwork and grass cutting, and enjoys these as much as navigating the boat, giving of himself in all these activities without need for calculated recompense.

Production, trade and use are grounded in a principle of redundancy in which non-equivalence, deferral and gratification coalesce to create a continual surplus upon which others may draw should the need arise, without wasting anything. Pleasure is found in the uplifting experience of doing a good job, in becoming skilled, in working towards what might be possible, and then giving the made things away, where there is felt need, without calculating what they might receive in return: the future returns are of little interest. The relations are melded on the basis that others feel similarly inclined towards giving, they too experience the bounty of working well, each at their tasks in the 'taskscape', each making what otherwise would not be made, whether it is a boot, a comfortable chair or a pleasant exchange in a shop. It is a society in which commercial exchange and moral duty are entwined by a creative spontaneity in, and collective responsibility for, provision. Gothic ornament evokes the form of such a society, it exudes growth that gives of itself, it reveals the natural ties that bind all life, it delights in openings, small surprises and niches, it refuses to be managed.

### Some Hints on Pattern Designing

It is in ornament that humans encounter a sensual, understandable expression of how it is that in successive acts of prehension (the dawning in awareness that the influence of what has gone before affords a rough understanding of what's to come) the present is always interlacing and converging with the past by taking it on: 'Ah, now I can go on'. It is a movement which generates a rich sense of possibility because in taking root in the present its growth is unimpeded by a goal and will always remain subject to the contingency of chance and accident. For many, Herbert Read among them, Morris' achievements were 'mainly in the sphere of applied ornament and decoration, and did not touch the more fundamental problems of form'.[42] Yet ornament *is* form. The twisting vine

---

[41] See Michelle Weinroth Morris' Road to Nowhere. In *To Build a Shadowy Isle of Bliss*. Edited by Michelle Weinroth and Paul Leduc Browne. Montreal: McGill-Queens University Press. 2015. 172–194.

[42] Herbert Read *Art and Industry*. London: Faber and Faber. 1934. 29.

emerges from earlier growth of the plant, utterly aware of its dependency on the past acts of robbery by which it took root and grew taught and robust, but not at all determined by that dependency, and alive with how it might be committing to further as-yet-unscripted acts of robbery (and being robbed from), each act giving onto the next, following Goethe's *Urpflanze*. Robbery is active, it requires a sense of an undertaking which is both vigorous and thoughtful. Far from being a superficial illustration to this robbery, ornament – the arboresque lines embellishing the edging along carpets, the burgeoning acanthus leaf pushing out from the flatness of printed chintz, the amiable maze of thistle and teasle confusing the vertical surface of a wallpapered wall – becomes its mediating force. Through ornament, the worker can perceive how patterns of nature, being ones of effortful robbery combining confinement with exuberance, tradition with novelty, energy with repose, entry with withdrawal, the rural with the urban, and creative mediaeval work with individual freedoms.[43] The perception is never complete or clear. Like William Guest, who acknowledges as he wakes from his dream state that he has much to unlearn before he could live in this future place, ornament is a sensory embodiment of the modulating, asymmetric rhythms by which any freedom must emerge within an experimental commitment to what is felt to have potential.

It is in their very propinquity with nature and its effulgent unfolding in patterns that Morris' Works were robbing from nature: they robbed from the river, from the indigo plants, from the trees to make the printing blocks, from the cotton plant picked by exploited labour. Yet the Works also gave, and arguably they gave more than they took, entering into the lives of the makers and the users as small revelations of natural force whose resonance was felt as an opening up or closing down, not as a fixed outcome. In the printed or woven trellis of a honeysuckle or in the yellow punctuation of bright pimpernels time does not perish into a fixed line and trajectory with a given end, it is not wholly ordered, but becomes a 'moving image of eternity', and one prone,

---

[43] In elaborating on the nature of work (which she distinguishes from labour, which is thoughtless or operational activity that meets our basic biological needs, Hannah Arendt (*The Human Condition.* Chicago: University of Chicago Press. 1958)) describes its incursion into nature as 'doing violence', with the justification that something lasting is made: a temple, a law or constitution, a piece of art or museum, all of which cohere into forms of civilization whose mark of distinction is they outlast the span of life to which their makers have been consigned: 'work, and its product, the human artifact, bestow a measure of permanence and durability upon the futility of mortal life and the fleeting character of human time' (Hannah Arendt, *The Human Condition.* 8) In contrast what is being produced by labour is immediately consumed by life processes which demand yet more, and no matter how abundant the forces of labour, how fertile, life always needs more (Hannah Arendt, *The Human Condition.* 308). The violence is a process of transforming the natural world to an artificial one.

potentially, to unforeseen motion.[44] The ornament pushes outwards, curls away, twists inwardly, intensifies and loosens, dies back, shrivels, connecting and un-connecting in alignments whose traveling repetitions are without definite purpose, diverging from their starting point, in perpetual motion, leading Nowhere.

In his lectures gathered under the unassuming title *Some Hints on Pattern Designing*, Morris elaborates on the sympathy between fulfilling and joyful work and the redundancy of ornament. Ornament emerges from work, the basic turn of a woven knot, the polishing of woodgrain, the folding of leather, the pressing of paper, the etching of copper, the bending of rushes or iron bars, the joining and binding of boards, the tightening of lids; all these gestures were the root movements of pattern. As these are pursued, embellishments and developments of the pattern occur, and these can be grafted to the further patterns that Morris associates with human emotional expressions enduring across cultures, the *pathosformel* which Aby Warburg was to describe as the expressive values carried in the far traveling symbols of motion (tree of life, winged birds, flames) carried deep within the collective memory of a culture, whether those of European Medieval towns, the Iran of *Shahnameh*, the Old Norse cultures described in the Sagas, or Victorian Britain, all of them cultures for which Morris was able to feel communion and love,[45] because all of them were cultures whose patterns had their origins in disorder. As the anthropologist Mary Douglas noticed from across her studies of many different cultures:

> Granted that disorder spoils pattern, it also provides the material of pattern. Order implies restriction; from all possible materials, a limited selection has been made and from all possible relations a limited set has been used. So disorder by implication is unlimited, no pattern has been realised in it, but its potential for patterning is indefinite. This is why, though we seek to create order, we do not simply condemn disorder. We recognise that it is destructive to existing patterns; also that it has potentiality. It symbolises both danger and power.[46]

The patterns upon which Morris settled bore the mark of an affective experience as well as being the site of a future one, they were determining as well as determined, they carried both the formal (*formel*) and emotive (*pathos*) within the fixed outlines of their gestural expression (Figure 60).[47] In the expressive suggestiveness of ornament there was no contained outcome, no

---

[44] Alfred North Whitehead *Process and Reality*. 338.
[45] Caroline Arscott. Pattern: Textiles and Wallpaper. In *Cambridge Companion to William Morris*. Edited by Marcis Waithe. Cambridge: Cambridge University Press. 174–187.
[46] Mary Douglas *Purity and Danger. An Analysis of Concepts of Pollution and Taboo*. London: Routledge. 2002. 95.
[47] S. Pearl Brilmyer and Filippo Trentin. 'Toward an Inessential Theory of Form: Ruskin', Warburg, Focillon *Criticism*. 2019, 61, 4, 481–508.

Figure 60 Edmund Hort New, *The Chintz Printing Rooms, Merton Abbey*, 1898. Pen and ink on paper. D 57. © William Morris Gallery, London Borough of Waltham Forest.

overarching completion, no fixed vision of an ideal world, indeed nothing whatsoever that was ulterior to the creative exchange of energy in which order encourages suggestiveness without relinquishing form.

Good ornament exhibits a strength of definite, mannered line that conveys a sense of visible growth and continuance so that where a pattern ends, the furtherance of growth is suggested, and at the suggestion of nature, rather than the whim of the designer. Ornament was how Morris avoided being caught in the whims of fashion: where the seasonal patterns of fashion herald diminishment and death, those of nature herald future growth. Echoing how Plato views the soul taking up the new patterns of life again and again, in its reasoned and disciplined patterning, ornament keeps hold of, and keeps alive, the eruptive force and density of new life taking hold. In this fusion of reasoned outline and imaginative drift comes an ability to convey the ongoing process of growth without being cowed by the demand for mimetic realism:

> You can't bring a whole country-side, or a whole field, into your room, nor even a whole bush; … These are limitations which are common to every form of the lesser arts; but, besides these, every material in which household goods are fashioned imposes certain special limitations within which the craftsman must work. Here again, is the wall of order against vagueness, and the door of order for imagination. For you must understand from the first that these limitations are as far as possible from being hindrances to beauty in the several crafts. On the contrary, they are incitements and helps to its attainment; those who find them irksome are not born craftsmen, and the periods of art that try to get rid of them are declining periods.[48]

The restrictions of material and tools are a boon to the lesser arts, they elicit thoughtfulness where otherwise there would be indulgence. Jesper Kouthfood at Teenage Engineering agrees: limits are a tool for people to work. A limited palette of colours, limited typefaces and restrained features to products eradicate the opportunity to prevaricate, to work within a restricted range of options to create beautiful things.[49] In Morris' patterns there is an acceptance that ornament only works by concentrating upon the basic tendencies, the strongest lines of force, the essentials as they reveal themselves under sustained concentration. Confusing ornament with superfluous excess was a tendency Morris worried would creep into the more unfettered aspects of craft work, such as painted decoration: 'In pottery-painting we are more than ever in danger of falling into sham naturalistic platitude, since we have no longer to stamp

---

[48] William Morris *Some Hints on Pattern Designing*. London: Chiswick Press/Longmans & Co. 1899. 10.

[49] Conversation between author and Jesper Kouthoofd, CEO and Head of Design, Teenage Engineering, 18 March 2021.

Figure 61 Unknown photographer, *May Morris*, early 1890s. Cyanotype. © National Portrait Gallery, London.

our designs with a rough wood-block on paper or cotton, nor have we to build up our outlines by laying square by square of colour, but, pencil in hand, may do pretty much what we will.'[50] And what we 'will' to do is give material expression to the feelings of community and continuity with natural forms steeped in repeating cycles of unscripted and unending growth and which we allow in, through a window so to speak, to brighten and provoke life (Figure 61).

[50] William Morris *Some Hints on Pattern Designing*. 33. Lecture delivered to Working Men's College at the College, Queen Square, Bloomsbury, December 1881.

## In between Presence and Absence: The Infrathin

It is in the gaps between things rather than the things themselves that Morris sensed the potency of pattern: it was in absence that the power of nature was strongest. Not just natural things, all things. The small, resonant interfaces between similar objects or objects being made similar by their historical, cultural and geographical context articulate difference and sameness at one and the same time. The traditional artistic struggle of form to dominate and then free itself from material is no longer apposite as it is in relation to things and their materiality that the potency of aesthetically organized life comes to the fore.

Marcel Duchamp labelled the in-between region of connexion the infrathin (*inframince*), and by way of expanding on his concept he listed numerous examples: the restless intimacy between liquid and its container, or between two objects made from the same mould and brought together after a prolonged separation, or between skin and its anticipation as it hovers over the surface of an icy lake, or the brief glance of one eye falling on another. The infrathin is barely there, it needs working at, it is an exposed space unavailable to accepted classifications and symbols. It is the space where poets can tread, scrutinizing the conjunctions of letters, paper, space, lines, sound, rhythm and punctuation to build a poem by allowing meaning to begin, again, and again. The writer Marjorie Perloff regards the infrathin as a place which avoids the mystical weight of symbolism. They do not reach for being a unity, or for unified meaning; their form emerges from going back into the 'taskscape' of the written-down word, the audible pause, the resonance of sound. The material thing of the poem – language – and its shape in sound and written down, are enough, and there is no certainty or completion in the use of language as it forms itself as something distinct, like a vase is formed from the earth to form a void whose presence is revealed as it is put to work in its multiple uses as an absence to be filled. The form of poems comes from their material shapes, and the everyday uses of this material, which can be multiple and which always move on (recalling the patterned vectors followed by Måås-Fjetterström apprentices, learning how to weave the Greek key motif) as the poem is seen and read anew.[51]

In Whitehead's technical (conceptual) language this 'moving on' occurs in creative acts of prehension, a grasping, from out of the present, an

---

[51] This recalls Merleau Ponty's insistence that meaning arises historically, from within the experience of practice: 'The meaning of a picture or a poem cannot be separated from the materiality of the colors or the words; it is neither created nor understood from the idea out.' (Merleau Ponty *Sense and Nonsense*. Translated by Hubert Dreyfus and Patricia Dreyfus. Evanston: Northwestern University Press. 130.)

arrangement of form that confers status to future possibility by moving both the poet and reader to places they otherwise would not go; the emptiness of the future is being put to work, nothing is confirmed, just suggested. It harks back to Noë's talk of entanglement, how the use value of things, their being ready to hand, comes forth and permeates and percolates through a regional setting of already organized cultural biological and social routines, norms and affections, and how it does so not by being more present, full and all encompassing, but through the movement of something that is empty filling up, and of something full being emptied, each being a force that engenders the other in the gathering of repeating lines that border a rug without enclosing it. There is no perfect, complete, causal or symbolic explanation for any of this.

Alive to the infrathin, the craft worker pushes a thing in the making towards its edges so nothing about it is left untouched (*toccata*) and along these edges comes an emptiness and incompleteness, an absence that invites further presence.[52] There is a continual calling forth of the thing which is also a continual installing of the thing – like a rug – into the ordinary circulations of being, a cycling and circulating of conforming and (potentially) contorting meanings. Its presence lingers continually between potential and actual and cannot be locked down and contained by signifiers or evaluative measures.

What excites Duchamp about the infrathin is its utter normalcy, its being outside of the art world, or what Heidegger called the 'art business'. There is, continues Heidegger, something creative about bringing art alongside a lack of art, so that the exercise of capacities and confirmation of genius so often associated with the former can be seen as never amounting to art. Art can only exist in the company of things that have been made without being means in an operation, without intent: art refuses to be organized and classified, especially by a gallery system.[53] The readymade for which Duchamp is renowned becomes art precisely because of its lack of art, it does not suffer from the indecision that bedevils all works of art that classify themselves to be such; namely, one can never really tell if the pleasure and provocation felt in its company is the upshot of its being without purpose, and so art, or of its being a product of irony and trickery packaged by business interests. The readymade confirms and underscores the aesthetic quality of all practice and the anonymization of the beautiful by announcing, first, that all material

---

[52] For an extended discussion of the non-symbolic alternations of presence and absence in Eastern worldview, see Francois Jullien *The Great Image Has No Form, On the Nonobject through Painting*. 81–83.
[53] Alva Noë *The Entanglement*. 100–105.

is material for art, and second, that all art is dependent upon contextual (woven) settings. In turn, the infrathin describes the aesthetic power uncovered in the readymade thing whose affective resonance resides in its no longer being easily classified as a 'this' or a 'that'.[54]

Erin Manning, writing about the infrathin, cites the artist Francis Alÿs: 'After a while … you start oscillating yourself. You forget about the mechanics of the piece and you are entering this kind of lullaby space. You just take a back seat and that is where eventually you accede to that different time perception, which is in between two worlds of space.'[55]

This in-between state of the infrathin is a state of being with both what is given and is giving over (the as yet unappointed and unallocated surplus). Under the attentive gaze of the artist striving to be alive to the infrathin, the thing enjoys a freedom of presence that is both fleeting form and formless, allowing the artist to play with what Manning calls 'the both-and of double articulation'.[56]

It is by listening in to this double articulation that craft works also exhibit the infrathin. All vessels, for example, are containers for sound: just as they are given form, they in turn give form to sounds, and sound emerges because of the absence made present by the vessel walls. A good pot rings like a bell; you flick its sides with a finger, it resounds. The potter Jane Lee can tell the age of the clay from the sound it makes when fired and formed as a vessel. A story ensues about the digging of the clay. In digging, the potter empties the earth, exposing the processes by which it was and is still being formed, how it is always coming and going, flowing, refusing to settle into being one thing. As it was dug it was still under formation, though imperceptibly. The emptying becomes an event which dislocates and fractures the continuing pattern of formation: the left clay, still present, continues in its slow transformation, the dug clay becomes the made thing, even though Lee sometimes leaves it fallow for 20 or 30 years before using it, allowing it to speckle, and to contribute to what it will become, a natural process set alongside the other processes of making: the pulling and pressuring of gravity during the wedging the clay; the firing and changing pockets of heat in the kiln as the oxides release themselves and flux and fill and burst open; the settling and hardening into a bell-hard bowl whose newly minted void fills with silence, before being flicked by a finger.

---

[54] Martin Heidegger *Contributions to Philosophy (from Enowning)*. Translated by Parvis Emad and Kenneth Maly. Bloomington: Indiana University Press. 1999. 356.

[55] Francis Alÿs and Siobhan Davies, 'Conversations', in www.siobhandavies.com/conversations/alys/transcript.php. Quoted in Erin Manning 'For a Pragmatics of the Useless'. *Political Theory*. 2017, 45, 1, 97–115.

[56] Erin Manning Creative Propositions for Thought in Motion. *Inflexions* May 2008.

It is this co-existence of presence and absence in the in-between sound that enticed the artist and craft worker Oliver Beer to arrange pots in a stalled choir of 'voices'. Like Alison Britton and Gillian Lowndes, Beer interrupts our habituated way of encountering made things like ceramic pots. Though fixed, the vessels structure and emit differing sounds depending on their shape, age and situation, and in collections they can 'sing' as might a sleepless, breathless choir. Beer's 'choirs' have been made up of all manner of vessels: toilet bowls vie with Meissen bowls, grave goods with creamers, storage jars with ceramic sculptures. Beer is clear that the gathering space of structure, void and sound – the infrathin – emerges from the vessels, the craft worker listens out, *physis* as much as *techne*, an in-forming to which the creative act accedes and makes efforts to retain in the work being formed, like birth marks. Duchamp also found sound in the infrathin: the legs of corduroy trousers rubbing against one another when walking, which he notated as '9v' in his list of examples, a sound he then contrasts with a 'pigeon blue fabric piece bought in Grenoble/changing silk (material of visible infra thin) in opposition to corduroy which rubbing with the same gives auditory infrathin' (11r).[57]

## Profane Objects

The glass of a shop window refracts and delays the relations it clearly admits and promotes. The glass reveals the insides as outside, and those looking in from the outside can also catch a glimpse of their looking-glass self, and so look upon themselves looking upon the goods with which they are merging in a mirror play of objects on display, each being made distinct in moments of comparison and choice. The glass gathers and holds these objects within its visible transparency, and Duchamp gathers these operations of the glass window in *Fresh Widow*, a handcrafted (by a cabinet maker) eight-panelled miniature of a hinged French window, its frame painted in teal blue, and signed by Duchamp 'Copyright Rose Sélavy, 1920', both a play on the French '*éros, c'est la vie*', and the legal claim to have title over such things as love and life. There is also the life that goes on after death, the life of the widows, newly single after the fighting of World War I had killed their men. They were being made available anew, back on display. Though Duchamp had the window-panes covered in black leather, which he suggested should be polished daily, giving a shine to what cannot be seen. The blacked-out windows,

---

[57] Marcel Duchamp *Notes*. Edited by Paul Matisse. Boston: G.K. Hall & Co. 1983.

reminiscent of war, of secretive things within, and of the cloth of mourning. The signs run rampant.[58]

Unlike art works, craft works are happy enough to live in shop windows and partake of commerce. There is a potency here often refused to art objects. Duchamp often bemoaned the difficulty of overcoming the 'frozen look of the public (who glimpses and forgets immediately)'.[59] The audience for art works cannot really get to the thing, or the artist to the audience, because the relationship is already mediated by the artist's reputation and targeted market value, and the audience is already scripted by the sacralizing habits associated with viewing art (look don't touch, be largely silent, circulate in an orderly fashion, respect the object's uniqueness), and by the cloying admixture of sycophancy and condescension that marks out a strict hierarchy of access. No matter how well the artist struggles, they must do so behind a mask. 'Every profound spirit needs a mask: even more, a mask is continuously growing around every profound spirit thanks to the constantly false, that is shallow interpretation of every word, every step, every sign of life he gives.'[60] Duchamp's tactic to overcome this frozen look is to accentuate the mode of display: the plinth, the vitrine, the dividing rope, the window frame, the signature, the moment of trade, the permission to touch, to the point where their mediating force become apparent, no longer working invisibly, but deliberately.[61] Duchamp, however, never seems to hit home, or maybe it is that when he 'hits home', nothing is sustained. Duchamp makes a deliberate move to make viewers aware of how the subject is continually becoming an object. Noë calls the move an episodic un-homing into ambiguity that loops down into everyday things and re-organizes them in ways that disorient us, encouraging aesthetic efforts at re-orientation. This is the only job of art. It is all it does, and when the art stops, so does the aesthetic struggle. The pause and severance instituted by art work, is contained within that world,[62] which leaves it vulnerable, at risk of falling back in with the art world, a falling which Adorno sees as inevitable:

[58] Dalia Judovitz *Drawing on Art: Duchamp and Company*. Minneapolis: University of Minnesota Press. 2010. 23.
[59] Marcel Duchamp *Notes* Transcribed and translated by Rebecca Loewen from the notes (46, handwritten) on *inframince*, held in the Cabinet d'Art Graphique archive, Centre Pompidou in Paris. 1912–1968. https://rebeccaloewen.com/inframince.
[60] Friedrich Nietzsche *Beyond Good and Evil/On the Genealogy of Morality*. Translated by Adrian Del Caro. Stanford: Stanford University Press. 2014. §40. 42.
[61] Dalia Judovitz *Drawing on Art: Duchamp and Company*. Minneapolis: University of Minnesota Press. 2010. 82–185.
[62] Alva Noë *The Entanglement*. 156–160.

Each statement, each piece of news, each thought has been pre-formed by the centres of the culture industry. Whatever lacks the familiar trace of such pre-formation lacks credibility, the more so because the institutions of public opinion accompany what they send forth by a thousand factual proofs and all the plausibility that total power can lay hands on. Truth that opposes these pressures not only appears improbable, but is in addition too feeble to make any headway in competition with their highly-concentrated machinery of dissemination.[63]

The only available response is to go again, to generate further 'moves' that question, destabilize and corrupt the established orders of value.

Under the established values of capitalist industrialism, however, this 'going again' art is being continually profaned as a sacred object, made useful as a distraction and compensation: the disturbance and reorganization as spectacle. Morris also thought art under capitalism was doomed. Yet whereas Adorno calls on art to recover its force by radical acts of separation, existing for its own sake, and bearing witness to the encroaching machination of all life, Morris goes the other way and looks to further integrate art and human practice, and to make artistic sensibility more, not less, central. Which is why what Morris was happy to call the 'lesser arts' are more potent, because it is through these – through craft work – that a re-organization of human relations, and the relations between things and humans, is *made* possible.

Adorno was not antithetical to craft work, yet he assigned it a subaltern role in art practice as the disciplined means of material manipulation that contributed to the capacity of art to sustain its own energy and authority. The role of art was to complete knowledge with what is excluded from knowledge, which it did by working deliberately and diligently beyond the prevailing classifications and concepts, as, say, twelve-tone composition in music did.[64] By employing skills in craft work, the artist affords themselves sufficient room (*Raum*) to incur the risks of losing form and meaning. Not just David Pye's technical risk, but the social and political risk of being unhomed and facing derision from those who cannot understand because they lack the epistemic structures to do so. In this sense Duchamp is akin to the twelve-tone composers, and he venerated craft. Indeed, far from diminishing or crowding out craft skills, John Roberts suggests Duchamp's readymades expanded their territory. By agitating for a recalibration of what constitutes artistic material, display and making, the readymade provided a fertile space to re-organize the struggle between appearance and reality. The readymade was admirable as a thing that allowed the

---

[63] Theodor Adorno *Minima Moralia*. §71.
[64] Theodor Adorno *Aesthetics*, 1970/2002. 54.

artist to complete knowledge by including what was excluded, and craft work helped sustain this transition.

Yet Adorno was insistent that once it was removed from the carapace of art and left to go it alone, craft work was doomed.[65] Only art can unhome because only art was freed from the 'law of pure functionality',[66] free because freedom from practice was its only purpose. Morris' project of installing craft work as a transformational riposte to the ills of capitalism would be, for Adorno, risible in its naivety. Yet if all we have as a 'way out' are the tactics of artists: any dialectic of opposition is doomed to alternating between temporary gestures of severance. Without space of their own, the artists only have tactics that feed from the proper spaces provided by majoritarian strategy, and those employing these strategies. Because they lack space of their own, artists lack the power to create and sustain their own knowledge in the modality of an idea and thought that is theirs: art is confined to the role of *la perruque*, grafting itself into the system to then sever from it in acts of bricolage, ironic protest, absurdity, intense scrutiny. These acts are illocutionary: the structures of meaning (knowing that) are disturbed by artistic interventions that push at and even topple them, upsetting their intensity or integrity, revealing contradictions.[67] But they are never displaced.

What Morris and Ruskin attempt to do is to create and preserve a strategic space for art, or the lesser arts, by going low. Avoiding grand gestures, the lesser artists are content to recur to the transitive spaces of function and find their something useful to which they might contribute. They learn to work at simple things like vases, tables, books, lights, clothes, knives, food preparation, programming, and to work well, and in the repetitions of this learning, on occasion, there is an experience of contingency and surplus, a pattern escapes from the historical binds of causal association, and something timeless, yet still placed, is made. For many craft workers these intransitive moments might be rare, but are always a possibility: the space becomes theirs, something Walter Benjamin evokes in the collection of quotations he collects in his *Arcades* project, this one from Franz Hessel:

It is the obscurely rising dream of northerly streets in a big city – not only Paris perhaps, but also Berlin and the largely unknown London – obscurely rising, in a rainless twilight that is nonetheless damp. The streets grow narrow and

---

[65] See Glenn Adamson *Thinking through Craft*. 10–11.
[66] Theodor Adorno *Minima Moralia*. 40.
[67] This distinction between the proper space created by strategic acts (a space which is necessary to determining the criteria for both knowing that and knowing how) and the derivative, temporary gains made by tacticians (see Michel de Certeau *The Practice of Everyday Life. Vol. 2*, section on Anaesthesia.)

the houses right and left draw closer together; ultimately it becomes an arcade with grimy shop windows, a gallery of glass ... As I advance a little further, however, I see on both sides small summer-green doors and the rustic window shutters they call volets. Sitting there little old ladies are spinning, and through the windows by the somewhat rigid flowering plant, as though in a country garden, I see a fair-skinned young lady in a gracious apartment, and she sings: 'Someone is spinning silk.'[68]

In experiencing redundancy, craft workers have the potential to generate surplus of the in-between which, like Adorno's artists, is unmanageable, but unlike these artists, it remains quiet, ordinary and part of everyday working lives. In its encouraging everyday experiences of beauty, utility and functionality, craft work is incompatible with the kind of capitalism that related to the world as though it were a scene of perpetual battle between resource-hungry monopolists for whom art worked as both a boast and form of compensation. Craft work incurs an aesthetic reforming of how workers sense the standard divisions of time and space by which work life is organized. What Duchamp came to call the infrathin – the in-between space between things – becomes apparent, as does the in-between space that divides work from leisure, language from experience, the urban from the rural, thought from the body, or life from death, even. In craft work – and this most apparent in the surplus and redundancy exemplified in 'useless' ornament – comes the potential for re-organizing what Jacques Rancière calls the hierarchical divisions that distribute the sensible (the manner and meaning of the ways we are permitted to sense the world). Through craft work Morris envisages the possibility for workers to re-form the character they have been allocated by the prevailing institutions to which they have been subjectified, and to do so through the lesser rather than higher arts (the schism with which Jude Fawley so fatally wrestled). Morris found in ornament the most precise and fulsome expression of this re-distributive potency: to follow the lines of things, to sense how in any form there was nothing stable, and how in any character or human body there is a similar instability working its way into growth, an insight re-iterated in the teaching of Paul Klee:

The character of work is set in processes of giving form Form must on no account ever be considered as something to be got over with, as a result, as an end, but rather as a genesis, growth, essence. Form as a semblance is an evil and dangerous spectre ... What is good is form giving. What is bad is form. Form is the end, death. Form giving is movement, action. Form giving is life.[69]

---

[68] Walter Benjamin. *The Arcades Project*. Translated by Howard Eiland and Kevin McLaughlin. Cambridge, MA: Belknap Press. 87.
[69] Paul Klee *The Notebooks. Volume Two*. Translated by Heinz Norden. Edited by Jürg Spiller. Lund Humphries: London. 1973. 269.

Form giving emerges from an ornamental impulse towards surplus that is 'of' nature, and 'of' humans. Adorno is right to question the baleful effects of machinery upon this impulse, but too quick to think craft work compromised. Whilst the spaces of craft work might, like the spreading canopy of Manley Hopkins' elm tree, present themselves in neat, smoothing arcs of compliance, there is, beneath, a tangle of unallocated growth stretching out, the lines widening, enriching.

# 8   Making Form in a Broken World

In their veneration and idealization of Medieval life, both Morris and Ruskin were criticized as dreamers and escapists. Critics were quick to argue their enthusiasm had little support in the historical record. Written evidence that workers in the Middle Ages were buoyed by a collective spirit of hearty good will and free expression was as intermittent and opaque as that sustaining the claim that working lives in the Renaissance were corralled by frigid rationalization or falsely inflated by the 'moody pride' of individualism. Medieval accounts of what it felt like to quarry and carve stone, to cut the timber for a gable end, to smithy a knife blade, to stitch a shoe, or to roll and colour glass are scant. The evidence from the archival records is full of gaps. Yet in allowing their imagination to take flight, Ruskin and Morris were prompted by a different sort of evidence: the work itself, notably Gothic buildings. Their archives were open to the sky and had to be read with the full range of the bodily senses, they had to be felt, dwelt in and then examined within an emotionally charged atmosphere of revivalist possibility. Their project was about social change, not science and what their thesis lacked in verifiability and replicability, it made up for in its provocation: the only scene of a sustained and just transformation in how humans relate to one another and their environment is in craft work.

The thesis and spirit of this book is similarly revivalist. Just as Ruskin and Morris hopped over generations of civilized progress to take their historical cue from a deliberately selective, hermeneutic reading of Gothic work, so I have hopped over much of the twentieth century to find in Ruskin and Morris a spur to re-think the organization of work practice. In imaginatively suggesting Ruskin was one of the first to document the effects of what has become known as the Anthropocene, I was attempting to justify this 'hopping over' by providing a bridge of sorts. He, like us, was experiencing a broken world. Arguably, the breaks seem far more apparent now. Environmentally this comes with the rapid breakdown of climate systems and erosion of biodiversity, and socially with the fracture of communities, forced (and frustrated) migration and an explosion in precarious labour. Yet rewind to Ruskin's time and colonial expansion, the growing urbanization of a landless poor working on piece rates, and landscape and workforce equally stained with soot suggest our contemporary human travails are not wholly novel. To repair what is broken seems not only wishful, but dangerous, given the solutions emerge from the same technological systems to which the breakage has been attributed. Yet situationally sensitive efforts to restore lost heritage, reconcile antagonistic cultures, and re-configure relations with the wider environment continue apace, often with a nod to learning from cultures deemed as being closer to nature.[1] By invoking Gothic and its placing of aesthetic relations at the heart of human interaction, Ruskin and Morris appear to do something similar, though with two profound differences.

First, theirs is an imaginative rather than evidential form of recall, and one that is situated within rather than outside of the culture that gave rise to industrial capitalism. The intent is to provoke, not prove, and to upset rather than re-calibrate the current order of things. Second, their diagnosis of what is 'broken' is not so much that once extant objects are now collapsing, cracking and splintering – though they accept that they are – but that the real source of what Ruskin called 'illth' is a pervasive system of knowledge and control in which things are broken down to their constituent parts and then re-assembled in tightly managed relations dedicated to the pursuance of specific ends. The broken world to which Ruskin and Morris attest, and against which they rail, is a world of parts, and parts of parts, a divided world made so by divisions in which things (including human things) have become so objectified that their identity, their potential and their history are as nothing unless they appear through acts of classification dedicated to the order and control of events: life is a vast woven network of factors held in linear chains and each link, each chain and each weave of chains can be broken and replaced, under the direction of a visible hand.

In Europe, this knowledge system took first flower in the genius of the Renaissance: the hand of 'Man' split from the hand of 'God', the Sistine ceiling is a narrative of departure, not union, the first break. The medieval, Gothic order of experience and common sense gave way under a weighty symbolism of human prowess and achievement. Humans are born again, without the naive dependency or ecological respect; the human was centre stage. Capitalist industrialism was a perverse expression of this centrality, an investment in division, standardization and mechanized power that elevated a few, but only on

---

[1] Duncan McLaren 2018. 'In a Broken World: Towards an Ethics of Repair in the Anthropocene', *The Anthropocene Review*, 2018, 5, 2: 136–154.

the prehension of their having promised yet more. The robbery went unabated, surplus was corralled and returns on investment were held fast in the unproductive state of private wealth. Hence, the return to Gothic was to be a recovery of place where we are in touch with things, to recur to what John Dewey called the aesthetic experience of grace in which a 'self' fluxes with other selves and their wider environment in ongoing transactional states of being.

Second, theirs is a joyous not penitent riposte. The revolution, such as it is, was to come from within and work was to be maintained. Humans lived and flourished as they dwelt in the practices of making things and using them well. In Gothic, Ruskin and Morris felt they had found and recovered what had been lost, namely the disciplined enjoyment of forming things and re-forming them in ongoing use. They enthuse about how the lesser arts were organized through communities bonded by common sensibilities and consciously and traditionally arranged distributions of bodies, cant/argots, places, activities, tools, workshops and markets, which were far more substantially alive than ever were abstract commitments to political dogma and positions.[2] The life and liveliness of these communities was grounded in a shared, personal willingness to bear the load of integrating work into their willing body; they carry the tools, they have *techne* without exposure to the abstractions of rational thought. The concern was not with why it worked, but with how and that it worked within everyday practice.

Recent critical readings of craft work aver from such naïve inspiration exhibited by Ruskin and Morris. They prefer to study craft work as a symptom of the broader social, economic and political forces encapsulated in the enterprise discourse. On these readings, any avowed commitment to preserving the distinctiveness of human experience places craft work in an uneasy relation to what Richard Sennett calls flexible capitalism.[3] The stabilizing workplace elites and social hierarchies of which Ruskin and Morris complained have given way to networks, career paths have become rhizomic in their open-ended multiplicity, work roles have become ambiguous and flexible, opportunities shimmer like mirages on the horizon of venturing businesses, and amid this flurry of uncertainty the risk taking of craft work appears as a potentially potent force. The willingness to allow materials a say, to broach strict commercial logic with an aesthetic and speculative sensibility, to enlist others in venturing through what Melinda Cooper neatly summarizes

---

[2] See Jacques Rancière 'From Politics to Aesthetics', *Paragraph*. 2005, 28,1, 13–25. Also see Martin Parker. Organizational Gothic. *Culture and Organization*. 2005, 11, 3, 153–166.

[3] Richard Sennett *The Corrosion of Character*. New Haven: Yale University Press. 2000. 160–161.

as a mixing of the unfree contract of mutual obligation with the legal contracts of transaction to then transform contingent labour into a necessary condition of innovation.[4]

Taking risks from within the bosom of family and community-based small ventures generates the creativity by which capitalism acquires what Luc Boltanski and Eve Chiapello have called its new spirit. The elevation of individual risk tasking in work is indicative of how an ever-lithe capitalism is extending its allegiances from standardized, predictable forms of manufacturing and logistics organized through computer-mediated micro-management towards customization and creative, self-governing makers.[5] In this transition control is being internalized through forms of publicly expressed self-discipline. Rather than being told what to do, workers found, within themselves and their immediate relations, the resources to make, mark and market products that have a unique, handmade touch, connecting with consumers in search of familiar, tangible, close relations with what they buy and use, and with those making them. The momentum for capital accumulation has extended into an inward sense of personal fulfilment through the networked pursuit of multiple and temporary projects.[6] It has, in other words, corralled the claim for authenticity in work, transforming it into a distracting and mollifying manoeuvre whose apparent earnestness belies what is, essentially, a compliance with the globalized forces of capital acquisition.[7] Firms committed to craft work like Morris & Co. were, arguably, early instantiations of this mercurial willingness of capitalism to absorb its contraries; it has appropriated the independence and liminality of a self-motivating, self-managing, self-claiming creative class, exploiting the communities, emotional force, creative energy and speculative imagination of workers, which it then institutes as a precariat dedicated to nothing other than its own transformation in the service of capital accumulation: it is what Peter Flemming rather neatly calls the inauthentic

---

[4] Melinda Cooper 'Workfare, Familyfare, Godfare: Transforming Contingency into Necessity', *The South Atlantic Quarterly*. 2012, 11, 1–4.

[5] Luc Boltanski and Eve Chiapello *The New Spirit of Capitalism*. Translated by Gregory Elliott. London: Verso. 2018.

[6] Luc Boltanski and Eve Chiapello *The New Spirit of Capitalism*.110. Also, Susanne Ekman. *Authenticity at Work: Questioning the New Spirit of Capitalism from a Micro-sociological Perspective*. In *New Spirits of Capitalism: Crises, Justifications, and Dynamics*. Edited by Paul de Gay and Glenn Morgan. Oxford: Oxford University Press. 2013. 294–315.

[7] See Kirstin Munro and Chris O'Kane 'The Artisan Economy and the New Spirit of Capitalism', *Critical Sociology*. 2022, 48, 1, 37–53. On how new markets in craft emerge see Rodolphe Durand and Mukti Khaire 'Where Do Market Categories Come from and How? Distinguishing Category Creation from Category Emergence', *Journal of Management*. 2017, 43, 87–110.

making of an authenticity machine.[8] The full-blown blossoming of what, in Morris & Co., could be read as an early spring bud, has been witnessed in an organizational kaleidoscope of movements: the march of the makers, craftivist summer camps, hackathons, platform-mediated upcycling craft markets and artisanal media broadcasting.

This appropriation of craft work by the enterprise discourse remains, however, an unfinished claim. There remain plenty of studies attesting to the persistence and resilience of craft work in which the slow and disciplined acquisition of expertise in hand work, a giving over to materials, and a sense of belonging and contributing to the difference-making repetitions sustained by the institutions of communal tradition come to the fore on their own terms.[9] It might well be the case that amid the enterprising discourse of 'the self', the pursuit of 'authenticity' has upended itself by becoming a useful compulsion for self-governance. But the freedom to which craft work attests, and of which Morris and Ruskin were so enamoured, is an aesthetic construction whose sufficiency retains an irony and self-deprecation that sits uneasily with the zestful enthusiasm presumed to riddle the enterprising self.

If we are to talk of craft and authenticity – and given its appropriation by branding campaigns, it is a treacherous association – the self-awareness and sense of responsibility for one's own actions to which craft work attests has two aspects: submission and refusal. First comes submission. Craft work is a site of practical puzzles and small successes and failures over which no-one has full control but from which a sense of self emerges when the environmental distributions of sensation can be woven with an immediacy of personal perception in such a way as to realize a sense of belonging to the rules of a practice that one might 'go on'. In discussions of Mead, Dewey and Simondon, along with Kierkegaard's refinement of the concept of grace, I have suggested how this handing over a sense of 'self' to the practice and process of work finds it an endlessly made thing being made amid other made things. It is a specific form of made 'self', one able to experience progress first hand in the acquisition and use of skills fostered by tools and instruments. Progress is a sensation, it is felt as an aesthetic accomplishment of greater and greater fit within immediate processes of making. In part, this fit is with

---

[8] Peter Fleming *Authenticity and the Cultural Politics of Work: New Forms of Informal Control.* Oxford: Oxford University Press. 2009.
[9] See Emma Bell, Maria Toraldo, Scott Taylor and Gianluigi Mangia (Editors) *Introduction: Understanding Contemporary Craft.* In *The Organization of Craft: Identities, Meanings and Materiality.* London: Routledge. 2019. 1–19. See also Roy Suddaby, Max Ganzin and Alison Minkus *Craft, Magic and the Re-enchantment of the World.* In *Management Research: European Perspectives.* Edited by S. Siebert. New York: Routledge. 2017. 41–72.

the raw materials, tools and instruments of the workshop, with its encapsulation of traditional rhythms and the collective assembly of makers gathered to see the making through. But following Mairet and Ingold, it is also a fit with other craft workers whose values are enmeshed with the continuation of the practices of making, with the suppliers of raw materials and with the multiple histories of human practices that make up the wider 'taskscape'. Finally, it is also a giving over to wider natural forces, to the broader ecological systems from which life 'robs' its substance (Dewey's 'grace'). In all this 'giving over', the technics organized through rational inquiry becomes muffled by an uncalculated trust in the process of 'going on' from within what has gone before, a process from which to stake a situational confidence in what will come.

In the furthest reaches of this giving over there is, as I tried to show, a resonance with the sense of self prevailing in much Japanese philosophy. For example, for Nishida:

> to follow the sincere internal demands of the self – to actualize the true personality of the self – does not mean to establish subjectivity in opposition to objectivity or to make external objects obey the self. Only when we thoroughly eliminate the subjective fancies of the self and unite with a thing can we satisfy the true demands of the self and see the true self.[10]

Experience does not happen to individuals, rather individuality arises because there is experience from which subject, object, meaning and judgment are being grammatically articulated and historically sedimented, as in, for example, the entwinement of Mead's 'me' and 'I', each robbing from the other. Life occurs in an open field of experience that 'can itself only be intuited in the same way the hidden lining of a kimono serves to keep form and shape and yet itself always remains unseen'.[11]

Second, and in equal part to this trusting submission, comes refusal. The craft worker refuses to be condemned by either the materiality of objects or the practicalities of experience. Though they acknowledge the structural and symbolic force of material, form and purpose detailed through already circulating ecological constraints, these are far from totalizing, even when these constraints have been taken up and intensified by technological mediation. There is in craft work a stalling of the giving over, a hesitancy, an opening of the eyes, a critical gaze being shed upon practice by workers animated in unsettlement, and unscripted by, say, an *idea* of functionality or good taste, or by self-elevation or self-improvement. There is a necessary sense of unease

---

[10] Kitarō Nishida *An Inquiry into the Good*. Yale University Press. 1992. 133.
[11] Robert Chia Kitarō Nishida (1870–1945). In *The Oxford Handbook of Process Philosophy and Organization Studies*. 298.

and suspicion through which both the subject (maker) and object (made thing) relate to one another without either taking precedence.

The attributes of Gothic attest to this stalled experience of 'giving over', to how extended communities of workers, in taking up the repetitions of machine-aided handwork, bond themselves to the practicalities of everyday experience. Their distinction comes from the surplus they generate as they 'give to life' by producing things that work well, and that bear the imprint of having been made thoughtfully. They avoid the role of isolate genius on the one hand, and a submission to a seamless state of grace on the other (Kierkegaard's refinement of Dewey's grace is important here).[12] To give over in this way is to expend, and expand in ordinary ways, rather than in abeyance to an artful idealization of will or to technical necessity. It is, as Peter Sloterdijk observes, a form of self-awareness that discloses a sense of freedom through a deliberate, because conscious, struggle with ecological demands to realize 'maximal grip' under the impress of a basic, self-imposed demand: 'go again'. It is not a self-reliance set against its wider milieu, but nor is it seeking efficient compliance with it. Rather, it is an ensemble of body and mind working on behalf of movement itself, one which remains alive to the symbolic possibilities of acting and sensing and feeling differently as it goes along in its keen, carefully observed, technical repetitions. It is a deliberate impoverishment of the enterprising (and Renaissance) idea of the 'self' as a confident, self-governing system, and it is in wilful avoidance of complete, environmental harmony espoused in Basho, and it is, potentially, far more generative because of these avoidances. The Gothic seeks the moment of hesitation in compliant repetition, and once found, it lingers and explores the multiplicity of forces that open there because, in 'going again', the work will always deviate a little.

Having felt the potency of Gothic work, keener still was the irritation Ruskin and Morris felt towards the spread of laissez-faire economics in the institutional framing of Victorian work practice and the symbolic recognition of worth and wealth in the form of abstract possessions like money. Wealth was becoming something calculated, and so compared, by reasoning subjects who claimed inviolable commercial and individual rights to accrue and hold what they might. Work became the pursuit of ends organized by contractual structures that separated ownership from production (and by extension, mind from body, management from labour, legal compliance from ethical concern, and reasoned decision from situational judgment). Through the light of a restricted, instrumental idea of reason, work was being analysed from the outside,

---

[12] Hannah Arendt *The Human Condition*. 210–211.

to the point where productive operations could as well be undertaken by combinations of metal and oil as by flesh and blood (or by relays as well as synapses, by protocols as well as values). In being squeezed out by machinery, a qualitatively different form of abstracted human individuality was being formed, one fed by acquisition, not experience.

Morris was spurred by Ruskin's emotionally hostility to the dominance of this calculated sense of wealth, and the wholesale and unexamined cheapening of production that it warranted. What could be so free about a system that permitted the commercial interests of a trading elite to dominate all life? What made the domination worse, argued Morris, was its continuance through war, a commercial war, which was quite as violent as a 'gunpowder war', and because of colonization, was far more global. It was a war between owners of capital for a share of the products of unpaid labour, a perpetual war of brisk capital transformation in which lives, and life itself, are laid to waste. The forms of waste are multiple, but Morris highlights two dominant forms: the waste of puffery and the waste of the cheap and useless.

Puffery is the empty expansion of commercial activity and objects, an inflation of presence through which managerial processes appear to be far more necessary than they need to be. It was the 'war' that made them necessary. In warring with one another, commercial organizations have to guard against incursion, so spend vast sums insulating themselves against risk: they hire accountants, lawyers, auditors and security services to avoid, where possible, the barbs of those with whom they are entangled and competing in the search for arbitrage (excessive rents). All this sundry, managerial work is useless, it generates nothing of value. It is one of the factors in why things cost so much more to buy than to make, a gap that widens further still when bearing the costs of yet further 'useless' activity: advertising. Brands and adverts designed to make of something more than it is, to inflate its worth with messages of promise and satisfaction that have little connexion to its inherent qualities, and so must be appended by sophistry which is carried by 'our newspaper and periodical press [that] are little more than puffing sheets when they are successful, sugared with a little news, a little politics and sometimes a little literature.'[13]

Even more corrosive than 'puffery' is the waste created in the production and consumption of cheap wares that are forced upon the market under the dictates of cost-effective necessity, disguised by the symbolism of fashion. It is in the interests of those prosecuting

---

[13] William Morris *Commercial War*. Speech given on 27 March 1885 before the Croydon branch of the Social Democratic Federation at Crown Hill, Croydon. BM Add. MSS. 45334. University of Iowa William Morris archive (http://morrisarchive.lib.uiowa.edu/).

the commercial war to enforce the division between themselves and those who work by confining workers to a place of relative poverty, whilst still expecting gratitude for the scant 'bones' they offer by way of wages. By cheapening the goods designed to meet human needs, they get their labour cheaper still, keeping the workers in a state of competition amongst themselves. Because they can only be made at a scale that requires intricate and efficient organization, and because cheapness is also a weapon against other owners of capital, forcing each into ever more refined improvements of this organizational machinery, to the point it has become no mean science: cheap wares force the worker to fashion and intensify their own poverty from within a discourse of thrift. It is a discourse that is spreading the world over. As the empire expands, so new markets open, into which the monopolists pitch themselves in competitive rivalry, forcing more and more humans to immiserate themselves in the progressive race towards efficiency.[14] The race is championed by the newspapers, authorized by law, and blessed by the church, an institutional triumvirate dedicated to the recognition of work and the promulgation of a language that served the furtherance of an already powerful commercial elite.[15]

How, then, to break the universalizing hold of this commercial spirit? One cannot oppose it with symbolism, certainly not through the idealistic creation of totalizing alternatives such as Robert Owen's factory at New Lanark in Glasgow. Owen's objectives were laudable: to improve the lives of workers and their families. Through the re-organization of the factory, the village and the school informed by the scientific analysis of human behaviour, Owen had instituted a system of production in which significant improvements in pay and conditions were accompanied by a transformation in moral character. Or so he had hoped. Yet

---

[14] Morris was one of the few who vocally supported the Sudanese in the Battle of Khartoum, arguing the British Army had neither moral right nor pragmatic necessity on their side, whereas the Sudanese were quite rightly trying to protect themselves from the ever-expanding reach of the commercial war. At an anti-war meeting of the Socialist League on 2 April 1885, Morris proposed the following rider to a broader resolution 'that this meeting believes that the invasion of the Soudan has been prompted solely by the desire to exploit the country in the interests of capitalists and stock jobbers; and warns the working classes that such wars will always take place until they (the workers) unite throughout the civilised world, and take their affairs into their own hands'. Quoted in Nicholas Salmon 'The Serialization of The Pilgrims of Hope', *Journal of the William Morris Society*, 12, 2, 14–25. 15–16.

[15] Abetted by cronyism, the race continues, and in its contemporary setting the colonial has morphed into a global presence of extractive activity through which elite corporate control remains dependent upon immiserated labour. See Laleh Khalili *Extractive Capitalism: How Commodities and Cronyism Drive the Global Economy*. London: Profile Books. 2025.

over the years – despite the reforms – Owen remained frustrated at the fragility of the moral and social order he was creating. The problem, as Morris was only too aware, was how entrenched and fixated upon their own immediate survival the mass of workers actually are, and how enmeshed in global wealth systems they have become. Even by 1800 when Owen opened New Lanark, the workers had been habituated into measuring and bargaining for the value of their labour in a mechanical system of division and exchange. Feeling had little to do with it, especially moral feeling. Their desires and interests, and the values and value expressions emerging from them, emerged from the established circulations of capital in the form of weekly (and weakly) wages that kept them and their family above the 'breadline'. Owen's New Lanark offered better terms, so they were inclined to stay on. The moral (and religious) symbolism with which Owen imbued his works never took hold, it was always an additional concern, a bolt-on, and the work, though the terms and conditions were far better, did not alter: it was repetitious, volume-based, thoughtless.[16]

By the time he was writing *News from Nowhere*, Morris was proposing an aesthetic, not a morally and religiously inspired transformation of work practice. It was the value inherent in experiences of work that was being brought to the fore, not the value that it might generate in terms of income or, in Owen's case, spiritual clarity and obedience. Just as capitalist industrialism failed to acknowledge how work lay at the root of human flourishing, so did Owen's religion: art and technics were being broken up and separated, the technical individual was being lost, work became either management or machine assistance, and values became compliance with moral principles. Morris' emphasis on the aesthetics of work practice restored the possibilities for technical individuals, freed from the dominance of either machinery (which was indifferent to life) or dogma (which was largely ignorant of it). The engraver Phillip Hagreen, a somewhat skeptical member of the Catholic Ditchling Guild, recalled:

> We have scores of priest friends. Some like to come here because they like to see Catholic families growing up, or because they like 'Gothic' vestments, or because they like good cooking. They praise work as long as they think it is drudgery, but

---

[16] Owen was less interested in changing the nature of work than alleviating poverty and morally impecunious behaviour. He wanted gainfully employed workers committed to a sober and thereby rewarding life riven with religious decency. To this paternalistic end he devised organizational techniques to standardize, control and monitor work practice; for example, the 'silent monitor', a device for telegraphing the conduct of each worker, showing black (bad) through blue and yellow to white (good) placed publicly above their workstation. In Morris' terms, this is an example of puffery. See Timon Beyes *Organizing Color*. 49–52.

when they see that we find it delightful & that our besetting sin is doing it on Sundays, they are shocked. They say that man should take a pride in his work – & sign it. That is the antithesis of what we mean. Should one take a pride in one's prayer & sign it? I suppose that the root trouble is that they are so used to the privation of beauty that they think of it, not as an inevitable attribute of rightly made things, but as a dangerous luxury.[17]

Morris would have shared Hagreen's skepticism. The rhythms of work were to have a shared shape and texture of intimate involvement with a (technical) thing being made; the swarf or shavings from machinery were to carry the odours and sounds of raw materials being worked; the community of workers' voices were to be animated by the sound and bodily anticipation of fulfilling a tradition; the made things were to stand with a density that invites and gathers functional and needful use; the ornament was to twist into individual details and pockets of distinction. If a god were involved, it would be confined to what might be revealed in the thing being made, nothing more: a shop can be as spiritual as a chapel.

Once made, the thing would be taken up and give to life, as when, in *News From Nowhere* the shopkeeper of a tobacconist's shop 'gives' William Guest a hardwood, bejewelled smoking pipe he becomes entwined in an open, endless circuit of making and exchange motivated by mutual feelings of pleasure and acknowledgement of need for which there is no final end or absolute criteria of evaluation. The pipe is made because the maker enjoys the difficulty of getting the pipe to function well enough to satisfy a need, to look beautiful, and to last. When pressed by William Guest on his experience of work and whether he had the opportunity to relax, Dick the waterman replies 'there is a kind of fear growing up amongst us that we shall one day be short of work. It is a pleasure which we are afraid of losing, not a pain.' There is a 'conscious, sensuous pleasure' in work that is done freely, and within the means of what each worker might do.[18] Nothing is made that workers do not want to make or is not wanted. As Morris elaborates, in plain, practical terms, what is made is being made because others have expressed a need for it, and given there is no buying and selling, there is no need or incentive to make things on a promise that they might sell, and given things are made for expressed use, there is every incentive to make things as well as one can, for then not only is the need met with minimal waste, but there is pleasure to be had in acquiring the skill of

---

[17] Quoted in Lottie Hoare *Phillip Hagreen: A Sceptic and Craftsman.* Winchester: Richie Press. 2009. 41.

[18] William Morris *News from Nowhere.* London: Longmans. 1908. Chapter XV.

doing things well, whether with machines where the labour is laborious or the exactitude of a machine is required, or with the hand where there is a need for expressive touch.

Incredulous, Guest cannot but smile inwardly at the naivety of such a system. Yet were he to look hard he would realize these impulses are already in play in his own world, in craft work, where these aesthetic concerns become the tap root of a transformed experience of work. The genius of Morris' later radicalism was that it took the word 'radical' seriously, going to the root of things to cut out the rot of laissez-faire relations. If one could cut out the rot then transformation could occur from within: 'It is the commercial system itself which will kill the commercial system, and we Socialists, hard as we shall have to work, shall only have to assist nature in that operation.'[19]

The assistance offered by Morris (thinking through Ruskin, who he acknowledged as 'the first comer, the inventor')[20] was the story of Gothic framed as a narrative thesis distilled from history. Though Morris enlisted the backing of what he called 'the modern school of evolutionary historians', it was Morris's feeling for the power of storytelling that emboldened him to propose Gothic as a cure to his coruscating diagnosis of the ills of the present age. In Morris' fabulizing imagination, Gothic began in the rhythmic twining of two ancient systems: Byzantine aesthetics and Northern European civic politics. The fusion of Eastern and Western sensitivities in Syria and other Byzantine cultures created forms whose mass and outline veered towards simplicity but whose ornament was 'bright and clear in colour, pure in line, hating barrenness as much as vagueness, redundant, but not florid'.[21] This aesthetic formed one narrative thread, which Morris wove with another, equally vigorous, emerging vibrantly from the free cities of Mediaeval Europe that had overthrown their aristocratic elites and were being governed by delegates from craft guilds who had fought for, and won, the liberty of weavers, joiners, masons, shop keepers and wrights.[22] At least for a brief

---

[19] William Morris *Commercial War*. See also Florence Boos 'William Morris's "Commercial War": A Critical Edition', *The Journal of Pre-Raphaelite Studies*. 2010, 19, 45–65.

[20] William Morris *The Collected Letters. Volume II, Part A. 1881–1884*. Letter 815. 126.

[21] William Morris *Gothic Architecture: A Lecture for the Arts and Crafts Exhibition Society*. London: Kelmscott Press. 1893. 27.

[22] In echo of Ruskin's encomiums to the craft workers of Florence, Morris invokes the weavers of Flanders. Ruskin's and Morris' enthusiasm for the Medieval past was bedded into a broader suspicion of a Victorian need to feel at home within the world, their world. Whilst Ruskin and Morris also extolled the benefit of organic vitality and of organizations at peace with their surrounds and principles, neither of them felt peace was all that generative, and more contentiously, they were suspicious of such a feeling, finding in Gothic a tendency towards expressive pleasure, to elevate the particular over the general and an urge to find rest in the restless. Ruskin's first rule for all work was

period, as the thirteenth gave way to the fourteenth century, there was a burgeoning of creative energy, not just in the building of churches, but in tapestry, wood carving, illumination, ballads, sagas and painting. There was a frankness to its prodigality, a vigour to its restraint, an honesty to its limits, an inclusivity to its heights. With the Renaissance, 'a Mediaeval Society of Status was in process of transition into a modern Society of Contract' sustained by the emergence of a bureaucracy fed by political (artificial) nationalities and rational science. It was, accepts Morris, 'a necessary instrument for the development of freedom of thought and the capacities of man; for the subjugation of nature to his material needs. This Great Change, I say, was necessary and inevitable, and on this side, the side of commerce and commercial science and politics, was a genuine new birth. On this side it did not look backward but forward'.[23] Contractual relations encouraged a consistency, clarity and independence of thought and action. But whilst in science and politics it embraced experiment, in aesthetics it shuttered it, preferring instead to look back to classical Greece and Rome and to invoke these models as timeless verities. The arts, once so integral to the co-operative self-understanding of a people, were sidelined to the role of a decorative support act for the rise of the machine. Since the Great Change, there have been many great individual artists, but for the mass of people in Europe there has been little need for art. The 'great army of artist-craftsmen who had produced the beauty of her cities, her churches, manor houses & cottages' had been transformed into 'human machines, who had little chance of earning a bare livelihood if they lingered over their toil to think of what they were doing: who were not asked to think, paid to think, or allowed to think.'[24]

In a world broken into units whose values are being compared and traded through contracts, there is little room for the progressive feelings of thoughtful work, and yet because the loss of thoughtfulness is still felt, there remain, in the remains, fallow spaces from which to effect the recovery of aesthetically charged work in which the experience of

---

never to make anything in which invention had no share. The *pathos* was prior to the *formel*. Morris went further still, willing the example of the medieval guilds of Flanders upon his peers. Refusing any authority save their own, the guilds oversaw work standards, ran schools and had their own saints and churches, contributed to town militias and resisted 'parasitic' aristocrats. To be sure, Morris was reading his own values into the historical record, but in support of his interpretation, see the Introduction to Maarten Prak, Catharina Lis, Jan Lucassen and Hugo Soly (editors) *Craft Guilds in the Early Modern Low Countries: Work, Power, and Representation.* Aldershot: Ashgate. 2006.

[23] William Morris *Gothic Architecture: A Lecture for the Arts and Crafts Exhibition Society.* London: Kelmscott Press. 1893. 50–51.

[24] William Morris *Gothic Architecture.* 57.

skill, the creation of carefully made, situationally appropriate things (including service relations) and a sense of personal complicity with the forming of one's own character are able to cohere. Amongst these fallow spaces are the workshops and studios of craft workers whose job in hand is to make work 'sing' by furthering the production of wealth, not waste. These places drive those who make into cohesion. As they acquire skill, craft workers' senses are heightened, expanding their dextrous, haptic and intellectual capacity to perceive and feel both the paucity and potential of making things that conform to, yet also aver from, regionally placed, functional needs. Whilst Morris talks of the beautiful as well as the functional, rather than define and classify 'beauty' he prefers to concentrate on the process not the outcome, and avoids the distinction that has, for centuries, plagued European aesthetics and its contemplated pursuit of perfection (beauty) at the expense of function (ornament, decoration, pattern). It was in pursuing this fusion of beauty and function that Morris felt he was complimenting rather than repeating Ruskin's work. Ruskin's 'Gothic' had eradicated age-old hierarchies and divisions. Prior to Ruskin's 'Gothic', the distinction claimed on behalf of art practice was its autonomy. Art pursued beauty and beauty lay in revealing the essence of materials and the perfection of form. Function was of no concern to art. After Ruskin's 'Gothic', function and beauty were twinned: beauty lay with what gave to life, and life gave most fully in the experience of making and using artful things. Morris got stuck in with practical programs that exemplified the possibilities for placing art at the centre of work.[25] The beautiful, such as it was, arose through an organization of work that was: cooperative to the point that one works alongside the other whilst being provoked by that otherness; sufficiently experimental and speculative to allow the made things to resist full and easy classification whilst still serving functional needs; undivided by commercial scansions (there are no hourly rates, no scripted leisure time, no overtime); and grounded in the discipline and skill associated with a tradition. It was a view of freedom quite distinct from the autonomous exercise of choice and the disciplined self-government being championed by advocates of laissez-faire liberalism.

---

[25] Writing to Robert Thompson, Morris suggests Ruskin's schemes would only work once a socialist system had been established: 'You must understand 1st that though I have a great respect for Ruskin and his works (besides personal friendship) he is not a socialist, that is not a practical one. He does not expect to see any general scheme even begun: he mingles with certain sound ideas which he seems to have acquired instinctively, a great deal of mere whims' William Morris *The Collected Letters. Volume II, Part A. 1881–1884.* Letter 985. 385.

For Morris (and Ruskin) liberal freedom had become: the freedom of choice sets and of unmolested right to accrue private income; the freedom to invest in forms of capital that required the enslavement of labour; the freedom to rationally program manufacturing processes so they might run to the pendulum swing of clock time; the freedom to strip working life of its errant, expressive detail; the freedom to enlist the huge variety and mass of human capacities and direct them towards the homogenous commercial interests of a few. It was, in short, a freedom that required active management and control, and it hid the stain of this contradiction behind the institutional structures of politics.

The freedom coursing through the body of Gothic societies had subsumed and dispensed with any need for politics. The shortest chapter in *News From Nowhere* is XIII titled 'Concerning Politics', made up of four short sentences, in which Guest's inquiry as to how they manage with politics is met with the reply 'we are very well off as to politics – because we have none'.[26] The kind of politics they avoided was the abstracted politics of position taking and bargaining undertaken by isolated individuals and policed by executive enforcements. Under laissez-faire systems, freedom had retreated into the object 'individual', an object made large by the idea of autonomous subjectivity and made small by the reality of its constrained experience. Politics became the outward organization of this inward movement: individuals would compete for access to institutional structures (they would vote, trade, accrue) that would authorize their individuality, reward followed effort; yet the potency of effort was contingent upon already existing distributions of instituted presence. The association of freedom with Gothic made by Morris and Ruskin was steeped in a phenomenological awareness that autonomy did not belong to, or emerge from, the organized bargaining of individuals holding onto pre-formed, particular interests, as though clutching a stack of chips, a measure of their worth, with which they could bargain and bet: cede some freedoms here, to maybe gain some there. In Gothic communities, freedoms were not brought to the game (the subject was not born with freedoms with which they could contract), they emerged from the playing, from riffing off situations, subduing the original intention, accepting and even revelling in inadequacy, for here was the open latticework for joyful, pleasurable expression. The demand that art be free is met from within the 'taskscape' rather than in severance from the everyday life of a community or from nature. In Whitehead's terms, freedom was a pattern of expressive openness emerging from the mutual entry and exit of already existing

---

[26] William Morris *News from Nowhere*. 87.

useful and arresting objects, traditions, material conditions, intensions, thoughts and feelings: freedom was made through work that served to both house and provoke life.[27]

In housing life, Gothic work, which was also art – 'genuine art', stated Morris 'is always an expression of pleasure in Labour'[28] – was the work of Simondon's technical individual making technical things. It was work that took place in workshops in which technics and art were brought together in animated collisions. Machines had a role. Morris himself was not averse to machinery that removed the drudgery of repetition. More generatively, he was even excited by the potential in emerging technology. It was the enlarged imagery made available by photographic technology, for example, that inspired him to establish the Kelmscott Press using a typeface he designed using detailed photographs of the fifteenth-century Venetian books published by the French printer Nicolas Jenson. What excited Morris was how Jenson's typeface no longer tried to imitate handwritten script, but instead – with what Mumford would call the humility of proper technics – allowed the medium (the metal punches, the need to track and re-rack moveable type, the available papers, inks and presses) to influence the form. The result was a near perfect, and in Morris' view never bettered, typeface that communicated clearly, was flexible and efficient in use, made full use of the available space without clutter, affordable to cut (and sell to other printers). The Kelmscott likewise would progress towards using cleaner and cleaner typeface, and whilst its books were never cheap, it inspired many other presses (like Pepler's) to commit to making work equally as beautiful – because of its considered and efficient use of perfect fonts on good paper – but less expensively bound.

Morris' concern with housing also prefigured biotechnics, at least insofar as his interest in specific tools and instruments extended to an awareness of the criteria or conditioning structures and atmospheres of their use. Gothic work was attentive to how bodies, histories, symbols, objects and patterns of their use were already organizing what humans experienced as autonomous expression, how these already scripted and edged how humans relate to the world. To clarify the distinction

---

[27] Jacques Rancière reads Ruskin's Gothic as a riposte to the Hegelian urge to equate progress with perfection, whether in symmetrical buildings or peaceful and contented societies. In both cases the freedom that comes from synthetic order is that of a designer who, having reached perfection and with nothing left to do, is at liberty to insist others comply with the divisions of the design. Ruskin regards this form of abstracted mimesis as a system of servitude. The autonomy experienced in Gothic is acquired in open expressions of life that grow through the institutional constraints of workshops, public buildings and domestic homes as honeysuckle grows through a trellis. *Aisthesis: Scenes from the Aesthetic Regime of Art*. Translated by Zakir Paul. London: Verso. 2013. 139.

[28] William Morris *The Collected Letters. Volume II, Part A. 1881–1884.* Letter 1005. 329.

between tool use and the context of use, the philosopher Günter Figal, uses the analogy of a library:

> the world of useful objects can be compared to a library. Though a library does not prescribe and thus determine particular readings, it nevertheless provides what can be read and thus defines particular possibilities of reading. Someone exclusively using a single library would read only books to be found in this library. In a complex and surely not constructible way, these books would organize the reading experiences, prejudices and insights of the library's users.[29]

Being such a library, the materials, worldviews and objects of Gothic life organized human freedom by elevating the regional communities and their living progress above the dead, cosmic life of state and government whose progress was measured by statistical representations. Both Ruskin and Morris took the striations of ornament and symbolism in medieval Gothic work and wove it into their own times, folding and twisting and stitching them into as many different collective movements as they could create or become associated with. Morris was especially vigorous, joining or creating groups of like-minded folk, many of them offshoots of one another, morphing, growing and dying back like organizational equivalents of the briars he loved so much: the Democratic Foundation, which he then left to found the Social Democratic Foundation, which he then left to found the Socialist League; then there was the Pre-Raphaelite Brotherhood; the Kyrle Society (dedicated to improving workers housing); the Society for the Protection of Ancient Buildings; the Commons Preservation Society (dedicated to preserving public, open spaces); and the Art Worker's Guild. None of them dominated Morris' life, and he never remained central to them for long, always moving, looking for other opportunities to fuse work, aesthetics and social organization.

There is, as Rancière comments, a risk in this socially charged understanding of art as a house of life, a house of being. In the gathering of art becoming life, and of the community becoming a work of art, totalitarian tendencies might emerge, ones for which artists (and craft workers) produce authorizing cultural objects, or at the very least become the source of decorative diversions and emotional compensation. It was one such trajectory of thinking of art as providing a house for being, for

---

[29] Günter Figal *The Vessel*. In Timon Beyes, Simon Denny, Robin Holt, Claus Pias and Bettina Steinbrügge *Proof of Stake: The Claims of Technology*. Milan: Lenz Press. 2023. 197–200. 198. The palimpsest script set within the kaolin walling of Edmund De Waal's *Library of Exiles* extends this observation into lost libraries, from ancient Alexandria to modern day Mosul, and the libraries being carried within the body and community of refugees and migrants as they roam (see https://libraryofexile.infoteca.it/start).

example, that compelled Heidegger into the dark pit of Nazism. His eulogy of tradition and craft work as a mode of being set fast against global commerce was fused into a broader politics of the *Volk* for which *Dasein* became an idealizing figurehead and projection of human unity. Craft work became part of Being, and revealing Being became an eclipsing, idealistic obsession that reached for transcendent appeals to destiny which, when they found political expression, became genocidal.[30] Yet, Rancière continues, we might also think of the more sober attempt of Morris as a benign, even uplifting alternative: 'William Morris was amongst the first to claim that an armchair is beautiful if it provides a restful seat, rather than satisfying the pictorial fantasies of its owner.'[31] The restful seat emerges from lesser arts dedicated to building well-built, situationally appropriate things with which users can dwell as both a shelter and place in which life is shown to the fullest extent, in all its fecund twisting, minute iridescence and solid dependability.

In addition to housing life, the lesser art of Gothic society also provokes it: it is an imagined community that gives rise to things.[32] For many, including many of the fellow socialists with whom Morris became frustrated, a civilization progresses as the need for its citizens to work diminishes. Even Marx, for whom labour was intimately associated with an idea of the whole person, envisages a communist utopia in which work is confined to the odd morning, leaving time to fish and read Plato. Likewise, Aristotle, despite his encomiums to human practice and praxis, argued the acme of human happiness was a state of contemplation freed from the working business of the household. For Morris (and Ruskin), however, it was only through the first-hand experience of work that civilization progressed, and this progression had to be lived out within the extended body of each thoughtful soul. It is experienced, to recur to Simondon's phrase, through tool-bearing work undertaken for its own sake, not work dedicated to stated ends, that they speak: an aesthetically charged, creative from of work that was inseparable from art and into which all human beings might lean were they given the room and encouragement to do so. They were set against capitalist industrialization because it diminished and devalued work by insisting that the 'taskscape' be broken into units to which there was no arc of entry and exit, no possible grace, and no thoughtful poise. In recovering

---

[30] Theodor Adorno *Negative Dialectics*. Translated by E B Ashton. London: Routledge. 2004. 76.
[31] Jacques Rancière The Aesthetic Revolution and Its Outcomes. In *Dissensus: On Politics and Aesthetics*. Translated by Steven Corcoran. London: Continuum. 115–133. 120.
[32] Emma Bell, Tina Dacin and Maria Toraldo 'Craft Imaginaries – Past, Present and Future', *Organization Theory*, 2021, 2, 1.

these qualities, craft work is not then in direct opposition to industrial machinery so much as a harbinger of the freedom to be experienced in the company of machines: studies of pattern cutting, vinyl record mastering, biotech laboratory work or digital electronic weaving attest to the multiplicity of overlaps.[33]

The experience of freedom comes in the form of immediate and often small, everyday epiphanies of surprise and achievement that need no external warrant for their existence. These small freedoms encourage people to work for its own sake. As workers, people who enjoy work *qua* work are ungovernable, unruly, they cannot be easily confined by contracts which exchange work for income nor are they impressed by the organizational scale and size of ensembles of powerful machinery. They work because they value the immediacy of work and the pleasure it brings, it is its own wealth, and it is a wealth that finds expression in making not just needed and provocative things, but in forming the communities and characters of those doing the making and using. Hence, the absence of politics. The functional work of housing life slips into the artful work of provoking it through the pointless experience of giving form, both materially and socially, both beautifully and ethically. Which is why Morris's insistence on the intimacy between work, the good and pleasure is so pivotal and remains so timely, because it is the deliberate and critical inclination to give form to things that makes human beings free: form giving – Klee's form giving, and not the abstraction called the individual, sovereign subject – is the tap root of all autonomy. Humans are makers, they are form-giving beings and are utterly equal in this respect, and Gothic art/work revels in this. Not just because the forms being made house life, but because they provoke it to reveal itself, not life as it is laid out for us according to functional necessities associated with needs (which tended to be where the teaching of the Bauhaus was concentrated, reflected in its gridwork, in its satisfaction that aesthetic creativity and function can be harmonized), but life itself, both inside and outside of us, irrespective of use-value.

The sense of provocation common to Gothic work comes with what David Jones – engraver and poet – called giving form gratuitously: the

---

[33] See Anna Piper and Katherine Townsend 'Crafting the Composite Garment: The Role of Hand Weaving in Digital Creation', *Journal of Textile Design Research and Practice*, 2015, 3, 1–2, 3–26; J. Harris 'Digital Practice in Material Hands: How Craft and Computing Practices Are Advancing Digital Aesthetic and Conceptual Methods', *Craft Research*, 2012, 3, 1, 91–112; Jesse Adams Stein 'Hidden between Craft and Industry: Engineering Patternmakers,' *Design Knowledge Journal of Design History*, 2019, 32, 3, 280–303; Robin Holt and Rene Wiedner 'Technology, Maturity, and Craft: Making Vinyl Records in the Digital Age', *Business Ethics Quarterly*. 33, 3, 532–564.

gratuitous act is both a hallmark and a sign system of human life.[34] The condition of gratuity emerges when repetitious patterns of skilled making move from what Jones called a transitive to intransitive movement. In this transition, work ceases to be wholly functional and makes room for the surplus speculation and experiment that characterize what Jones calls the endless end common to all arts. The endless end, he continues, is a process of attaining an adequate, and maybe even a close to perfect fit, between materials and form. The thing is offered up to itself, and a whole or unity is created, a gathering of parts which articulates itself as a fitting together on its own terms (autonomy) from which all manner of further ends become possible because the form has reached a self-sufficient, *Gestalt* state (the whole is distinct from the sum of its parts, viz. it operates both in ways that cannot be reduced to the operations of its constituent elements, and in ways that cannot be explained by graceful reference to the determinations of wider social, economic and cultural forces). The materials can range from the words, ink, spaces and lines that make up a poem (Jones was as much a poet as he was an illustrator and engraver, and his poems have a distinct and conscious spatial meaning) to the steel and brass components in a door handle. Both poem and handle, if they have been worked well enough to achieve 'fit', will then move back into a transitive state as they give themselves over to purpose (both symbolic and functional), as when, for example, Morris' poems conveyed an atmosphere of Mediaeval chivalry or of nostalgic loss, or when open doors convey people through a building. Having moved back into use, however, these made things still retain in themselves the mark of having been borne along by an intransitive (artistic) process, an experience of creative immersion which acts as its own warrant and contains its own logic of extension into the present.

It is an artfulness that gives itself over to an intense consideration of its own adequacy. There is no yardstick against which to compare itself, no ideal utopia, no Platonic form from which to take a cue and to authorize or absolve one's own complicity in the making. The adequacy is secured in the execution and admiration of the process by which a thing is being brought into being, into *existenz* to recall the 'becoming' part of what Heidegger called the transitive regions of useful things. Jones, like Heidegger, reaches for a vocabulary of loosened nouns and equivocal adverbs to describe this artful fitting together of materials and form. For example, once made artfully, a door handle passes over into transitivity as it brings about a certain 'door-handle-ness' by affording an effective and efficient way of opening and closing a gap. It becomes known

---

[34] David Jones. *Art and Sacrament*. In *Epoch and Artist*. London: Faber and Faber. 2017. 148.

8   Making Form in a Broken World

through its functioning as part of a wider regional setting, and typically only appears in moments of breakdown in this setting, as when we reach out and find a mechanism sticks, or that the handle is incorrectly placed and strikes other objects in a room, or that somehow, unaccountably, the handle is absent. But if we attend carefully, as we would if we were a craft worker, or an obsessive user like the philosopher Ludwig Wittgenstein, who was taking time off from revolutionizing philosophy to concentrate on the materials and form of door handles in the Viennese villa he was designing for his sister, we might then notice, as did Wittgenstein, a need for the asymmetric pairing of handles so one side might bend and accommodate the windowsills which would abut the doors when fully open, and how this 'fit' then demands a more intransitive concern with how to shape and spin the tubular metal so on each side of the door the pair of handles might follow different lines without losing mutual sympathy, or unity (Figure 62).

Whilst Heidegger attends to these unallocated aspects of a thing's inherent thinglyness – the aspects that are beyond its 'in order to' functionality – he slips into a thicket of etymological excurses that frustrate as

Figure 62  Ludwig Wittgenstein, door handle. Photograph. Doorhandle from Haus Wittgenstein, Vienna. 2024. Photography: Max Ronnersjö.

easily as they can beguile the reader. Jones manages to put his Catholic commitment to trans-substantiating mystery in parenthesis, and is altogether more prosaic, perhaps because, as an illustrator as well as author, he made a living from making arresting and functional things. As an exponent of both higher and lesser arts he felt able to suggest, with the ordinary authority that comes from experience, that the making of objects like door handles was no different from making books or marble statues as they all belonged to the field (or taskscape) of making. 'For within that field' he observed, 'are things as dissimilar as: the Diesel engine, boot-making, English prose, radar, horticulture, carpentry and the celebration of the Sacred Mysteries.'[35] What connects these arts is not just the often skilful working through of form and materials to meet the needs of living, but the potential for its slippage into a state of gratuity: it is the making of things for the experience of making them, and in this process of making, something of significance is made, a thing that has been grained by the uncertain and risky effort of re-presenting experience through the process of making to bring about new, fitting things which are, as yet, shorn of any reason to exist. For it is in everyday things that 'the anonymous and inevitable quality we associate with the works of the great civilizations where an almost frightening technical skill for a rare moment is the free instrument of the highest sensitivity'.[36] These well-made, everyday things find their place in the rituals and commerce of domestic and public life, fomenting it whilst lacing it with slivers of unfamiliarity something sacred in the profane, and they do so without the protection of an art industry whose only raison d'etre is to authorize and then then commercialize the artist's claim for complete autonomy.

Manufacturing, and more broadly industrial capitalism, has tended to organize in outright hostility towards instransitive movement and the gratutious. Gothic relishes them given what matters above all in Gothic is the housing and provoking of life. Most objects mediating the human lives in industrialized economies might be experienced as functionally impressive and desired for their allure, and many have been created with immense technical skill, sometimes even through apprenticeships then expert skill, but they remain – as heirs of the *Rock Drill* – held fast in a regional setting of calculation and control. The working experience is shuttered from spaces that are fallow, overlooked and unused, and ushered away from temporalities of sauntering and lingering, or of energetic exploding. They may well build upon others' achievements respectfully, but they do not emerge from the gratuitous

---

[35] David Jones. *Art and Sacrament*. In *Epoch and Artist*. 2017. 153.
[36] David Jones quoted in Fiona MacCarthy *Eric Gill*. 185.

task of beginning again, which is a task of abiding with things that belongs to each craft worker alone, not to a tradition. As a harbinger of things that house and provoke life, craft work runs askance from, not in opposition to machine production, and it does so through continual exposure to the transitions between transitive and intransitive working practice. It is this movement that animated Gothic form, and that unified culture, work and society not as an organizational or managed whole, but in each working self. It is an experience of self that has a unity that has been broken time and time again by work, but which need not be, would we be prepared, in our work life, to envelop finalities with beginnings, and fragment stipulation with curiosity.

# Index

Aalto, Alvar, 122–124
  great outdoors, 133
  meeting Ethel Mairet, 271
  naturalism, 139–140
  Paimo, 133–135
Abuja, 167
Adamson, Glenn, 52, 107–108, 231, 314
Adorno, Theodor, 38, 80, 138, 170, 249, 251, 282, 284–285, 312–316, 334
Agamben, Giorgio, 68, 74
*agon*, 158–159
Albers, Annie, 84, 120, 275
Albers, Josef, 273–275
*aletheia*, 211
Anthropocene, 6, 317–318
*Antigone*, 169
apprenticeship, 154, 223, 245, 254–255, 264
Arabia (Iittala), 30, 38
architecture, 16, 26–27, 212, 228–231
  as archive, 317
  Gothic revival, 289
Arendt, Hannah, 79–80, 83, 86, 303, 323
Aristotle
  *Eudemian Ethics*, 221
  functionality, 221–222
  *Nicomachean Ethics*, 221
art
  art object, 238–239
  freedom, 312–314
  relation to craft, 85
  relations with craft, 52, 57, 312, 330
*art brut*, 207
Arts and Crafts Movement, 294
Ash, Barnaby, 189–190
Ashbee, C. R., 258, 260, 262, 294
Atget, Eugène, 80
atmosphere, 72, 98, 101, 229
Auerbach, Frank, 159–160, 163
*augenblick*, 238

Bachelard, Gaston, 90
Bakhtin, Mikhael, 184
Baselitz, Georg, 77
Bateson, Gregory, 54–55, 115
  difference, 54
  pathology, 168
  pattern, 116
  trans-contextual, 167–168
Batterham, Richard, 231–232
Bauhaus, 78, 272–275, 277, 335
  modern person, 78–79
  weaving, 273
beauty, 332
  anonymity, 309
  blemish, 188
  and function, 296–297, 330
  ineffable, 170
  ugliness, 187–188
Beckett, Samuel, 138
Beer, Oliver, 311
Belloc, Hilaire, 259
Benjamin, Walter
  *Arcades*, 314
  aura, 79
  collecting, 80
  folk literature, 83
  photography, 80
  war, 76–77
Berger, Otti, 275
Bertoia, Harry, 272
Beyes, Timon, 110–111, 115, 204, 326, 333
birch, 134–136, 271
Black Arts Movement, 154
black box, 141, 241
Bogost, Ian, 131
Bolaño, Roberto, 129
Boltanski, Luc, 320
Bornholm, Denmark, 195, 197
Böttger, Frederik, 114
Bourdieu, Pierre, 16
Brecht, Bertolt, 96, 185

340

# Index

Britton, Alison, 36–38, 125
bronze, 36, 99, 154, 239
brown pot movement, 152
Browne, Thomas, 213
  *Urne Burial*, 214
Buddhism, 142
burial ritual, 215
Burne Jones, Edward, 289
business
  as a company, 288–290
  venture, 250–251

calligraphy, 171, 185
capitalism, 315
  market, 140
  speed, 11–12, 261
Cardew, Michael, 51–52, 56, 63
Carson, Anne, 169
Carter, Angela, 83
Cartesian, 24
Certeau, Michel de, 75–76, 314
Cézanne, 146, 237–238
*Chajing*. See tea ceremony
Chattopadhyay, Kamaladevi, 254
Chatwin, Bruce, 81, 278
Chesterton, G. K., 259
Chiapello, Eve, 320
Chipping Camden, 258
Chojiro. *See* raku
Christian
  society, 251
Christianity
  Catholic, 256, 259, 338
  criminality, 257
  factory system, 326
  the Fall, 111
  guild, 256
  Mary, 111
  revelation, 202
  sin, 111
  suffering, 178
  Thomism, 16
Cibachrome, 240–242
class production, 250–251
classification, 42
clay, 24, 29, 36, 39, 49, 71, 197
  human form, 161, 166–167, 233
  kneading (*kikuneri*), 192
  void, 279
cobbler, 222–223
Cobden Sanderson, T. J., 257
collage, 42
Collingwood, R. G., 9, 150
Colomina, Beatriz, 71, 74
colour, 53, 65, 275
  black, 151, 241, 311

blue, 153, 193
brown, 153
dye, 120, 241
Falu Röd, 109
harmony, 162
organizationl force, 326
red, 109–115, 255
communities, 258, 323, 335
  cult, 258
  patriarchy, 258
composition, 157
  music, 58–59
Compton, Surrey, 244
consciousness, 43, 177, 239
Constable, John, 13
Cooper, Melinda, 229
Cotswolds, 294
*Craft Horizons* journal, 170
creamware, 155
Crivelli, Carlo, 111–112
cyborg, 282

Daitokuji Temple, 141
d'Alembert, Jean, 102
Dalman, Robin, 44–45
dance, 89
Dante, 132–133, 135, 137, 166, 168, 183, 239
*De Stijl*, 159
De Waal, Edmund, 114, 170, 233, 237, 333
Dean, Tacita, 57, 169
death, 217, 220
Deleuze, Gilles, 29, 95–96, 98–101, 130, 133
Descartes, Rene, 22–23
design, 56
  anaesthesia, 69, 71
  comfort, 73–74
  contingency, 66–67
  problem solving, 67
Dewey, John, 39, 53–54, 57
  grace, 164–167, 178, 322
  organism survival, 163–164
  transdermal transactions, 165
Dickens, Charles, 129–130, 252
Diderot, Denis, 102
difference, 65
digital, 173
  digital-analogue relations, 172–173, 175–177
  media, 58
disease, 188
Distributism, 258–260
Ditchling, 253, 255–256, 258–260, 264, 270, 326

Dodgson, Charles, 202
Dōgan Kigen, Eihei, 142
Douglas, Mary, 304
Doves Press, 257
Drake, David, 155–157
Dreyfus, Hubert, 85
Dubuffet, Jean, 207
Duchamp, Marcel
  *Fresh Widow*, 311
  infrathin, 308
  *Notes*, 312
Dürer, Albrecht, 102, 183
  *Adam and Eve*, 279

Eames, Charles, 74, 77, 272
Eames, Ray, 74, 77, 272
Elers brothers, 56
Eliot, George, 32
Eliot, T. S., 93–94
emsubi, 167
endozoochory, 296
Enlightenment, 260, 263
enterprise culture, 319, 321
Epstein, Jacob
  *Rock Drill*, 282–285
Erhart, Michel, 111, 114
Espersen, Maria Bang, 195

fashion, 81
fiction, 153–154
Figal, Günter, 333
film, 16mm, 57
Firm, the. *See* Morris, William
Florence, 328
folding, 118
foliage, 218
folk art. *See Mingei*
folk tales, 83, 184
folk world, 184
fool, 184–185
form, 36, 43, 49–50, 56, 109, 149, 159–161, 225
  atmosphere, 230
  grace, 169
  human character, 221–222
  as ornament, 302
  relational, 159
  robbery, 303
  topology, 229, 237
fragments, 208
Frank, Kaj, 30
Freud, Sigmund, 72
Fritsch, Elizabeth
  form, 160
  metaphysical ware, 160
  *Piano Pot with Counterpoint*, 162

Gadsby, Florian, 99
gallery, 309
  beyond the gallery, 155
Galloway, Alexander, 74, 140, 172–173, 176–177
gansey sweater, 220
gardens, 8
Gates, Theaster, 158
  *Afro-Ikebana*, 154
  black *Mingei*, 154
  *Plate Convergence*, 153–154
  To Speculate Darkly, 155–157
Geddes, Patrick
  eutopia, 265–266
  The Notation of Life, 267
genius, 130, 184
  of the artist, 79, 84–85, 309
*Gestalt*, 25, 31, 163, 225–226, 228–230, 232
  outline, 163
Ghandi, Mahatma, 253–254
Gill, Eric
  monastic lifestyle, 256
glass-blowing, 90–91, 114, 122, 196
glaze, 193
Goethe, J. W., 53, 62, 65
  *The Metamorphosis of Plants*, 291
  *Urpflanze*, 291, 303
*The Golden Bowl*. *See* James, Henry
Goldmark Gallery, 236
Goldstein, Kurt
  adequate fit, 229
  good form, 225–228
gothic
  architectural style, 16
  changefulness, 61, 110
  disturbed imagination, 217
  Erwin Panofsky, 16
  as fabulation, 328
  form, 18
  gratuitousness, 183–184
  grotesque, 179–184, 203
  naturalness, 126
  obstinacy, 253
  ornament, 218, 286
  qualities, 14, 328
  rudeness, 19–20, 23, 47
grace, 166, 236
  environmental fit, 164–167
  openness, 169
Greek key, 94, 96, 308
grid, 161, 240, 252, 275

Hagi ware, 188
Hagreen, Philip, 256, 258, 326–327
Hamada, Shoji, 236

Hamburger, Michael, 58
Haraway, Donna, 209–210
Hardy, Thomas
  *Jude the Obscure*, 281
Harman, Graham, 133, 135–136, 139
Heaney, Seamus, 108–109, 160
Hegel, Georg Wilhelm Friedrich
  *Aesthetics: Lectures on Fine Arts*, 204
  suits, 204
Heidegger, Martin
  *Being and Time*, 23, 27
  *Dasein*, 24
  language, 29, 31, 127
  National Socialism, 28, 334
  regions, 31–33, 47, 336
  *technē*, 127–128
  useful things, 31
Hepworth, Barbara, 59–60
Heraclitus, 188
Herbert, George, 14
hermeneutics, 103
Hicks, Sheila, 89–90
Hirai, Akiko, 61
  *Shibui*, 216
Hjortshøj, Anne Mette, 197
Hoffmann, Josef, 69–72, 234
Holman Hunt, William, 218
Holmes, Oliver Wendell, 131
Home Arts and Industries Association, 244
Homer, 150
Hopkins, Gerard Manley, 163
Hui, Yuk, 22, 65, 67, 83
  contingency, 286

imaginary, 154
industrial capitalism, 1, 6, 12, 14, 80, 127, 152, 169, 242, 255, 260, 287, 295, 318, 338
industrialized capitalism, 256, 259
infrathin, 311
Ingold, Tim, 85
instress, 243
Ise, shrine, 212

James, Henry, 45
Janus, 209
Jekyll, Gertrude, 245
  planting, 248
  political campaigner, 246
  social class, 250
  *Wood and Garden*, 249
Jennings, Humphrey, 208
joints (wooden), 11, 194
Jones, David, 256
  *Epoch and Artist*, 336
  transitive-intransitive, 336

Jones, Owen
  *The Grammar of Ornament*, 290
jug, 26, 28–34, 36, 43, 125, 159
  Bellarmine, 33–34
Jullien, Francois, 124, 187–188, 236, 309
Jungersen, Gitte, 187, 193

*Kamogawa*, 49, 120
Kandinsky, Wassily, 275
Kandyan craft workers, 253
Kant, Immanuel, 54
  art, 84–85
  purposive, 98
Kavanagh, Patrick, 131
Kawabata, Yasunari, 142
Keats, John, 165, 238
Keeler, Walter, 38
Kierkegaard, Søren
  desire, 82
  *Either/Or*, 81, 140, 198, 211
  folk literature, 184
  grace, 178
  hope, 198
  *Journals and Notebooks*, 178
  sensual, 140
Kilbride, Valentine, 256
kimono, 117
Kindersley, David, 171, 173–174, 232, 269
*kintsugi*, 195
Klee, Paul, 129, 273–275, 315
knife, 44–45
Knoll, Florence, 272
knowledge
  embodied, 91, 137–138, 232
  knowing that, knowing how, 92–93
  knowledge that, knowledge how, 108
  questionability, 103
  Western, 147
*Kohiki*, 61
Kotiahkeruus, 272
Kouthfood, Jesper, 306
Kui, Zhong (Shoki), 185
Kunckel, Johannes, 114–115
Kuo, Shen, 185
*kwabstijl*, 86–87
Kyoto, 48, 65–66, 118, 120, 141, 143, 197, 206

*la perruque. See* tactician
lacquerware, 61, 147
laissez-faire, 1, 18, 287, 295, 323, 328, 330–331
language game, 94–95
Laozi, 124, 188, 236
Larkin, Philip, 17, 166
*Lazoi*, 187

Le Guin, Ursula, 35–36
Leach, Bernard, 152–153, 231
  *A Potter's Book*, 202
Lear, Jonathan, 223
Lee, Jaejun, 63
Lee, Jane, 63, 154, 178, 310
Liberty, London, 245
Lingis, Alfonso
  *The Imperative*, 249
Lloyd Wright, Frank, 290
London Group Show 1915, 284
Lowndes, Gillian, 39–43

Mååås-Fjetterström, Marta, 96–98
  *Bruna Heden*, 109
  Swedish folklore, 101
MaCarthy, Fiona, 289–290
machine, 7, 66, 105
  apparatus, 74
  hostility to, 23, 234, 259–260, 262, 332
  house as, 81
Magritte, René, 173
Mairet, Ethel
  *Handweaving Notes for Teachers*, 254
  machine learning, 260
  *Vegetable Dyes*, 255–256, 258, 270
*The Maker's Eye* exhibition, 169, 171
Manley Hopkins, Gerard
  The Wreck of the Deutschland, 243
Manning, Erin, 310
manufacturing, 56, 107, 148
Marks, Grete
  *Haël- Werkstätten fur Künstlerische Keramik*, 274
Martin bros.
  disturbed imagination, 206
  grotesque, 199–200
  origins, 198–199
  Wally Birds, 199
Maruwa, manufacturer, 278
Maruyama, Masao, 157–158
Marx, Karl, 300
  *Grundrisse: Foundations of the Critique of Political Economy*, 301
mass observation movement, 208–209
  *Mantelpiece Directives*, 209
Massey, Doreen, 266
materials, 229, 336
  light, 240–242, 277
Mead, G. H., 251
  appearance of the subject, 251
  'me' and 'I', 248–249
Mediaeval, 317, 328, 336
*Meiji Ishin*, 147
Meissen, 114, 278, 311

Merleau-Ponty, Maurice, 88–89
  flesh, 145, 165
  horizon, 146
  *Phenomenology of Perception*, 146
  subject, 128, 145
  subjectivity, 146
metal, 60, 62, 99
metempsychosis, 210–211
Michikawa, Shozo, 192–193
Milner, Marion, 125
*Mingei*, 184
  characteristics, 141–142
  natural elites, 157–158
Nishida, 152
  origins, 141–142
  subject, 177
Mitsuko, Asakura, 117–121
Moeran, Brian, 152
Mondrian, Piet, 159
Morris, May, 295, 307
Morris, William
  contradictions of production, 292–295
  exchange value, 300
  Merton Works, 288, 294–295
  Morris & Co., 288–290, 294, 320–321
  nature of work, 17
  *News from Nowhere*, 299–300, 326–327, 331
  pattern, 292
  robbery, 304
  *Some Hints on Pattern Designing*, 302, 304
  Strawberry Thief, 292–293
  wallpaper, 289–290, 294–295
Mulhall, Stephen, 140
Mumford, Lewis
  biotechnics, 263–264
  eutopia, 268
  symbolism, 268–269
Munch-Petersen, Ursula, 24, 31, 36
myth, 35, 155

negative capability, 165
Neruda, Pablo, 287
Nishida, Kitarō, 143, 145, 147–152, 158, 164, 322
  *Basho*, 150–152
  Being, 150
  *kaibutsu*, 149
Noë, Alva, 91–92, 95, 98–99, 309, 312
Noh theatre, 143

oak, 10–11
  medullary, 164
objectivity
  appearance, 146–147

# Index

language, 137, 140, 240
  objects 135, 139, 208–209, 235, 238–239, 338
  process, 296–297
  sensual object, 136
  understanding, 136
O'Connor, Erin, 90–91
Odundo, Magdalene, 166–167
ontology of things, 137
ornament, 72
Oswald, Alice, 240, 251
Otagi Nenbutsu-ji Temple, 206
Owen, Robert
  New Lanark, 325–326

Paimo, 271
Palladio, 22, 24, 26, 78
Palmyra, Syria, 194
Panofsky, Erwin, 16–17, 124–125
paper, 273
Park, Jongjin, 192
pattern, 173
  gansey sweater, 220
Peirce, C. S., 260
Penty, A. J., 259–260
Pepler, Hilary, 256
perception, 135
Perloff, Marjorie, 308
pewter, 56, 65
phenomenology, 138–139, 225, 231
philanthropy, 252
Phipps, Howard, 189
*physis*, 126–128, 133
  organic life, 163
Plato
  *Cratylus*, 135, 149–150, 210–211, 267, 306, 334
  *Meno*, 210–211
  *Republic*, 210
  *Theatetus*, 135
  *Timaeus*, 149–150
playfulness, 203, 209
Plumb, Dru, 189–190
politics, 313, 325, 331
*Porzellankrankheit*, 114
Potters Arts Guild, 245
Pound, Ezra
  Hugh Selwyn Mauberley, 205
Pre-Raphaelite Brotherhood, 199, 288–290, 333
printing, 257
  styles, 257–258
professions, 52
Prometheus, 198
prosthesis, 226

prosthetics, 227, 250
Proust, Marcel, 179–182
  Rouen cathedral, 179
  Ruskin's imaginative power, 180
punch'ong, 142
Purkersdorf Sanatorium, 72–73
Pye, David, 105–108, 169–171, 176
  reluctance to write on craft, 170

Radigue, Eliane, 58–59
Rainier, Priaulx, 59
raku, 50
Rancière, Jacques, 319
  *Aisthesis*, 332
  *Dissensus*, 334
  on William Morris, 334
raw state, 36, 49–50
recursion, 65
  recovering the dead, 181
Redmayne, George, 244
reflexivity, 105, 109
*Rembrandt van Rijn*, 86
repetition, 58
  contingency, 62, 65, 84, 98
  folk tale, 83
  generations, 158, 215
  *Komainu*, 157
  *Mingei*, 142
  pause, 89–90
  prayer, 257
  reciprocity, 90
  recursion, 66
  rhythm, 59–60, 88, 95
  seasonal cycles, 142, 248
*res cogitans* and *res extensa*, 24–28, 41, 52, 68, 89, 177, 228, 230
Ricoeur, Paul, 102–105
Rie, Lucie, 71, 171–172, 274
Rilke, Rainer Marie
  *Dinggedichte*, 232–233, 235
  *Duino Elegies*, 233
  on machinery, 234
  *Sonnets to Orpheus*, 234
risk, 106–108, 176, 313
Rodin, Auguste, 232–233, 237–239
Rogers, Phil, 33, 236
Rousseau, Jean Jacques, 17
Ruskin, John
  beauty, 191
  Brantwood, 1, 3, 7
  clouds, 3, 5–6
  Coniston Mechanics Institute, 8, 10
  *Crown of Wild Olive*, 280
  education, 2, 10
  Florence, 9

346    Index

Ruskin, John (cont.)
  freedom, 176
  grotesque, 182–183, 191–192
  Guild of St George, 1–2, 7, 245
  on J. M. W Turner, 3
  masons, 22
  *Modern Painters*, 3, 5, 43, 132
  nature, 218
  nature of business, 8
  obstinacy, 223
  obstinate work, 224
  ornament, 287
  pathetic fallacy, 131–132
  perspective, 124
  railroad, 11
  Renaissance, 22–23, 27, 124–125, 317
  Rouen cathedral, 15, 179
  sky, 13–14
  St Giorgio Maggiore, 20–22
  *The Stones of Venice*, 10, 12, 18, 22–23, 61, 87, 125, 161, 182–184, 191–192, 217–218, 223–225, 288
  *The Storm Cloud*, 6
Ryle, Gilbert, 92–93

Saarinen, Eliel, 272
Salmenhaara, Kylliki, 38
Sartre, Jean Paul
  *Nausea*, 151
Sawada, Shinichi, 207
scaling production, 57, 157, 254, 272, 275, 325, 335
Schäfer, Michael, 263
Schiller, Friedrich, 159
Schlemmer, Oscar, 78
science, 52–53, 133, 139, 164, 259
  commercial science, 325, 329
Scott, Paul, 191, 194
Sebald, W. G, 55–56, 58, 213, 215
self formation, 100, 107, 158–159, 170, 178, 226
  authenticity, 235, 320–321, 323
  autonomy, 236, 285, 331
  care, 257
  character, 222–223, 228, 325
  doubt, 223
  improvisation, 146, 264
  *khôra*, 150
  mortality, 216
  Nishida, 143–145
  nothingness, 150–152
  space (*khôra*), 175
  subject object relations, 136, 138, 151, 238–239, 322
  technical individuals, 260–261, 326

self-organization, 285
Sennett, Richard, 58
  bricklaying, 264
  skill as critique, 88
Sex Pistols, 206
sheep, 270
*Shikinen Sengū*, 212
Shimizu, Shiro, 197
Shinto, 118, 142, 152
  kami, 212
*Silas Marner*, 32, 47
silver/goldsmith, 86
Simondon, Gilbert, 229, 260–261
  technical objects, 261
Simpson, Arthur, 9–11, 24
Sistine Chapel, 318
skill, 13, 23
  acquisition, 85
  analogue, 176
  discipline, 106, 161–162
  experiment, 62, 134, 164, 263–264, 273
  failure, 13, 62, 212, 223
  genius, 93
  grip, environmental, 43, 89, 226–227, 247, 299
  immersive flow, 84, 88
  materials, 51, 57, 88, 91, 137, 192, 198, 242, 271, 277, 292
  precision, 22, 67, 74, 162, 261, 275, 282
  reticence, 105–106
  Ruskin, 108
  suspicion of writing about, 169–171
  thoughtfulness, 90–91, 141, 160, 269, 330
  writing about, 102–105
  written record, 65, 241
Slee, Richard, 208–210
Sloterdijk, Peter, 91, 323
Sozan, Suwa, 64
speculative realism, 131, 135–136
Spira, Rupert, 137, 178
Spuybroek, Lars, 229
St Dominic's Press, 256
St Michele of Lucca, 191
St Michele of Pavia, 191
steel, 44–45
Stiegler, Bernard, 126–127
Stoke-on-Trent, 56, 208
Stölzl, Gunta, 275
stone, 60
stone masons, 22, 125–126, 176, 207, 218
Straub, Marianne, 272
Strengell, Marianne, 272
Studio Ghibli, 207

### Index

*The Studio* magazine, 244
suffragism, 250
Sung dynasty, 142
*svastika* (Sanskrit), 266
symbolic representations, 176
symbolism, 326
synthesizer, 59, 106

tactician, 76, 81, 314
tailoring, 92
Tang dynasty, 48, 50, 185
taskscape, 85, 88–89, 92, 94, 109, 115, 261, 277, 281–282, 302, 308, 322, 331, 334, 338
tea bowl, 48
tea ceremony, 48
technē, 91–92, 94, 127–128, 133, 222
Teenage Engineering, 106–107, 306
terracotta, 245
tool use, 64–65, 106, 143, 227, 241, 257
   experiment, 263
   ritual, 212
   social conditions, 271
   symbolism, 227
tools, 66, 106, 175
   instruments, 260
Topp, Leslie, 72
tradition, 39, 86
   common sense, 86
   originality, 93–94
   political, 157
truth
   beauty, 165
   Cartesian, 27
   correlationism, 128, 135, 140
   feeble, 313
   in repetition, 211
   verisimilitude, 227
Turner, J. M. W., 3
   *Loch Fyne*, 4
   *Slavers Throwing Overboard the Dead and Dying – Typhoon Coming on*, 2
Twain, Mark, 6
Twomey, Clare, 196
typography, 99, 171

Ulm, Germany, 111
urushi. *See* lacquerware
utility, 13, 29, 40, 43, 222

Van Cleeve, Joos, 113
Van Essen, Tamsin, 188
Vienna Exposition 1873, 147
vitalism (new materialism), 175
Vitruvius, 21, 27

Wandle (river), 280, 289, 291–292, 294
Warburg, Aby
   *pathosformel*, 304, 329
waste, 197, 208, 324
   as material, 41, 196
Watts, G. F., 244
Watts, Mary Compton, 244–245
Watts Gallery, 190
weaving, 89, 96–98, 100–101, 117–121
   knitting, 218, 220
Wedgwood, Josiah, 263
Westwood, Vivienne
   drunken shirt, 203–205
   punk, 205
Whitehead, Alfred North
   prehension, 298, 302
   robbery, 296–297
   societies, 296–298
*Wiener Werkstätte*, 69, 72
Wigley, Mark, 71, 74
Williamson, Rupert, 194
willow, 111
Wittgenstein, Ludwig, 94–95, 136
wood carving, 9, 61, 329
woodwork, 105
wool, 269–270
Woolf, Virginia, 225
Wordsworth, William
   *The Excursion*, 12
   on exploited labour, 12
work
   exploited, 303
   intrinsic value, 222–223, 334–335
   machine relations, 12, 57
   recognition value, 52, 264, 325
   surplus, 286
   violence, 303
workshop, 262
   division of labour, 153
   factory, 261
   place of education, 10–11, 101, 258–263
   symbolism, 269
   as tool, 66

Yanagi, Muneyoshi, 141–142
Yixing ware, 56
Yu, Lu, 48, 50
Yue ware, 50

Zumthor, Peter, 229–230
   *Atmospheres*, 229
   dwell, 265

Printed in the United Kingdom by TJ Clays Ltd.